Bankrupt

Bankrupt

THE INTELLECTUAL AND MORAL
BANKRUPTCY OF TODAY'S DEMOCRATIC PARTY

David Limbaugh

Since 1947
REGNERY
PUBLISHING, INC.
An Eagle Publishing Company • Washington, DC

Library of Congress Cataloging-in-Publication Data

Limbaugh, David.
   Bankrupt : the intellectual and moral bankruptcy of today's democratic party / David Limbaugh.
     p. cm.
   Includes bibliographical references and index.
     ISBN 1-59698-017-6
     ISBN 1-59698-526-7
     1. Democratic Party (U.S.) 2. United States—Politics and government—2001- I. Title.
     JK2316.L53 2006
     324.2736—dc22

                    2006023108

Published in the United States by
Regnery Publishing, Inc.
One Massachusetts Avenue, NW
Washington, DC 20001

First paperback edition published in 2007

www.regnery.com

Manufactured in the United States of America

10 9 8 7 6 5 4 3 2 1

Books are available in quantity for promotional or premium use. Write to Director of Special Sales, Regnery Publishing, Inc., One Massachusetts Avenue NW, Washington, DC 20001, for information on discounts and terms or call (202) 216-0600.

To my son, William ("Will") Limbaugh

CONTENTS

I wrote *Bankrupt* as a warning about what might happen if the American people—in their understandable anger at Republicans who had abandoned their principles of reducing government spending, controlling the border, and promoting a robust national defense—elected a Democratic congressional majority. If the Republicans in 2006, with their scandals and out-of-control spending, were badly flawed, the Democrats—as I pointed out—were morally and intellectually bankrupt.

Since the disastrous 2006 election, many Republicans seem to have gotten the message about cleaning up their act and renewing their commitment to conservative principles—though there are admittedly far too many stragglers. But the Democrats have lived down to my expectations and proven just how unworthy they are of political power. Here are just a few of the lowlights of the Democrats' recent control of Congress.

Usurpation of Executive Power

Remember Nancy Pelosi's attempt to make herself commander in chief? In one of her first significant acts after the Democrats gained control of Congress, House Speaker Pelosi made an unauthorized trip to Syria—even though President Bush had asked her not to go.

America's official foreign policy is that we will not negotiate with Syria, which supports terrorists in Iraq as well as Hamas, Hezbollah, and other terrorist organizations. Syria is also allied with Iran and is dedicated to the destruction of our ally Israel. Pelosi said her mission's purpose was merely "fact-finding," but it's more accurate to say she conspired with the Syrian regime to alter the president's policy toward it. One member of her delegation, Tom Lantos, boasted that the meeting "reinforced sharply" the potential benefits of talking to Syria. "This is only the beginning of our constructive dialogue with Syria, and we hope to build on this visit," Lantos said.

The Constitution confers on the president the authority to conduct foreign policy. President Bush has attempted to isolate Syria and has urged our allies to follow suit. Pelosi, however, acted as if Syria is part of the international mainstream, and thus, as the highest-ranking member of the House, she colluded with a terrorist-sponsoring regime to undermine and humiliate our commander in chief and countermand his foreign policy. The Democrats have constantly berated the president for allegedly overstepping his constitutional authority, but they had nothing but praise for Pelosi's unconstitutional usurpation of the commander in chief's privileges. The Democrats have also constantly berated President Bush for harming America's image in the world, but were unmoved when Pelosi denigrated our nation's foreign policy and publicly undercut the nation's commander in chief in Syria.[1]

If that weren't embarrassment enough, Pelosi officiously intermeddled with Israeli foreign policy, implying that Israel had softened its stance against Syria and wanted to renew peace negotiations. This incensed Israeli prime minister Ehud Olmert, who strongly denied that he had changed his position. He reiterated that until Syria changes its terrorist sponsorship, peace talks would be meaningless.[2]

Iraq

In *Bankrupt* I point out that for all their partisan sniping, the Democrats have never created—not in 2004 and not in 2006—a plan to deal with the Iraq war. Of course, this didn't stop them, after they took over Congress, from immediately claiming a mandate to withdraw our troops from Iraq.

What is interesting is that as of this writing (summer 2007), the Democrats still have not settled on a plan. They've been energetic in attempting to pass legislation that would undermine the president's authority, force him to begin withdrawing the troops on certain arbitrary timetables, mandate greater time off for troops between deployment tours, and various other schemes. But they've never had a cohesive, intelligible plan, and they've never been able to pass any such legislation.

Despite their criticism of almost every Bush policy and action in Iraq, the Democrats have never bothered to address the critical question of what consequences might follow if we precipitously withdraw our troops from Iraq. They have been content merely to rehash their bogus propaganda that "Bush lied, people died," and that Bush has grossly mismanaged the war.

Even certain mainstream media players have seemed to express bewilderment at the Democrats' refusal to offer anything constructive to the mix. ABC News's Jake Tapper posed this question to Senate Majority Leader Harry Reid: "Is there not a moral obligation of the United States to make sure that the Iraqi people are safe before the U.S. withdraws?" Tapper said, "I tried to get an answer. . . . I did not succeed."[3]

Tapper might also have asked Reid—though he wouldn't have answered this either—how withdrawal or a drastic drawdown of our troops would advance the security interests of the United States. If quelling terrorist violence in Iraq required a "surge" of U.S. troops, does it not logically follow that withdrawing large numbers of troops (as leading Democrats want to do) would ease the pressure on al Qaeda in what the terror group considers its front-line battle? Wouldn't that be enormously reckless?

Vice President Dick Cheney made news when he exposed the absurdity and disingenuousness of the Democrats' approach to Iraq by highlighting Harry Reid's three distinctly different positions on the matter—all within five months. Cheney had finally had enough of Reid, who had unilaterally declared that we had lost the war in Iraq. Cheney noted that Reid had gone "from pledging full funding for the military, then full funding but with conditions, and then a cutoff of the funding . . . on the most important foreign policy question facing the nation and our troops."

When conservatives say Democratic policies are detrimental to our national security, Democrats characteristically whine that conservatives are challenging their patriotism. It is typical of the Democrats to regard any criticism of them as "unfair." But it's also hard to examine the Democrats' behavior toward the war without concluding that they are indeed invested in the defeat of our troops.

As I show in this book, when it comes to the war, the Democrats have consistently taken a defeatist line, and instead of behaving as the "loyal opposition" have attempted to raise antiwar sentiment and turn it against President Bush and the Republicans. Even though they voted unanimously to approve General David Petraeus as the commander of our forces in Iraq, they have refused, from the beginning of his command, to support his decisions, and they were quick to call his "surge" strategy a failure. While the Democrats had long criticized President Bush for not following the advice of generals, they changed course when Bush followed the advice of General Petraeus. The Democrats, of course, were very selective in whose advice should be followed: they meant only retired generals who had soured on the war or opposed it from the beginning.

General Petraeus promised to deliver a progress report on the surge in September 2007, at which time, presumably, politicians could evaluate its relative success. Early news on the surge was favorable, but Democrats declared it a failure even before all the troops had arrived. In mid-July, after the full complement of U.S. troop reinforcements was finally in place in Iraq, President Bush reported in a news conference that we were beginning to see marked changes on the ground in Iraq.

Areas formerly believed irretrievably lost to al Qaeda were recaptured by American and Iraqi security forces. Sectarian violence began to decline. Tribes that had supported al Qaeda turned against it, because they no longer thought it was dangerous to entrust their security to American and Iraqi forces. Thanks to the infusion of troops, American forces could not only capture territory but also hold it.

Indeed, General Peter Pace, chairman of the Joint Chiefs of Staff, reported that Iraq had undergone a "sea change" in security in recent months. "It's no longer a matter of pushing al Qaeda out of Ramadi, for example, but rather—now that they have been pushed out—helping the local police and local army have a chance to get their feet on the ground and set up their systems."[4]

But were these revelations good news to Democrats? Did they meet them with rejoicing and applaud the president, General Petraeus, and our troops? No, they focused exclusively on the president's admission that not all the "political" benchmarks had yet been accomplished. They reiterated their defeatist battle cry that the surge was a failure. They redoubled their demands that we begin withdrawal immediately.

The Democrats—and an increasing number of fainthearted Republicans—didn't want to hear the good news. The House went into overdrive almost immediately and voted 223–201 for a Democratic proposal to force the withdrawal of U.S. troops by spring 2008.[5] The Senate followed suit a few days later when Senate Majority Leader Harry Reid forced the chamber into a theatrical all-night "debate" on the Iraq war on July 17. The sleepover led into the Senate's scheduled vote on July 18 on legislation by Democratic senators Carl Levin and Jack Reed that would require President Bush to begin withdrawing American troops from Iraq within 120 days.[6] So far, enough Republicans have held together to prevent the

Democratic Congress from undercutting the heroic—and successful—efforts of troops.

Investigations

The Democrats' ongoing war against President Bush is about more than Iraq. They're still after him on every conceivable front, as if their primary mission is to destroy his presidency. Predictions that a Democratic victory in November 2006 would result in an explosion of investigations against the president—for an assortment of reasons—have been vindicated. The Democrats have initiated more than 300 investigations, 350 document and interview requests, and have held more than 600 oversight hearings in about one hundred days, according to White House spokesman Scott Stanzel. Though Harry Reid disputed these figures, Stanzel said he came up with the numbers by canvassing departments and agencies concerning such inquiries and investigations since Democrats took control of Congress.[7]

Perhaps the most ludicrous and outrageous examples of the Democrats' mischief along these lines were their purely partisan investigations of the administration's firing of eight U.S. attorneys and President Bush's commutation of Scooter Libby's jail time.

Everyone, including Democratic congressmen, knows that U.S. attorneys serve at the pleasure of the chief executive, who may fire them at will—even for political reasons. The congressmen also know that Bill Clinton, in an unprecedented move near the beginning of his first term, fired all ninety-three U.S. attorneys even before their replacements had been selected. Nary a word of protest issued from Democratic ranks.

In response to the Democrats' fishing expedition in 2006, the White House asserted executive privilege and refused to turn over documents concerning the attorney firings in the interest of pre-serving the executive's independence from the overreaching legisla-tive branch. While Democrats complained that President Bush was using the privilege to conceal the truth, they were obviously afflicted again with selective amnesia, this time about their past reaction to another president's invocation of the same privilege. Not only did they not object that time, but they also vigorously defended Presi-dent Clinton's assertion of executive privilege and various other privileges (some of which he made up as he went along, like the bogus "protective function" privilege).

As for the president's clemency for former White House aide Scooter Libby, the Democrats knew that the chief executive has complete authority to commute sentences. Regardless of whether they agreed with his decision to spare Libby jail time, it was noth-ing more than circus politics for them to initiate an investigation into the matter. They fabricated absurd excuses to justify their witch hunt, such as that the administration was granting leniency to Libby to buy his silence against Vice President Cheney. But there was not a scintilla of evidence to warrant suspicion that Bush had acted improperly or illegally, as contrasted with the rash of highly questionable pardons Bill Clinton granted at the end of his term.

Censorship

Many also predicted that in the event of a Democratic victory in November 2006, the Democrats would resurrect the "Fairness Doc-trine," an FCC regulation in force from 1949 to 1987 requiring broadcasters to present "both sides" of controversial issues. It is more accurately described as a plan designed to shut down conservative talk radio in the name of injecting "balance" into the media. Senator James Inhofe claims he once overheard Senators Hillary Clinton and Barbara Boxer on a Capitol elevator discussing a "legislative fix" for the "right-wing extremists" on talk radio, though the two Democratic senators deny it.[8]

Liberals have not been able to compete in the marketplace of ideas on talk radio, despite pouring huge amounts of money and effort into it. Their response has not been to lick their wounds and take it like grown-ups, but to demand that the federal government force stations to alter the content of their conservative talk shows to accommodate a liberal message.

Basking in their newfound control of the legislative branch, Democrats started making noise about bringing back the Fairness Doctrine not long after they resumed control of Congress. Democratic congressman Maurice Hinchey has sponsored the Media Ownership Reform Act, which includes reinstatement of the Fairness Doctrine. Other liberal senators, like Democrat Dianne Feinstein, have indicated they're considering bringing back the rule. Complaining about conservative talk radio, Feinstein said, "It pushes people to, I think, extreme views without a lot of information.... There ought to be an opportunity to present the other side. And unfortunately, talk radio is overwhelmingly one way."[9] Likewise, Senator Dick Durbin said, "It's time to reinstitute the Fairness Doctrine. I have this old-fashioned attitude that when Americans hear both sides of the story, they're in a better position to make a decision."

When Republican senators tried to pass a version of the House legislation sponsored by Republican congressman Mike Pence to maintain a free marketplace of ideas and prevent reestablishment of the Fairness Doctrine, Democratic senators blocked the measure.[10]

Typical of their myopia, Democrats have no intention of making "fairness" applicable to other media, broadcast or print, despite the fact that most mainstream media television news broadcasts are decidedly liberal and have been for decades. Indeed, one sure reason conservative talk radio has been so successful is that predominantly conservative talk radio audiences had been starved for a balanced message from the media for these many years. What has made the mainstream media's liberal bias even more unpalatable to conservatives is that they disguise and deny it. They select news based on their bias, they slant their reports to conform to their bias, and they editorialize while purporting to be engaged in objective reporting. With conservative talk, at least, the hosts are overwhelmingly transparent and honest about their conservative tilt and don't deny that they are editorialists. Even the FOX News Channel, which liberals condemn as conservatively biased, scrupulously presents both sides of controversial issues.

While liberals continue to blatantly deny liberalism's monopoly on the mainstream media, data consistently bears it out. Accuracy in Media reported that an examination of political donations by journalists from the 200 largest newspapers in the country revealed that of 143 donations from editors, columnists, reporters, and editorial cartoonists, 125 went to Democrats or liberal groups, 16 to Republicans or conservative groups—while two gave to both.[11]

Those Ephemeral Values Voters

While the Democrats still decry the Republicans for bringing religiously held moral values to bear on policy, they themselves have continued to woo "values voters." When Republican politicians invoke Christian images and language, the media and the Left become hysterical. When Democrats talk about faith, the media and the Left are almost congratulatory, presumably because they understand that such talk is largely a cynical ploy to garner political support from Christian voters.

No one batted an eye when CNN and the liberal evangelical group Sojourners sponsored a forum on faith, which was an undisguised Democratic effort to make inroads into the Republicans' seeming lock on "values voters." John Edwards proudly intoned, "We are all sinners. We all fall short, which is why we have to ask for forgiveness from the Lord." Hillary Clinton related how prayer warriors sustained her through tough times at the White House. Barack Obama discussed the nature of good and evil.[12] And the media didn't flinch. But imagine if a Republican candidate talked about sin the way Edwards did or invoked the support of prayer warriors the way Hillary did.

The Left's Ongoing Stranglehold

The entire Democratic field is tilting further and further to the left, whether the issue is Iraq, gay rights, health care, taxes, or energy policy. Democrats are openly talking about funding socialized medicine (they call it universal health care) and environmental initiatives to combat global warming with increased taxes. They are also pushing to repeal the Defense of Marriage Act and to eliminate the ban on homosexuals serving in the military openly.[13] On Iraq, while many Democrats were at least supportive of the overall mission in Iraq in 2004, today all the candidates oppose Bush's commitment to persevere until victory is achieved.

Even if Democrats decided to become less strident and more reasonable in the political arena, they would have a very difficult time pulling it off. Their base—which energizes and funds their elections—is made up of extremist, uncompromising leftists. Successful Democratic presidential contenders don't dare buck these people too often, especially not during the campaign season, which seems perpetual these days.

The Democratic base is not one cohesive group but a collection of interest groups, some overlapping and some entirely independent, from the gay lobby to the feminists to the greens. Recent examples of the politicians' deference to these groups were the decisions of many Democratic presidential candidates to participate in a debate centering on homosexual issues, their uniform pandering to black activist groups, and their kowtowing to "progressive" activists at the annual three-day "Take Back America" conference in Washington, D.C. While high-profile Democratic presidential hopefuls Hillary Clinton, Barack Obama, and John Edwards refused to participate in a debate hosted by FOX News Channel, they jumped at the chance to debate on LOGO-TV, an outlet identified with the homosexual lobby. In the August 9 event, the candidates debated homosexual-related issues, including gay "marriage," civil unions, discrimination based on sexual orientation, hate crimes, gays in the military, and HIV/AIDS. This unapologetic nod toward the gay lobby is a significant change from the 2004 campaign, when candidates were reluctant to guarantee they would fight for gay rights and when John Kerry was booed at the Human Rights Campaign's forum for affirming his support for traditional marriage.

The Take Back America conference was a leftist lovefest where extremist liberal groups gloated over their influence. Conference organizer Robert Borosage boastfully stated, "We really do believe we're driving the debate right now. It's a historic turn, a repudiation from the last twenty-five years of conservative dominance."

Economic Policy

The Democrats have stubbornly refused to give President Bush or his tax-cutting policies credit for the long period of economic growth—including low unemployment and nominal inflation—that America has enjoyed during his presidency. Nor have his policies been given credit for the drastically reduced federal budget deficits. The Democrats denied all these positive signs, or chose to distort them, by claiming that economic growth was disproportionately benefiting the wealthy. The facts were of no consequence to these charlatans peddling their demagogic class warfare message. But according to tax data cited by economist and TV talk-show host Larry Kudlow, the top 1 percent of income producers pay some 37 percent of federal income taxes, and the lowest 40 percent pay virtually no taxes and are even subsidized.

Despite the objective evidence confirming the success of the tax cuts, Democrats refuse to extend them. One of the first actions the new Democratic congressional majority took was to change legislative rules, implemented by a 1994 Republican House, requiring a super-majority vote to increase taxes. They also indicated their intention to change a 185-year-old House rule to allow the government to increases taxes and government spending without having to vote—notwithstanding their pledge, through Speaker Nancy Pelosi, to deliver the American people the "most honest and most open government." House Minority Leader John Boehner said, "This is an astonishing attempt by the majority leadership to duck accountability for tax-and-spend policies the American people do not want."[14]

But no one is engaging in more egregious class warfare than presidential candidate John "two Americas" Edwards, who embarrassingly advanced a plan to eliminate poverty in America within thirty years.[15] Nor is anyone engaging in worse hypocrisy than Edwards, who while railing against the disparity of income among Americans lives in a 28,000-square-foot mega-mansion in North Carolina and luxuriates in $400 haircuts.

The Environment

Many have noted, quite accurately, that the environmental movement today is a quasi-religious phenomenon, replete with prophets of doom and apocalypse. While they claim to have unswerving allegiance to science and the scientific method, they notoriously violate the spirit of scientific inquiry in their approach to environmental issues by attempting to shut down debate. They declare that their doomsday scenarios are settled matters of fact denied only by crackpots and corporate stooges, and they decline to hold their prophets, like Paul Ehrlich, accountable for some of their already disproved prophecies of doom. The Hollywood Left has fully embraced the radical environmentalist agenda, glorifying former vice president Al Gore's bizarre documentary *An Inconvenient Truth*.

One signature of the leftist is his claim to moral superiority based on policies he advocates rather than the way he conducts his life, and nowhere is this more pronounced than in the Left's approach to environmental issues. From Robert Kennedy Jr. to envirodemigod Al Gore himself, these greens routinely use private jets to gallivant around the nation to rail against the rest of us for using gas-guzzling automobiles that don't emit a fraction of the carbon pollution their jets produce.

But the granddaddy of all is the enviro-Left's newfound "carbon credit" concept, through which they confer absolution on themselves for any and all environmental infractions by simply acquiring so-called carbon offsets, which purport—speciously—to counter any negative effect of their enviro-unfriendly activity. It doesn't matter that they aren't practicing what they preach in environmental policy. What matters only is that they are preaching and saying the right things.

And when it comes to that sort of hypocrisy you have a pretty good description of why the Democrats remain morally and intellectual bankrupt.

Why the Democrats Deserve to Lose

The oldest continuous political party in the world is bankrupt.

While the Republican Party is far from perfect and could do much better on immigration, domestic spending, and other issues, it does stand for principles beyond winning. It is the only party that can be safely entrusted with the most important issue of our day: the War on Terror. What weaknesses it has could be vastly reduced with a renewed commitment to conservative ideals across the board.

Democrats, on the other hand, have few policies beyond attacking President Bush and have long lost any legitimate right to claim they are a responsible opposition party. The "Scoop Jackson" Democrats of the 1970s who understood the need for a strong national defense are long gone, with few exceptions, like Senator Joseph Lieberman, whose responsible statements on the war have led to his ostracism by the party elites. The 1970s Catholic, Southern, and blue-collar Democrats who stuck by their traditional moral values are now mostly "Reagan Republicans."

In their desperation to regain the power they held for decades, Democrats have seized on a few isolated scandals and manufactured others, trying to paint Republicans as fostering a culture of corruption. But the real systemic corruption is in the Democratic Party, from its highest positions of leadership to the bowels of its Bush-hating, antiwar base.

The party's decline took firm root in the late 1960s and 1970s, but has accelerated dramatically over the last decade. Today's Democratic Party—the party of Al Gore, John Kerry, Howard Dean, Harry Reid, Joseph Biden, Edward Kennedy, and Hillary Rodham Clinton—is the party that sacrificed all moral principle to defend Bill Clinton in the 1990s no matter what the scandal. It is the party that adopted the Clinton mode of conducting politics as an art of personal assassination—while accusing the other side of doing it.

It is the party that tried to steal the presidential election in 2000, then convinced itself that Republicans *did* steal it—and has been paralyzed with bitterness and conducting revenge politics ever since. It is the party that demands bipartisanship and reconciliation, but whips President Bush with the olive branch he extended at their behest.

It is the party whose ex-presidents routinely violate the long-standing tradition against criticizing their successors—and even do so on foreign soil.

It is the party that falsely claims President Bush is trampling on the Constitution—while making no secret of its own willingness to subordinate the Constitution to its own political ends, most notably through using the judicial branch to "legislate" policy it cannot achieve through democratic means.

It is the party that isn't honest about its core convictions, knowing that honesty will render it even less electable in a center-right America. It denies its liberalism in favor of the euphemistic "progressivism." But while "progressive" implies "forward-looking," Democrats are mired in the past, reactionary on issues from Social Security (don't change a bankrupt system) to Iraq (don't defeat a hostile dictatorship and try to make it a democracy).

It is the party of elites who look down their noses at red-state America. It is the party that snubs Christians and "values voters" yet claims to be their authentic representatives. It is the party that can't decide whether its electoral difficulties stem from its failure to effectively articulate its message or from the wholesale stupidity of an electorate that's too Christian, too much in favor of traditional family values, and too patriotic.

It is the party that often doesn't even bother to offer alternative policies, but chooses instead to slander President Bush and obstruct his policies. In the last few decades the party has increasingly engaged in the destructive partisan politics of class and race warfare, further alienating and dividing Americans. But it has sunk to new lows more recently with the egregious practice of playing partisan politics with our national security.

What follows is an indictment of today's Democrats—in their own words, and meticulously documented—revealing them to be a party of moral and intellectual bankruptcy with little promise of redemption in sight. Our country needs a responsible opposition party—a party willing to participate in an honest policy debate—but sadly, the Democrats fall way short of the mark.

PART I

The Intellectual and Moral Bankruptcy
of the Democratic Party in the War on Terror

CHAPTER ONE

Iraq: Democrats Lied, and Their Credibility Died

Nothing in recent politics has been more disheartening and maddening than the Democrats' behavior on the Iraq war. We have come to expect the Democratic Party to politicize domestic and social issues. But it is still rather shocking that they also play partisan politics over life and death issues involving our national security.

We are way past the point where today's Democratic leaders even pretend to respect the long-accepted adage that "politics stops at the water's edge." They might as well have substituted "no holds barred" as their guiding philosophy on issues of national defense and foreign policy. They politicized the Iraq war even before it began but denied doing so and reversed the charge—falsely— against Republicans. Senator Hillary Clinton said, "The exercise of playing politics with war...carries with it a very high cost, and those who choose to play that game are squarely in the wrong."[1] If only she and her colleagues could follow their own advice.

Democrats complain loudly and often about perceived challenges to their patriotism. But one cannot closely follow the news without noticing that in the War on Terror, especially in the Iraq theater, the Bush administration is fighting terrorists and insurgents on the one hand and the leadership of the Democratic Party on the other. At every turn the Democrats can be counted on to oppose and obstruct President Bush regardless of the consequences to the national interest.

With respect to President Bush's policies on Iraq, Democrats "hear no good and see no good." No matter how positive certain developments are in Iraq, they find something to complain about. There are basically two reasons for this. One is that they truly disagree—philosophically—with the hawkish bent of the Bush administration. They are appeasement-oriented to a fault, especially when their party does not control the presidency.

So they would be against President Bush on the Iraq war even if they weren't playing partisan politics. But they are—the second reason for their unmitigated opposition. It's as if they sense the horrifying potential of a smoothly run, unopposed war to boost the popularity of a commander in chief and his party. They simply cannot allow him his due on any aspect of the Iraq war, because to praise him is to elevate him politically.

From the very beginning of our attack on Iraq, the naysayers had their say. They were beside themselves that we didn't give the UN weapons inspectors more time. They predicted tens of thousands of American casualties. They were hysterical over Bush's preemptive attack. They complained that we acted unilaterally and strained relations with our European allies. They said we were alienating more Muslims than we were liberating and creating more terrorists than we could kill or capture.

They shouted "quagmire" when a sandstorm hit Iraq shortly after our invasion. They said our ground forces were moving through the desert efficiently all right, but too efficiently—so quickly that they had outrun their supply lines, resulting in unarmed and unfed soldiers. They said our drive toward Baghdad had stalled and a longer war would be likely.[2] They said we didn't sufficiently equip and arm our troops.[3] They said we sent too few troops.[4] They said we sent too many troops.

We were being greeted, said the critics, not as liberators, but as occupiers. We were killing innocent Iraqi women and children. They implied we didn't care about "collateral damage," though our entire prosecution of the war was carefully designed to minimize injury and death to innocent civilians. They said we were destroying the Iraqi infrastructure. They said we didn't anticipate and guard against the looting of the National Museum in Baghdad.[5] They said we allowed stockpiles of munitions to be removed from Al-Qaqaa, a former Iraqi military installation, even though signs indicated that most of those weapons had been removed before our troops arrived in the spring of 2003. (The *New York Times* reported the munitions removal as a scandal of prewar planning incompetence, but it was given repeated, exhaustive coverage—sixteen separate stories in the eight days before the election—even though it was actually old news. The *Times* curiously discontinued reports on the story following the election.[6])

The naysayers said we attacked Iraq for oil. They said we attacked because we are an imperialistic nation. They said President

Bush bribed other nations to commit troops and other resources to help rebuild Iraq.[7] They said we might have had a plan to win the initial phase of the war, but had no idea how to win the peace. They said we sowed the seeds of our ultimate difficulties with the terrorists and insurgents by the very nature of our rush to Baghdad, letting Iraqi troops retreat to the countryside to fight us later. They characterized isolated cases of abuse and humiliation as a systematic policy of torture and attributed it to the Bush administration. They demanded constitutional rights for enemy combatants. They mischaracterized intercepts of international communications of terrorists as domestic spying on innocent American citizens. They were quick to rush to judgment upon news of alleged Marine atrocities in Haditha.

They say we should have anticipated the insurgency that followed the war because this was obviously Saddam's plan. Yet a recent U.S. military history study, "The Iraqi Perspectives Project," concluded that Saddam did not, in fact, plan the insurgency, mainly because he was convinced the U.S. would never invade his country and that we would never dare enter Baghdad. The study said, "As far as can be determined from the interviews and records reviewed so far, there were no national plans to embark on a guerilla war in the event of military defeat. Nor did the regime appear to cobble together such plans as its world crumbled around it."[8]

Mission Accomplished

A perfect example of the Democrats' orchestrated pessimism was their refusal to join President Bush in celebrating the triumph of our initial rout of Saddam. They ridiculed him for piloting a jet onto the USS *Abraham Lincoln* on May 1, 2003, standing in his flight suit in front of a banner reading "Mission Accomplished" and declaring an end to "major combat operations" in Iraq. Though some say Bush didn't actually utter the phrase "mission accomplished," he admittedly did say, "America sent you on a mission to remove a grave threat and to liberate an oppressed people, and that mission has been accomplished."[9]

Sometime later, with the full benefit of hindsight, liberals triumphantly condemned Bush for that "premature" assessment. They spun it as a reckless distortion, when at face value it was accurate. Saddam was removed—in short order, no less—and the Iraqi people were liberated from him. That terrorists and insurgents launched an action to undo what America had already accomplished didn't invalidate Bush's statement that we had effected a regime change.

Iraq was certainly not a terror-free zone, but it had become a free society on its way to constitutional self-rule. Perhaps it is fair game to criticize the administration for its failure to anticipate the degree to which terrorists would begin a reign of horror designed to break our will, though it remains unclear how anyone, including Nostradamus, could have predicted that with certainty.

It is unfair to say that Bush was intentionally overstating the military's accomplishment in Iraq. Indeed, it is difficult to imagine what conceivable motive Bush would have had to make such a statement if he knew upcoming events would undermine our victory. Why would he voluntarily subject himself to the inevitable ridicule of his ever-eager detractors? Even if he had anticipated the nature and degree of the insurgency, there is nothing wrong and everything right with his congratulation of our troops for their accomplishment—and it was a magnificent accomplishment.

We Let Osama Escape

One of the Left's most frequently uttered antiwar mantras is that Iraq is not part of the global War on Terror and that Bush decided to attack it for personal reasons. In doing so, he diverted our resources and focus from Osama bin Laden—our real enemy. *New York Times* columnist Maureen Dowd wrote, "Iraq never threatened U.S. security. Bush officials cynically attacked a villainous country because they know it was easier than finding the real September 11 villain, who had no country."[10] Senator Kennedy said that though Bush mentioned terror twenty-seven times in his State of the Union address, he never mentioned the man who launched the September 11 attacks. "What world is he living in?" asked Kennedy. "He started a war we never should have fought. He stopped fighting a war we hadn't won, and left our greatest enemy in the world still at large, planning his next September 11."[11]

One of Senator Kerry's favorite campaign slogans was that Bush outsourced the job of capturing Osama bin Laden in Tora Bora in 2001 to Afghan warlords. General Tommy Franks refuted this canard, saying that our Special Forces units were on the ground in hot pursuit of bin Laden. In an op-ed for the *New York Times*, Franks wrote, "As commander of the allied forces in the Middle East, I was responsible for the operation at Tora Bora, and I can tell you that the senator's understanding of events doesn't square with reality." Franks rejected Kerry's contention that we allowed bin Laden to escape after having him surrounded, saying "we don't know to this day whether Mr. bin Laden was at Tora Bora in December 2001."

Nor, according to Franks, did we "outsource military action." President Bush never "took his eye off the ball" when it came to Osama bin Laden. Perhaps most important, Franks affirmed that "the war on terrorism has a global focus" and "cannot be divided into separate and unrelated wars, one in Afghanistan and another in Iraq."[12]

"Bush Lied, People Died"

No other accusation against Bush was as slanderous as the repeated allegation that he lied about the intelligence on Iraqi WMD in order to drag us into an unnecessary, unjustified war. This was a particularly egregious tactic by those who accused Bush of hurting our national image. Their false charges not only discredited President Bush, but damaged the image and standing of the United States in the world. If American leaders—opposition party or not—consistently tell the world that the nation's commander in chief concocted a false version of events to justify attacking a sovereign nation, without provocation, how can the world possibly think America's hands are clean in Iraq?

Certain Democrats began accusing President Bush of misconduct in the War on Terror well before we invaded Iraq in 2003. Congresswoman Cynthia McKinney, donning her conspiracy hat, asked shortly after the September 11 terrorist attacks, "What did this administration know and when did it know it, about the events of September 11?" Senator Hillary Clinton was not far behind, asking on the floor of the Senate, "What did Bush know and when did he know it?" DNC chairman Howard Dean, not to be outdone, related his theory on WAMU radio that the president "was warned ahead of time by the Saudis [about the September 11 attacks]."[13] The *New York Times* reported, "President Bush was told more than a month before the attacks of September 11, 2001, that supporters of Osama bin Laden planned an attack within the United States with explosives and wanted to hijack airplanes, a government official said Friday."[14]

All of this hype was sparked by a single Presidential Daily Briefing on August 6, 2001, which didn't mention a word about plans for hijacked planes to be flown into buildings. It did mention that Osama had aspired to conduct terrorist attacks in the U.S. since 1997, and told his followers that he wanted to target Washington, D.C. But, as the briefing made clear, Osama had made this statement "after US missile strikes on his base in Afghanistan in 1998," which was three years before September 11. This is why the White House was correct in referring to the intelligence contained in the briefing as "historical."[15]

The briefing did refer to bin Laden's desire to "hijack a US aircraft," and stated that the FBI had detected al Qaeda activity suggesting "preparations for hijackings or other types of attacks." But the purpose of such hijackings was "to gain the release of 'Blind Shaykh' 'Umar' Abd al-Rahman and other US-held extremists." The briefing mentioned that terrorists had engaged in recent surveillance of federal buildings in New York."[16] Later that evening the *New York Times* clarified its reporting to admit that "the briefing did not point to any specific time or place of attack and did not warn that planes could be used as missiles." But the damage had already been done. The fact remains that there was absolutely nothing in the memo that could have alerted the administration that the plane attacks were coming—or when or where. But that didn't keep the liberal press and Bush-hating Democrats from painting the picture that Bush virtually knew about the attacks in advance, could have prevented them, and chose not to do so.

Democrats also began accusing President Bush of lying about Iraq before we attacked in 2003. Three Democratic congressmen, Jim McDermott, David "Baghdad" Bonior, and Mike Thompson went to Iraq in September 2002, denouncing the United States and President Bush on enemy soil. They weren't just criticizing Bush, but supporting a U.S. enemy in a way reminiscent of Jane Fonda's trip to Vietnam to support the Viet Cong.

McDermott said he believed President Bush was willing "to mislead the American people" about Iraq. "I believe that sometimes they give out misinformation," said McDermott "... and they've shifted. First they said it was al Qaeda, then they said it was weapons of mass destruction. Now they're going back and saying it's al Qaeda again."[17] Not only did McDermott trash his own president while in Iraq, but made statements supportive of Saddam Hussein's position on WMD. "[Iraq] said they would allow us to go look anywhere we wanted. And until they don't do that, there is no need to do this coercive stuff where you bring in helicopters and armed people and storm buildings." He said we "should take Iraqis on their face value."

Bonior, the second highest-ranking House Democrat, implied moral equivalence between Iraq and the United States. He said, "We've got to move forward in a way that's fair and impartial. That means not having the United States or the Iraqis dictate the rules to these inspections."[18] No one was alert enough to point out to Bonior that the rules had already been dictated to Iraq as a part of the treaty Saddam agreed to after being defeated in the Gulf War.

Not only did the Democratic hierarchy fail to reprimand these misfits, other top party officials were busy competing to make similarly destructive statements. Senate Majority Leader Tom Daschle said that the White House was "too narrowly focused on terrorism and Iraq and has steered the economy into the worst trouble since the Great Depression."[19] Senator Robert Byrd said that President

Bush's plans to invade Iraq were a conscious effort to distract public attention from domestic issues. Senators Hillary Clinton and Bill Nelson said Byrd's remarks were "the height of patriotism."[20]

The Big Lie

Next came the Democrats' big lie about the big "lie": "Bush lied about Iraqi WMD." This claim has been particularly exasperating both because of its preposterousness and its effectiveness. As Norman Podhoretz said, "What makes this charge so special is the amazing success it has enjoyed in getting itself established as a self-evident truth even though it has been refuted and discredited over and over again by evidence and arguments alike. In this it resembles nothing so much as those animated cartoon characters who, after being flattened, blown up, or pushed over a cliff, always spring back to life with their bodies perfectly intact. Perhaps, like those cartoon characters, this allegation simply cannot be killed off, no matter what."[21]

Democrats, who prided themselves on not caring a whit about presidential falsehoods during the Clinton scandals, suddenly had a collective epiphany over Bush's alleged lies about Iraq. His lies were different, they said, because people died as a result. Bush hadn't lied—and Democratic Party leaders knew it. But they were in a pickle. Most of them had supported the Joint Resolution to Authorize the Use of United States Armed Forces Against Iraq, which they insisted be brought to a vote, and needed to explain away their votes to their rabid antiwar base.

At the time of the resolution, public support for the war was strong. A *Washington Post* poll in January 2003 showed that 57 percent of the public supported military action against Iraq. President Bush had decided to attack Iraq and Democrats in Congress were in an uproar because he hadn't sufficiently consulted them. When President Bush agreed to bring them in on the decision, they were forced—because of the pro-war mood of the country—to support the resolution, many while holding their noses.

But it didn't take Democrats long after the invasion of Iraq to accuse President Bush of lying about Iraqi WMD. As soon as it became apparent that we weren't going to find major stockpiles of WMD, Democrats charged that our failure to find them meant they were never there and that Bush had lied about Saddam having them. They were not the slightest bit deterred from making allegations against the commander in chief during war.

Senator Edward Kennedy said, "The Bush administration misrepresented and distorted the intelligence to justify a war that America should never have fought."[22] Senate Minority Leader Harry Reid said, "The Bush White House manufactured and manipulated intelligence in order to bolster its case for the war in Iraq and to discredit anyone who dared to challenge the president." Senator John Kerry and former president Jimmy Carter accused President Bush of lying us into war in Iraq during their speeches at the Democratic National Convention. Earlier, Kerry had called the Bush administration "the most lying, corrupt group of guys."

The Democrats didn't discontinue their "Bush lied" propaganda after their 2004 presidential election defeat. On NBC's *Meet the Press* in November 2005, DNC chairman Howard Dean, often referring to the administration as corrupt, said, "I think Democrats always have to stand up and tell the truth and that's what we're doing. The truth is that the president misled America when he sent us to war."[23] That same month Senator Kennedy said, "In his march to war, President Bush exaggerated the threat to the American people."[24]

Hoisted by Their Own Petards

While they have had the effrontery to lambaste President Bush over his WMD assertions, scores of Democrats are on public record making similarly strong statements about Iraqi WMD. Indeed these quotations are too voluminous to cite in toto.[25]

President Clinton, while he was still in office, was quite clear in his opinion that Saddam had WMD, and he publicly endorsed a policy of regime change for Iraq. That he didn't follow through on it says more about Clinton's fecklessness and lack of principle than whether Saddam was in fact a threat.

Democratic sabre-rattling against Saddam started even before President Bush began his bid for the Republican nomination. On February 4, 1998, Clinton said, "One way or the other, we are determined to deny Iraq the capacity to develop weapons of mass destruction and the missiles to deliver them. That is our bottom line."[26] On February 17, he said, "If Saddam rejects peace and we have to use force, our purpose is clear. We want to seriously diminish the threat posed by Iraq's weapons of mass destruction program."[27]

On December 16, 1998, Clinton said, "Earlier today I ordered America's armed forces to strike military and security targets in Iraq.... Their mission is to attack Iraq's nuclear, chemical, and biological weapons programs and its military capacity to threaten its neighbors."[28] The same day, Vice President Al Gore said, "If you allow someone like Saddam Hussein to get nuclear weapons, ballistic missiles, chemical weapons, biological weapons, how many people is he going to kill with such weapons? He's already demonstrated a willingness to use these weapons."[29]

Clinton's secretary of state Madeleine Albright said in February 1998, "Iraq is a long way from [here], but what happens there matters a great deal here. For the risks that the leaders of a rogue state will use nuclear, chemical, or biological weapons against us or our allies is the greatest security threat we face."[30] On November 12, 1999, Albright said, "Hussein has...chosen to spend his money on building weapons of mass destruction and palaces for his cronies."[31] In February 1998, Clinton's national security adviser Sandy Berger said, "[Saddam] will use those weapons of mass destruction again, as he has ten times since 1983."[32]

Democratic senators Carl Levin, Tom Daschle, John Kerry, and others sent Clinton a letter on October 9, 1998, in which they told him, "[W]e urge you, after consulting with Congress, and consistent with the U.S. Constitution and laws, to take necessary actions (including, if appropriate, air and missile strikes on suspect Iraqi sites) to respond effectively to the threat posed by Iraq's refusal to end its weapons of mass destruction programs."[33] On December 16, 1998, Congresswoman Nancy Pelosi said, "Saddam Hussein has been engaged in the development of weapons of mass destruction technology which is a threat to countries in the region and he has made a mockery of the weapons inspection process."[34]

Years later, Democrats continued to insist that Saddam had WMD. Former president Bill Clinton told Larry King several months after we had invaded Iraq, "It is incontestable that on the day I left office, there were unaccounted for stocks of biological and chemical weapons. We might have destroyed them in 1998. We tried to, but we sure as heck didn't know it because we never got to go back in there."[35]

Senator Bob Graham, chairman of the Senate Intelligence Committee, signed a letter to President Bush dated December 5, 2001, saying, "There is no doubt that...Saddam Hussein has invigorated his weapons programs. Reports indicate that biological, chemical, and nuclear programs continue apace and may be back to pre–Gulf War status. In addition, Saddam continues to redefine delivery systems and is doubtless using the cover of an illicit missile program to develop longer-range missiles that will threaten the United States and our allies."[36] Later, Senator Graham said, "We are in possession of what I think to be compelling evidence that Saddam Hussein has, and has had for a number of years, a developing capacity for the production and storage of weapons of mass destruction."[37]

Senator Carl Levin said on September 19, 2002, "We begin with the common belief that Saddam Hussein is a tyrant and a threat to the peace and stability of the region. He has ignored the mandate of the United Nations and is building weapons of mass destruction and the means of delivering them."[38] Al Gore, on September 23, 2002, said, "We know that [Saddam] has stored secret supplies of biological and chemical weapons throughout his country. . . . Iraq's search for weapons of mass destruction has proven impossible to deter and we should assume that it will continue for as long as Saddam is in power."[39]

Senator Kennedy, at the Johns Hopkins School of Advanced International Studies on September 27, 2002, said, "We have known for many years that Saddam Hussein is seeking and developing weapons of mass destruction."[40] On October 6, 2002, on CBS's *Face the Nation*, he said, "Saddam Hussein is a dangerous figure. He's got dangerous weapons."[41] Senator Robert Byrd, around the same time, said, "The last UN weapons inspectors left Iraq in October 1998. We are confident that Saddam Hussein retains some stockpiles of chemical and biological weapons, and that he has since embarked on a crash course to build up his chemical and biological warfare capabilities. Intelligence reports indicate that he is seeking nuclear weapons."[42]

Senator Jay Rockefeller said, "There is unmistakable evidence that Saddam Hussein is working aggressively to develop nuclear weapons and will likely have nuclear weapons within the next five years. We also should remember we have always underestimated the progress Saddam has made in development of weapons of mass destruction."[43]

Senator Joseph Biden said on NBC's *Meet the Press* on August 4, 2002, "First of all, we don't know exactly what he has. It's been five years since inspectors have been in there, number one. Number two, it is clear that he has a residual of chemical weapons and biological weapons.... We know he continues to attempt to gain access to additional capability, including nuclear capability. There is a real debate how far off that is, whether it's a matter of years or whether it's a matter of less than that, and so there's much we don't know."[44]

Hillary Clinton said, "In the four years since the inspectors left, intelligence reports show that Saddam Hussein has worked to rebuild his chemical and biological weapons stock, his missile delivery capability, and his nuclear program.... It is clear, however, that if left unchecked, Saddam Hussein will continue to increase his capacity to wage biological and chemical warfare, and will keep trying to develop nuclear weapons."[45] Hillary also said, "I voted for the Iraqi resolution. I consider the prospect of a nuclear-armed Saddam Hussein who can threaten not only his neighbors, but the stability of the region and the world, a very serious threat to the United States."[46]

Senator John Edwards said, "Serving on the Intelligence Committee and seeing day after day, week after week, briefings on Saddam's weapons of mass destruction and his plans on using those weapons, he cannot be allowed to have nuclear weapons. It's just that simple. The whole world changes if Saddam ever has nuclear weapons."[47] Later Edwards said he had made a mistake in supporting the Iraq war resolution and sharply criticized President Bush, Dick Cheney, and Donald Rumsfeld—a clear attempt, which was successful—to get himself back into the good graces of his party's leftist antiwar base.[48]

But the granddaddy flip-flopper of them all, John Kerry, said, "I will be voting to give the president of the United States the authority to use force—if necessary—to disarm Saddam Hussein because I believe that a deadly arsenal of weapons of mass destruction in his hands is a real and grave threat to our security." Later, Kerry said, "Without question, we need to disarm Saddam Hussein. He is a brutal, murderous dictator, leading an oppressive regime....He presents a particularly grievous threat because he is so consistently prone to miscalculation. And now he is miscalculating America's response to his continued deceit and his consistent grasp for weapons of mass destruction....So the threat of Saddam Hussein with weapons of mass destruction is real."[49]

How the Lies about Lies Began

Author David Horowitz argues in his book *Unholy Alliance: Radical Islam and the American Left* that the Democrats have consistently tried to destroy Bush's credibility as commander in chief since at least June 2003.[50] This was just two months after Saddam was ousted and the terrorists began their campaign to take Iraq. Horowitz notes that the Left began its relentless assault on President Bush's credibility during the war, completely aware that a commander in chief's credibility is his most essential asset.

On July 10, a television attack ad produced by the Democratic National Committee began to air across the nation concerning the president's famous sixteen-word statement in his 2003 State of the Union address about Saddam's alleged efforts to buy yellow cake uranium from Niger. The sixteen words were: "The British government has learned that Saddam Hussein recently sought significant quantities of uranium from Africa."

But in their television ad titled, "Read His Lips: President Bush Deceives the American People," Democrats deliberately omitted, as Horowitz points out, the critical reference to the British government. They asserted that the president's statement was false and that he, the CIA, and the State Department knew it was false, because it had been disproved a year before.[51] The British, however, stood by their claim, which made Bush's statement undeniably true. And the Butler Report—the results of the British government's inquiry into prewar assessments of Iraq's nuclear weapons program—confirmed a year later that President Bush's statement was "well founded."[52]

A Bush administration spokesman later said—disappointingly—that the administration shouldn't have included the statement in the president's address[53] because, though factually accurate, director of Central Intelligence George Tenet still had reservations about it. In fact, reportedly at Tenet's urging,[54] the statement was removed from a presidential speech in Cincinnati three months earlier.

Ironically, Tenet later took responsibility for the statement's inclusion in the SOTU speech because the CIA cleared the speech without insisting the statement be removed.[55] There was no indication that the president made the claim in anything but good faith. Even the findings of the retired American ambassador who investigated claims that Iraq was seeking yellow cake lent credence to, rather than detracting from the president's statement, according to the bipartisan Senate Intelligence Committee. But the ambassador, Joseph Wilson, later changed his tune to become a prominent anti-Bush critic and Democratic celebrity.[56] The fact is, to any reasonable observer, the president's statement, in its entirety, remains irrefutably true. The British government had learned of Saddam's efforts, and it later reaffirmed the correctness of its findings. It still stands by its statement.

Then National Security Adviser Condoleezza Rice confirmed that the president's statement, though accurate and supported by a number of other sources, shouldn't have been included because the administration has a "higher standard" for presidential speeches, and includes only those things in which the intelligence community has "high confidence." In addition, she said, the alleged acquisition of yellow cake was but a small part of a large body of intelligence pointing to Saddam's efforts to continue his WMD program.[57] She added that Saddam's pursuit of WMD was not the only reason we went to war.

The Lie Continues Through the 2004 Campaign

Democrats continued wrongly to accuse Bush of lying about WMD throughout the 2004 presidential campaign. John Kerry stuck to that strategy but had to be careful that it didn't cause him to look too dovish, especially during wartime. Though he had been soft on defense throughout his political career, he tried to prop himself up as a pro-war candidate, highlighting his "heroic" war record—which would later be obliterated by John O'Neill and the Swift Boat Veterans for Truth.[58]

But the meteoric rise of Howard Dean in the Democratic primaries put a monkey wrench in Kerry's plans to have it both ways on the war. Dean had grown in popularity primarily because of his militant stance against the war. And he was directing his attack against his primary opponents, like Kerry, as much as President Bush. Kerry and other primary contenders, John Edwards, Dick Gephardt, and Joe Lieberman were all taking heat from the antiwar Democratic base for their support of the resolution to go to war. In 2003, at the Democratic National Committee's winter confab, an audience member heckled Gephardt, yelling, "Shame." Both Lieberman and Edwards had met similar fates in speeches in Manchester, New Hampshire, and Los Angeles, respectively.[59]

Caught between mainstream American opinion, which supported the war, and the antiwar base of the Democratic Party, John Kerry needed to bolster his justifications for voting for the Iraq war resolution or Dean would continue to hammer him over his vote. So Kerry repeated the false charges that Bush lied about Iraqi WMD and claimed a direct connection between Saddam and September 11. But Kerry also manufactured the story that he only voted for the resolution because President Bush promised he would not attack Iraq unless he built a broader multilateral coalition and further exhausted diplomatic avenues. This claim was convenient, but absolutely ludicrous. The resolution was unconditional. Moreover, the resolution was not just about WMD. As David Horowitz has pointed out, there were twenty-three "whereas" clauses in the resolution "articulating the rationale for the use of force," only two of which mentioned WMD stockpiles. Twelve of them addressed Saddam's violations of UN resolutions.[60]

Kerry's lies about the conditionality of the war resolution, coupled with his refusal to support the $87 billion supplemental appropriations bill for our troops in Iraq (he voted for it before he voted against it), sufficiently mollified the base. But they were evidently not enough to convince the general electorate of his fitness for commander in chief, even with all the military hype he engineered at the Democratic Convention that culminated in his hokey salute-studded announcement: "Reporting for Duty."

Harry Reid's Stunt

The Democrats' failure in the 2004 presidential campaign didn't discourage them from continuing their WMD lies. Never once did Democrats, including presidential and vice presidential candidates Kerry and Edwards, ever apologize for slandering the president. "Bush Lied and People Died" remains part of their talking points propaganda against the president and "his war," as Congressman John Murtha uncharitably dubbed it.

Al Gore famously said that George Bush "betrayed this country. He played on our fears. He took America on an ill-conceived foreign adventure dangerous to our troops, an adventure preordained and planned before September 11 ever took place."[61] Democratic presidential contestant General Wesley Clark said, "I think we're at risk with our democracy. I think we're dealing with the most closed, imperialistic, nastiest administration in living memory. They even put Richard Nixon to shame."[62]

Senator John Kerry also kept up the propaganda after the election. In November 2005, when President Bush was giving a series of speeches, finally answering his critics' bearing of false witness against him, Kerry fired back. "This administration misled a nation into war by cherry-picking intelligence and stretching the truth beyond recognition....It's a dangerous day for our national security when an administration's word is not good." His fellow Massachusetts senator, Ted Kennedy, said Bush's speeches were "a campaign-like attempt to rebuild his own credibility by tearing down those who seek the truth about the clear manipulation of intelligence in the run-up to the Iraq war."[63]

Senate Minority Leader Harry Reid, in a quintessentially cynical and highly unusual move, called for a closed-door meeting of the Senate to discuss the various claims against Bush concerning Iraq. Reid claimed—deceptively—that Majority Leader Bill Frist had reneged on his pledge to investigate thoroughly whether the administration hyped the prewar intelligence. Senator Dick Durbin said, "I seconded the motion Senator Harry Reid made last week. Republicans in Congress have refused, despite repeated promises, to investigate the Bush administration's misuse of prewar intelligence, so Senate Democrats are standing up and demanding the truth."[64]

Senate Intelligence Committee chairman Pat Roberts was outraged at Reid's maneuver, relating that just twenty-four hours before Reid called for the meeting, his staff had informed Democrats on the committee that they were moving toward closure on those issues. Referring to Reid's move, Roberts said, "If that's not politics, I'm not standing here."[65] Significantly, the reason the Intelligence Committee's investigation was delayed—which is supposedly what led to the frustration giving rise to Reid's stunt—was the discovery of a secret memo of Senator Jay Rockefeller revealing the Democrats' plan to exploit the committee's findings for political gain.[66] The memo, originally reported by FOX News's Sean Hannity, discussed the Democrats' plan to time the investigation of prewar Iraqi intelligence to maximize embarrassment to the Bush administration and thereby damage the president's re-election efforts.[67] In announcing the meeting, Reid expressed absolute certainty that Bush lied about WMD:

> The Libby indictment provides a window into what this is really about: How the administration manufactured and manipulated intelligence in order to sell the war in Iraq and attempted to destroy those who dared to challenge its actions. As a result of its improper conduct, a cloud now hangs over this administration.[68]

Senator Dick Durbin added his own incendiary allegations: "It is clear now that the American people were not informed properly before the invasion of Iraq. Intelligence information was distorted, was misused, and we have seen as late as last week the lengths which this administration has gone to try to silence and discredit their critics of the misuse of this intelligence information."[69] DNC chairman Howard Dean sent out a group e-mail applauding Reid's move: "We must demand accountability for manipulated intelligence on Iraq and the White House cover-up." Dean then asked for a special financial contribution.[70]

Did Saddam Have (and Move) WMD after All?

The yellow cake flap was just one small aspect of the "Bush lied" controversy. What about other evidence bearing on whether Bush fabricated, manipulated, or exaggerated intelligence on Iraqi WMD? What about the charges that he pressured our intelligence agencies to overstate the case? What about the Democrats' claims that Bush acted unilaterally? How valid is the charge that he was unjustified in preemptively attacking Iraq?

Before answering these questions, we must address a few preliminary issues. First, our failure to find WMD stockpiles does not mean they were not there or that Saddam was not desperately trying to acquire them. Second, even if there were no WMD stockpiles, that doesn't mean that President Bush lied about the weapons or that we were not justified in attacking Iraq.

The weapons could have been moved to Syria, Iran, or elsewhere. All kinds of stories have circulated and some books have been written asserting that those weapons did exist and were moved prior to our invasion. Israeli officer Lieutenant General Moshe Yaalon, chief of staff of the Israel Defense Forces from 2002 to 2005, insisted that Saddam moved his chemical weapons into Syria right before the war began.

Author Kenneth R. Timmerman tells the story of former deputy undersecretary of defense John A. Shaw, who was responsible for tracking Saddam Hussein's weapons programs before and after the 2003 U.S.-led invasion of Iraq. According to Timmerman, Shaw reported at an "Intelligence Summit" in Alexandria, Virginia, that WMD Saddam bought from the Russians were moved to Syria and Lebanon before the war. "They were moved by Russian Spetsnaz [special forces] units out of uniform," said Shaw, "that were specifically sent to Iraq to move the weaponry and eradicate any evidence of its existence." Shaw said the evacuation of the WMD was "a well-orchestrated campaign using two neighboring client states with which the Russian leadership had a longtime security relationship."[71]

In addition to many WMD being moved from Iraq before the war, Timmerman also claims that many chemical weapons *were* found in Iraq.[72] Senator Rick Santorum and Congressman Peter Hoekstra reinforced Timmerman's claim in June 2006 in a press conference in which they reported that documents developed by our intelligence services revealed the discovery of around five hundred munitions containing degraded weapons of mass destruction in Iraq. The discovery of these sarin- and mustard-filled projectiles— though they were believed to be pre–Gulf War chemical munitions—proved that Saddam lied about his WMD and that he violated his agreement to dispose of all such weapons. Senator Santorum called the find "incredibly" significant and added, "The idea that, as my colleagues have repeatedly said in this debate on the other side of the aisle, that there are no weapons of mass destruction is in fact false."[73]

Also, the U.S. Survey Group reported in late 2004 that a major French arms maker was offering to refurbish surface-to-air missiles for Iraq just weeks before we attacked. Such sales would have violated UN sanctions, assuming the French government was behind them or permitted them. The Duelfer Report, prepared by chief U.S. arms inspector Charles Duelfer, described how Saddam obtained arms from foreign arms dealers and certain foreign nations, including Russia. From 2001 until we attacked Iraq in 2003, there was a charter flight from Moscow to Baghdad every Monday carrying smuggled high-tech military gear, "such as radar jammers, GPS jammers, night vision devices, avionics, and missile components."[74]

Perhaps the most persuasive evidence that Saddam was aggressively pursuing WMD and concealing his activities and weapons was that contained in the revealing book by Saddam's former general Georges Sada.[75] Sada was a Christian member of Saddam's inner circle, who had earned Saddam's trust. In *Saddam's Secrets*,

Sada gives his own compelling eyewitness account of Saddam's mysterious WMD. Sada said Iraqi engineers had become very proficient at manufacturing chemical weapons for various delivery systems and ordnance. Even in 2002, when Saddam was convinced America would attack, he kept producing these weapons systems until he realized he would have to get rid of the evidence. He then whisked the weapons out of the country.[76]

Sada wrote:

> The point is that when Saddam finally grasped the fact that it was just a matter of time until Iraq would be invaded by American and coalition forces, he knew he would have to take special measures to destroy, hide, or at least disguise his stashes of biological and chemical weapons, along with the laboratories, equipment, and plans associated with nuclear weapons development. But then, much to his good fortune, a natural disaster in neighboring Syria provided the perfect cover story for moving a large number of those things out of the country.[77]

Sada says he knows the names of some of those who were involved in smuggling WMD out of Iraq in 2002 and 2003, and the names of the officers of SES, the front company that received the weapons. Sada notes that Israel is well aware that Saddam had WMD and transferred them to other countries in the region. He says that some Americans know these things too, but are not making the information public, possibly for diplomatic reasons. That's why, Sada says, media accounts are dominated by opponents of the Iraq war who have a vested interest in denying the existence of Iraqi WMD. Sada wrote, "When I speak here about weapons of mass destruction, I am referring to the biological, chemical, and nuclear weapons that Saddam had built or was trying to build. Everyone in the international arms community knew that Saddam had them and that he was spending like a sailor to buy more."[78]

The *Boston Herald* editorialized that "there have been just too many recent reports, impossible to brush off, that [Iraqi WMD] were transferred to Syria shortly before the beginning of the U.S. invasion of Iraq in March 2003." The place to start an investigation into the claims "is the two million documents captured by U.S. forces in Iraq along with more than 2,500 hours of audiotapes of Saddam Hussein's meetings with underlings." According to the *Herald*, the general who oversaw Pentagon spy satellites confirmed that large truck convoys were seen traveling from Iraq to Syria as the war began.[79] President Bush eventually decided to release most of the documents.[80]

Saddam's Burden of Proof

To lie is to say something you know to be false. If President Bush believed Iraq had WMD at the time he made his assertion, which the evidence clearly indicates he did, he was not lying about it. More important, his justification to attack Iraq did not depend upon the existence of Iraqi WMD. What is paramount is that Saddam provoked the United States into attacking him. The United States did not have the legal or moral burden of proving that Saddam was still manufacturing and stockpiling WMD. Saddam had the burden of proving that he disposed of the weapons we know he had and used on his own people, and wasn't producing any more of them.

Following the Gulf War, he was on probation. He signed postwar treaties promising to disgorge himself of WMD and not to produce any more. He was to permit UN weapons inspectors to verify that he was not in breach of his promises. He was also not to interfere with our enforcement of the no-fly zones.

But following the war, for twelve years he repeatedly violated the treaties. He defiantly denied weapons inspectors the latitude to do their jobs. He repeatedly shot at our aircraft in the no-fly zones. He violated seventeen Security Council resolutions requiring that he rid himself of WMD. The United Nations' ultimate refusal to exhibit the moral courage to enforce its resolutions is an indictment of the United Nations, not proof that President Bush acted imperiously in "going it alone" against Iraq. We did the right thing, as did our coalition partners, while the UN and many nations of Old Europe did not.

On November 8, 2002, the United Nations adopted Resolution 1441 by unanimous consent of the fifteen-member Security Council. The resolution affirmed the world's certainty that Saddam possessed weapons of mass destruction. It declared that Iraq had repeatedly breached its obligations under UN Resolution 687 by failing to disclose fully and accurately its WMD and long-range missile programs. It stated that Iraq had repeatedly obstructed UN inspections and finally terminated them altogether. It gave Iraq a final chance to comply with its treaty obligation to disarm, but warned that Iraq would be considered in further material breach and face serious consequences if it made false statements or omissions in its required declaration as to its disarmament.[81]

This meant that Iraq was required to show us its weapons caches or produce a paper trail demonstrating that it had disposed of the weapons. Instead, on December 8, Saddam delivered a 12,000-page document full of disinformation. He was required to prove to us that he no longer had WMD, but instead openly defied us, just as he had the weapons inspectors. Even if the UN lacked the fortitude and principles to follow through on its warnings, President Bush did not. Ultimately, his attack on Iraq was not unprovoked. It was in response to Saddam's refusal to comply with his agreements and his continual defiance of UN weapons inspectors, the United States, and the rest of the world.

Regardless of whether Saddam still possessed stockpiles of WMD, *he was behaving as though he had them.* Indeed, one theory from those who believe he didn't have WMD is that he wanted the world to believe he did—and, in fact, many of his own generals did believe him. One report indicated that Saddam rejected a suggestion by someone in his inner circle that he come clean about having no WMD, for fear that Israel might attack in the absence of a nuclear deterrent.[82]

If Saddam acted as though he had WMD, it was reasonable for President Bush to assume he did, especially since CIA director George Tenet, a Clinton appointee, told President Bush that it was a "slam dunk" that Saddam had WMD. All fifteen intelligence gathering agencies for the United States, and the intelligence services for many other nations, including Germany, France, Britain, Russia, China, Israel, and Jordan, were convinced Saddam had WMD.[83]

At a UN Security Council meeting on February 5, 2003, French foreign minister Dominique de Villepin declared, "Right now, our attention has to be focused as a priority on the biological and chemical domains. It is there that our presumptions about Iraq are the most significant. Regarding the chemical domain, we have evidence of its capacity to produce VS and Yperite. In the biological domain, the evidence suggests the possible possession of significant stocks of anthrax and botulism toxin, and possibly a production capability."[84] On NBC's *Today Show* on February 26, 2003, German ambassador to the United States Wolfgang Ischinger said, "I think all of our governments believe that Iraq has produced weapons of mass destruction and that we have to assume that they still have weapons of mass destruction."[85]

The National Intelligence Estimate of 2002 expressed with "high confidence" the conclusion that "Iraq is continuing, and in some areas expanding its chemical, biological, nuclear, and missile programs contrary to UN resolutions." Even the Bureau of Intelligence and Research of the State Department agreed, despite reports to the contrary. It is true that they didn't believe Saddam's nuclear program was operational, but they did believe he had other WMD.[86]

Plus, we had a history of erring on the side of underestimating the nuclear capabilities of other nations, including the Soviet Union, China, Pakistan, India, North Korea, and Iraq (before the first Gulf War).[87] And our virtual absence of human intelligence necessarily added to our anxiety about Saddam's intentions and activities.[88]

What was especially exasperating about the Democrats' criticism of Bush for attacking Iraq without being one thousand percent sure Saddam possessed WMD was that they wanted to have it both ways. With their earlier conspiracy theories they argued that Bush failed to connect the dots before September 11 and ignored crucial intelligence that could have led to preventing the attacks. According to them, he should have known exactly where, when, and how we were going to be attacked on September 11 and prevented it— though we had no advance warning on any of the specifics. But though all of our intelligence agencies and many key European and regional intelligence agencies agreed Saddam had WMD, Democrats now say it wasn't enough to warrant an attack.

CHAPTER TWO

The Defeatocrats

Democratic congressmen had access to substantially the same intelligence on WMD as President Bush and came to the same conclusions. Democrats falsely deny this, saying the Presidential Daily Briefing (PDB) was superior to the National Intelligence Estimate (NIE) provided to Congress. But the Robb-Silberman Commission concluded that, if anything, the PDB was "more alarmist" and "less nuanced" than the NIE, though the intelligence in the two was not "markedly different."

Did the President Pressure the CIA?

Democrats also falsely claim the president pressured the intelligence agencies, including the CIA, to overstate the case for WMD. The bipartisan Senate Select Committee on Intelligence found, based on hundreds of interviews with intelligence officials, that the president did not exert pressure on the CIA. Its Conclusion 83 stated, "The Committee did not find any evidence that Administration officials attempted to coerce, influence or pressure analysts to change their judgments related to Iraq's weapons of mass destruction capabilities." Conclusion 84 stated, "The Committee found no evidence that the Vice President's visits to the Central Intelligence Agency were attempts to pressure analysts, were perceived as intended to pressure analysts by those who participated in the briefings on Iraq's weapons of mass destruction programs, or did pressure analysts to change their assessments."[1]

Similarly, the Robb-Silberman Commission found no evidence of presidential coercion of the intelligence services. The report concluded, "The Commission found no evidence of political pressure to influence the Intelligence Community's pre-war assessments of Iraq's weapons programs. As we discuss in detail in the body of our report, analysts universally asserted that in no instance did political pressure cause them to skew or alter any of their analytical judgments. We conclude that it was the paucity of intelligence and poor analytical tradecraft, rather than political pressure,that produced the inaccurate pre-war intelligence assessments."[2]

Finally, the Butler Report commissioned by the British government concluded, "We should record in particular that we have found no evidence of deliberate distortion or of culpable negligence."

Tenet's Reflective Assessments

In a speech at Georgetown University on February 5, 2004, CIA director George Tenet addressed how the U.S. intelligence community evaluated Iraq's WMD programs leading to the National Intelligence Estimate of 2002.[3] Before discussing the specific evidence, Tenet made a very important point about intelligence collection and analysis in the real world, which is consistently omitted in today's discussions. "By definition," he said, "intelligence deals with the unclear, the unknown, the deliberately hidden. What the enemies of the United States hope to deny, we work to reveal." He emphasized that it is an inexact science where certain conclusions are few and far between.

Tenet said that the purpose of the NIE was to answer whether Iraq had chemical, biological, and nuclear weapons and delivery systems. Its conclusions were that Iraq did have some WMD; and those it didn't have, such as nuclear, Saddam was trying to develop. Tenet conceded that intelligence analysts were not in agreement on all these conclusions, but said that dissenting opinions were spelled out clearly in the NIE. Tenet affirmed, like President Bush, that the CIA never said there was an "imminent" threat, but analysts "painted an objective assessment for our policymakers of a brutal dictator who was continuing his efforts to deceive and build programs that might constantly surprise us and threaten our interests."

Tenet said intelligence agencies had three important "streams of information." First, Iraq's history of possessing and using WMD. Saddam had used chemical weapons against Iran and his own people at least ten different times. Also, we know that in the early 1990s, Saddam was but a few years away from developing a nuclear weapon, and that the world "had significantly underestimated his progress." To believe Saddam had no interest in reconstituting his program would have required our agencies to ignore history.

The second stream of information was that the United Nations was unable to account for all the weapons we know Saddam had.

Saddam behaved deceptively, uncooperatively, and defiantly toward
the weapons inspectors for eight years, which "undermined efforts
to disarm him." More important, "To conclude before the war that
Saddam had destroyed his existing weapons, *we would have had to
ignore what the United Nations and allied intelligence said they
could not verify.*"

Don't forget that Saddam kicked out the weapons inspectors. The
third stream of information was the data gathered after the inspectors left Iraq in 1998: from human agents, satellite photos, and
communications intercepts. In those intercepts, "we heard Iraqis
seeking to hide prohibited items, worrying about their cover stories,
and trying to procure items Iraq was not permitted to have." Also,
satellite photos "showed a pattern of activity designed to conceal
movement of material from places where chemical weapons had
been stored in the past." Analysts detected reconstruction of dual-
purpose facilities where chemical and biological agents had been
made in the past. Sources told of Iraq's efforts to acquire and hide
materials used to produce chemical and biological weapons.

Indeed, a source "who had direct access to Saddam and his inner
circle" reported that Saddam was "aggressively and covertly" developing a nuclear weapon. Iraq's Nuclear Weapons Committee, which
Saddam chided for not yet having a weapon because "money was
no object" and "they had the scientific know how," assured the dictator that once they acquired fissile material they could make a
bomb within eighteen to twenty-four months. And, they assured
him, the return of the weapons inspectors would not delay them
because they were experts in denial and deception. The source also
said Iraq was stockpiling chemical weapons and that insecticide-
producing equipment, under the Oil-for-Food Program, had been

diverted to chemical weapons production. Other sources reported Saddam was producing chemical and biological weapons.

Tenet admitted that the accumulated intelligence did not make a perfect picture or answer every question, but did provide a solid basis upon which to prepare the "estimate." To have arrived at different conclusions than they did would have required them "to ignore all the intelligence gathered from multiple sources after 1998."

Perhaps the most revealing part of Tenet's speech was his report on what we actually found upon entering Iraq. We discovered that

- Iraq had an aggressive missile program that had been concealed from the international community. The Iraq Survey Group concluded Iraq was committed to delivery system improvements that, in the absence of our invasion, would have dramatically breached UN restrictions imposed on Iraq after the Gulf War.
- Iraq was well on the way to producing liquid propellant missiles with ranges up to 1,000 kilometers, which threatened large portions of the Middle East, and which had been hidden from the United Nations. Also, the Iraq Survey Group confirmed our prewar intelligence indicating that Saddam had been in secret negotiations with North Korea to obtain dangerous missile technology.
- Iraq was working on several unmanned aerial vehicle designs that a senior Iraqi official has admitted were intended for delivery of biological weapons.
- Though Saddam did not have nuclear weapons, David Kay confirmed that "the testimony we have obtained from Iraqi scientists and senior government officials

should clear up any doubts about whether Saddam still wanted to obtain nuclear weapons." Tenet said that there is no question Saddam wanted nuclear weapons and intended to reconstitute his nuclear program at some point. But Tenet was emphatic that the CIA *never* claimed before the war that Saddam did have nukes. In fact, he said, "We made two judgments that get overlooked these days: we said Saddam did *not* have a nuclear weapon, and probably would have been unable to make one until 2007 to 2009." Most agencies, he said, did believe Saddam had reconstituted his nuclear program, but disagreed on other issues, all of which were laid out in the NIE. In the end, admitted Tenet, we don't know if Saddam had reconstituted his nuclear program, but we may have overestimated the progress he was making.

- Iraq intended to develop biological weapons and research and development work was in progress that "would have permitted a rapid shift to agent production if seed stocks were available." We don't know if production actually took place, nor had we found biological weapons. But we did find evidence that Iraq was deliberately concealing its research and development of biological weapons. The Iraqi Survey Group also located a network of laboratories and safehouses that contained equipment for chemical and biological research that were not disclosed to the United Nations.

- Saddam had the intent and capability to quickly convert the civilian industry to chemical weapons production but we did not find the chemical weapons stockpiles we expected to find.

Secret Documents

Voluminous documents that were obtained from Iraq's intelligence services after we deposed Saddam in 2003 point to Saddam's nuclear weapons aspirations. Kenneth R. Timmerman said that among those documents "were transcripts of Saddam's palace conversations with top aides in which he discussed ongoing nuclear weapons plans in 2000, well after the UN arms inspectors believed he had ceased all nuclear weapons work." Former FBI translator Bill Tierney, according to Timmerman, said, "What was most disturbing in those tapes was the fact that the individuals briefing Saddam were totally unknown to the UN Special Commission."

Tierney revealed that there were tapes of conversations between Saddam and his aids in 2000 concerning ongoing plasma separation programs—plans to enrich uranium—that our intelligence services had dismissed as "old programs" that were disbanded years before.[4] Also on the discovered tapes—twelve hours of conversations from the early 1990s and 2000 between Saddam and his top advisers— were revelations that Saddam was conspiring to deceive UN inspectors concerning WMD destruction and discussing how the weapons might be used against the United States.[5]

In addition, a discovered memo from 2002 details "the transfer of Top Secret and Very Important WMD documents from the Iraqi National Monitoring Agency to more secure locations" to make it more difficult for weapons inspectors to find them.[6]

The Iraq/al Qaeda Connection

Another major prong of the Democrats' unrelenting policy of attacking President Bush on Iraq is their assertion that he duped the American people into supporting an invasion of Iraq by falsely suggesting that Saddam was involved in September 11. President Bush did not say Saddam was involved in the September 11 attacks, but quite the opposite. Bush said, "We've had no evidence that Saddam Hussein was involved with September 11."[7] Nor did Condoleezza Rice, contrary to liberal propaganda, make such a connection. She said on ABC's *Nightline*, "We have never claimed that Saddam Hussein had either...direction or control of September 11. What we have said is that this was someone who supported terrorists, helped train them. But most importantly, that this is someone who, with his animus towards the United States, with his penchant for and capability to gain weapons of mass destruction, and his obvious willingness to use them, was a threat in this region that we were not prepared to tolerate."[8]

What the administration also said was that Saddam was friendly to and supportive of terrorists. On this, many Democrats agreed. The Clinton administration, in 1999, included Iraq on a list of nations that were supporting terrorists. Secretary of State Madeleine Albright said, "Governments on the list that would like to see their names removed know exactly what they must do: stop planning, financing, and supporting terrorist acts and stop sheltering and interfering with the apprehension and prosecution of those who commit them." Senator Hillary Clinton said on the floor of the Senate, "[Saddam] has given aid, comfort, and sanctuary to terrorists, including al Qaeda members, though there is apparently no evidence of his involvement in the terrible events of September 11, 2001."

The *Washington Post* reported in August 2002, based on U.S. intelligence reports, that "At least a handful of ranking members of al Qaeda have taken refuge in Iraq."[9] The Senate Intelligence Committee corroborated the president's conclusion that there were ties between al Qaeda and Iraq. So did the Butler Report, citing "meetings...between senior Iraqi representatives and senior al Qaeda operatives."[10] The Butler Report concluded that after al Qaeda was expelled from Afghanistan, senior al Qaeda figure Abu Musab al Zarqawi "was relatively free to travel within Iraq proper and to stay in Baghdad for some time. Several of his colleagues visited him there." Indeed, it is undisputed—confirmed by the Senate Intelligence Committee—that "Zarqawi was in Baghdad with two dozen al Qaeda associates nearly a year before the war." Zarqawi, according to General Tommy Franks, "had received medical treatment in Baghdad." Yet after American bombs killed Zarqawi, the *New York Times* featured a thirty-five-point list of "Key Events in the Life of al Zarqawi," in which it conspicuously left out his time in Baghdad.[11]

The 9-11 Commission also made some interesting findings about al Qaeda's interactions with Iraq. It said, "There is evidence that around [1997] bin Laden sent out a number of feelers to the Iraqi regime, offering some cooperation." And, "in March 1998, after bin Laden's public fatwa against the United States, two al Qaeda members reportedly went to Iraq to meet with Iraqi intelligence.... Similar meetings between Iraqi officials and bin Laden or his aides may have occurred in 1999 during a period of some reported strains with the Taliban. According to the reporting, Iraqi officials offered bin Laden a safe haven in Iraq."[12]

The "reports describe friendly contacts and indicate some common themes in both sides' hatred of the United States." "Bin Laden," according to the commission's report, "was also willing to explore possibilities for cooperation with Iraq, even though Iraq's dictator, Saddam Hussein, had never had an Islamist agenda—save for his opportunistic pose as a defender of the faithful against 'Crusaders' during the Gulf war of 1991."[13]

The *Weekly Standard*'s Stephen F. Hayes has done a great deal of invaluable research and writing concerning the ties between Iraq and al Qaeda. In his book *The Connection: How al Qaeda's Collaboration with Saddam Hussein Has Endangered America*, Hayes contends it was common knowledge that there were strong ties between the two, though public opinion on the matter has changed. Hayes noted that before the war, Senator Jay Rockefeller "pointed to Zarqawi's presence in Iraq as a 'substantial connection between Iraq and al Qaeda.' Yet he, too, now insists that Saddam Hussein's regime 'had nothing to do with Osama bin Laden, it had nothing to do with al Qaeda.'" Hayes also documented that "Saddam Hussein's regime provided financial support to Abu Sayyaf, the al Qaeda-linked jihadist group founded by Osama bin Laden's brother-in-law in the Philippines in the late 1990s, according to documents captured in postwar Iraq."[14]

According to Hayes and Thomas Joscelyn, writing for the *Weekly Standard*, whatever their relationship before, "the relationship between Iraq and al Qaeda intensified in 1998.... On February 3, 1998, Ayman al Zawahiri, bin Laden's Egyptian deputy, came to Baghdad for meetings with Iraqi leaders.... We do not have reporting on when, exactly, Zawahiri left Baghdad. But we do know from an interrogation of a senior Iraqi intelligence official that he did not leave empty-handed. As first reported in *U.S. News & World Report*, the Iraqi regime gave Zawahiri $300,000 during or shortly after his trip to Baghdad."

Hayes and Joscelyn note that documents retrieved after the war, which U.S. intelligence have verified as authentic, "provide another window into the relationship between the former Iraqi regime and al Qaeda." Some of these documents show that two days after Clinton gave a speech preparing the nation for a confrontation with Iraq in February 1998, "the Iraqi Intelligence Service finalized plans to bring a 'trusted confidant' of bin Laden's to Baghdad in early March." The documents, which were a series of communications between Iraqi intelligence divisions, indicated that the "trusted confidant" of bin Laden's would be assisted with travel arrangements and that Iraq would "carry all the travel and hotel expenses inside Iraq to gain the knowledge of the message from us to bin Laden, the Saudi opposition leader, about the future of our relationship with him, and to achieve a direct meeting with him."

Just a few days later, bin Laden, Zawahiri, and leaders of four other terrorist groups announced the formation of a group that would later "become better known as al Qaeda." The grievances in their fatwa, according to Hayes, focused on Iraq, protesting, "the great devastation inflicted on the Iraqi people by the crusader-Zionist alliance."[15]

The authors conclude, "We know that in the context of a decade-long confrontation with the United States, Saddam reached out to al Qaeda on numerous occasions. We know that the leadership of al Qaeda reciprocated, requesting assistance in its endeavors. We know that reports of meetings, offers of safe haven, and collaboration persisted. What we do not know is the full extent of the relationship. But we know enough to know that there was one. And we know enough to know it was a threat."[16]

In addition, FOX News reported that "a newly released document" captured in Iraq shows further terror links to Saddam's inner circle. The document "appears to provide evidence that in

1999 the Taliban welcomed 'Islamic relations with Iraq' to medi-
ate among the Taliban, the Northern Alliance, and Russia, and that
the Taliban invited Iraqi officials to Afghanistan." The document
"provides evidence of a cooperative, operational relationship
agreed to at the highest levels of the Iraqi government and the Taliban."[17] Other captured documents show that Saddam's inner circle "not only actively reached out to the Taliban rulers of
Afghanistan and terror-based jihadists in the region, but also
hosted discussions with a known al Qaeda operative about creating jihad training 'centers,' possibly in Baghdad."[18] FOX News also
reported that an Arab regime—most likely Saddam's—supplied
training manuals for Taliban and al Qaeda terrorists in Afghanistan
prior to the September 11 attacks.[19]

Sadly, Democrats are determined to deny there was any relationship between al Qaeda and Saddam because if a relationship can be
demonstrated it will prove Iraq was part of the War on Terror and
that our attack was justified. As *U.S. News & World Report*'s
Michael Barone observed, despite "evidence of contacts between al
Qaeda and Saddam's regime [that] went back to the 1990s and were
cited, without murmur of dissent, by President Bill Clinton . . . the
Democrats fear more Americans would support Mr. Bush and the
war effort if they believed there was [a connection between al
Qaeda and Saddam]."[20]

Imminent Threat

Democrats have persistently asserted that Bush misidentified Iraq as
an "imminent threat" to bolster his case for war. On *FOX News Sunday*, Senator Joseph Biden accused Vice President Cheney and "the
administration" of describing the Iraqi threat as "imminent."[21] When

host Chris Wallace challenged him on the point, Biden was adamant, "Oh, he did. No, no, he did [describe the threat as imminent.]"

The following week on the program, Wallace reported, "Well, we checked and could find no instance when the vice president ever said Saddam was an imminent threat. So we asked Senator Biden to back up his claim. This was the best his office could come up with." Wallace then played a clip in which Cheney said there was no doubt Saddam "now has" WMD and that he was "amassing them to use against" the United States, its friends, and allies. Wallace then summarized Cheney's statement, "Certainly a threat, but nothing about an imminent threat."[22]

Wallace was correct. President Bush often described Iraq as a "gathering threat," but not an imminent threat. At a speech at the Cincinnati Museum Center on October 7, 2002, he said, "America must not ignore the threat gathering against us. Facing clear evidence of peril, we cannot wait for the final proof—the smoking gun—that could come in the form of a mushroom cloud."[23] In a national press conference on March 6, 2003, he said, "If I thought we were safe from attack, I would be thinking differently. But I see a gathering threat."[24]

Interestingly, a few weeks before Biden appeared on *FOX News Sunday*, another Democratic senator found himself trapped by his own words on the same program. Senator Jay Rockefeller was the guest and Chris Wallace played him a prewar clip of Rockefeller declaring, in an October 2002 speech, "I do believe that Iraq poses an imminent threat, but I also believe that after September 11 that question is increasingly outdated." Wallace pointed out that with that statement, Rockefeller "went further than the president ever did" in actually assessing Iraq as an "imminent threat."[25]

"Unilateralism"

One of the Democrats' longest standing criticisms of Bush administration foreign policy is that President Bush has been arrogant toward other nations and has acted unilaterally. Even before the Iraq war, Democrats like Senator John Kerry complained that Bush's "unilateral approach" to foreign policy was hurting America's war against terrorism. As the United States was contemplating military action against Iraq, Senator Edward Kennedy said that unilateral military action would undermine the international coalition needed in the war against al Qaeda.[26] When we did attack Iraq, Democrats complained that we had acted unilaterally. The charge is false. President Bush did build a substantial coalition. It is true that certain European nations didn't support various aspects of President Bush's policy toward Iraq. But that is not to say they were right and he was wrong, which the Democrats usually presume. Liberal Democrats never seem to question the wisdom and propriety of foreign dissent. They don't consider the consequences of deferring to the United Nations or the so-called international community when it's contrary to America's strategic interests.

Whenever a strong Republican president is in office articulating clear foreign policy positions and taking decisive action, Democrats get nervous that other nations will disapprove. Remember how they shuddered in horror when President Reagan dubbed the Soviet Union "an evil empire"? The Left has been similarly critical of President Bush's "axis of evil" designation. They have also denounced him for not signing on to the Kyoto climate change treaty and the International Criminal Court, notwithstanding his justifiable concerns over their potential for compromising American sovereignty. The Democrats' complaint is always that America is snubbing its nose at foreign governments, when in reality it is just acting in its own national interests, as every nation has a duty to do.

Howard Dean, when vying for the Democratic nomination, slammed President Bush for his "go-it-alone approach to every problem" and his "radical unilateralism." Bush had "created a new rallying cry for terrorist recruits." Dean said, "We find ourselves, too often, isolated and resented." The Bush administration, said Dean, "seem[s] to believe that nothing can be gained from working with nations that have stood by our side as allies for generations." Revealingly, he added that he "would not have hesitated" to attack Iraq "had the United Nations given us permission and asked us to be a part of a multilateral force."[27]

Democrats charged that our "unilateral action" against Iraq not only alienated our allies, but diminished our chances for success, because we lacked vital support from other nations. Senator Carl Levin, on *FOX News Sunday*, said, "We can't go it alone [in Iraq]."[28] In an op-ed for the *Washington Post*, Senator Joseph Biden wrote, "We have one last chance to bring the world into Iraq. It would require a genuine U-turn away from the unilateral model we've been following for securing and rebuilding Iraq."[29]

Former president Jimmy Carter said that by acting unilaterally, President Bush had alienated and isolated the United States from its potential allies in the War on Terror. He said Bush's extremist policies have resulted in America losing our "reputation as the most admired champion of freedom and justice."[30]

Former president Clinton, in accepting an award for "international understanding," said that America's image had cratered in the entire Muslim world, except, of course, where he personally had made an impact: in Indonesia with his work on tsunami relief. "It's a big argument," he said, "for doing things in a cooperative way rather than in a unilateral way." Clinton characterized Bush's attitude toward foreign nations as "cooperate when there's no other alternative.... We should still have a preference for peace over war, a preference for cooperation over unilateralism, a preference for investing more to build a world with more partners and fewer terrorists." The unmistakable inference was that President Bush's "unilateral approach" was creating more terrorists. It wasn't the Saudi madrassas or terrorist recruitment efforts, or Islamic radicalism transferred from generation to generation, but President Bush's cavalier foreign policy.[31]

In fact, Bush formed a coalition of some thirty-two nations to attack Iraq. And he tried very diligently to persuade France, Germany, and Russia to join us—and they refused, which some believe was partly because of their corrupt involvement in the United Nations Oil-for-Food scandal. Those who have accused President Bush of "going it alone" in Iraq with American troops have also greatly demeaned the profound sacrifice of Iraqi soldiers. As of late 2005, Iraq had committed 212,000 soldiers and police to fighting the insurgency and had suffered enormously higher casualties than America.[32]

Regardless, President Bush can't be blamed for the failure of some of our allies to do the right thing, especially when they agreed that Saddam was a menace who had WMD and was trying to develop nuclear capabilities. When it comes to foreign policy, we are not engaging in some international popularity contest, but acting to protect our national security. John Kerry repeatedly said that he would not give other nations veto power over our national security. But at the same time he was criticizing President Bush for attacking Iraq without the joinder of these unreasonably recalcitrant nations. He can't have it both ways.

Besides, France and Germany made it quite clear that they were unpersuadable. Kerry's implication that if he had been president he would have been more successful at building the coalition was absurd, especially when he couldn't even build an intelligible policy on Iraq. He believed Saddam was a threat, authorized the war, and then called it "the wrong war, [at the] wrong place at the wrong time," hardly coalition-building words.

Rooting for Defeat?

Democrats continued to fight President Bush every step of the way on Iraq. It was almost as if they were rooting for America's defeat and humiliating withdrawal in Iraq, just for the deliciousness of discrediting President Bush. As columnist Mona Charen observed, "There are any number of liberal congressmen, commentators, and opinion leaders who, like their European counterparts, actively wish America to fail in Iraq because it will mean the failure of the hated Bush presidency."[33]

They don't just highlight the bad news coming out of Iraq. In every item of good news they find something overpoweringly negative, such as their refusal to acknowledge the triumph of the January 2005 Iraqi elections for a transition government and the remarkable turnout of voters despite their great risk of personal harm. They could only complain that a certain segment of voters—the Sunnis—did not participate, so the elections were not that successful.

The *Washington Post*'s Jefferson Morley asked, "Who deserves credit for the first free election in Iraq in fifty years?" He said that while some give Bush the credit, "the more common view is that the election vindicated the political vision of Ayatollah Ali Sistani, the spiritual leader who insisted that elected Iraqis control the country's future. Patrick Cockburn, Baghdad correspondent for the *Independent* of London, claimed that the Bush administration, far from supporting democracy, originally 'thought it could rule Iraq directly with little Iraqi involvement.'"[34]

DNC chairman Howard Dean saw no hope for a successful outcome in Iraq. He actually said on WOAI radio in San Antonio, "The idea that we're going to win the war is an idea which is just plain wrong." Dean then compared Iraq to Vietnam.[35]

Just days before the January Iraqi elections, Senator Kennedy, in a speech at the University of Massachusetts–Boston, predicted, gloomily, that the elections could increase the violence in Iraq. "Sunday's election is not a cure for the violence and instability," said Kennedy. "Unless the Sunni and all the other communities in Iraq believe they have a stake in the outcome and a genuine role in drafting the new Iraqi constitution, the election could lead to greater alienation, greater escalation, and greater death for us and for the Iraqis."[36]

After the election, *The Hill* reported that a group of some twenty Democratic congressmen (the "Iraqi working group") met at the behest of Minority Leader Nancy Pelosi to formulate the party's response to the successful Iraqi elections, as if they viewed the success as their failure and political problem.[37]

After the constitutional referendum in Iraq on October 15, 2005, President Bush said the vote would deal a severe blow to the terrorists' plans to thwart Iraqi democracy. Former Democratic presidential candidate retired general Wesley Clark didn't see it that way. He said that while the large turnout "seems to be an important step" for the country, "let's not kid ourselves about the difficulties that lie ahead."[38]

Democratic leaders displayed the same pessimism and negativity toward the Iraqi elections in December 2005 to establish a permanent government for Iraq. They greatly understated the profound significance of the adoption of the Iraqi constitution and installation of the government by the Iraqi people. Senators Harry Reid, Carl Levin, and Jack Reed held a press conference after President Bush's speech before the elections to report on our progress in Iraq. The forlorn senators disputed that we were winning the war. "[Bush] hasn't leveled with the American people or laid out a strategy for success. He continues to say: Stay the course. He continues to say we're winning. But based on his three speeches, if this were a baseball game . . . he would already be struck out."

To the senators, the American people, in order to support the mission, "need to know the remaining political, economic, and military benchmarks, maybe a reasonable schedule for achieving them."[39] This prompted the *Weekly Standard*'s Bill Kristol to say Democrats were "crazy" if they didn't think Americans wanted to win in Iraq. "This nation roots for success. If the war goes badly, they'll blame President Bush, and rightly so. But they looked defeatist, like they are half-rooting for failure."[40]

After the elections, Nancy Pelosi paid grudging lip service to Iraq's progress toward democracy but then issued a statement berating President Bush for invading Iraq instead of pursuing bin Laden. Pelosi also said, "There are ways for the United States to make Iraq more stable that do not require 160,000 U.S. troops in Iraq and which would make the American people safer and the Middle East more secure."[41]

One day after the successful December 2005 Iraqi elections, Democrats had a chance to prove their unified commitment to victory in Iraq by voting in favor of House Resolution 612, "Expressing the commitment of the House of Representatives to achieving victory in Iraq." The resolution also rejected setting an "artificial timetable," which would be "fundamentally inconsistent with achieving victory." While many Democrats acknowledged that a specific timetable for withdrawing our troops would be unwise, 108 Democrats voted against the resolution and thirty-two abstained.[42] Democrats called the measure a political stunt and offered an alternative resolution that congratulated Iraqis for their three successful 2005 elections, but refused to mention a commitment to victory. Congressman John Murtha said the Republican resolution in calling for "complete victory" was too "open-ended, and therefore means that our troops could be there for ten or fifteen years."[43] History repeated itself in June 2006, when House Republicans called for a vote on a resolution affirming that it was *not* in the national security interest of the United Sates to set an arbitrary withdrawal or redeployment date for Iraq. Though 150 out of 192 Democrats voted against the measure, it passed 256 to 153.[44]

Downplaying the Results

Democrats have grossly understated or ignored the many successes we've had in the War on Terror. After the United States deposed Saddam Hussein and captured him in a spider hole, we kept up pressure on Libya to end its nuclear proliferation program. Then undersecretary of state for arms control and international security John Bolton, in his June 2003 testimony before the House International Relations Committee, voiced the U.S. concern "about Libya's long-standing efforts to pursue nuclear, chemical, and biological weapons, and ballistic missiles." Bolton said, "Libya must understand that improved relations with the United States means forgoing its WMD and missile programs." The message came through loudly and clearly to Libya's dictator, Colonel Muammar Qadhafi, who announced, on December 19, 2003, that Libya was abandoning its weapons of mass destruction and long-range missiles programs "because it's in our own interest and security."[45] This development and the U.S. restoration of diplomatic relations with Libya were a direct result of our successes in the War on Terror.

Another such success was Pakistan's placement of its national hero, A. Q. Kahn, Pakistan's top nuclear scientist and father of its nuclear weapons, under house arrest. Kahn is responsible for selling nuclear secrets to rogue nations such as North Korea and Libya.[46]

Democrats seemed underwhelmed with these achievements and were similarly unimpressed when we intercepted a message from Abu Musab al Zarqawi, al Qaeda's leader in Iraq, saying, "Our enemy is growing stronger day after day and its intelligence information increases. By God, this is suffocation."[47]

When American bombs killed Zarqawi, liberals not only downplayed the event, but also used it as an excuse to renew our demands that America withdraw her troops from Iraq.[48] The *New York Times*, for example, all but dismissed Zarqawi's death and the "confirmation of the last three members of the Iraqi cabinet." In an editorial titled "Too Soon to Cheer in Baghdad," the *Times*, instead of celebrating the "modest piece of encouraging news" that American forces had killed Zarqawi, chose to complain about "the already overstretched American forces" in Iraq and that "Meanwhile, millions of Iraqis go without electricity at least part of the day, thousands of families have had to flee their homes, and Iraqi women have seen their rights to an independent life and livelihood significantly diminished."[49] A little more than a week after Zarqawi's death, Democrats were focusing on the news that 2,500 American troops had now died in Iraq. Congresswoman Nancy Pelosi emphasized American deaths instead of positive news, calling the Iraq war a "grotesque mistake," and renewing her calls for withdrawal of American troops.[50] Congressman John Murtha also ignored the good news. He said on NBC's *Meet the Press* that we needed to "change direction" in Iraq. Murtha reiterated his opinion that "We can't win a war like this."[51]

Democrats were hardly more impressed when the U.S. military discovered even more damning admissions from Zarqawi in documents found at his hideout following his death. Zarqawi said that National Guard forces "have succeeded in forming an enormous shield protecting the American forces and have reduced substantially the losses that were solely suffered by the American forces." Zarqawi admitted that time was on America's side because we had restricted the resistance's financial outlets, confiscated its ammunition and weapons, undertaken massive arrest operations, begun a media campaign against the resistance, and taken advantage of the resistance's mistakes. One way out of this "crisis" and "current bleak situation," said Zarqawi, was to "involve the U.S. forces in waging a war against another country [like Iran] or any hostile groups."[52]

The discovery of these documents and their contents lent credence to other documents discovered by coalition forces in which al Qaeda similarly lamented that it was losing the war. The captured documents contained these admissions: "The Americans and the Government were able to absorb our painful blows, sustain them, compensate their losses with new replacements, and follow strategic plans which allowed them in the past few years to take control of Baghdad as well as other areas one after the other. That is why every year is worse than the previous year as far as the Mujahidin's control and influence over Baghdad." Another: "The current commander of Northern al-Karkh (Abu-Huda) is very concerned because of his deteriorating security situation caused by being pursued by the Americans, since they have his picture and voice print. Therefore, his movement is very restricted and he is unable to do anything here."[53] Such good news was *bad news* for Democrats.

Democrats have also refused to acknowledge that our technological espionage efforts have severely impeded al Qaeda communications, causing the terrorists to regress to less sophisticated methods, such as couriers.[54] They've downplayed other successes we've had, such as preventing at least three hijack plots by al Qaeda, as revealed by the Department of Homeland Security.[55] When the FBI uncovered a terrorist plot to blow up a New York tunnel,[56] Senator Chuck Schumer didn't seem too grateful. He said, "It was caught by the terrorists talking to one another. So this is one instance where intelligence was on the ball.... These don't seem to be the brightest bulbs in the terrorist lot."[57]

They just can't bring themselves to rejoice at any good news, but there is, indeed, good news. Zarqawi's death turned out to be a watershed event in more ways than one. It led to the discovery of crucial intelligence information, which in turn led to 452 military raids against insurgents in the week following his death. In those raids, 104 insurgents were killed, 759 "anti-Iraqi elements" were captured, and twenty-eight "significant" arms caches were seized.[58] Shortly after Zarqawi was killed, another senior member of al Qaeda, Mansur Sulayman Mansur Khalif, known as Sheikh Mansur, was killed in a coalition airstrike. A few days later, American-led forces captured yet another senior al Qaeda member in the Baquba area of Iraq.[59] Not long after, they captured another al Qaeda member—Yousri Fakher Mohammed Ali, known as Abu Qudama, who was suspected in the bombing of a Shiite shrine.[60]

President Bush had announced in his acceptance speech at the Republican convention in 2004 that "more than three quarters of al Qaeda's key members and associates have been detained or killed."[61] In Iraq alone, as of October 2005, coalition forces had captured or killed all but eleven of the fifty-five "deck of cards" featuring Saddam Hussein and fifty-four of his lieutenants. Coalition forces had also captured or killed all eight of al Qaeda's top leadership committee operating in Iraq.[62]

Apart from the military front, reconstruction and economic progress have occurred much more quickly than they did in postwar Germany and Japan—notwithstanding continuous insurgency and terrorist efforts to stifle progress. Toward the end of 2005, the Iraqi economy was beginning to grow at a healthy pace. Real GDP was believed to have grown at 3.7 percent in 2005 and was projected to grow 16 percent in 2006.

The World Bank reported that Iraqi per capita income had doubled since 2003 and private investment had stimulated strong private sector growth. Over 30,000 new businesses had registered since the war began and thousands more unregistered ones were believed to have launched. Infrastructure progress, despite the daily tolls of war, was also beginning to occur.[63] The Iraqi media has begun to thrive, with around one hundred newspapers, seventy-two radio stations, and forty-four television stations, not to mention the proliferation of Internet blogs.[64]

Not only has the brutal, despotic Iraqi government been eliminated as a chief sponsor of terrorism; international terrorists have gravitated toward Iraq like flies. It is folly to debate whether Iraq is part of the War on Terror when we have evidence that the terrorists have invested so much in thwarting Iraq's struggle for freedom and democracy. It is also not true that we have created more terrorists by attacking Iraq. It is not America's aggressiveness that has caused Islamist terrorism against America, but the terrorists' misapprehension that we are weak. Osama bin Laden came to believe we were a paper tiger, largely based on our cutting and running in Somalia at the direction of former president Clinton.

Toward the end of 2005, the Pew Research Center released polling results demonstrating the great disparity between the views of the liberal media and academia on the one hand and those of military leaders and the American public on the other. The poll revealed that 63 percent of news media people and 71 percent of those in academia or think tanks believed the Iraqi experiment in democracy would fail. Military opinion leaders, by contrast, believed by a margin of 64 percent to 32 percent that it would succeed, as did the American people 56 percent to 37 percent—notwithstanding the relentless barrage of negative reporting.[65]

More Good News

Defense Secretary Donald Rumsfeld reported that the Iraqi people have a high degree of confidence in their burgeoning democracy, demonstrated by their high voter turnout—"from 8.5 million in the January 2005 election to nearly 12 million in the December election"—public opinion polls, and the fact that "tips to authorities from ordinary Iraqis have grown from 483 to 4,700 tips in a month."[66] Rumsfeld pointed out that Iraqis now see a different Iraq than Saddam's "brutal dictatorship where the secret police would murder or mutilate a family member sometimes in front of their children, and where hundreds of thousands disappeared into Saddam's mass graves."[67]

The Defense Department's quarterly report to Congress in May 2006 showed "continued momentum on the political, economic, and security fronts and evidence that those attempting to derail it are failing." The report described Iraq's unity government, formed May 20, 2006, as "the culmination of the democratic process." Efforts to incite large-scale ethnic or sectarian violence were described as unsuccessful. The major violence was concentrated in four of the eighteen Iraqi provinces, especially in Anbar, but "substantial improvement" is occurring "even in the toughest locations."

In addition, 111 Iraqi army and special operations battalions were conducting counterinsurgency operations, which represented a 9 percent increase since the previous progress report. Seventy-one Iraqi battalions were leading operations. Iraqi forces—soldiers, sailors, airmen, and police numbering 263,000—were trained and equipped. Saddam loyalists were becoming irrelevant, according to the report, and the greatest remaining threats were terrorists and foreign fighters. The economy, while still experiencing peaks and valleys, was trending toward macroeconomic stability.[68]

Despite the difficulties experienced by our enemies in Iraq and our steady progress, Democrats were stubbornly unwilling to acknowledge any positive signs. Senator John Kerry attempted to completely reverse the White House argument that keeping terrorists busy fighting in Iraq has helped prevent attacks on American soil. Kerry preferred to give al Qaeda credit, rather than our military, intelligence services, and Homeland Security. He said the reason we haven't been attacked more in America is that al Qaeda is having so much success against our forces in Iraq. Kerry said on ABC's *This Week*, "Many people surmise that one of the reasons we haven't been attacked here is because they are being so successful at doing what they need to do to attack us in Iraq and elsewhere."[69] Indeed, the Left seemed determined to proclaim our efforts, not just in Iraq, but in the overall global War on Terror, "a failure." In a survey of some one hundred American foreign-policy analysts, 86 percent of them said the world has grown more dangerous despite President Bush's claims that the United States was winning the War on Terror.[70]

Withdrawal Mania

Democratic leaders persistently complained about the slow speed at which Iraqi security forces were being trained and that American troops were not being permitted to leave Iraq soon enough. This was not that long after they were complaining that we had too few troops in the theater of war in Iraq. Senator Joseph Biden was one of the fiercest critics of the rate at which Iraqis were being trained. He insisted the administration was not leveling with the American people about this lack of progress—yet another example of the Democrats' accusing the president of lying.[71] Senator Ted Kennedy said, "If America can train the best military in the world in thirteen weeks, why can't we train the Iraqis in eight or twelve or fifteen months to fight and die for their country?"[72]

Democrats were energized by the steady and significant decline in President Bush's approval ratings. Though complaints about Iraq didn't work for them in the 2004 elections, they sensed the tide was turning and saw serious potential for exploiting Bush's unpopularity on Iraq in the 2006 elections. Feeling their oats, Democrats ratcheted up their attacks on President Bush and began a steady drumbeat urging withdrawal of our troops. Republicans accused Democrats of playing politics with a life-or-death issue. Republican National Committee chairman Ken Mehlman asked, "Are the Democrat attacks designed to help us win the War on Terror or help them win the next election?"[73]

On November 17, 2005, Congressman John Murtha introduced a bill calling for a phased withdrawal of U.S. troops from Iraq. Murtha said America's efforts were a lost cause. "Our military has done everything that has been asked of them, the U.S. cannot accomplish anything further in Iraq militarily," he said. "It's time to bring them home."[74]

The media showered accolades on former Marine Murtha for his "courage," highlighting his military record and arguably misrepresenting him as a strong defense hawk, to bolster his credibility in calling for a complete pullout. Democrats have a tendency to exploit ex-military politicians' credentials when they become antiwar, with the expectation that their nonsensical, even dangerous recommendations will be treated as sacrosanct and above criticism. Yet this is the same "war hawk" who indicated he didn't want it to look like we won in Iraq. Murtha said, "I worry about a slow withdrawal which makes it look like there's a victory when I think it should be a redeployment as quickly as possible and let the Iraqis handle the whole thing."[75]

The White House noted that Murtha was endorsing positions of the extreme liberal wing of his party. "Nowhere does he explain how retreating from Iraq makes America safer," said a White House statement. But Murtha insisted our presence in Iraq was "impeding" progress there because our troops had "become a primary target" of the insurgency[76] and he called Iraq a "civil war." Along the lines of John Kerry's statement that al Qaeda wasn't attacking us in America because they were killing us in Iraq, he said, "The only people who want us in Iraq are Iran and al Qaeda . . . and China. . . . Why? Because we're depleting our . . . troop resources and our fiscal resources."[77]

The day after Murtha introduced his withdrawal motion, House Republicans called the Democrats' bluff by scheduling a surprise vote on the measure. The House, Democrats and all, rejected the measure by a resounding 403 to 3 vote.[78] It wasn't just this surprise vote. When push came to shove Democrats just couldn't come to a consensus on their withdrawal demands. House Minority Leader Nancy Pelosi was solidly behind Murtha, while the Democrats' second in command at the House, Steny Hoyer, was silent. Senator Hillary Clinton's refusal to join the withdrawal frenzy brought her a rebuke from antiwar fringe activist Cindy Sheehan: "I think [Senator Clinton] is a political animal who believes she has to be a war hawk to keep up with the big boys." Meanwhile, two of Hillary's potential presidential rivals, Senators Russ Feingold and John Kerry, offered their own proposals for withdrawal.[79]

When Republicans pressed Democrats on the dangerousness of a withdrawal timetable, Senator Kerry denied they were seeking an "artificial date for withdrawal," but were interested, rather, in "a *timetable for success*, which will permit the withdrawal of our troops."[80] What Kerry meant by this distinction is anyone's guess.

In June 2006, Senate Republicans challenged their Democratic counterparts to put their money where their mouths were. When Senator Mitch McConnell called for a vote on Kerry's resolution to withdraw the troops from Iraq, the resolution suffered a stunning 93–6 vote defeat.[81]

In the end, Democrats had twisted themselves into pretzels. One day Democrats would demand withdrawal; the next, when Republicans called them on it, they would deny they were advocating a date certain, but rather some nebulous benchmarks or "timetable for success."

Howard Dean even claimed it was not incumbent on his party to come up with a plan; demonizing President Bush was sufficient. Congressman Rahm Emanuel, chairman of the Democratic Congressional Campaign Committee, said that "at the right time, we will have a position" on Iraq.[82] Congressman Thomas M. Reynolds, National Republican Congressional Committee chairman, responding to Emanuel's casual statement, said, "With the same stench of political opportunism, Democrats have moved from playing politics with the terrible human tragedies of the Gulf Coast hurricanes to attempting to score political points off our men and women serving in Iraq."

Congresswoman Nancy Pelosi took it a step further than Dean or Emanuel. She said Democrats should not seek a unified position on an exit strategy in Iraq, because the war was a matter of individual conscience and that different positions among caucus members could help strengthen the party.[83]

A Floundering Party

Liberals desperately long for coherence on foreign policy and national security issues, but are haunted by ghosts from their past and conflicts in the present. They wax nostalgic for their war-protesting days of the Vietnam era, relying on those times for spiritual strength in their effort to unite against the Iraq war. But the forced comparisons fall flat. The romance is gone. As liberal stalwart Michael Kinsley has noted, the Vietnam-era antiwar movement was unequivocally against the war and unequivocally for bringing our troops home—yesterday. By contrast, the antiwar Democrats today are unequivocally against the war, but ambivalent—as a group—about when our troops should be withdrawn. The antiwar folks today, says Kinsley, "are in some kind of existential opposition to the war but aren't doing much about it and aren't very clear about what they would like to see happen.... Most of them deplore the war, but only a tiny fraction favor an immediate pullout."[84] Kinsley is right. The Democrats can't even get their act together on an issue that excites them above all others.

The Democrats' plight on the war issue is best typified by John Kerry's meandering approach to it during his presidential campaign. He said that Iraq was "the wrong war, the wrong place, at the wrong time," yet couldn't bring himself—until much later—to recommend withdrawing the troops. Kerry had put himself on the political map on returning from Vietnam by grandstanding in Congress and demanding to know "How do you ask a man to be the last man to die for a mistake?" Yet today, after having pronounced Iraq a mistake, he refused to apply the same glorified standard of his youth. If Kerry truly believed Iraq was a mistake, how could he continue to ask all those soldiers to be among the last to die for that "mistake"?

In late March 2006, after being ridiculed for their naysaying-only posture on national security issues, the Democrats finally came up with a "plan" they smarmily called "Real National Security," which was not a plan at all, but little more than a statement of broad goals, most of which were already being pursued by the Bush administration. They proposed to make 2006 "a year of significant transition to full Iraqi sovereignty, with Iraqis assuming primary responsibility for security and governing their country and with the responsible redeployment of U.S. forces." This vague language on Iraq further revealed the Democrats' inability to arrive at a consensus on the issue. After all their carping about withdrawal, they couldn't demand an immediate pullout. Their "plan" was insulting in its absence of strategies and tactics and in its tone.

In promoting their plan, Democrats played cynical, semantic games, promising that their plan was "strong and smart" and "tough and smart." Even more juvenile was their assurance that they would put more resources into capturing Osama bin Laden—while offering no specifics as to how they would increase the likelihood of his capture.[85] Democrats were basically asking the American people to unlearn everything they had come to know about the Democratic Party: its intrinsic softness on defense, its decades-long opposition to military spending, and its obstruction of the president in nearly every particular in the War on Terror.

In the end, the "plan" proved nothing except how partisan the Democrats had become. In producing a plan that was just a restatement of the administration's goals, the Democrats were de facto admitting the president's course of action was prudent and that they had been playing politics with America's national security. In trying to make themselves relevant, they only confirmed their consummate intellectual and moral bankruptcy.

The Height of Politics

The Democrats' true colors were on display in March 2006 when it was revealed that they had mapped out a political battle plan for the March congressional recess. Senate Minority Leader Harry Reid devised the plan, which was set out in a six-page memo passed out to Democratic senators. The plan called Democratic senators to stage press events with active duty military personnel to attack President Bush's national security policies.[86] It also called for staged town hall events at weapons factories, military bases, National Guard units, fire stations, and veterans' posts.

The plan advised senators to hold town hall meetings where they could ask local National Guard members "to offer input on how security and response at home is compromised by long deployments." It also encouraged them to "work with [veterans] organizations . . . to find recently returned Iraq and Afghanistan veterans willing to discuss the mental effects they or their fellow veterans have experienced." The senators were urged to "Tour a factory in your state that manufactures military equipment like Humvees or body armor and hold a press availability afterwards with Iraq and Afghanistan veterans on the importance of protective equipment." Also, "Visit the home of a military family that has purchased body armor on their own for a family member serving in Iraq or Afghanistan and hold an open press [conference] on the issue. . . . Ask the family if they would be willing to hold the open press conversation/town hall meeting in their yard, on their front porch or in their home."

The plan further directed the politicians to "ensure that you have the proper U.S. and state flags at the event, and consider finding someone to sing the national anthem and lead the group in the Pledge of Allegiance at the start of the event."

With behavior like this, it's amazing Democrats accuse Republicans of politicizing the war. Democrats have been doing it from the beginning.

CHAPTER THREE

King George

The Democrats' animus toward George Bush and Republicans is largely due to their frustration over Republican control. Democrats held a virtual monopoly on congressional power for forty years and don't cheerfully accept minority status, especially when the GOP also holds the executive branch. Economist Arthur Laffer believes "the unprecedented hatred directed at Republicans in general and President Bush in particular" comes from the Democrats' "hostility, intense jealousy, and disappointment" over the Republicans controlling the presidency, the Senate, the House, the Supreme Court (it's true that seven of the nine justices are Republican appointees, though the Court retains a liberal majority), the Federal Reserve Board chairman, and the majority of state governorships and legislatures.[1] To judge by their rhetoric, Democrats think this Republican domination is more dangerous than the threat posed by Islamist terrorists.

Senator Patrick Leahy has complained that the constitutional "checks and balances that have served to constrain abuses of power for more than two centuries in this country" are at risk when Republicans control the legislative and executive branches.[2] Leahy and his colleagues are particularly annoyed that President Bush insists on running the executive branch without taking orders from them. They have consistently charged that he has unduly expanded his executive powers and suppressed civil liberties through the Patriot Act, the NSA eavesdropping program, the alleged abuse and torture of enemy combatant detainees at Gitmo and Abu Ghraib, and even his executive decision-making style. Some have tried to censure President Bush for his "power-grabs" and others have threatened to initiate impeachment proceedings against him[3] and probably would if they could acquire majority control of the House.

Democrats have regularly impeded President Bush's prosecution of the War on Terror and shown a reflexive sympathy for allegations—even from terrorist propagandists—against the United States, the American military, and the Bush administration. Liberals can always be counted on to make bad news worse, to create bad news where little or none exists, and to put partisan politics ahead of national security. Almost from the beginning of the war, liberals complained about the unlimited detainment of terrorist prisoners without charge, preferring to treat them as criminal defendants entitled to the full panoply of constitutional civil rights rather than prisoners of war.[4]

Abu Ghraib

Under Saddam Hussein, Abu Ghraib prison housed up to fifty thousand prisoners. The torture of prisoners was routine, as were weekly executions. After coalition forces deposed Saddam they took over the facility and converted it into their own military prison. Early in 2004, reports surfaced that U.S. military personnel had mistreated and abused prisoners there, which resulted in the suspension of General Janis Karpinsky, the officer in charge of our military prisons in Iraq, and an investigation ensued. The results of the investigation were recorded in a March 9, 2004, report written by Major General Antonio M. Taguba.[5] The report, supported by witness statements and photographs, chronicled multiple acts of "sadistic, blatant, and wanton criminal abuses." Two military intelligence officers and two private contractors who oversaw interrogations might have been "either directly or indirectly responsible."[6]

The alleged acts of abuse were: breaking chemical lights and pouring the phosphoric liquid on prisoners, pouring cold water on prisoners, beating them with a broom handle and a chair, threatening them with rape, allowing a guard to stitch a prisoner's wound (acquired when he was thrown against the wall), sodomizing a detainee with a chemical light and maybe a broomstick, and using dogs to scare prisoners, with one actually being bitten. In addition, prisoners were forced to get naked and pile on top of each other in a pyramid. Others were forced to simulate performing oral sex.

Defense Secretary Donald Rumsfeld said the abuses were "totally unacceptable and un-American," but denied the Pentagon authorized them. The military had responded swiftly to the allegations "to hold accountable those that may have violated the code of military conduct and betrayed the trust placed in them by the American people."[7] President Bush was reportedly so upset over the news that he criticized Secretary Rumsfeld in an Oval Office meeting for not telling him about the photographs. But he was quick to express his confidence in Rumsfeld, who still had "his full support."[8]

Democrats immediately tried to exploit the news for partisan political gain. Senator Joseph Biden said, "This is a disaster of significant proportions. It calls for accountability—and quickly." He said that if the blame led to Secretary Rumsfeld's office, he should resign.[9] Presidential candidate John Kerry said the Abu Ghraib story should not be politicized, but then sent mass e-mails attacking President Bush over it and initiating a petition drive calling for Rumsfeld's resignation.[10] Senator Edward Kennedy said that "Saddam's torture chambers reopened under new management, U.S. management." Senator Harry Reid said, "Let's not have a few of the non-officers be the scapegoats for a war on this country.... We cannot allow a few underlings to take the fall for what obviously was a concerted action."[11]

While Rumsfeld accepted responsibility and apologized for the incidents, it wasn't enough for the Left, who wanted his head—and that of President Bush. The *New York Times* was outraged the administration had the audacity to assert—via the Senate testimony of undersecretary of defense for intelligence Stephen Cambone—that Rumsfeld was deeply committed to the Geneva Conventions protecting prisoners' rights and that any violations of those rights occurred at "the command level."[12] Democratic sugar daddy George Soros said that Abu Ghraib was worse than the September 11 attacks. Senator Hillary Clinton, who was on the stage with Soros, let the comment pass without challenge.[13]

Al Gore, in a speech at New York University, blamed the Abu Ghraib abuses directly on President Bush, saying they were not the result of "a few twisted minds at the lowest ranks of our military enlisted personnel," but the administration's systematic disregard for the Geneva Conventions. "What happened at the prison, it is now clear, is not the result of random acts of a few bad apples. It was the natural consequence of the Bush administration policy."[14]

"Private...England did not make the decision that the United States would not observe the Geneva Convention," said Gore. "Specialist Charles Graner was not the one who approved a policy of establishing an American gulag....These policies were designed and insisted upon by the Bush White House."[15] Gore said that President Bush "has created more anger and righteous indignation against us as Americans than any leader of our country in the 228 years of our existence as a nation."[16] He demanded the resignations of six high-ranking officials, including Secretary Rumsfeld, National Security Adviser Condoleezza Rice, and CIA director George Tenet.[17]

There is no question that gratuitous acts of abuse are indefensible and no one can justify the outrages that occurred at Abu Ghraib. But such actions were not authorized by the Bush administration or the Pentagon, nor attributable to its policies on the treatment of enemy detainees. Nor did most of the acts rise to the legal definition of "torture," though some did constitute abuse. It was shameful that opportunistic Democrats compared these isolated abuses to the torture inflicted in that very prison at Saddam's direction. These abuses did not remotely compare to what occurred in Soviet gulags. As Norman Podhoretz noted, while the harassment and humiliation of the detainees was wrong, none of the detainnes, as far as we knew, "were even maimed, let alone killed."[18]

The Democrats' hyperbole and baseless attribution of these acts to the Bush administration doubtlessly contributed to Muslim hatred for America—an effect they profess to avoid at all costs—

and undermined the war effort. Norman Podhoretz argued that they also contributed to "a great wave of defeatist gloom that was deepened by the nervous tactical shifts they produced in our military planners (such as the decision to hold back from cleaning out the terrorist militias hiding in and behind holy places in Falluja and Najaf.)"[19]

Gitmo

Nor was there any actual torture at the U.S. naval base in Guantánamo Bay, Cuba ("Gitmo"), according to a military investigation released in the summer of 2005. The Gitmo flap began in 2002 when FBI agents assigned to the facility reported abusive treatment and the Pentagon ordered an investigation.

Testifying before the Senate Armed Services Committee, Air Force Lt. Gen. Randall M. Schmidt said, "We looked at this very, very carefully—no torture occurred. Detention and interrogation operations across the board...looking through all the evidence we could, were safe, secure, and humane." One "high-value" al Qaeda operative was subjected to "abusive and degrading treatment" in being forced to wear a brassiere, perform dog tricks, and stay awake for twenty hours a day.[20]

Schmidt said the investigation involved surveying all 498 FBI agents who had worked at Gitmo. Investigators found that of 24,000 interrogations there were only nine cases of alleged abuse, though all were "relatively minor." Seven of those were substantiated, five being authorized by the Army Field Manual or Defense Secretary Rumsfeld, and two being unauthorized. In a few of the "substantiated" cases, it's difficult to see what all the fuss was about. In one a detainee was briefly chained to the floor, to protect the guards, and in another they placed duct tape over the mouth of a prisoner who wouldn't quit chanting.[21]

The most famous of the reported cases involved the would-be twentieth hijacker for the September 11 attacks, Mohammed al Kahtani, who had resisted all conventional interrogation techniques, prompting Secretary Rumsfeld to approve a tougher approach. He was reportedly forced to wear women's clothes. He was called a homosexual, insulted about his family, interrogated for twenty hours a day, and touched suggestively by women. Though the Geneva Conventions prohibit sexual humiliation of prisoners, President Bush's policy was that the Gitmo prisoners were terrorists, classified as "enemy combatants," and not subject to the conventions' guarantees.[22] The military said that the techniques produced "solid intelligence gains," including information on how Osama bin Laden planned the September 11 attacks, and how he recruited terrorists, financed his operations, and entered the United States.[23]

Democrats, of course, refused to believe (and publicize) anything but the worst from the military and the administration. "It is clear from the report that detainee mistreatment was not simply the product of a few rogue military police on a night shift," said Senator Carl Levin. "Rather, this mistreatment arose from the use of aggressive interrogation techniques."

But the money quote came from Senator Dick Durbin, the assistant Democratic leader. "If I read this to you and did not tell you it was an FBI agent describing what Americans had done to prisoners in their control, you would most certainly believe that this must have been done by Nazis, Soviets in their gulags or some other mad regime—Pol Pot or others—that had no concern for human beings." But as columnist Jack Kelly noted, "There are some differences worth noting. About 9 million people died in Nazi concentration camps, 2.7 million in Soviet concentration camps, and about 1.7 million Cambodians (out of a population of 6 million) were killed by Pol Pot. The number of detainees at Gitmo who have died is zero. The number of detainees who have suffered serious injuries at the hands of guards or interrogators is also zero." And, the Nazi and Soviet victims committed such unforgivable sins as expressing the wrong opinions, or being Jewish or Christian. Gitmo prisoners were proven or suspected terrorists who murder innocent human beings.[24]

In *Gulag Archipelago*, Aleksandr Solzhenitsyn said the prisoners of the Soviet camps were generally not those who had taken up arms against the state or collaborated against the regime; nor were they arrested on the battlefield while waging war against the mother country. They were often political prisoners, who might have criticized the repressive government—even privately. Gulag prisoners had dissented from a government that repressed liberties; Gitmo prisoners were opposing liberty and democracy and killing those fighting for it or enjoying it. Solzhenitsyn told about real torture in the gulag. It involved prisoners having their skulls squeezed with iron rings, or being lowered into acid baths, or being trussed up naked to be bitten by ants and bedbugs, or having their anal canals invaded with heated ramrods or their genitals slowly crushed by jackboots, or severe beatings.[25]

Though Senator Durbin was credited with having apologized for his unconscionable remarks, he expressed no contrition and didn't retract them. He blamed others for misunderstanding his words, but stood by their content. "I am sorry if anything I said caused any offense or pain to those who have such bitter memories of the Holocaust, the greatest moral tragedy of our time. Nothing, nothing should ever be said to demean or diminish that moral tragedy. I am also sorry if anything I said cast a negative light on our fine men and women in the military. . . . I never ever intended any disrespect for them. Some may believe that my remarks crossed the line. To them I extend my heartfelt apology." (Note: He said, "Some may believe," not "I did in fact cross the line.")

Another Gitmo feeding frenzy occurred after *Newsweek* reported that a Gitmo guard had deliberately flushed a prisoner's Koran down a toilet. *Newsweek* was forced later to retract the story when it proved untrue, but not before it had led to violent protests and deaths in the Islamic world.[26]

Democrats loudly demanded that Gitmo be shut down, without expressing any concern over where the prisoners—"the worst of the worst"—would be taken or whether they would be freed to return to the battlefields and streets to kill innocents again. As U.S. attorney general Alberto Gonzales said, "You capture people on the battlefield fighting against your country. What are we supposed to so with them? Do we simply release them, and have them come back and fight against our soldiers?"[27] (In fact, a dozen or so terrorists released from Gitmo returned to terrorism or jihad.[28])

Minority Leader Nancy Pelosi said, "I think that we need a fresh start . . . a clean slate for America in the Muslim world." Senator Joe Biden called Gitmo "the greatest propaganda tool that exists for the recruiting of terrorists around the world."

Former president Jimmy Carter, in keeping with his policy of violating the tradition that ex-presidents not publicly criticize their successors, slammed the administration's detention of terror suspects at the Guantánamo naval base as a "disgrace to the United States." Carter said it "has given impetus and excuses to potential terrorists to lash out at our country and justify their despicable acts."[29] Carter said, "To demonstrate clearly our nation's historic commitment to protect human rights, our government needs to close down Guantánamo and the two dozen secret detention facilities run by the United States as soon as practicable."[30]

Former vice president Al Gore chimed in as well and on foreign soil. In a speech at the Jiddah Economic Forum in Saudi Arabia in February 2006, Gore told his mostly Arab audience that the United States had inflicted "terrible abuses" on Arabs following the September 11 attacks. He said the U.S. had "indiscriminately rounded up" Arabs and held them in "unforgivable" conditions. He also attacked President Bush, saying that by blocking Saudi visa applications he was playing into al Qaeda's hands.[31]

Following this hand-wringing chorus, four senators visited Gitmo and toured the facilities. Democrats Ron Wyden and Ben Nelson and Republicans Jim Bunning and Michael D. Crapo all agreed that no abuse was occurring. Nelson said, "Everything we heard about operations there in the past, we'd have to say, was negative. What we saw firsthand was something different." A delegation from the House also visited the camp and made similar findings. Congressman Joe Wilson said, "The detainees' meal was as good as any I had in my thirty-one years of Army Guard service, and I can see why the prisoners this year gained five pounds over last year." The Republican senators said the prisoners were treated as well as or better than the Geneva Conventions would require for war prisoners.[32]

Retired Army major Dana R. Dillon, a former military officer and Heritage Foundation senior policy analyst, reported that more than one thousand journalists, seventy-seven congressmen, and ninety-nine congressional staffers have visited Gitmo. But, "despite a plethora of available eyewitness testimony to the humane conditions in American military detention facilities, Amnesty International denounced Guantánamo as the 'gulag of our times,' and Human Rights Watch compared Abu Ghraib to Darfur."[33]

The United Nations, never to be outdone in America-bashing, in May 2006 recommended that Gitmo be shut down.[34] (No one from the UN Commission on Human Rights had actually visited Gitmo.[35]) On the same day—which many believe was no coincidence—Gitmo prisoners staged a riot, in an orchestrated response to a staged suicide attempt. The prisoners spread urine and feces on the floor so that the guards would slip upon entering the cell where the fake suicide was occurring. Base spokesman U.S. Navy Commander Robert Durand said that many prisoners admitted that part of their plan was to ambush the guards, and then rally other prisoners to fight by spreading a false rumor that a Koran had been abused. They hoped this "cover story" might be picked up by the media. But Durand said, "The Koran is shown tremendous respect at Guantánamo. Our guard force does not touch or handle the detainees' Korans, period." A review determined that the guard force "acted appropriately and with minimal force."[36]

The Koran publicity scheme was not unlike the prisoners' hunger strike that many believe was designed to get media attention and damage America's image. "The hunger strike is consistent with al Qaeda practice," said Durand. It "reflects detainee attempts to elicit media attention to bring international pressure on the United States to release them back to the battlefield." Obviously, the scheme worked, as the usual suspects—Amnesty International and Human Rights Watch—cited the strike in renewing their calls to close Gitmo down.[37]

The next month, three prisoners did succeed in committing suicide. Some believe the deaths were not motivated by despair, but to further their jihad by making the United States look bad. Rear Admiral Harry Harris, Gitmo commander, said that the prisoners are people who "have no regard for human life, neither ours nor their own. . . . I believe this was not an act of desperation, but an act of asymmetric warfare against us," by terrorists who have run out of weapons to use against America. Some speculated that the three could have been trying to influence a Supreme Court decision concerning lengthy detentions of enemy prisoners without trial. And, Gitmo prisoners, according to reports, had been spreading rumors that the three envisioned the facility being closed down after their deaths. The Pentagon confirmed they all had close links to terrorism.[38]

The *New York Times*, of course, sided with the terrorists. "It was the inevitable result of creating a netherworld of despair beyond the laws of civilized nations, where men were to be held without any hope of decent treatment, impartial justice or, in so many cases, even eventual release," wrote the *Times*. "It is a place where secret tribunals sat in judgment of men whose identities they barely knew and who were not permitted to see the evidence against them. Inmates were abused, humiliated, tormented and sometimes tortured."[39]

"Domestic" Spying

Though many Democrats had voted for the Patriot Act, they were later apoplectic over some of its provisions, including those that gave the FBI more power to collect information. The Democrats delayed renewal of the act, threatening at one point to filibuster it in the Senate. The Democrats went ballistic because "enemy combatants" might be detained for the duration of the war without judicial review of their detention.[40] And when word leaked of a National Security Agency (NSA) warrantless surveillance program, Democrats thought they could make political capital by accusing the Bush administration of violating civil liberties.

In December 2005, the *New York Times* reported that President Bush issued an executive order in 2002 secretly authorizing the National Security Agency to conduct warrantless surveillance of international telephone and Internet communications of suspected terrorists.[41] Under the order the agency *never* monitored entirely domestic communications without first obtaining a warrant. There had to be an international connection. But from the beginning Democrats deceptively characterized the surveillance practice, "warrantless *domestic* spying." The agency reportedly eavesdrops without warrants on around five hundred people at a time inside the United States and between five thousand to seven thousand people overseas with suspected ties to terrorists.

The Bush administration explained that it started the program after September 11, because the NSA could not act quickly enough to thwart terrorist attacks, coordinated by disposable cell phones and other electronic communication techniques, if it had to be subject to the usual time-consuming legal and bureaucratic restrictions. The NSA needed to monitor "urgently" large batches of numbers simultaneously, which would make obtaining individual warrants from the Foreign Intelligence Surveillance Act (FISA) Court impracticable.[42] Officials said the program was a "critical tool in helping disrupt terrorist plots and prevent attacks inside the United States."[43]

The Justice Department did apply for warrants when it sought to expand its eavesdropping to include purely domestic communications. While Democratic leaders feigned outrage that they had been kept in the dark about the program, the administration had briefed congressional leaders and alerted a principal judge on the Foreign Intelligence Surveillance Court about it. Vice President Dick Cheney, NSA director Lt. Gen. Michael V. Hayden, and CIA director George Tenet briefed Democratic and Republican congressional leaders on the program in Cheney's White House office shortly after the program began.

The program had helped foil an al Qaeda plot against the Brooklyn Bridge and Islamist attacks on British pubs and train stations. Indeed, the program accelerated in early 2002 partly because of information from captured al Qaeda operatives. The government wanted to monitor those numbers and other identifying data immediately.

Democrats asserted that the NSA had previously limited its "domestic" eavesdropping to foreign embassies and missions, had left domestic spying to the FBI, and was now conducting unlimited domestic surveillance. But the NSA's program wasn't arbitrary or unlimited at all. It focused solely on suspected terrorists whose names were obtained from captured databases and other intelligence gathering, and at least one party to any of the monitored communications had to be outside American soil.

While Democrats cried that President Bush's program was in clear violation of the law and conducted in reckless disregard for the people's rights, the president had not implemented the program whimsically or without civil liberty safeguards. He sought and obtained classified legal opinions that the program was lawful, both under the congressional resolution authorizing the campaign against terrorism and the president's inherent constitutional authority. A Justice Department brief in one case argued that "the Constitution vests in the president inherent authority to conduct warrantless intelligence surveillance (electronic or otherwise) of foreign powers or their agents, and Congress cannot by statute extinguish that constitutional authority."[44]

Its argument was based, in part, on a number of federal appellate cases[45] in which the courts recognized the president's inherent power to conduct warrantless electronic surveillance to collect foreign intelligence information. In the 1984 case of *United States* v. *Duggan*, the Second Circuit Court of Appeals stated: "Prior to the enactment of FISA, virtually every court that had addressed the issue had concluded that the president had the inherent power to conduct warrantless electronic surveillance to collect foreign intelligence information, and that such surveillances constituted an exception to the warrant requirement of the Fourth Amendment."[46]

The FISA Court itself, in 2002, ruled, "We take for granted that the President does have [inherent authority to conduct warrantless searches to obtain foreign intelligence information] and, assuming that is so, FISA could not encroach on the President's constitutional power."[47] The administration was reportedly reluctant to seek additional congressional authority because it didn't want to risk disclosure of the program's existence, which would alert terrorists and render it much less useful. President Bush reported that he personally conducted oversight of the program, "reviewing it every forty-five to sixty days and renewing the original executive order more than three dozen times."[48]

In addition, a panel of former FISA judges, testifying before the Senate Judiciary Committee, said the president clearly has "constitutional authority to spy on suspected international agents under an executive order," which is not overridden by the Foreign Intelligence

Surveillance Act.[49] Judge Allan Kornblum, magistrate judge of the U.S. District Court for the Northern District of Florida and one of the authors of FISA, said, "If a court refuses a FISA application and there is not sufficient time for the president to go to the court of review, the president can under executive order act unilaterally, which he is doing now. I think that the president would be remiss exercising his constitutional authority by giving all of that power over to a statute."[50] But, the judges conceded, the president's inherent constitutional authority was not absolute.[51]

Democrats started screaming bloody murder over the program, claiming that President Bush wanted to eliminate our civil liberties. Since news of the program was reported the very week the Patriot Act was to be voted on for renewal, some Democrats used the news as an excuse to filibuster the bill's reauthorization. Others demanded the program be terminated and that congressional and criminal investigations be initiated. Senator Chuck Schumer said, "Today's revelation that the government has listened in on thousands of phone conversations is shocking."[52]

Senator Edward Kennedy said the program was "Big Brother run amok." Senator Russ Feingold said news of the program "ought to send a chill down the spine of every American and every senator." He added, "You want to talk about abuses? I can't imagine a more shocking example of an abuse of power, to eavesdrop on American citizens without first getting a court order based on some evidence that they are possibly criminals, terrorists, or spies."[53]

Senator Patrick Leahy said, "My concern is for peaceful Quakers who are being spied upon and other law-abiding Americans and babies and nuns who are placed on terrorist watch lists."[54] Leahy contended that Bush had made some of the most expansive claims of power since the nation rid itself of King George III's oppressive rule.[55] He and other Democrats parroted this theme repeatedly during the confirmation hearings for Judge Samuel Alito, charging that Bush was trying to consolidate power in the executive and that Judge Alito, if confirmed to the Court, would conspire to facilitate Bush's power grab. He would become, they feared, a "rubber stamp" for President Bush's nefarious schemes.

Al Gore, in a speech for the American Constitution Society and Liberty Coalition, said that in his "pervasive wiretapping" Bush was repeatedly breaking the law and accumulating a dangerous amount of authority. "A president who breaks the law is a threat to the very structure of our government," said Gore.[56]

Gore failed to mention a few facts. The Clinton administration in which he was vice president conducted a warrantless search of the home of CIA spy Aldrich Ames. In 1994, a high official in the Clinton-Reno Justice Department, Jamie Gorelick, testified to the Senate Intelligence Committee that "the Department of Justice believes, and the case law supports, that the president has inherent authority to conduct warrantless physical searches for foreign intelligence purposes."[57]

Gore didn't mention that his old boss Bill Clinton, like other presidents beginning with Jimmy Carter, signed an executive order explicitly authorizing the attorney general "to approve physical searches, without a court order, to acquire foreign intelligence information for periods of up to one year." Gore also neglected to mention Clinton's Echelon surveillance program, through which almost every electronic conversation around the world and in the United States was monitored. The NSA program, by contrast, involved the interception of e-mails and phone calls in which at least one party to the communication was always outside the United States and at least one party was always a terrorist, a suspected terrorist, or had ties to terrorists.[58]

But the liberal media would hear none of it, convinced they had caught Bush red-handed in an attempt to install himself dictator. The *Philadelphia Inquirer* wrote, "Through history, tyranny has not always foamed at the mouth. In the beginning, it often wears an earnest, sincere face. Eventually, though, it begins to harp incessantly about threats and enemies; it comes to treat dissent as treason, and civil liberty as an unwise luxury."[59] The *New York Times* said that instead of giving the legal grounds for its wireless eavesdropping program, the administration engaged in political spin, historical revisionism, dismissals of concerns about civil liberties, lies, and "cynical attempts to paint dissents as anti-American and pro-terrorist."[60]

Leftist pundits picked up on the "Bush-wants-to-be-dictator" theme. Tom Engelhardt, in Salon.com, above a cartoonish image of Bush in a royal robe and wearing a red, white, and blue crown, said, "It is slowly becoming clear that the Bush administration's real goal is not winning the right to torture, or to spy on Americans, or to lock people up without recourse. It is absolute power."[61] *The Nation* was no less extreme in its piece titled "Madness of King George."[62]

This was nothing new for the Left. Shortly after our invasion of Iraq, liberal author and columnist Eric Alterman conducted a "Name That President" contest. One of the participants picked "George III," saying, "He actually is our third president named George, and he's as imperious and perhaps as mad as his British namesake supposedly was."[63] British historian Niall Ferguson, in

Vanity Fair, wrote of "The Monarchy of George II," where President Bush justified an invasion "with recondite claims," waged "war with a tyrant's zeal," and bankrupted his country.[64]

Abuses and Usurpations

In February 2006, eighteen House Democrats, in a letter to President Bush, demanded that Attorney General Alberto Gonzales appoint a special counsel to investigate the legality of the surveillance program.[65] In April, Senator Russ Feingold made a motion to censure the president for the NSA surveillance program. On *FOX News Sunday*, Feingold told Chris Wallace that Bush was thumbing his nose at the laws of this country. The purpose of the *impeachment* remedy, he said, was to keep the president in check and make sure he didn't acquire power "like King George III."

Feingold echoed Leahy and Gore's concern about the GOP controlling the legislative and executive branches. But like Leahy and Gore, it apparently slipped his mind that voters had chosen, under no duress, to put Republicans in charge. Feingold said, "We have this problem of one-party rule in our system of government right now," and "we have a Republican president and two houses of Congress run by the Republicans."[66] Feingold's language was apparently carefully chosen, given his interest in censuring and possibly impeaching President Bush. "King George III" evokes more than the garden variety imagery of a power-hungry ruler. In our nation's history, King George III was the tyrant against whom the Declaration's signatories aimed their bill of particulars, justifying America's independence from the Crown. Those "particulars" involved "abuses and usurpations" of the king and, according to the Left, President Bush has committed analogous "abuses and usurpations."[67]

While Democrats publicly fret over civil liberties encroachments, they cannot point to any examples where either the Patriot Act or the NSA surveillance program victimized an innocent U.S. citizen. They refuse to acknowledge the distinction between these wireless intercepts used against the enemy for wartime purposes, and those of law enforcement officials against suspected criminals. It's not as though President Bush is using spy agencies to eavesdrop on *his* political enemies. Indeed, the reason there aren't any legal challenges is that the targets are not suspected criminals, but the enemy. In short, the Democrats are playing politics with our national security, which is why they were so shameless as to mischaracterize the program and to falsely claim they weren't briefed on it—a program that has prevented terrorist attacks and saved American lives.

Data-mining

In May 2006, the Left tried to manufacture one more scandal over another alleged "massive intrusion on personal privacy." This one involved three major U.S. telecommunications companies that had helped the National Security Agency build a terrorist tracking database. No calls were being monitored. Rather, as the *Wall Street Journal* editors explained, the government was keeping "track, after the fact, of most calls placed to and from a great many phone numbers in the U.S. In other words, the scary government database contains the same information you see on your monthly phone bill—slightly less, in fact, since names aren't attached to numbers and never will be unless government computers detect activity suspicious enough to warrant some being singled out of billions of others."[68]

The government would use these records—if at all—as a tool and if something looked suspicious, they would seek a warrant to monitor purely domestic calls. It was simply an informational tool to help the government identify terrorists. It involved no surveillance or intercepts of communications, so the FISA statute didn't apply to it, nor were warrants required—unless follow-up surveillance was pursued. As the *Wall Street Journal* pointed out, the program raised no right to privacy concerns. The Supreme Court ruled in 1979 that the government can legally collect phone numbers because callers have no reasonable expectation of privacy with information that is already known by their phone companies.[69]

Nevertheless, Democrats—and some Republicans—expressed outrage over the program. Senator Dianne Feinstein huffed about "a major constitutional confrontation."[70] Democratic National Committee spokeswoman Stacie Paxton said, "This is another example of the Bush administration misleading the American people."[71] Senator Edward Kennedy said the program was "abusive." "Today's shocking disclosures," Kennedy added, "make it more important than ever for the Republican Congress to end its complicity in the White House coverup of its massive domestic surveillance program." Senator Hillary Clinton claimed to be "deeply disturbed."[72] Democrats were again scaremongering for partisan political purposes to the detriment of the national interest and covering for the liberal media in leaking data that would aid and abet our terrorist enemies.

After the faux scandal died down, questions were raised about the timing of the story. *USA Today* placed the story on its front page immediately before confirmation hearings for CIA nominee General Michael Hayden were to be held. The reporter who broke the story for *USA Today*, Leslie Cauley, was shown to have strong ties to the Democratic Party.[73] As it turned out, this was largely a recycling of old news; the *New York Times* had reported the essential facts the previous December. The only semblance of a scandal that emerged from the story was when BellSouth asked *USA Today* to "retract the false and unsubstantiated statements" concerning the company that were included in its May 11 story.[74]

Tracking Terrorists

In June 2006, the *New York Times*, over the administration's strenuous objections, publicly disclosed the existence of another secret government program to investigate terrorists. When President Bush articulated his strategy for conducting the War on Terror shortly after the September 11 attacks, he promised to include "intelligence" and "financial" components. He made clear that to shut down international terrorists it would be essential to track and disrupt their financial operations. Unbeknownst to the public—prior to the *Times* leak—the administration initiated the Terrorist Finance Tracking Program (TFTP), whereby the CIA would track the international financial transactions of those with suspected ties to al Qaeda by examining data of the Society of Worldwide Interbank Financial Telecommunication (SWIFT).

SWIFT is a Belgian cooperative owned by more than 2,200 organizations that oversees the routing of funds between banks, brokerages, stock exchanges, and other institutions. Under TFTP, the CIA examines wire transfers and other methods of moving money overseas and into and out of the United States, but not most routine financial transactions within the United States. For example, the CIA could track transfers from the personal bank account of a terrorist in the Middle East to a mosque in a U.S. city. The government uses the data acquired exclusively for terrorism investigations, not for investigations of tax fraud, drug trafficking, or other suspected criminal activity.[75]

There was very little doubt that TFTP was legal.[76] The Supreme Court ruled in 1976 that the right to privacy does not protect information in the possession of third parties, such as SWIFT, involving financial transactions. Nor does the 1978 Right to Financial Privacy Act apply to TFTP because SWIFT is not a financial institution.[77]

The TFTP has been instrumental in our prosecution of the War on Terror, leading to the capture of al Qaeda operative Riduan Isamuddin, known as "Hambali," who was likely behind the 2002 bombing of a Bali resort. It also led to the prosecution and conviction of Uzair Parachu, a Brooklyn man, on terrorism-related charges, for laundering $200,000 through a Karachi bank to assist an al Qaeda terrorist in Pakistan.[78]

Administration officials pleaded with the *Times* not to disclose the program. Even the entreaties of "several current and former officials, both Democrat and Republican," who vouched for the program's value, did not persuade the *Times*. The *Times*'s attitude was curious given its own editorial endorsement of just such programs shortly after the September 11 attacks. On September 24, 2001, its editors wrote:

> Organizing the hijacking of the planes that crashed into the World Trade Center and the Pentagon took significant sums of money. The cost of these plots suggests that putting Osama bin Laden and other international terrorists out of business will require more than diplomatic coalitions and military action. Washington and its allies must also disable the financial networks used by terrorists.... Much more is needed, including...

greater cooperation with foreign banking authorities.... The Treasury Department also needs new domestic legal weapons to crack down on money laundering by terrorists. The new laws should mandate the identification of all account owners, prohibit transactions with "shell banks" that have no physical premises and require closer monitoring of accounts coming from countries with lax banking laws.... If America is going to wage a new kind of war against terrorism, it must act on all fronts, including the financial one.[79]

The administration warned that publicizing the program would severely compromise it by alerting terrorists to its existence and causing them to make adjustments to get around it. But *Times* executive editor Bill Keller said, "We have listened closely to the administration's arguments for withholding this information, and given them the most serious and respectful consideration. We remain convinced that the administration's extraordinary access to this vast repository of international financial data, however carefully targeted use of it may be, is a matter of public interest." Under this bizarre test, it is hard to see how any classified information coming into the press's hands could ever be off-limits from public disclosure no matter how damaging to the national interest or dangerous to American lives. If the *Times* had access to our nuclear launch codes, would it publish them because the information "may be... a matter of public interest?" As FOX News's Brit Hume noted, what is a matter of public interest "can apply to almost anything.... Women with their breasts exposed are a matter of public interest to some people."[80]

What *might be* a matter of public interest was, to the *Times*, more than sufficient to outweigh what *would certainly be* a detriment to the public interest. The *Times*'s refusal to stand down clearly exposed a program that was saving American lives. Under the excuse of protecting privacy interests, it again abetted our terrorist enemies.

President Bush was furious over the *Times*'s publication of the story, calling it "disgraceful. For people to leak that program and for a newspaper to publish it does great harm to the United States of America." It "makes it harder to win this war on terror." Bush said that Congress had been briefed on the program and that it was fully authorized under the law.[81]

The Left, which feigned outrage over the alleged "outing" of CIA employee Valerie Plame by the Bush administration, was not outraged by this leak of information to the *Times* or the *Times*'s seditious decision to publish it. Some Democrats, like Congressman Dennis Kucinich, even defended the *Times*'s publication of the story. So long as it helped to build the case against President Bush as a civil rights–destroying executive, what was a little collateral damage to the national interest?

PART II

The Intellectual and Moral Bankruptcy
of the Democratic Party on Judges,
Values, Race, and the Economy

CHAPTER FOUR

We Have Values Too

Democratic senator Christopher Dodd, stunned by the defeat of Senate Minority Leader Tom Daschle in 2004, said, "We have lost the ability to connect with people's value systems and we're going to have to work to get that back." Congressman Richard Gephardt echoed similar sentiments. Democrats, he said, had failed "to speak our faith, and to relate to people that we share their faith."[1]

But Democrats were ambivalent. On one hand, they criticized "values voters" for being too rigid, doctrinaire, judgmental, and borderline theocratic. They believed these voters were trying to use government to impose their values on the rest of society and suppress civil liberties. On the other hand, Democrats disputed that conservatives had a monopoly on "values." They had their own values—thank you very much—and these values were superior: tolerance, inclusiveness, and compassion, for starters.

So Democrats vacillated between trashing "values voters" and claiming them as their own. In fact, many of them in their heart of hearts weren't convinced "values voters" did them in. Democratic pollster Mark Mellman, for example, dismissed their impact. He said, "People assumed moral values meant abortion and gay marriage. That is completely unsupported by the data."[2] (Instead, some Democrats thought it was that last-minute surprise videotape that Osama bin Laden released that defeated Democrats. Or maybe it was conspiracy: GOP suppression of black voters or Republican-driven computer voting errors in Ohio and Florida.)

But in the end, it wasn't that complicated. Few would deny that leftists have values. But it is a mistake not to recognize that, in general, they promote a different set of values than conservatives. As columnist Ellen Goodman wrote:

> Anyone who isn't a member of the antiabortion, anti-gay-rights, fundamentalist right is categorized—or caricatured—as someone who checked her values one hundred yards from the polling booth. Well, speaking for the designated "immoral minority," there are a whole lot of folks who believe that starting a preemptive war on false premises is a moral issue. There are a whole lot of people who believe that giving tax cuts to the rich and a deficit to the grandkids is a matter of values. There are a whole lot who put our faith, secular and sacred, in the most religiously diverse country in the world.[3]

The 2004 presidential exit polls confirmed that the more observant voters of any religion were more likely to vote Republican and the less observant, Democrat. According to the Pew Research Cen-

ter, "Americans who regularly attend worship services and hold traditional religious views increasingly vote Republican, while those
who are less connected to religious institutions and more secular in
their outlook tend to vote Democratic." President Bush beat Kerry
64 percent to 35 percent among voters who attend church more than
once a week, and 58 percent to 41 percent among those who attend
once a week. Those less engaged—attending just a few times a
year—favored Kerry 54 percent to 45 percent. But those who never
attend worship services favored Kerry 62 percent to 36 percent.[4]

Liberals fail to grasp that they cannot ridicule conservative
Christians—as DNC chairman Howard Dean did by calling same-sex
marriage opponents "bigots"[5]—and then expect to ingratiate themselves when it comes time to vote. Just as moderate Muslims rarely condemn Islamic suicide bombers, moderate liberals rarely criticize—and
often embrace—verbal attacks by liberals on conservative Christians.

The official website for the Washington State Democrats, for example, sold bumper stickers depicting the Christian fish symbol and
the cross "emblazoned with the word 'hypocrite' on a background of
hellish flames."[6] Columnist Maureen Dowd likened Christian conservatives to "a vengeful mob—revved up by rectitude—running
around with torches and hatchets after heathens and pagans and
infidels."[7] Bill Moyers suggested that "Christian fundamentalists
may believe that environmental destruction is not only to be disregarded but actually welcomed—even hastened—as a sign of the
coming apocalypse."[8]

God's Politics

Liberals can protest until they're blue in the face that *their* "values"
more authentically reflect the Christian faith than do those of

conservative Christians. The Reverend Jim Wallis, author of *God's Politics*, can continue his mission to "rescue religion from the Right." But in the process he's going to have to explain the Left's denigration of moral absolutes, its celebration of secular humanism, its dilution of the uniqueness of the Gospel, and its derision of central elements of the Judeo-Christian ethic. He's going to have to explain why the Left even supports partial-birth abortion—the grotesque, abominable procedure of killing a baby that is halfway out of its mother's body by crushing its skull.

Most voters can usually detect counterfeit peddlers of faith and morality. For candidates to resonate on faith issues they must do more than specialize in empty rhetoric or wrap their policy positions in artificial recitations of Scripture. It will take more than "reclaiming some language," as recommended by Reverend Robert Edgar, general secretary of the leftist National Council of Churches. As Janice Shaw Crouse of Concerned Women for America said, "The moral values that were a top priority in this election—abortion, embryonic stem cell research, same-sex unions—are rooted in deep religious beliefs."[9]

Wallis would have to be politically tone-deaf not to realize it is liberals, who, in the name of tolerance, inclusiveness, and religious freedom, suppress the religious liberties of Christians. It is liberals who radically oppose the government's *slightest recognition* of Christianity but are silent when the government *endorses* secular values and those of other religions. It is liberals who fight to remove legitimate and traditional Christian influence on politics and policy, and who deny the historical Christian role in the development of our constitutional system and political culture.[10] How many liberals are upset at public grade schools prohibiting teachers from using

American historical documents, including the Declaration of Independence, in class because of their references to God or Christianity? Actually, liberals are at the forefront of efforts to censor references to Christianity from public school American history textbooks. The Left even supported the New Jersey Education Association's proposed ban of a portrait of George Washington in public schools.[11] The Left celebrates secular values—not Christian values—as the backbone of our freedom tradition. Is it any wonder observant Christians are suspicious of liberalism and its "values"?

The Left impugns conservative Christians as science-rejecting and reality-challenged bigots. It even equates "fundamentalist" Christians with the Taliban. No less a prominent Democratic figure than Robert Reich, former U.S. labor secretary under President Clinton, goes further, writing:

> The true battle [of the twenty-first century] will be between modern civilization and anti-modernists; between those who believe in the primacy of the individual and those who believe that human beings owe their allegiance and identity to a higher authority; between those who give priority to life in this world and those who believe that human life is mere preparation for an existence beyond life; between those who believe in science, reason, and logic and those who believe that truth is revealed through Scripture and religious dogma. Terrorism will disrupt and destroy lives. But terrorism itself is not the greatest danger we face.[12]

The Left's institutional hostility toward the Christian religion isn't lost on "values voters." The Pew Research Center released another survey in July 2005, showing that only 29 percent of the respondents believed the Democratic Party is generally friendly toward religion (down from 40 percent in 2004) and 44 percent believed secular liberals have too much influence in the Democratic Party.[13] It also showed that people believed, by a margin of 51 percent to 28 percent, that Republicans were more concerned with protecting religious values.[14] The Democrats' problem is not that they have failed to get their message out about their values. It is that they have articulated their message very clearly, despite their efforts to obfuscate at election time. The problem isn't that Christians don't understand where the Left is coming from; it's that they do.

Looking Down Their Nose

Senator Joseph Biden, as a guest on HBO's *Real Time with Bill Maher*, made a surprisingly candid admission. "I think the problem with a lot of elites in the Democratic Party, quite frankly," said Biden, "is they communicate they don't respect people's faith. People out there don't want them to believe like they believe but they want to know that they respect them....We have too many elites in our party who look down their nose on people of faith....That's the big problem with my party."

Biden's words are encouraging—even if he is running for president and being careful not to unduly offend conservative Christians. But he went on to criticize President Bush and the Republicans' particular "usage" of religion. "This guy [Bush] uses it in a way, I think, to avoid having to know the hard things....The idea that you would pray whether or not you should go to war or pray after making a difficult decision, I understand that. But...Republicans seem to use prayer as a political organizational tool, not a road to redemption."

On the same program, actor Ben Affleck agreed that the president substitutes religion for learning and informing himself about issues that matter. "It's because he doesn't have anything else to tout, and touting religion absent any thought is a terrible mistake and really, almost criminal."

Affleck was, to a degree, echoing something host Maher had said earlier to initiate the discussion. Maher said, "I constantly read things in the news about how the president or someone high up in his administration didn't know something really kind of crucial about Iraq like that there are Sunnis and Shiites, something really big, and my guess is that he was praying when he should have been learning. I don't say that as a snarky remark; I really mean it."

Biden, while chiding the arrogance of the "elites" of his party toward people of faith, nevertheless applied his own brand of arrogance in assessing President Bush, whom he obviously believes is intellectually lazy, to put it charitably (a seemingly unanimous view on the Left).

Biden is correct that Republicans target Christian conservatives for political support. But for the most part it's anything but cynical. Though some less religious Republican politicians may opportunistically pander to that portion of the base, most of the influence is the other way around. Christian conservatives have far more influence on policy than certain insincere politicians have on Christian conservatives, who generally believe what they believe as a matter of conscience, and who are not for sale. For most Christian conservatives, their faith is fundamentally more important than their politics. Joe Biden is mistaken. In a word, it *is,* above all, about redemption. Democrats—even those few like Biden who seem to recognize and disapprove of his party's contempt for practicing Christians—fail to grasp this at their political peril.

It is the Democrats, not the Republicans, who are cynically trying to figure out how they can appeal to "values voters" by superficially repackaging rather than changing their policies. As Rabbi Daniel Lapin said, "What do you do if you are devoted to the Democratic Party, which has spent years defining itself as the party of secularism, and you suddenly discover that Americans are becoming more religious? Answer: you learn to sound spiritual."[15]

For proof this is occurring, we need look no further than Howard Dean's pandering to Christians when vying for the Democratic presidential nomination. The *Washington Post* reported that "Dean said frequent trips to Bible Belt states such as South Carolina, where evangelical Christianity flourishes...are prompting him to more candidly discuss his faith."[16] As Rabbi Shmuley Boteach noted, "Now, there's a man of conviction for you, bringing God out of the closet in order to attract voters."[17]

After a few sessions with linguistics consultant George Lakoff, Democrats had "[spun] out a new morality play in which everything, from Social Security to the driest spending cuts, is cast in terms of right and wrong." And, "Democrats are freely quoting the Bible."[18] Demonstrating they were quick studies, congressional Democrats stood in front of the Capitol Christmas tree as they urged support for increasing the minimum wage. They said it was the key to the "true meaning of Christmas—hope, generosity, and goodwill toward others." On another occasion, they said Republican budget cuts would hurt the poor, which would be an affront to Christian voters.[19] But no matter how vacuous Democrats assume Christian conservatives to be, they will not be fooled by phony overtures.

To get a flavor of what Biden is referring to as the "elites" in his party and elsewhere on the Left, we should consider the statements of Democratic politicians and liberal editorialists in the mainstream media and the liberal blogosphere. Most everyone by now is familiar with Michael Weisskopf's description of the followers of Jerry Falwell and Pat Robertson as "largely poor, uneducated, and easy to command."[20] But that was a tame indictment compared to the steady onslaught against Christian conservatives that has followed. Senator John Kerry said, "I am sick and tired of a bunch of people trying to tell me that God wants a bunch of conservative judges on the court."[21]

Columnist Maureen Dowd, during the Terri Schiavo controversy, wrote, "Oh, my God, we really are in a theocracy."[22] Dowd compared Christian conservatives to Muslim "religious fundamentalists" in Iraq. The *New York Times*'s Paul Krugman likened Christian "extremists" in America to "religious extremists" in Israel who "have already killed one prime minister."[23] The *New York Times* columnist Nicholas Kristof devoted a column to denigrating the "Left Behind" series and calling Christianity's exclusive truth claims, in essence, "bigotry." "Silly me," wrote Kristof, "I'd forgotten the passage in the Bible about how Jesus intends to roast everyone from the good Samaritan to Gandhi in everlasting fire, simply because they weren't born-again Christians."[24]

New York University's William Thatcher Dowell wrote a particularly offensive op-ed in the *Los Angeles Times* comparing Christians defending Ten Commandments displays to Muslim extremists. He said that Christians feel like they are failing in their effort "to blur the boundaries between church and state" much as, in the Middle East, Islamic fundamentalists fear they are losing out to "Western values." He said that the school districts' elevation of religion over scientific theory in biology class, American tax dollars allocated to faith-based initiatives, and the use of the Ten Commandments as a "putative founding document" are comparable to Arab insistence on the establishment of Islamic law as the foundation for policy. But the kicker was his suggestion that President Bush had to make a Faustian bargain, of sorts, with evangelicals. In exchange for their support he is now beholden to their demands, just as Saudi Arabia's "founder" had to make a bargain with the "fanatical ultrareligious Wahhabi movement."[25]

Columnist Ellis Henican wrote, "The Party of God is now fully in charge of the City of Earthly Advantage, and the faith-based finger-pointing has only begun. It's another four years for a leader who considers himself as God's own prophet, a man who says he can't even imagine someone serving in the White House 'without a relationship with the Lord.'"[26] Bill Moyers wrote, "One of the biggest changes in politics in my lifetime is that the delusional is no longer marginal. It has come in from the fringe, to sit in the seat of power in the Oval Office and in Congress. For the first time in our history, ideology and theology hold a monopoly of power in Washington."[27]

Novelist Jane Smiley contributed a piece for Slate.com, titled, "Why Americans Hate Democrats—A Dialogue: The unteachable ignorance of the red states." Referring to ignorant red-staters, Smiley wrote, "Here is how ignorance works. First, they put the fear of God into you—if you don't believe in the literal word of the Bible, you will burn in hell. Of course, the literal word of the Bible is tremendously contradictory, and so you must abdicate all critical thinking, and accept a simple, but logical system of belief that is dangerous to question. A corollary to this point is that they make sure you understand that Satan resides in the toils and snares of complex thought and so it is best not [to] try it."[28]

New York Times columnist Thomas Friedman also spoke to the values dichotomy between the red and blue states. "Is it a country that does not intrude into people's sexual preferences and the marriage unions they want to make? Is it a country that allows a woman to have control over her body? Is it a country where the line between church and state bequeathed to us by our Founding Fathers should be inviolate? Is it a country where religion doesn't trump science?"[29]

"A Word to the Faithful"

Liberals are offended by the suggestion that Republicans have a corner on the morality market. DNC chairman Howard Dean has expressed outrage—his natural state—over what he perceives to be the Republicans' claim to the moral high ground. "How can Republicans get to talk about moral values when they don't have any?" he asked. "I don't want to hear any lectures about Christian values from the Republican Party. They are the Pharisees and the Sadducees."[30] This was the same Howard Dean who once referred to pro-lifers in the state of Vermont as common criminals he didn't care to meet.[31] Pennsylvania governor Ed Rendell, one of Dean's predecessors as DNC chairman, voiced similar sentiments. He admitted he is not a Bible scholar, but said, "You have to look awfully hard" to find anything about abortion or gay marriage in the Bible. But what is in every chapter of the Bible, the Koran, and the Torah, Rendell said, are references to the Golden Rule. The Democratic philosophy, he added, more closely reflects the rule than the Republican philosophy, what with the Republicans' tax policy that benefits the wealthiest people.[32]

Following the 2004 elections, Senate Minority Leader Harry Reid, a Mormon, took it upon himself to lead the charge to corral religious voters into Democratic folds. In a move Joe Biden would decry if initiated by a Republican leader, Reid launched a website titled "A Word to the Faithful," which shamelessly pictured Reid among a group of Protestant ministers with his head bowed in prayer. The website directly couched Democratic positions in moral terms and denounced Republican positions as immoral. President Bush's move to privatize Social Security was portrayed as immoral, as were his proposed budget "cuts" on programs for the "needy." Perhaps most cynical was Reid's identification with "people of faith"—those he and his party are usually fond of ridiculing. Reid said on the website, "People of faith and Senate Democrats can work together to lift our neighbors up and achieve our common goals."[33]

Beyond establishing the website, Reid carved out a new position on his staff to head up "faith-based affairs," and he convened a faith-based services symposium in Las Vegas. In what must have been considered a betrayal by his church/state separation colleagues and supporters—unless they realized he was just "using" religion for political purposes—he procured a Las Vegas pastor to deliver the Senate's opening prayer in July 2005. Carrie Gordon Earll of Focus on the Family expressed what many conservative Christians thought of Reid's sudden bow to religion. "This looks like a reaction to November's election and if that's the case, it's unfortunate it took losing an election to see that faith is important to Americans," said Earll. Democrats "will not reach values voters with their current positions on social issues. If they are aiming for more mainline voters who might be more liberal they probably have those voters already."[34]

"I'm Sick of Values"

Liberal columnist Michael Kinsley, as usual, was more honest than many of his ideological kin. He expressed disgust at all the post-election talk about values. Kinsley wrote, "It's been less than a month since the gods decreed that, due to the election results, American political life henceforth must be all about something called 'values.' And I gave it my best. Honest. But I'm sick of talking about values, sick of pretending I have them or care more about them than I really do. Sick of bending and twisting the political causes I do care about to make them qualify as 'values.'"

But, like Dean and Reid, Kinsley defended liberal positions as being just as values-oriented (moral) as conservative ones. He said, "Why does an ideological position become sacrosanct just because it gets labeled as a 'value'? There are serious arguments and sincere passions on both sides of the gay marriage debate. For some reason, the views of those who feel that marriage requires a man and a woman are considered to be a 'value,' while the views of those who believe that gay relationships deserve the same legal standing as straight ones barely qualifies as an opinion."

But Kinsley exhibited even more intellectual honesty on the morals question when he confessed that he didn't care about whether government leaders had good values—and that no one else should either. What really matters, he said, is whether they are competent. Like other liberals of the Clinton mold, he argued that our morality should be a private matter and that values shouldn't be particularly relevant to governance—and the government definitely has no business interfering with our personal values.

This is where Kinsley and others conflate the government/morality and church/state question. Whether he realizes it or not, liberalism is a religion.[35] Its entire impetus—as misguided as conservatives believe it to be—is morally based. Government is morally required to redistribute wealth and income. Government should impose race- and gender-based preferences to equalize the playing field—as a matter of values. And, as Thomas Friedman opined, government should sanctify homosexual unions and protect a mother's right to terminate her pregnancy—because liberals believe those are the morally superior positions. So morally superior that they must be imposed on society at all costs and through any means, including unconstitutional judicial "legislation."

As noted, conservatives have no corner on "values voters," if by that term we mean people whose political positions are based largely on their ideas about what is moral and right. But if we're talking traditional values—those generally emanating from the Judeo-Christian tradition—liberals not only have little claim to them, they openly scorn them.

The liberals' disdain for traditional values was in plain view during the Clinton era, when they even ridiculed the idea that a president's moral character matters. Clinton's defenders insisted the president's private life was irrelevant to his public life and should be of no concern to the body politic. As long as we have peace and prosperity—"It's the economy, stupid"—nothing else matters. Most conservatives, however, believe it is sheer sophistry to suggest that one's private character will not affect his governance.[36]

But since liberals routinely dismiss the importance of character and reject many traditional values, their effort to repackage their positions to make them appear more palatable to traditional "values voters" should be understood as a gross deception.

"We Cannot Tolerate the Intolerable"

The liberals' disregard for traditional values is further revealed in their uniform opinion that conservatives who hold those values are judgmental and intolerant.[37] Yet every fiber of the liberal's being bristles with moral superiority and intolerance toward opposing views. Liberals are the ones who impose speech codes on college campuses, support the Fairness Doctrine to suppress conservative speech, and seek to criminalize thought through hate crimes.

They are the ones—three professors—who filed a "sexual harassment" claim against a reference librarian at Ohio State University-Mansfield for suggesting that students read four conservative-oriented books: *The Marketing of Evil*, by David Kupelian; *The Professors*, by David Horowitz; *Eurabia: The Euro-Arab Axis*, by Bat Ye'or; and *It Takes a Family* by Senator Rick Santorum.[38] They are the ones—a New Jersey state assemblywoman—who wanted Ann Coulter's book *Godless: The Church of Liberalism*, banned from all New Jersey bookstores.[39] They are the ones who seek to suppress the free exercise of religion by Christian conservatives with whom they disagree. In my book *Persecution* I detail countless examples of this, including one where a professor was disciplined for making available to her class Christian-oriented magazines as part of a discussion about how public school teachers could approach the issue of homosexuality. In a letter of reprimand, an administrator explained that the university "cannot tolerate the intolerable."[40]

If by "tolerance" liberals mean that conservatives should be required to believe and pronounce the equal validity of all ideas then conservatives will readily plead guilty to intolerance. But if they mean that conservatives will in any way suppress the liberals' expression of those ideas, they are wrong.

"I'm Pro-Choice, But against Abortion"

A curious anomaly concerning the liberals' certainty of moral superiority is their readiness to run from their convictions at election time. They frequently boast that the majority of Americans are aligned with them on the abortion question, which is probably untrue and getting worse for them over time as advancements in medical technology make it more difficult to deny the humanity of the unborn. If anything, the Democrats' hard-line position on abortion, as Ramesh Ponnuru observes, might be helping to reduce them to a minority party.[41]

Democratic politicians must have a sense that this is true, since they often go to great efforts to conceal their unwavering support for abortion during national campaigns. Perfect examples of this were John Kerry's various pronouncements during the 2004 campaign. In an interview on Spanish TV, the host asked Kerry if he would be going against the teachings of the Catholic Church by supporting abortion. Kerry reportedly responded, "I am against abortion."[42] In the second presidential debate, Kerry implied he was personally against abortion but wouldn't use the government to impose his views on others. Likewise, President Carter's oldest son, Jack, in announcing his candidacy for the U.S. Senate in Nevada, took a similar position on abortion. "I'm a personal freedoms person. I don't want the government to come in and tell my child or whoever it is that they can't have an abortion. I'm pro-choice as far as a woman choosing, but I'm against abortion."[43] One wonders whether Carter is against stealing, assault, or even the murder of already-born human beings, but opposed to the government imposing its moral views and declaring these actions to be crimes.

If Kerry, Carter, and other like-minded liberals don't believe a baby in the womb is a human life but just an unviable tissue mass not entitled to protection, why are they personally opposed to it? Do they have a fondness for unformed tissue mass? But with Kerry the issue became even more convoluted. He went so far as to say, "I believe life does begin at conception."[44] So Kerry's position, distilled to its essence, is that he believes a pregnant woman is carrying a human life but the mother and doctor should be allowed to kill it anyway.

A Pristine Wall of Separation

Liberals claim they want a strict separation of church and state, saying it's what the Framers advocated, what the Constitution mandates, and that we owe our religious freedom to it. They are wrong on all counts. More importantly, they apply the separation principle selectively to advance their agenda and impede that of the conservatives.

Liberals zealously cite the First Amendment "Establishment Clause" to oppose the slightest endorsement of the Christian religion by any agency or subsidiary of government. We see this most often in the context of public schools, where they object to almost any reference to Christianity, even when the students voluntarily invoke the references themselves, such as during commencement speeches. Such occurrences are endorsements of religion by the state, they say, and strictly forbidden. Yet when Islam is taught in a public school or when a public school promotes secular values, they remain silent and unconcerned about the intersection of church and state.

In addition to this double standard, liberals also argue that the separation principle not only precludes government's endorsement of religion, but should limit the involvement of Christians in politics. Of course, they apply a double standard to this as well, withholding their objections when Christians or churches are used to promote *their* causes.

When the Christian Right mobilizes its forces to engage in grass-roots political efforts they cry foul. After the Democrats' resounding defeat in the 2004 elections, House Minority Leader Nancy Pelosi lamented that "the Democratic message was eclipsed by so-called values pronouncements. As a devout Catholic, I observe with great regret the intervention of some Catholic bishops who joined evangelical leaders in the political arena." This political activism by the bishops, said Pelosi, helped to blur the separation of church and state, "and that is wrong."[45]

Yet not a peep was heard from Pelosi or other Democrats when Roger Cardinal Mahony publicly instructed his priests to ignore immigration laws, citing Scripture. In this case, the cardinal was involved in politics every bit as much as the Catholic bishops Pelosi criticized. Indeed, Mahony's actions were easily more extreme and intrusive. Some of his critics even accused him of sedition, saying his exhortations to violate the law amounted to the "federal crime of advocacy of insurrection against the government."[46] Whether sedition or merely an exercise in civil disobedience, it is undeniable that Mahony was injecting his religion—with the imprimatur of Church authority—into politics and the liberals turned the other cheek. Democrats also never object when their leaders enter black churches and politic to their hearts' content.

More recently, liberals have tried to extend the separation principle to extreme and ludicrous lengths. When President Bush admits he prays over difficult decisions, they say he's unstable or a messianic militarist. They insist it's improper for a public official to allow his religion to affect policy decisions—as if it is possible, or even desirable, for a public official to separate his worldview from his deliberative processes and governance. In light of this nation's heritage of faith-driven presidents, the liberals' position is astounding.

Besides, liberals are as "guilty" of this as conservatives. Their core moral convictions drive their views and policies on issues ranging from abortion to taxes to war. Sometimes they might not describe their policies as being religiously based, but that does not alter the fact that they are based every bit as much on a particular worldview as those of conservatives.

As we've seen, John Kerry's stance on abortion during the 2004 presidential campaign is a perfect example. When the Catholic Church criticized Kerry for his pro-abortion position, Kerry, between speeches in which he lamely cited Scripture, said religious affiliation should not be an issue in politics. His campaign spokesman, David Wade, said, "The decisions he will make as president will be guided by his obligation to all the people of the country and to the Constitution of the United States. Every American—whether they be Jewish, Catholic, Protestant, or any other faith—must believe their president is representing them."[47] Thus, Kerry articulated the specious argument that to advocate a position that happened to align with the church's teachings would be tantamount to representing exclusively Catholics, instead of all the American people. The idea that a politician can represent all Americans on any divisive issue (almost every issue today) is fantasy and intellectually dishonest. Kerry's commitment to appoint only judges with a pro-abortion ideology[48] puts the lie to his statement that he would divorce his values from his governance.

Secular liberals argue that President Bush's open admission that he allows his faith to influence his policies is proof we are tilting toward a theocracy—as columnist Maureen Dowd hysterically observed.

They act as though Bush has turned over the reins of government to an Established Church and is suppressing religious freedom. As Catholic League president William Donohue noted, "Bush mentions Jesus as his favorite philosopher, and the secularists go mad. The president turns to God for wisdom, and the elites get nervous. There is more than a phobia at work here—it's a deep-seated hostility to any public expression of religion."[49] August 2004 Pew Research polling data confirmed just how out of touch liberals are on this issue. A whopping 72 percent of respondents said they believed the president should have strong religious beliefs, an increase from the already whopping 70 percent among respondents in 2000.[50]

Legislating Morality

Democrats were quite concerned with exit polling data revealing that in the 2004 elections 22 percent of the voters said that "moral values" were the primary consideration in their votes.[51] Even worse news was on the horizon, because a later Pew Research poll indicated that the percentage of "values voters" was substantially higher: 27 percent.[52]

Democrats, sensing before the election that "values voters" were wise to them, began cynically citing Scripture, as witnessed by John Kerry's frequent recitations of chapter and verse. In fact, Kerry, while he and his party otherwise pretended to disdain the interplay of faith and politics, said during the 2004 campaign, "My faith affects everything that I do, in truth."[53] He proceeded to quote Scripture freely on the campaign trail. Quoting Jesus Christ, he said, "My faith, and the faith I have seen in the lives of so many Americans, also teaches me that, 'Whatever you do to the least of these, you do unto me.'"[54] Beliefnet.com assimilated a long list of Kerry's Scriptural allusions.

The mainstream media, who unmercifully criticized Bush as some fire-breathing colonial Puritan whose faith is dangerous to the integrity of a faith-free government, gave Kerry a pass for his utterances. Could that be because they doubted his conviction?

Be that as it may, Kerry also stepped into a common error among liberals concerning the intersection of religion and politics: the idea that it is wrong to "legislate morality." Again, during the second presidential debate, Kerry said, "I can't take what is an article of faith for me and legislate it for someone who doesn't share that article of faith, whether they be agnostic, atheist, Jew, Protestant, whatever. I can't do that."[55]

Kerry is wrong. Almost all our laws, criminal and civil alike, are based on morality. We forbid murder, stealing, and pedophilia because they are immoral and because we believe that human beings are creatures with intrinsic worth and moral significance. We forbid speeding and other activites that could lead to human injury because we value life, as a collective moral judgment. In fact, conservatives and liberals both vote to enact legislation based on their respective moral beliefs. Liberals are even in favor of the judiciary "legislating" morality from the bench.

When liberals claim they don't believe in "legislating morality," what they really mean is that they don't want laws forbidding abortion, which they characterize as a private matter between a woman and her doctor, a formulation which completely ignores the only innocent party in the equation: the unborn human being. They also mean that the government should sanction same-sex marriage. This is a private matter between the individuals.

But their position necessarily involves the imposition of their values on the public at large. By insisting on society's validation of same-sex marriage, they are "legislatively" imposing their moral judgment that society has no legitimate interest in preserving the institution of marriage between a man and a woman. The conservative position doesn't prohibit homosexual behavior or cohabitation. It just strenuously opposes the public affirmation of such behavior and the denigration of the institution of traditional marriage.

Support of traditional marriage is not born of so-called homophobia, or bigotry, but a genuine belief that the institution is one of the pillars of our society and that its erosion will result in its decline and disintegration. For conservatives, this matter, like many moral issues, transcends the "privacy" and "freedom" of individuals. It impacts the very survival of our society.

Just as with abortion, liberals pretend they are in the majority on the gay marriage issue. When President Bush stood with Christian conservatives announcing his support of the Marriage Protection Amendment, Democratic leaders said Bush was promoting the traditional marriage amendment to deflect attention from his difficulties on other issues, including Iraq. The liberal media sang in unified chorus that Americans don't care about gay marriage and that it is "way down on the list" of their priorities.[56] But they protested too much. Liberals know that the conservative base is highly motivated on this issue and that it hurts Democrats at the ballot box. Indeed, 2004 presidential exit polls revealed that only 25 percent of voters support gay marriage and 35 percent favor civil unions.[57]

It's Our Bible Too

Not long after disparaging Republicans as "pretty much a white, Christian party," Howard Dean invoked the Bible, favorably. "Let me remind those Republicans," said Dean, that the Bible mentions helping the poor "three thousand times. I have not yet seen gay marriage mentioned in the Bible. That is a Republican issue."[58]

Following the 2004 election, Hillary Clinton was determined to position herself for a presidential run in 2008. She wasn't just going to paint herself as a hawk in the war; she was also determined to connect with that large bloc of "values voters" the polls had revealed were mostly voting Republican. During a speech in Albany, New York, in January 2005 she stated that "religious and moral values" were important in combating teenage sex.[59] Later that month she told the National Ten Point Leadership Foundation—a group that advocates faith-based remedies for gang criminality— "I've always been a praying person" and she made multiple references to God. She also said, "There is no contradiction between support for faith-based initiatives and upholding our constitutional principles." There must be room for people of faith, she said, "to live out their faith in the public square." These statements prompted the liberal *Boston Globe* to report that Clinton "embraced an issue some pundits say helped seal a second term for George W. Bush: acceptance of the role of faith in addressing social ills."[60]

In 2006, as the immigration issue was heating up in Congress and around the country, Hillary sought to ridicule Republicans' religious values and, at the same time, assert those values herself. She criticized a Republican immigration proposal in biblical terms, saying, "It is certainly not in keeping with my understanding of the Scriptures. This bill would literally criminalize the Good Samaritan and probably even Jesus Himself."

CHAPTER FIVE

The Values Blues

What "values" does the Democratic Party really stand for?
While Democratic politicians might cite the Bible at opportune
moments before the cameras, their animating worldview is anything
but traditional. They promote abortion on demand, affirmative
action, and special rights for homosexuals. Democrats don't even like
the Boy Scouts—as witnessed by their booing the Boy Scouts during
the Democratic National Convention.[1] What's next? Apple pie?

As we've already seen, liberals are not always completely candid
about these matters. Bill Clinton promised to make abortion "safe,
legal, and rare" and proceeded to remove obstacles to it. He
appointed pro-abortion judicial activists to the federal bench, like
Ruth Bader Ginsburg, and advocated such an expansive definition
of the "mother's health" exception to abortion restrictions as to render those restrictions virtually meaningless.

The Supreme Court, in *Stenberg* v. *Carhart*,[2] invalidated a Nebraska statute prohibiting partial-birth abortion. Though the statute contained an exception to protect the *life* of the mother, it did not include an exception for the mother's *health*, which was unacceptable to the liberal majority on the Court. The Court ignored arguments from pro-life advocates that the requirement of a broad, nebulous "mother's health" exception is a ruse because the procedure *never* jeopardizes the mother's health. As Justice Antonin Scalia wrote in his dissent, the "Court must know...that demanding a 'health exception'...is to give live-birth abortion free rein." Justice Clarence Thomas, in his dissenting opinion, wrote:

> But such a health exception requirement eviscerates *Casey*'s undue burden standard and imposes unfettered abortion-on-demand. The exception entirely swallows the rule. In effect, no regulation of abortion procedures is permitted because there will always be *some* support for a procedure and there will always be some doctors who conclude that the procedure [partial-birth abortion] is preferable. If Nebraska reenacts its partial-birth abortion ban with a health exception, the State will not be able to prevent physicians like Dr. Carhart from using partial-birth abortion as a routine abortion procedure.... The majority's insistence on a health exception is a fig leaf barely covering its hostility to any abortion regulation by the States—a hostility that *Casey* purported to reject.[3]

When Congress was considering its Partial-Birth Abortion Ban Act of 2003, it found that "partial-birth abortion is never necessary to preserve the health of a woman." In fact, the procedure itself poses serious health risks to the woman. But liberals on and off the court continue the charade that the mother's health exception is legitimate and not just a way to emasculate reasonable restrictions on abortion. While claiming to be working toward making abortions rarer, they are doing precisely the opposite.

Promoting the Death Culture

It will take far more than semantics to persuade voters that today's Democratic Party, which has become the home for those pushing the "culture of death," attaches sufficient reverence to human life. As Ramesh Ponnuru notes in his book *The Party of Death*, "[The Democratic Party] did not make a decision, sometime in the late 1960s, to become the chief political vehicle for all those who think that the inviolability of human life is an outdated or oppressive concept. But it is today the party of abortion on demand, euthanasia, and embryo-killing research. And it is the party of those for whom abortion has become a kind of religion."[4]

Conservatives have been warning for years that legalized abortion, immoral in its own right, would lead to a devaluation of life across the board and would result in a slippery slope toward euthanasia and other horrors.[5] Euthanasia advocates present it as innocuous, even compassionate. But gradually, there has been an insidious relaxation of our attitudes toward life-ending decisions as our culture has devalued life. We are gravitating toward the point—if not already there—where we'll begin to terminate life, not just to spare the elderly and ill pain and discomfort, but to avoid expenses, inconvenience, and disruption to others. As a society, we are becoming desensitized.

One repulsive example of this was the attempt by former students and faculty to dedicate a memorial student lounge to Villanova professor Mine Ener. Ener, in a state of postpartum depression, had killed her six-month-old daughter (who had Down Syndrome), and then committed suicide while in jail. Many alumni and others were outraged that a Roman Catholic school with a mission statement upholding "the sacredness of each person" would even consider honoring a woman who had murdered her baby and committed suicide. But Villanova spokesman Barbara K. Clement defended the move, saying that Ener's friends "simply want to honor her work as a dedicated scholar and enthusiastic mentor, and hope to raise awareness about postpartum depression.... She loved that baby very, very, very much. It was a disease. We have to focus on the fact that she was a wonderful teacher and researcher."[6] While postpartum depression can be serious, it is inconceivable—outside the context of a "culture of death"—that a woman who murdered her child could be treated as a mere victim and glorified for her work.

The trend toward the devaluation of life operates to the detriment of newborns as well. MIT psychology professor Steven Pinker questions whether the penalty for infanticide, in some cases, should be reduced. Pinker wrote, "To a biologist, birth is as arbitrary a milestone as any other.... No, the right to life must come, the moral philosophers say, from morally significant traits that we humans happen to possess. One such trait is... an ability to reflect upon ourselves as a continuous locus of consciousness, to form and savor plans for the future, to dread death and to express the choice not to die. And there's the rub: our immature neonates don't possess these traits any more than mice do."[7]

As such, "neonaticide"—the murder of infants—should not, say certain "moral philosophers," be classified as murder. Pinker was not arguing for full-blown legalization of baby-killing, but that mothers who kill their children shouldn't be judged as severely as those charged with murdering older human beings. Some appear to go further. Pinker quotes University of Colorado philosophy professor Michael Tooley, who rationalizes infanticide "during an interval after birth." Personhood, according to Tooley, does not begin at birth. Rather, "an organism possesses a serious right to life only if it possesses the concept of a self as a continuing subject of experiences and other mental states, and believes that it is itself such a continuing entity."[8]

It's not that the Democratic Party has yet embraced such chilling thoughts. But the liberalism that drives their party is comfortable with those ideas; it installs professors promoting them in major institutions, and it ridicules as officious, religious zealots those who denounce this culture of death. The late columnist Michael Kelly lamented that the *New York Times Magazine*, which published Pinker's thoughts, "treated [them] as a legitimate argument."[9] Pinker is a respected scientist, hardly considered by the Left to be on the fringe. Yet he wrote, "A new mother will first coolly assess the infant and her situation and only in the next few days begin to see it as a unique and wonderful individual." One has to wonder what mothers Pinker has encountered. Michael Kelly quoted George Orwell to capture Pinker's thinking. "You have to be an intellectual to believe such nonsense. No ordinary man could be such a fool." Sadly, these "non-ordinary people" are well placed in influential universities throughout the nation.

Even if Pinker represents the extreme of current liberal thought, there is a curious mindset among many liberals that sympathizes with those aggressively promoting the death culture. We saw it in the liberal community's response to the Terri Schiavo saga. There is certainly nothing wrong with the sentiment of wanting to spare one's loved ones or other fellow human beings pain. But some on the Left—not just "Dr. Death" Jack Kevorkian—virtually glamorize death, as when George Felos, Michael Schiavo's attorney, described the starving Terri as looking "beautiful." His statement went well beyond euphemism, according to the accounts of Terri's immediate family, who described her as emaciated, with flaking skin, sunken and bleeding eyes, bleeding mouth, and "like someone who is coming out of a bunker at Auschwitz."

Perhaps some in our society innocuously motivated by so-called privacy rights in their fierce opposition to the government encroaching on the freedom of individuals and their families to make end-life decisions. But there are some leftists who actually seem to prefer to err on the side of death. Aside from what many considered to be the excesses of the Right over Schiavo, it was hard not to notice where the unquestioning sympathies of the Left resided. They were all too ready to "close the case" on the flimsy basis that Terri had—supposedly—verbally expressed her will not to be kept alive to a man who was living with another woman with whom he had sired children. While they insisted they were just trying to vindicate the privacy and freedom of the patient—to honor her allegedly expressed intentions—they didn't seem open to considering that Terri might want to live, or that her estranged husband may have had other motives.

They didn't seem to be bothered that no matter what Terri may have told her husband, it is highly doubtful she said anything specific about wanting to be starved to death. Liberals were remarkably incurious about other troubling aspects of the case, such as that Terri's lack of written instructions or her immediate family members swearing she never expressed a will to die. Perhaps the Left's willing deafness to these and other anomalies was due to their revulsion toward "intermeddling" conservatives. But it also may have been because of their desensitization to life.

Safe and Legal, but Not Rare

A column by E. J. Dionne illustrates the liberals' misapprehension of the depth of the conservatives' conviction on the sanctity of human life and other issues. It demonstrates why liberals are misguided in thinking they can make inroads among traditional "values voters" merely through repackaging. Dionne praised fellow liberal Teddy Kennedy for encouraging Democrats, after the 2004 election, not to shy away from their "values," or "[retreat] from their core principles, but" to demonstrate "that those principles [are] consistent with the values held by many Americans who call themselves conservative." He noted that Kennedy used the abortion issue as an example, saying, "Surely, we can all agree that abortion should be rare, and that we should do all we can to help women avoid the need to face that decision."[10]

Liberals aren't being sincere about making any meaningful effort to make abortion rare. Beyond that, what Dionne and Kennedy miss is that pro-life conservatives aren't going to be pacified by a nominal reduction in the number of abortions. That entirely skirts the moral issue. To pro-life advocates, abortion, except to protect the life of the mother, is murder. They are not going to rest until they achieve social reform on the magnitude of ending slavery. Other things being equal, many of them are not going to vote for pro-abortion Democrats or Republicans just because they promise, emptily, to reduce the number of abortions.

But these "subtleties" are lost on many liberals, including 2008 presidential aspirant Hillary Clinton. In her current quest for the White House, she has adopted her husband's slogan "safe, legal, and rare."[11] She peppers her speeches with Scripture and feigned deference to the consciences of pro-lifers when it suits her audience, but in the meantime continues to promote abortion-friendly policy and judges who'll "legislate" it.

The pro-abortion lobby thrives on disinformation. In speech after hysterical speech they have warned that a reversal of *Roe* v. *Wade* would send us back to the days of back-alley and coat hanger abortions with thousands of woman dying as a result. But, as Ramesh Ponnuru points out, it turns out that those numbers were literally made up.[12] Nevertheless, abortion-friendly politicians continue to cite these statistics. To be sure, some women died from illegal abortions, but the numbers reported are grossly exaggerated.[13]

While "pro-choice" activists insist they really aren't pro-abortion, but just want to maximize the mother's freedom and sovereignty over her own reproductive rights—itself a gross euphemism—they do nothing to better inform women contemplating an abortion about the potential consequences of an abortion. If their motive were truly to maximize freedom they would ensure that women make informed decisions. But when they work to withhold important information from them one has to question whether they are trying to expand or suppress "choice."

It turns out that "legal" abortions are not as safe as advertised, and abortion advocates often try to conceal the inherent dangers. There is a possible, though disputed link between abortion and breast cancer[14] and there is evidence that the legalization of abortion has increased the incidence of sexually transmitted diseases[15] by increasing sexual promiscuity. There is also mounting proof that women who have abortions encounter long-term emotional problems. According to the *American Journal of Psychiatry* a study of five hundred post-abortive women found that 43 percent had immediate negative emotions due to the experience. A later review indicated the number was 50 percent. Also, some 10 percent of the women reportedly encountered "serious psychiatric complications." One psychiatrist noted, "Since abortion was legalized, I have seen hundreds of patients who have had the operation. Approximately 10 percent expressed very little or no concern. Among the other 90 percent there were all shades of distress, anxiety, heartache and remorse."[16]

Another study found that suicide rates for women who have had an abortion are significantly higher than those who carried the baby to term.[17] And, researchers at the University of Minnesota reported that teenage girls who have had an abortion within the last six months are ten times as likely to attempt suicide as those who have not.[18]

Admittedly, there is hardly unanimity on these findings. Other studies have shown there are no increased incidents of depression following elective abortions.[19] But a pro-abortion bias may be getting in the way of further objective study. As the authors of one study concluded, "strong emotions infiltrating the academic study of this topic render the conduct of research that is free from moral, political, and philosophical biases a difficult ... goal. However, in the interest of millions of women who undergo one of the most common surgical procedures currently available in the United States and elsewhere throughout the world, it is evident that more probing and substantive research should be conducted."[20] At any rate, the pro-abortion lobby and the Democratic Party that houses it has a vested interest in suppressing information that might discourage women from choosing abortion. Such is the disposition of the modern "party of death."

Even when certain mavericks attempt to break ranks with the Democratic Party on abortion they are met with a wave of hostility from their pro-abortion base. When the Democratic Senatorial Campaign Committee indicated its support for two pro-life candidates: Pennsylvania treasurer Robert Casey, running against Senator Rick Santorum, and Congressman James Langevin, to unseat liberal Republican senator Lincoln Chafee, it did not sit well with pro-abortion groups. NARAL president Kate Michelman described it as "disturbing" that the party would "anoint someone who doesn't share the party's core values."[21]

As a last resort in their desperate efforts to justify abortion, Democrats often point to the conservatives' support for capital punishment, which they believe renders conservatives' condemnation of abortion inconsistent and hypocritical. Again, they are at odds with the American people and logic. They are the ones guilty of inconsistency. Their extraordinary concern for the lives of convicted murderers—the least innocent among us—is at striking odds with their absence of concern for the lives of unborn babies—the most innocent among us. Many conservatives support the death penalty precisely because of their reverence for human life. When a human being murders another human being, the ultimate sanction of execution is justified as a societal statement that innocent life is so precious that those who murder forfeit their right to it.[22]

Repackaging Their Positions Won't Work

But it's not just on the abortion issue that the Democrats' effort to repackage their "values" will fail. Another good example is contained in E. J. Dionne's column praising Senator Kennedy's efforts to restate the party's positions to make them more palatable to moderates and conservatives. Dionne wrote, "If you are for family values, how can you oppose Kennedy's call to give all employees at least seven days of paid sick leave a year so they don't face 'a cruel choice between losing their job, or neglecting their sick child or sick spouse at home.' Who can disagree that companies should make it easier for parents to 'attend a PTA meeting or a school play or sports contest'? Why, in short, shouldn't liberals challenge the economic marketplace to be more friendly to the needs of families?"[23] Dionne and Kennedy miss the point. Liberals aren't just *challenging* the marketplace to be friendlier. They are using the coercive power of government to force employers to comply with these circumstances.

Conservatives believe in showing compassion toward people and most would favor employers *voluntarily* granting such leave. The same thing applies to universal health care, another issue Kennedy (through Dionne) cites. Conservatives want everyone to have health care coverage, but they generally oppose increased government control over the health care industry, which they believe is not only wrong, but results in higher costs and inferior care in the long run. Besides, most Americans, regardless of their economic status, are eligible for emergency medical care. Not having health insurance is not the same as not having some degree of medical care. Liberals like Dionne and Kennedy continue to underestimate the people's ability to discern substance over form, and to see through superficial repackaging efforts.

Promoting Radically Different Values

While liberals regard conservatives as the aggressors, they are the ones attempting to alter radically our cultural norms from classrooms to corporate boardrooms. This is especially true with their promotion of the homosexual agenda. Traditional marriage is not their only target. They are attempting, in school districts throughout the nation, to aggressively promote "alternative" lifestyles as normal and indoctrinate students on the "normalcy" of homosexuality and homosexual behavior. They have created "safe zones" and "bullying policies" that are partially designed to intimidate contrary views.

Liberals didn't complain when Newton High School in Newtonville, Massachusetts, held a "Transgender, Bisexual, Gay and Lesbian Awareness Day (To BGLAD Day)." Students were allowed—some would say "encouraged"—to attend workshops and assemblies in lieu of their regular classes, in which speakers would "make students feel good about homosexuality, bisexuality, and transgenderism."[24] How's that for getting back to the curricular basics? We know how liberals would react if the school were to conduct a seminar on the virtues of military life and the nobility of our cause in Iraq—to make students feel good about the military and liberty in the Middle East.

What is occurring in our schools is also occurring in our corporations, where liberals are trying to suppress dissenting opinion through such tactics as demonizing those who disagree as hate-filled bigots and sending them to sensitivity training seminars.[25]

Private Parts

Liberals are also somewhat selective in their attitude toward "privacy." They don't have respect for the "privacy" of parents with regard to decisions concerning their children. In many places, especially in more "progressive" states like California, they are flagrantly disrespectful of parents' wishes on the types of sensitive information that is imparted to their children at school. The school district in Palmdale, California, conducted a survey to assess psychological barriers to learning. It submitted questions to students, without their parents' permission or knowledge, directly relating to sex. The survey included such questions as whether they engaged in "thinking about having sex" and "thinking about touching other people's private parts."

When outraged parents sued the school district and two district officials, the federal district court dismissed their claims and the infamous Ninth Circuit Court of Appeals affirmed. The Court stated, "We . . . hold that there is no fundamental right of parents to be the exclusive provider of information regarding sexual matters to their children, either independent of their right to direct the upbringing and education of their children or encompassed by it. We also hold that parents have no due process or privacy right to override the determinations of public schools as to the information to which their children will be exposed while enrolled as students."[26] It takes a village, right?

While not all liberals are actively promoting a radical sexual agenda in our schools, liberals enable such developments by ignoring or repudiating parents who try to stop this madness, often rejecting them as ignorant religious zealots. Moreover, it is liberals who appoint and support federal judges who legislate against traditional moral values from the bench, and as long as they do, they'll fail to win traditional values voters.

"Who Does He Think He Is—Switzerland?"

No discussion of the values question would be complete without considering the parties' respective attitudes toward America, Western

Civilization, multiculturalism, national sovereignty, and patriotism. Liberals are extraordinarily defensive about their own patriotism, often rushing to defend themselves against accusations that were never made. While most seem to possess a blame-America-first mentality, from foreign policy to nuclear proliferation to environmental policy, they insist that their criticism proves love of country. But you would never catch a conservative television executive—assuming there are any, other than FOX News's Roger Ailes—telling a group of journalism students that he didn't think, as a journalist, he should offer any opinion on whether the Pentagon was a legitimate target for the terrorist attack on September 11, as did ABC News president David Westin.[27]

You would never catch a major conservative news anchor telling a student at Northwestern University, "I don't think it's appropriate for a journalist to wear a flag. It suggests that you approve of whatever the government is doing at that time." But NBC's Tom Brokaw did.[28] And would a conservative journalist ever refuse to be de-briefed by the U.S. military like CNN's Bernard Shaw did during the Gulf War, pronouncing that he was "neutral" in the conflict?[29] Shaw's position prompted actor Charlton Heston to ask, "Who does he think he is—Switzerland?"[30]

Try as they might, liberals cannot escape their well-earned image of being soft on defense and national security. Bill Clinton proudly gutted our military and scrapped important weapons systems during his military-loathing tenure. Democrats are well aware of their image problem on the military. In June 2006, they conducted a seminar for Democratic congressional staffers to help them learn how to better communicate with people in the armed services. The featured speakers, authors Kathy Roth-Douquet and Frank Schaeffer, spoke to the "great disconnect" between liberals and military culture.[31]

Democrats, as we have documented, have opposed President Bush at almost every turn in the War on Terror. They always have their excuses, from concerns over "unilateralism," to abuse, torture, unlimited detainment of enemy prisoners, wireless interception of enemy communications, and other alleged invasions of privacy through the Patriot Act. But the fact remains that they represent steadfast obstacles to the prosecution of the war. And as much as they protest being labeled as anti-American, they break bread with people who are openly hostile to America, like Michael Moore, and elevate them to positions of respect.

Many liberals scoff at the idea that American culture and American ideas could be superior to those of other nations. They bristle at the notion that it is even possible for certain cultures to be superior to others, no matter how civilized the former and how barbaric the latter. The dogma of multiculturalism teaches that cultures and the values they promote are equal and it is morally wrong to suggest otherwise. We have multiple ethnicities in this nation and we should celebrate that diversity, they say, instead of encouraging them to unite in the proverbial melting pot. They see nothing wrong with a balkanized America with people from different ethnic backgrounds speaking different languages—even though the growing trend toward bilingualism ushered in by waves of illegal immigration greatly threatens any sense of national identity and harmony.

They have little affinity for such antiquated and unenlightened concepts as national pride and national sovereignty. Many of them prefer transnationalism—where intellectuals and elites proclaim themselves citizens of the world. The more extreme among them consider the very idea of nation states as regressive. National entities are prideful, jealous, and warmongering and we must rise above them if we are to live in peace. They see flag waving and sentimentality over recitations of the Pledge of Allegiance as chauvinistic and intolerant toward other cultures.

While they vigorously defend the "constitutional right" of anti-American militants to burn the flag, they don't seem bothered by the act itself. In their heart of hearts, many of them probably think the whole idea of patriotism is outmoded and unduly threatening to other nations who don't have our power, wealth, or resources. But it is multiculturalism, which the Left unequivocally celebrates, that "saps and undermines serious efforts at civic education."[32] It works directly against the inculcation of national pride, patriotism, and a meaningful consensus about our national identity.

America, the Stingy

It is the Left that instinctively sides with the United Nations, which regularly criticizes and demonizes America. When Jeffrey Sachs, the economist appointed by the United Nations' Kofi Annan to direct the Millennium Project, harshly criticized the United States for not contributing enough to this "Project" to support poor countries, the *New York Times* couldn't have agreed more. In its editorial "America the Indifferent," the *Times* excoriated the United States as "the world's richest nation" for not contributing a sufficient percentage of its national income to foreign aid. "But no one is impressed when a billionaire writes a $50 check for a needy family," wrote the *Times*. "The test is the percentage of national income we give to the poor, and on that basis this country is the stingiest in the Group of Seven industrialized nations."[33]

So in the view of the *Times*, America is stingy. Further showing its colors, the *Times* derided America for spending thirty times more on the military ($450 billion) annually than on the development of poor countries ($15 billion). It quoted Sachs, approvingly, describing the U.S. as "all war and no peace in our foreign policy." The liberal flagship thus reveals its considered opinion that America is a warring nation, whose military expenditures are purely selfish and imperialistic. The *Times* obviously doesn't recognize that our government has a constitutional duty—and moral duty—to protect and defend itself and that unless it does so, it will not be in a position to help anyone.

Nor does the *Times* see any altruism in U.S. foreign policy, whether in defending Kuwait or unseating Saddam Hussein. Apparently, the only thing that qualifies for benevolence is direct transfer payments to other nations. The *Times* is obviously impervious to the idea that providing other nations the tools to create their own wealth is a far greater gift. Freeing Iraq and helping it to establish self-rule—not to mention helping to rebuild its infrastructure and educational system—will be of enormously greater value in the long run than just throwing billions of dollars at it.

The *Times*'s opinion about America's "stinginess" was not that unusual for the "progressive media." Even before the aftershocks of the ocean-based South Asian earthquake could be felt, liberals in the mainstream media and at the United Nations were condemning President Bush because he didn't speak quickly, loudly, and compassionately enough to the tsunami victims. United Nations official Jan Egeland said of Western nations, "It is beyond me why we are so stingy." The *Minneapolis Star Tribune* wrote, "As the Bush administration is wont to say, actions speak louder than words, and America's actions in recent days have painted the United States as a rich, self-absorbed and uncaring nation that had to be shamed into anything approaching appropriate concern about this catastrophe."[34] The *New York Times* piled on, coming to Egeland's defense. In an editorial titled, "Are We Stingy? Yes," the *Times* challenged President Bush's statement that Egeland's criticism was "misguided and ill informed." "We beg to differ," wrote the *Times*. "Mr. Egeland was right on target."[35]

Liberals also believe that "stingy" America greedily consumes an obscenely excessive percentage of the world's resources. Sometimes their arguments border on the absurd. The diet police on the Left have recently proposed a new tactic against the "plague" of obesity: to treat it as an environmental problem. The *Washington Post* reported that 140 million American adults are overweight or obese and that, collectively, they possess four billion pounds of extra fat—caused by having eaten fourteen trillion excess calories. Since "health attempts" to control obesity haven't met with much success, they are suggesting that we should also employ marketplace approaches. "The first step is realizing that, nationally, weight gain is not a medical problem, it's a pollution problem."[36] "Food calories" are so readily available they should be considered a "pollutant." They compare the obese person's consumption of calories with the asthmatic's inhalation of the air around him. Neither can help ingesting too much because air and calories are just too pervasive. But since emissions allowances have worked in reducing air pollution, perhaps similar emission allowances could be instituted to target foods with high caloric density. The bottom line, as with so many liberal-spawned proposals, is the intervention of "big brother" to tell us what we can eat and how much of it. Where are the pro-choice, freedom-loving liberals on these ideas?

"Read My Ears"

Some on the Left are just openly hostile to America and what it stands for. Former *Time* magazine White House correspondent Nina Burleigh, most noted for her statement, "I'd be happy to give [Clinton oral sex] just to thank him for keeping abortion legal," wrote, "I cringed as my young son recited the Pledge of Allegiance. But who was I to question his innocent trust in a nation I long ago lost faith in?" To "counteract any God-and-country indoctrination" her child was receiving in kindergarten at a "traditional and conservative" school, Burleigh and her husband "began our own informal in-home instruction about Bush, Iraq, and Washington over the evening news." One day on a drive into New York City, Burleigh gave her son—"trapped in the back seat of our car"—a civics lesson. "In simple language, I told my son that our president had started a war with a country called Iraq. I said that we were bombing cities and destroying buildings. And I explained that families just like ours now had no money or food because their parents didn't have offices to go to anymore or bosses to pay them. 'America did this?' my son asked, incredulous. 'Yes, America,' I answered. He paused, a long silent pause, then burst out: 'But Mommy, I love America! I want to hug America!' "[37]

As noted, the Left also often sides with European countries who criticize American policy in the War on Terror. When France, Germany, and Russia would not join the "coalition of the willing" to attack Iraq, Democrats criticized Bush as a "unilateralist" for beginning the war without them. It never occurred to Democrats to question the judgment and good will of those nations in refusing to join the alliance, even though their intelligence agencies agreed that Saddam had stockpiles of WMD.

New York Times columnist Thomas Friedman typified this attitude in a column about President Bush's planned trip to Europe.[38] "I have one small suggestion for President Bush.... When he comes to Europe to mend fences next month he [should] give only one speech... and it should consist of basically three words: 'Read my ears.'... There is nothing that Europeans want to hear from George Bush, there is nothing they will listen to from George Bush that will change their minds about him or the Iraq war or U.S. foreign policy.... In such an environment, the only thing that Mr. Bush could do to change people's minds about him would be to travel across Europe and not say a single word—but just listen." Friedman went on to say of the European criticism, "Some of it is very heartfelt, even touching."[39]

This kind of thinking—along with a visceral antipathy toward George W. Bush—led Congressman John Murtha to tell a North Miami audience in June 2005 that the American presence in Iraq is more dangerous to world peace than nuclear threats from North Korea or Iran.[40]

This is the same kind of thinking that leads Hollywood and academic leftists to romanticize Fidel Castro. It is the same kind of thinking that prompted former president Bill Clinton—also while U.S. soldiers were fighting and dying in Iraq—to tell an audience of Arab students at the University of Dubai that the United States made a "big mistake" by invading Iraq.[41] It's the same kind of thinking that drove failed presidential candidate John Kerry to tell U.S. troops he was visiting in Baghdad in January 2005 that their commander in chief had made "horrendous judgments" and "unbelievable blunders" that had undermined the war effort.[42] It's the same mentality that drove former president Jimmy Carter, while in Britain, to call the U.S. attack on Iraq "unnecessary and unjust."[43]

This kind of thinking also compelled Carter to condemn U.S. foreign policy as "arrogant." Carter said, "There is a sense that the United States has become too arrogant, too dominant, too self-centered, proud of our wealth, believing that we deserve to be the richest and most powerful and influential nation in the world." Carter suggested it was hypocritical for us to prohibit other nations from developing biological weapons "that we ourselves have." The United States, according to Carter, has given other nations reasons to scorn and resent us. Carter also mocked the faith of President George W. Bush in attacking his foreign policy. Carter said, "We worship the prince of peace, not of pre-emptive war."[44] Carter attacked the United States for its lack of charity, saying that we only give one-thousandth of our gross national product toward international assistance, while the average European nation gives four times as much. He declined to point out that our contribution in actual dollars dwarfs those of European nations.[45]

This kind of leftist thinking is also what was behind University of Washington student Jill Edwards's objection to her fellow student senator's proposal to erect a campus memorial in honor of World War II hero Pappy Boyington, an alumnus of the school. Edwards challenged the appropriateness of honoring someone who killed other people and said U.S. Marines were not the kind of people the university should want to produce. Her fellow senator Ashley Miller chimed in that there were already enough monuments at the school honoring "rich white men."[46] These are the "values" that institutions of higher learning are instilling in our students—values that those who end up in the academy will teach future students.[47]

As author Midge Decter said in a lecture to the Heritage Foundation, "[These] arbiters of culture have refused to bless the

American system, both its government and its economy.... The country went one way and its privileged aristocracy and thinkers and artists went another."[48] Liberals deny that America's universities are driven by a leftist ideological bias, apparently believing that red-state parents, who might just send their children to these state-sponsored indoctrination camps, won't be discerning enough to see through their empty denials.

Those Heartless Conservatives

We also cannot leave the values discussion without briefly expanding on the Left's claim to moral superiority in the compassion department, usually measured by government fiscal and tax policies. Howard Dean told ABC's George Stephanopoulos, "The truth is the Democrats are the party of moral values. We're altruists." Dean described President Bush's effort to tackle Social Security as his "attack" on Social Security—"a fundamental attack on the notion that America is one community and that we have responsibility for each other."[49]

Liberal commentator Bill Press, in his book *How the Republicans Stole Christmas*, wrote, "I think [the Christian Right] get[s] the Bible ass-backward, ignoring the most important teachings of Jesus, which place love and compassion above greed and intolerance."[50] It is the Left's enduring philosophy that government exists to equalize economic outcomes through wealth redistribution. It is no accident that it took Bill Clinton three times to sign the welfare reform bill into law. Though they deny it, Democrats have a soft spot for socialism, and a distrust of capitalism that most often manifests itself in their hostility toward corporate America, which they tend to see as one big giant "Enron."

"An Historically Great Party"

We began this discussion of values by chronicling liberal astonishment at the rise of the "values voter" in the 2004 elections. The mainstream media and political commentators were beating their heads against the wall trying to figure out what unleashed the morals freight train that ran over Democrats, who were standing paralyzed on the tracks like deer in headlights. Conservative Christian activist Gary Bauer, who has studied and promoted "values" issues his entire adult life, offered some simple but profound insights on this question.

The "experts" had been asking the wrong post-election question, he said. "The oddity on Election Day," wrote Bauer, "was not that millions of Middle Americans showed up who love their country and still believe in reliable standards of right and wrong. Those folks have been around since the beginning of the republic. The mystery is what sustains these radicals who hate America and hate their fellow citizens. The mystery is why an historically great party, the party of my parents and grandparents, the Democratic Party of the 'working man,' can't or won't find the courage to kick this gang of malcontents out of their 'big tent.'"[51] Indeed, the party has traveled a long way off the path in the past four decades, into the abyss of moral and intellectual bankruptcy.

CHAPTER SIX

The "Living Constitution"

The courts' assigned function is to interpret the laws and resolve legal disputes in actual cases. But their usurpation of the legislative function through decades of judicial activism has made them enemy number one among social conservatives because they have encroached on the people's sovereignty and dismantled the Constitution, brick by brick. The Left, being unable to implement its policy agenda through proper democratic processes, has seized on the courts to impose its will on the people—all in the name of vindicating "fundamental rights." "Fundamental rights" is code for those rights not guaranteed by the Constitution but created by an unrestrained judiciary.

Liberal justice Stephen Breyer, during a speech at the University of Chicago Law School, admitted that he frequently makes decisions about a law's constitutionality using standards other than merely interpreting the Constitution. "I tend to emphasize purpose and consequences," said Breyer. "Others emphasize language, a more literal reading of the text, history, and tradition—believing that those help you reach a more objective answer." As an example, he defended his inconsistent rulings on two cases involving Ten Commandments displays in front of courthouses in Kentucky and Texas. Because the displays in Kentucky would allegedly cause religious conflict, he decided they were unconstitutional. But since the Texas monument had been on display for years and would not cause conflict, he ruled it constitutional.[1]

Liberals have so much invested in the judiciary as a policy-making branch that they have been willing to go to almost any lengths to ensure that liberals are placed on the federal appellate bench and that conservative, Constitution-respecting judges are not. As a practical matter, this means they have been willing to assassinate the characters of perfectly honorable and exceptionally competent jurists, like Robert Bork, Clarence Thomas, and Charles Pickering. Their assaults have been so vicious, with outrageously unwarranted accusations of racism, corruption, or any other imaginable sins, that many qualified candidates have decided not to apply for positions on the court, unwilling to sacrifice themselves as expendable pawns in the Left's scorched earth campaign.

Liberals defend judicial activism by saying conservatives do it too. Liberals even assert that by appointing judges pledged to interpreting the original intent of the Constitution ("originalists"), President Bush is trying to pack the courts with right-wing extremists.[2] Conservatives, they say, appoint judges who will also impose their policy views, such as prohibiting abortion, on the people. Senator

Kennedy, for example, warned that if Judge Alito were confirmed to the Supreme Court, he "could very well fundamentally alter the balance of the court and push it dangerously far to the right, placing at risk decades of American progress in safeguarding our fundamental rights and freedoms."[3]

To the contrary, conservatives advocate the appointment of judges who practice judicial restraint, who strive to interpret the Constitution according to its original intent and who interpret the laws rather than making laws—the very reverse of judicial activism. For example, though most of President Bush's judicial appointees are doubtlessly pro-life personally, they don't "legislate" their views by creating a federal ban. Since the Constitution is silent on abortion, the farthest they might go is to overturn *Roe* v. *Wade*, which created a federal right to abortion out of whole cloth, and return the matter to the states. Conservatives believe that laws should come from the people's elected legislators, not from judges creating "fundamental rights" out of "a living Constitution."

"Evolving Standards of Decency"

One of the modern Court's most significant decisions establishing the Constitution as an ever-evolving document was *Planned Parenthood* v. *Casey*[4] in 1992. The case is widely recognized for reaffirming *Roe* v. *Wade*, while allowing some inroads into the Court's restrictions on the state's right to regulate abortion, such as permitting parental notification provisions. But the case was arguably as important for its flagrant endorsement of moral relativism and other secularist and humanist precepts. The Court wrote, "At the heart of liberty is the right to define one's own concept of existence, of meaning, of the universe and of the mystery of human life. Beliefs about these matters could not define the attributes of personhood were they formed under the compulsion of the State."[5]

In *Lawrence* v. *Texas*[6] (2003), which invalidated a Texas sodomy statute, the Court cited approvingly *Casey*'s liberty formulation. Few conservatives were upset with the demise of state sodomy statutes, which were almost never enforced anyway. But other aspects of the Court's ruling gave them serious cause for concern. The Court actually bowed to the customs, values, and practices of other nations and suggested they were relevant to our own constitutional interpretation. The Court stated, "To the extent [an earlier Supreme Court case] relied on values shared with a wider civilization, the case's reasoning and holding have been rejected by the European Court of Human rights, and that other nations have taken action consistent with an affirmation of the protected right of homosexual adults to engage in intimate, consensual conduct. There has been no showing that in this country the governmental interest in circumscribing personal choice is somehow more legitimate or urgent."

Henceforth, American jurisprudence could be held hostage to pronouncements of foreign judicial bodies. Since other countries have affirmed certain rights, America dare not deny them absent a showing of a compelling governmental interest. Not only have liberal judges ratified the erosion of our traditional values by placing the Court's imprimatur on moral relativism; they have endorsed the relativist values of more "progressive" nations and grafted those into our own Constitution.

Justice Antonin Scalia, in a speech on the growing influence of international law on our Supreme Court jurisprudence, asserted that the Court's increasing willingness to refer to international law in interpreting the Constitution is tied to the current "'living Constitution' paradigm" prevailing on the court, and in the legal community at large. Under this approach to jurisprudence, which Scalia strongly opposes, the Court's task is to ensure the Constitution comports with "the evolving standards of decency that mark the progress of a maturing society." "Once you assume the power to revise what the Constitution requires in order to keep it up to date,... there is no reason whatever not to consult foreign materials in doing it." "You are," after all, "engaged in the process of writing the Constitution."

It just so happens, Scalia explained, that judges inclined toward the "living Constitution" approach believe "there really is a brotherhood of the judiciary" throughout the world whose function is to determine the meaning of human rights. It is only natural that they should consult each other and that American judges consult their foreign counterparts. "And that's why, I think if you are a living constitutionalist, you are almost certainly an international living constitutionalist."[7]

A number of the liberal justices on the Court make no secret of their advocacy of resorting to international law in constitutional interpretation. Justice Ruth Bader Ginsburg openly favors it and has strongly criticized Republican congressional proposals to bar the practice. In a recent speech she said, "We refer to decisions rendered abroad... not as controlling authorities, but for their indication, in Judge Wald's words, of 'common denominators of basic fairness governing relationships between the governors and the governed.'"[8]

Likewise, Justice Stephen Breyer has endorsed the practice.[9] Ditto Justice Sandra Day O'Connor, who said that judges should refer to the "principles and decisions of foreign and international law...

[because of] globalization. No institution of government can afford any longer to ignore the rest of the world."[10] And Justice Anthony Kennedy's "embrace of foreign law," according to legal analyst Jeffrey Toobin, "may be among the most significant developments on the Court in recent years—the single biggest factor behind his evolution from a reliable conservative into the likely successor to Sandra Day O'Connor as the Court's swing vote."[11] Justice David Souter, of course, joined in Justice Kennedy's opinion in *Lawrence* v. *Texas*, indicating his favorable attitude toward foreign law as well.

It is these types of disturbing trends that make control of the federal appellate courts an enduringly pivotal issue to social conservatives and advocates of originalist constitutional interpretation. For conservatives there is a higher principle involved in constitutional interpretation than effectuating desired policy results through court decisions. They believe the Constitution established the best governmental structure ever conceived by human beings and produced the freest and most prosperous nation in the history of the world. This structure involves a division of governmental power that is preserved by competing branches and levels of government checking and balancing one another. When any branch usurps power of the other branches, that balance is threatened and the freedoms it guarantees are jeopardized. The safest bet for preserving this carefully designed governmental framework is for all three branches of the federal government to honor the Constitution and to respect its plain meaning, its original intent, and the limitations it imposes.

Since 1803, the judiciary has been the final, unchecked arbiter of the Constitution's meaning and thus has a special duty to honor its integrity. If activist judges dominate the Court, the implosion of our liberties is inevitable because judge-made law and constitutional revisionism is like building—and continually remodeling—a house on a foundation of sand. That is why conservatives are adamant that originalist judges be appointed to the bench. Our entire system of government depends on it.

Racial Judicial Politics

As a testament to the moral and intellectual bankruptcy of the Democratic Party you only have to look at how the Democrats have treated George W. Bush's judicial appointees. During the confirmation hearings for Janice Rogers Brown, a conservative black woman on the California Supreme Court, to the U.S. Court of Appeals for the D.C. Circuit, Senator Dick Durbin accused Brown of being "the lone dissenter in a great many cases involving the rights of discrimination victims, consumers, and workers. In case after case," said Durbin, "you come down on the side of denying rights and remedies to the downtrodden and disadvantaged." This must have been hard for the fifty-four-year-old Brown to take, since she grew up in the segregated community of Greenville, Alabama, with "poor sharecropper parents who had little formal education."[12] Many conservatives thought Brown was actually being discriminated against by Democrats who can't stand the idea of a conservative African American.

As despicable as the Democrats' behavior was toward Brown, their treatment of Judge Charles Pickering, President Bush's nominee for the U.S. Fifth Circuit Court of Appeals, was arguably worse.[13] For a while Senate Minority Leader Daschle put a virtual freeze on the president's judicial nominations. Though Pickering somehow managed to get a hearing, he was eventually denied a vote—through filibuster. The usual suspects—NARAL Pro-Choice America, People for the American Way, and Alliance for Justice—stridently opposed Pickering, claiming he was an enemy of civil rights, which is what they say about almost every conservative judge.

Senator John Edwards, as he was positioning himself for his upcoming presidential run, paid homage to these leftist groups by joining the smear campaign against Pickering on the floor of the Senate. Edwards twisted the facts—based on the evidence, it is truly hard to believe Edwards was unaware he was misrepresenting the record—to indict Pickering as an unmitigated racist. But Pickering not only was not a racist, he had courageously stood up for blacks at great personal risk to himself and his family. Edwards, like many of his colleagues, accused Pickering of having been lenient on criminal defendants convicted of crimes against blacks. Edwards referred to a case in 1994 where three men reportedly burned a cross—KKK style—in front of a home occupied by a white man and his black spouse.[14]

It did not sit well with Pickering that the two other defendants involved in the crime, who had played a much greater role and were more culpable, were being offered probation by prosecutors, while they were recommending seven and a half years of jail time for the least guilty of the three. Pickering wrote, "The recommendation of the government in this instance is clearly the most egregious instance of disproportionate sentencing recommended by the government in any case pending before this court. The defendant clearly had less racial animosity than the juvenile." Pickering agonized over the inequity of the situation and the mandatory sentencing issues that were unclear in the law, but eventually sentenced the defendant to twenty-seven months in jail.

As Byron York said, this "was a real-world solution to the kind of real-world problem that the justice system deals with every day."[15] Pickering's remarks to the convicted defendant at his sentencing make clear his position on racism. "You're going to the penitentiary because of what you did. And it's an area that we've got to stamp out; that we've got to learn to live, races among each other. And the type of conduct that you exhibited cannot and will not be tolerated.... You did that which does hinder good race relations and was a despicable act.... I would suggest to you that during the time you're in the prison that you do some reading on race relations and maintaining good race relations and how that can be done."

This was hardly the language of a David Duke. Yet demagoging Democrats portrayed Pickering as a racist. Senator Edwards, during his grandstanding cross-examination, accused Pickering of unethical conduct for initiating a call to his old friend at the Justice Department, Frank Hunger, over the case.[16] Pickering flatly and firmly denied any unethical conduct, saying that Hunger had no decision-making responsibility in the case. With total disregard for the facts, Edwards painted Pickering as so driven by racism that he engaged in unethical conduct to protect—in the words of Byron York—"a young cross-burner in Mississippi."[17]

Once Edwards and other Senate Democrats tagged Pickering as a racist, he was placed in the nearly impossible position of having to prove a negative. Still, a number of black acquaintances of Pickering's vouched for him, including federal judge Henry Wingate and Charles Evers (brother of murdered civil rights leader Medgar Evers). Another friend, Thaddeus Edmonson, a former president of the Laurel chapter of the NAACP, said, "I can't believe the man they're describing in Washington is the same one I've known for years."[18]

Pickering had a long record of working to enhance race relations in his community and in the nation as a whole. But by far the most compelling item of evidence—even reported by the *New York Times*[19]—was that in 1967, Pickering testified against Ku Klux Klan leader Sam Bowers, who was being tried for the firebombing death of a local civil rights leader, even after being warned by the FBI that his testimony could place him, his wife, and their two small children in danger from the Klan.[20] The *Times* reported that Pickering "is a widely admired figure" in "his small and largely black home-town.... Though few black residents here subscribe to Judge Pickering's staunchly Republican politics, many say they admire his efforts at racial reconciliation. "[21]

As despicable as the Senate Democrats' behavior was toward Judge Pickering and the confirmation process itself, they had been just as ruthless against Miguel Estrada. And it seemed they never had to pay a price for their abuses. In fact, they grew more vicious as time passed, gaining power from their successes. Their general theme was always the same: the president's nominee was a conservative ideologue, far outside the mainstream of American thought and must be stopped—at any cost.

"He Isn't Hispanic Enough"

When President Bush appointed Miguel Estrada to the D.C. Court of Appeals—the court many believe next in importance to the Supreme Court—Republicans thought they could overcome Democrats' shenanigans through force of their majority. They succeeded in voting Estrada out of the Judiciary Committee on a 10 to 9 party line vote. What the Republicans didn't anticipate was that Democrats would resort to a filibuster in the full Senate to block the nomination, though the unwritten rules of the Senate prohibited fili-busters of judicial nominations.

The Democrats fought dirty. It didn't matter that Estrada was a "minority" of Hispanic descent. Justice Clarence Thomas was derided as an "Uncle Tom." Miguel Estrada, according to Congressman Bob Menendez, "isn't Hispanic enough. Being Hispanic means for us much more than having a surname."

Estrada was eminently qualified for the position. Though he was not fluent in English when his family moved to the United States, he excelled in high school, eventually graduating magna cum laude from Harvard Law School. He earned prestigious clerkships, working for a Court of Appeals justice and Supreme Court Justice Anthony Kennedy. He appeared fifteen times before the Supreme Court to argue cases and was assistant solicitor general in the George H. W. Bush and Bill Clinton administrations.[22] He received the American Bar Association's highest rating.

Though Estrada had fifty-five senators willing to vote for him, he wasn't afforded the decency of a vote by the full Senate. The Democrats filibustered no fewer than seven times.[23] Sixty votes are required for cloture (ending debate), but Republicans couldn't muster more than fifty-five because of Democratic solidarity. This set the precedent that, in the face of unbending minority opposition, a super-majority would henceforth be required for confirmation—a result certainly not contemplated by the framers of the Constitution. Estrada finally withdrew his name from consideration in September 2003, after being abused and suspended in limbo by a militant Democratic Senate minority for nearly two and a half years. President Bush called the Democrats' treatment of Estrada "disgraceful," while Senator Kennedy boasted that it was a "victory for the Constitution."[24]

Democrats offered two phony excuses for blocking Estrada, both centering on their supposed inability to find out enough about him, which, by the way, was transparently inconsistent with their unqualified assertion that Estrada was "outside the mainstream of American thought."[25] One was that he was not sufficiently forthcoming, especially on the issues of abortion and affirmative action. But that objection was nothing new for nominees. Since the Democrats' merciless savaging of Robert Bork, most nominees have been more circumspect lest they knowingly sacrifice themselves on the altar of Democratic character assassination. Besides, the Democrats' charge was disingenuous. It later came to light that though the White House had offered to have the nominee answer questions, Democrats declined to submit any.[26]

Their other bogus excuse was that the Bush administration refused to release Estrada's intra-office memoranda written when he was serving as assistant solicitor general from 1992 through 1997. The Democrats' posturing on the memo disclosure issue was also in bad faith. Though they demanded these documents, they never questioned any of the former Clinton officials with or for whom Estrada worked about the requested documents.[27] More important, they knew that releasing private memos would set a dangerous precedent, which would have a chilling effect on the willingness of government counsel to give frank advice.

All seven living former solicitors general, three of whom had served in Democratic administrations, agreed that such memoranda were "highly privileged."[28] They joined in sending a letter to Democratic senator Patrick Leahy, urging him to back off in his demand for the confidential memos. They said, "Any attempt to intrude into the Office's highly privileged deliberations would come at the cost of the Solicitor General's ability to defend vigorously the United States' litigation interests—a cost that also would be borne by Congress itself....Although we profoundly respect the Senate's duty to evaluate Mr. Estrada's fitness for the federal judiciary, we do not think that the confidentiality and integrity of internal deliberations should be sacrificed in the process."[29] Nevertheless, the Democrats pretended the administration's reason for withholding the papers was that it (and Estrada) had something important to hide.

"A Closet Bigot?"

Democrats employed the same underhanded tactics on Supreme Court nominee Samuel A. Alito, Jr., depicting him as a racist, a sexist, and unethical on the bench. Democratic senators on the Judiciary Committee, while pretending to interrogate Alito to assess his knowledge, intellect, demeanor, and character, spent most of their allotted time speechifying before the television cameras. When Alito finally was given an opportunity to speak between Senators Biden, Schumer, and Kennedy's offensive sermons, he emerged as a calm, unflappable gentleman with a powerful intellect and a storehouse of legal knowledge. Democrats were frustrated they couldn't lay a glove on this man, who was reputed to be as conservative as Judge Scalia, thus earning him the disparaging moniker "Scalito."

Though it was rather obvious they weren't going to be able to block Alito's confirmation, some Democrats on the committee proceeded to smear him anyway with half-baked innuendo and wholesale distortions. Their gratuitous defamation centered on a handful of allegations. The first concerned his alleged association—some thirty-five years before (around the time Ted Kennedy had an accident at Chappaquiddick,[30] but admittedly a few decades after

Senator Robert Byrd began his membership in the Ku Klux Klan[31])—with the Princeton University alumni organization Concerned Alumni of Princeton (CAP).

CAP was started by those upset with Princeton's conspicuous opposition to ROTC during the Vietnam War. In the hearings, Alito testified he had no recollection of membership in the organization, but conceded that in 1985 he had affirmed his membership in it in an application for a position at the Reagan Justice Department. He opposed the anti-military mentality on campus that had led some protestors to bomb the ROTC buildings, and that had led the university to expel ROTC from campus, though it was later allowed to return.

Democrats were incredulous that Alito couldn't remember his association with such a dastardly organization and so dispatched staffers to the Library of Congress to comb through the private papers of William Rusher, a former publisher of *National Review*, in search of the smoking gun to prove Alito was more involved in CAP than he was letting on.[32] Senator Specter also sent staffers to examine the records. The next morning, after the researchers had pored through the records until 2 a.m., Specter reported that Alito's name did not appear anywhere in them.

Democrats seized on CAP because the group had opposed the admission of women to the formerly all-male Princeton. Inevitably, the Democrats also accused CAP of being racist. Senator Kennedy led the charge, demanding to know why Alito claimed (in his 1985 application) membership in this "radical group" that discriminated against women and minorities.[33] Senator Dick Durbin asked, "How could you identify with a group that would discriminate against women and minorities?"[34]

Likewise, Senator Leahy accused Alito of being "less than candid" and expressed concern that Alito had "proudly proclaimed affiliation" with a group that "excluded women, African Americans, and other minorities." In a stunning display of self-indulgence, even for a sanctimonious U.S. senator, Leahy said, "My parents tried to instill in me the idea that such discrimination, and all discrimination, is wrong. . . . I have tried my best to promote tolerance and inclusion."[35]

Alito assured the committee he would not have joined CAP had he known of any of its supposed positions against women and minorities. Senator Kennedy was hardly satisfied and cited an excerpt from a 1983 editorial in *Prospect*, CAP's magazine, to discredit him. Kennedy said, "So a 1983 *Prospect* essay titled 'In Defense of Elitism,' stated, quote, 'People nowadays just don't seem to know their place. Everywhere one turns, blacks and Hispanics are demanding jobs simply because they're black and Hispanic. The physically handicapped are trying to gain equal representation in professional sports. And homosexuals are demanding the government vouchsafe them the right to bear children.' "

When Kennedy demanded to know whether Alito was familiar with the essay, Alito quickly and firmly responded that he disagreed "with all of that. I would never endorse it. I never have endorsed it. Had I thought that that's what this organization stood for I would never associate myself with it in any way."[36]

As it turned out, the editorial was a tongue-in-cheek satire. As FOX News's Brit Hume reported, "But the magazine's editor at the time [Dinesh D'Souza] says the article was pure satire, a send-up of what liberals think conservatives think. He added, quote, 'I think left-wing groups have been feeding Senator Kennedy snippets and he has been mindlessly reciting them,' unquote." As the weblog "Newsbusters" pointed out, though mainstream media outlets NBC, CNN, and the *Washington Post* all highlighted Kennedy's quoted material from the essay, none of them—almost a week later—had clarified that the material was satirical.[37] And it was rarely mentioned in the media that for an organization that allegedly discriminated against women and minorities, its magazine *Prospect* had been edited by women and minority members.

Finally, the Democrats' accusations got to Judge Alito's wife, Martha, who was sitting behind him during his inquisition. Republican senator Lindsey Graham had had his fill of the cheap shots and was seeking to rehabilitate Alito during his questioning time. He asked Alito, rhetorically, "Are you really a closet bigot?" Alito answered that he was not and Graham said, "No, sir, you're not. Judge Alito, I am sorry that you've had to go through this. I am sorry that your family has had to sit here and listen to this." At that point Martha Alito rose from her chair and left the room in tears.

"Shifting Excuses"

Democrats also smeared Alito over his investment in Vanguard, a stock and mutual fund company. During his confirmation hearings for the federal appellate bench fifteen years before, Alito had signed a written promise to recuse himself from "any cases involving the Vanguard companies." In 2002, Alito initially failed to recuse himself from a case in which Vanguard was a party. He and two other judges ruled in Vanguard's favor by affirming the dismissal of a complaint that Vanguard had illegally seized and blocked assets to certain private accounts. The case was later re-opened on the motion of the owner of the account, who alleged Alito's ownership of investments in the company made his involvement in the case improper.[38] The case was transferred to a new Third Circuit panel, which reissued the same opinion.

Indignant Democratic senators grilled Alito on why he sat on the case, especially after having promised not to. Alito explained that the court's screening process failed to flag the case and call to his attention the potential conflict of interest. He said that in pro se cases—where a party represents himself without an attorney—the monitoring system for conflicts of interest was different.

Alito said that after this incident he instituted a new monitoring system in pro se cases using his own forms, to avoid a recurrence of this problem in the future. He said that when the motion was filed alleging his conflict of interest he "took it very seriously," and researched it thoroughly. He concluded that the ethical code did not require him to recuse himself, but he decided to do so anyway because questions had been raised. He asked that the initial decision of the court be vacated and that the widow get a new appeal.[39]

Alito said it was inconceivable that the outcome of the case could have affected the value of his personal holdings in Vanguard. "There was absolutely no chance [that I would benefit financially no matter how the case came out]," he said.[40] As Senator DeWine pointed out in his questioning of Alito, Vanguard "was not accused of any wrongdoing. It didn't stand to lose anything. Really, the only question was whether Vanguard would transfer some of the funds it held for one person over to another. . . . Nothing about this case could realistically have affected Vanguard as a company, let alone affected your mutual funds."[41] And that is the crux of the matter in evaluating the propriety of Alito's failure to recuse himself.

The governing law (28 U.S.C. Se. 455(b)(4)) requires a judge to disqualify himself when "he knows that he...has a financial interest in the subject matter in...a party to the proceeding, or any other interest that could be substantially affected by the outcome of the proceeding." But a subsection clarifies that ownership in an investment fund that holds securities—like Vanguard—does not translate to an ownership interest in the securities themselves, unless the judge helps manage the fund.

As George Washington University Law School professor Thomas Morgan, co-author of the nation's most widely read ethics textbook, said in a letter to committee chair Arlen Specter, "In my opinion there is no basis for suggesting [Alito's] action was in any way improper.... The best technical argument that Judge Alito did something wrong seems to be that he had a 'financial interest' in 'a party to the proceeding,'... The argument collapses, however, in view of the clear statement in Section 455(d) that ownership of a mutual fund is expressly *not* a financial interest 'unless the judge participates in the management of the fund.'"[42]

Professor David McGowan of the University of San Diego Law School agreed, saying, "The purpose of the rule is to guard against the risk that a judge will rule based on his or her economic interest rather than the law."[43] By all reasonable accounts Judge Alito was correct that the outcome in the case on which he sat couldn't have affected the value of his interest in Vanguard. Moreover, Alito testified that a number of legal experts had looked into the issue and determined that he was not required to recuse.[44] Senator Hatch cited several other experts who agreed that Alito had done nothing improper, including Professor Geoffrey Hazard of the University of Pennsylvania Law School, Ronald Rotunda of George Mason University Law School, and others.[45] However, Professor Deborah Rhode of Stanford Law School disagreed.[46]

But the near consensus that Alito hadn't committed an ethical breach didn't keep Democratic senators from demagoging the issue and painting Alito as a man who wouldn't honor his promises and who flagrantly disregarded ethical rules. Senator Patrick Leahy accused Alito of giving "shifting excuses" for sitting on the Vanguard case, saying he had earlier blamed a computer glitch and later retracted that explanation.[47] But during the hearings, Alito made clear that his answers had not been inconsistent. He was not blaming the computer for failing to detect a conflict, but the screening system the court had in place for pro se cases. Though Leahy virtually called Alito a liar, Alito had no motive *not* to recuse himself in the case and more than made up for it anyway, when he later saw to it that the party involved got "an entirely new appeal."

"A Unitary Executive"

Democrats also attacked Alito for being a proponent of a strong executive—too strong, under their view of the Constitution. This was a particularly delicious angle for Democrats, who had been depicting President Bush as a power-hungry president trying to consolidate executive power and wrest power from Congress. They argued that if confirmed to the Court, given his past writings on the subject, Alito would use his vote to facilitate Bush's executive power grabs. Columnist Robert Kuttner wrote, "Alito would serve as Bush's enabler. He would give Bush effective control of all three branches of government and the hard right long-term dominance of the high court."[48]

Democrats pointed to Alito's support of a "unitary executive," and expressed grave concerns that such support signaled that Alito favored the executive branch having expansive powers. When given an opportunity by Republican senator Jon Kyl to clarify, Alito explained that the concept of the "unitary executive" has nothing to do with expanding executive power vis-á-vis the other two branches. It in no way limits the checks and powers of the other two branches on the executive, nor stands for the executive usurping the proper constitutional authority conferred on those branches. (In fact, Alito provided examples of where he had ruled against the executive branch.) It just holds that the president, under the Constitution, has control over the executive branch. It certainly means that the president does not, for example, have to defer to members of his cabinet. But it doesn't mean that he can defy Congress in cases where the Constitution might require his deference.

As Alito stated, "[the idea] is that the president should be able to control the executive branch, however big it is or however small it is. It has to do with control of whatever the executive is doing. It doesn't have to do with the scope of executive power. It does not have to do with whether the executive power that the president is given includes a lot of unnamed powers or what's called inherent powers. So it's the difference between scope and control."[49]

Alito's clarification didn't deter Democrats from misrepresenting his position. Senator Harry Reid said Alito had "professed his strong belief in the so-called unitary executive theory of constitutional law, a theory embraced by those who advocate for expanding executive powers at the expense of the judicial and legislative branches of government."[50] Reid's statement was delivered a full three weeks after Alito had denied he favors an enhancement of the executive power at the expense of the other two branches.

The Democrats opposed Alito not because he was willing to support an extra-constitutional power grab by the executive branch, but because he would interfere with their scheme to preserve the judiciary as a liberal policy-making branch, unaccountable to the people.[51]

"You Better Win Elections"

Democrats also charged that Alito had a history on the bench of protecting the rich and powerful over the interests of the individual. Senator Reid said, "In disputes between ordinary American citizens and large powerful entities like corporations and the government, Judge Alito is too often on the side of the powerful and against the interests of the individual."[52] Senators Biden and Stabenow made nearly identical allegations.[53] Many other Democratic leaders echoed this charge, but it was little more than a thin veil for class warfare. They cited anecdotal examples of his rulings in certain cases in which corporate litigants prevailed. Of course, Alito provided examples where he ruled against corporate and government interests as well.

The Democrats' selective citing of cases is especially specious, because there is no way you can glean anything about a judge's jurisprudence by looking merely at results, without carefully examining the facts and law in each case. It is particularly unfair in evaluating judges like Alito, who try meticulously to interpret the law rather than to achieve a desired outcome.

This line of attack shouldn't be taken any more seriously than Senator Kennedy's embarrassing Senate rant where he contemplated (out loud) whether Alito, if confirmed, would side with big polluting corporations who were causing more children to die of asthma. Kennedy asked whether Alito would "come on out for that mother who has a child that's got asthma or that parent who's seen the pollution that's taken place in a pond, in a lake, and whose child has been affected by those kinds of poisons?"[54]

Perhaps the most ridiculous objection to Alito concerned his ruling in a case involving the strip-searching of a ten-year-old girl. In the case, the police had obtained a warrant to search a man at a certain address for possession of illegal drugs. They also searched the suspect's wife and daughter, even though the warrant did not specifically mention them. Senator Leahy was angry that Alito, on appeal, voted to approve the search since it "went beyond the four corners of the search warrant" signed by the magistrate.[55]

Democrats and the liberal media not only criticized Alito for approving expansive police powers in the case, but for condoning the strip-search of a little girl—as if he were indifferent to what occurred, or perhaps was even a bit perverted, as the loony Left bloggers suggested. One liberal group ran a thirty-second TV spot saying that Alito "even voted to approve the strip search of a ten-year-old girl."[56] Alito insisted he "was not pleased that a young girl was searched in that case, and I said so in my opinion. That was an undesirable thing."

Alito said his decision turned on "the technical issue" of whether the policemen's affidavit used to obtain the search warrant—which expressly mentioned searching other people on the premises—"was properly incorporated into the warrant for the purposes of saying who could be searched." Alito noted that the affidavit included a statement by the police officers that "We have probable cause to believe that this drug dealer hides drugs on people who are on the premises. And, therefore, when we search, we want authorization not just to search him, but to search everybody who's found on the premises, because we have reason to believe he hides drugs there."[57] Alito thought the magistrate intended that the allegations in the affidavit were to be included in the warrant so that the police could search other people on the premises, even though the face of the warrant itself didn't say so. He said he believed that judges are "supposed to read warrants in a common-sense fashion," especially since they're often prepared under serious time pressure.

In the end, the Democrats' efforts to demonize and block Alito were fruitless. He had established too strong a record and a reputation for integrity and performed very well under intense partisan pressure at the hearings. Democrats delayed his confirmation as long as they could, to no avail. Senator Kerry, in a grandstanding move from his ski slope in the Swiss Alps, tried to "call in" Alito's impeachment, but his effort barely made a whimper, except to the Democratic base to which Kerry was pandering.

After Alito was confirmed, the *New York Times* reported that though Democrats knew they had little chance of defeating Alito, "they were dismayed that a nominee with such clear conservative views" would stir so little opposition. Democratic leaders, demonstrating their obliviousness to their own extremist views, said it was disappointing that the White House could place on the court any qualified candidate of its choosing, no matter how "ideologically out of step with the country." This defeat for Democrats just increased their resolve to take back the White House and Congress, which they view as their only chance to stem the tide of conservatism in all three branches. Former Clinton adviser turned Illinois congressman Rahm Emanuel succinctly summarized the Democrats' plight. "George Bush won the election," said Emanuel. "If you don't like it, you better win elections."[58]

CHAPTER SEVEN

"Extraordinary Circumstances"

Democrats deny they've obstructed President Bush's judicial nominees, saying they've confirmed a great percentage of his picks. But statistics can deceive. When you add in trial judge appointments, they can claim a high percentage. But appellate judges have a much greater impact on the course of the law—and the integrity of the Constitution. In his first fifteen months in office, President Bush succeeded in having only seven of his twenty-nine circuit court nominees confirmed. In a similar period, nineteen of President Clinton's twenty-two circuit court nominees were confirmed.[1] At a later point Democrats had blocked twelve out of forty-one of Bush's appellate nominees. During the 107th Congress, Bush's appellate nominees were confirmed at a rate 45 percent lower than previous presidents and Bush's appeals court vacancies averaged 50 percent higher than Clinton's when the Senate was under Republican control.[2]

Senator Mitch McConnell noted that more than 90 percent of the circuit court nominees from Carter through Clinton received a Judiciary Committee hearing during a president's first Congress, but only 37.9 percent of Bush's did. Eighty-six of the nominees from Carter through Clinton got a committee vote, contrasted with 34.5 percent for Bush nominees. And, 86 percent of circuit court nominees from Carter through Clinton were voted on by the entire Senate, contrasted with only 27.6 percent for President Bush's nominees.[3]

The appellate court vacancy rate in late 2002 was more than twice what it was in 1997. But Democratic senator Patrick Leahy thought the 1997 vacancy rate constituted a "crisis" that interfered with the administration of justice.[4] In Leahy's words, "Any week in which the Senate does not confirm three judges is a week in which the Senate is failing to address the vacancy crisis. Any fortnight in which we have gone without a judicial-confirmation hearing marks two weeks in which the Senate is falling further behind."[5] But, of course, that was when we had a Democratic president.

From Blue Slips to Filibusters

Democrats have grossly politicized the judicial appointments process in other ways. In the midst of their years-long filibustering marathon of Miguel Estrada, they also conspired to abuse a long-standing Senate practice of deference to senators of the states in which the nominee resides. Customarily, the home-state senators voice their acceptance or rejection of a nominee on a "blue slip"—

a practice that works if senators exercise it in good faith and limit their acceptance or rejection to the nominee's qualifications.

But at one point in 2003, both Michigan senators, Democrats Carl Levin and Debbie Stabenow, used their negative blue slips to block, categorically, all of the president's nominees from Michigan—Richard Griffin, David McKeague, Susan Bieke Neilson, and Henry Sadda—to the Sixth Circuit Court of Appeals. As *National Review*'s Byron York noted, this was an especially remarkable move, since a virtual judicial emergency existed with more than half of the sixteen seats on that court vacant at the time. Levin and Stabenow were trying to hold the president's appointment power hostage, demanding by way of ransom that he renominate two former Clinton appointees Republicans had "unfairly" blocked. White House counsel Alberto Gonzales rejected their "unprecedented" demand, reminding them that when George H. W. Bush's term ended in 1992, fifty of his nominees were left suspended without Senate action. Yet Republicans never demanded that President Clinton renominate any of them based on "fairness."[6]

As we have seen, Democrats resorted to the extraordinary measure of filibustering President Bush's nominees, something that had never been done in the history of the republic to a judicial nominee who had clear majority support in the Senate. Democrats claimed that Republicans filibustered two of Clinton's judicial nominees, Richard Paez and Marsha Berzon. While Republicans did stall their nominations in the Senate Judiciary Committee, neither was filibustered, and both were eventually confirmed. In fact, when one Republican senator—Bob Smith—tried to filibuster the nominees, forty Republicans joined Democrats in voting against a filibuster for

Paez and forty-one did the same for Berzon. As Byron York observed, "There was never any filibuster, because Republicans would not support it."[7]

The only previous filibuster of a judicial nominee occurred under President Lyndon B. Johnson. Johnson's nominee, Abe Fortas, was subjected to a filibuster, but he likely did not have support of a majority of the full Senate[8] (though some dispute this).[9] Former chief counsel to President George H. W. Bush C. Boyden Gray notes that "at least forty-nine senators—a majority of the ninety-five senators whose positions were identified in the Congressional Record—either opposed allowing a confirmation vote or opposed confirmation on the merits. This evidence...casts doubt on the likelihood that a committed plurality of fifty senators (who, with vice president Humphrey, would have constituted a majority) would have voted for Justice Fortas's confirmation had the filibuster not prevented it."[10] In any event, Republicans have not triggered a filibuster of a Democratic president's nominee for some four decades, notwithstanding the extremely leftist views of many of those nominees.

Democrats not only resorted to filibuster, but also used the tactic of refusing to vote a number of nominees out of the Senate Judiciary Committee to give them a hearing before the full Senate. Republicans never refused to vote a Clinton judicial nominee out of committee.[11]

The "Nuclear" Option

Finally, Republicans were fed up and decided to take action to prevent further filibustering. Senate Majority Leader Bill Frist proposed an amendment of the Senate rules to forbid judicial filibusters—an idea shrewd Democrats successfully mislabeled—the "nuclear option." Though Democrats painted it as a radical departure from precedent and a presidential power-grab, it was Democrats who had engaged in a radical break with past practice by initiating judicial filibusters.[12] The past statements of Democratic senators opposing judicial filibustering are instructive. Senators Biden, Boxer, Daschle, Durbin, Feinstein, Kennedy, Leahy, and Levin are all on record as having opposed the practice.[13]

Democrats were so worried Republicans might invoke "the option," they wouldn't even pause their public campaign against it in deference to the breaking news of Pope John Paul II's death. Instead they played an old radio address of former Democratic senate majority leader George Mitchell attacking Republicans on the issue.[14]

The Gang of Fourteen

Unfortunately, a group of seven Republican senators joined forces with a like number of Democratic senators, forming the "Gang of Fourteen," and effectively blocked Frist's prudent plan to preserve the integrity of the judicial nomination process. The fourteen senators, who together could likely control the deciding votes on either a filibuster or a full up or down vote in the Senate, crafted a compromise to avert a formal rules change that would prevent the "outlawing" of the judicial filibuster. Their compromise involved an agreement—after a two-year delay—to permit an up or down vote on nominees Janice Rogers Brown, William Pryor, and Priscilla Owen, plus a commitment (among these fourteen) not to filibuster future judicial nominees except under "extraordinary circumstances."

Conservatives were quite unhappy with what amounted to yet another Republican capitulation to Democratic heavy-handedness. They believed Republicans had the votes to invoke the option and that the compromise validated the precedent of judicial filibustering, since it preserved it in "extraordinary circumstances," though it was constitutionally unjustified under any circumstance.

The Gang of Fourteen deal did not uphold the "traditions of the Senate" as claimed. But it did give Democrats a public-relations victory by implying it was Republicans, not Democrats, who were breaking with historical precedent and violating the spirit of the Constitution. Republicans had the moral and historical high ground and voluntarily surrendered it to a militant Democratic minority by tacitly agreeing to a false version of the facts and history.[15]

Conservatives recognized that "extraordinary circumstances" was a highly subjective term, particularly since the agreement provided that each of the fourteen signatories had the right to decide for himself what would qualify as such and that each would exercise his advice and consent responsibilities "in good faith." Members said they would respect the "conscientious decisions" of fellow members. Thus, if Democratic gang members claimed extraordinary circumstances existed, Republican members would arguably be honor bound *not* to invoke the option.

One of the gang, Republican senator Lindsey Graham, denied this was a concern because under no circumstances could a Democratic member be in good faith in claiming that ideological differences with a nominee could constitute "extraordinary circumstances." But it didn't take long before Democratic gang member Ben Nelson conceded that the nominee's ideology could be an "extraordinary circumstance" if it was "the extreme of either side."[16] Since Democrats uniformly consider conservative judges as falling "outside the mainstream of American thought," Nelson's statement exposed "extraordinary circumstances" as the exception that swallows the rule.

Democratic gang member Joseph Lieberman confirmed that "extraordinary circumstances would include not only extraordinary personal behavior but also extraordinary ideological positions."[17] Democratic member Mary Landrieu agreed, saying "A nominee's political ideology is only relevant if it has been shown to cloud their interpretation of the law.... A pattern of irresponsible judgment, where decisions are based on ideology rather than the law, could potentially be 'extraordinary.'" Though Landrieu certainly didn't mean to imply this, her formulation would virtually disqualify all liberal activist nominees. Democratic member Ken Salazar also refused to be boxed in from ruling out a filibuster for a strong conservative, such as Janice Rogers Brown. "[The agreement] didn't set a standard. We would leave it up to each person to define what extraordinary circumstances means."[18]

Later, after Graham and fellow Republican member Senator Mike DeWine threatened to vote against a filibuster of Judge Alito, with DeWine going so far as to say he would vote to invoke the "nuclear option" in the event of a Democratic filibuster, the full gang took the two to the woodshed. After they emerged from the meeting, Graham and DeWine said they would take a "wait-and-see" approach.[19]

Judicial Philosophy versus Political Ideology

Lost in this discussion was that the proper scope of inquiry should be a nominee's *judicial* philosophy, not his political ideology. If judges honored their duty to interpret, rather than rewrite the Constitution and other laws, their political ideology would be far less relevant. But since liberals rely on the courts for policy making, the political ideology question is critical, even indispensable, to them.

It used to be that liberals like Nan Aron of the liberal Alliance for Justice admitted that a president has the right and "duty to... appoint jurists who share his views." Today, they invariably apply litmus tests on issues like abortion, affirmative action, or the nominee's faith—though they'll never admit it—to block nominees.[20] Even Senator Chuck Schumer confessed that "Ideology is not the only factor in determining how we vote, but for most of us, whether we want to admit it or not, it is a factor."[21]

Legal scholars disagree on whether a nominee's political ideology is a proper subject for Senate scrutiny.[22] But in practice, Republicans and Democrats are playing by a different set of rules, to the great disadvantage of Republicans—and originalist nominees. With few exceptions, Democrats have strenuously resisted every one of President Bush's federal appellate court nominees precisely because of their presumed conservative ideology, labeling many of them "extremists, far outside the mainstream of American thought." Republicans have opposed some nominees based on ideology, but to a much lesser extent. If Republicans intend to establish an equal playing field on judicial nominations in the future, they must develop a coherent confirmation philosophy. You can be sure that Democrats will maintain theirs.

In fact, most judicial activism over the last fifty years has issued from liberal judges. As Professor Lino Graglia wrote in 1996, "almost without exception, the effect of rulings of unconstitutionality over the past four decades has been to enact the policy preferences of the cultural elite on the far left of the American political spectrum."[23] Robert Bork agrees. In *The Tempting of America*, he admitted that judicial activism has been a part of the Court's tradition almost since the inception of the republic, but its pace has greatly accelerated in modern times. "In each era the Court responded to the ideology of the class to which the Justices felt closest. . . . The intellectual class has become liberal, and that fact has heavily influenced the Court's performance. For the past half-century, whenever the Court has departed from the original understanding of the Constitution's principles, it has invariably legislated an item on the modern liberal agenda, never an item on the conservative agenda."[24]

So for Democrats who want to enact their liberal agenda and for conservatives who want to defend the Constitution, the stakes are enormously high in federal appellate court positions—and leftist interest groups, especially the pro–abortion rights organizations, will heavily pressure Democrats to continue to use whatever tactics are available to maximize liberal influence on the courts. They even make the ludicrous argument that a nominee must be weighed against the justice he is replacing. Senator Biden said to Judge Alito concerning his possible replacement of Justice O'Connor, "You are replacing someone who has been the fulcrum on an otherwise evenly divided court. . . . This goes beyond you. It goes to whether or not your taking her seat will alter the constitutional framework of this country by shifting the balance 5–4, 4–5, one way or another." Senator Kyl called Biden on the absurdity of his statement. Kyl said, "Of the 109 justices to sit on the Supreme Court, nearly half—forty-six to be exact—have replaced judges appointed by another political party." Kyl pointed out that the very liberal Justice Ginsburg replaced Justice Byron White, a "centrist."[25]

Leaked Memos

Mysterious and damning memos of Democrats on the Senate Judiciary Committee were leaked in November 2003 to the *Wall Street*

Journal editorial page, showing that senate Democrats were working in concert with liberal special interest groups to thwart President Bush's judicial nominations. Democrats immediately took control of the story, converting the focus from the content of the memos to the impropriety in leaking them—and demanding an investigation into who leaked them.

Two memos, dated November 6 and November 7, 2001, were written by Senator Durbin's staff to the senator. Three others were written to Senator Kennedy by his staff in 2002. The *Journal*'s editorial page published all five memos and excoriated Democrats for letting special interest groups direct their moves in the confirmation process.[26]

The memos reveal collusion between Democratic committee members and liberal special interest groups who finance their campaigns and support their causes, including People for the American Way, NARAL Pro-Choice America, Alliance for Justice, Leadership Conference on Civil Rights, NAACP Legal Defense and Education Fund, American Association of University Women, National Women's Law Center, and the National Partnership.

In the November 6 memo, Durbin's staff informs the senator he will be meeting with members of the liberal interest groups and "the primary focus will be on identifying the most controversial and/or vulnerable judicial nominees. The groups would like to postpone action on these nominees until next year, when (presumably) the public will be more tolerant of partisan dissent." The November 7 memo singles out nominee Miguel Estrada "as especially dangerous, because he has a minimal paper trail, he is Latino, and the White House seems to be grooming him for a Supreme Court appointment. They want to hold Estrada off as long as possible."[27]

But a leaked memo of April 17, 2002, to Senator Ted Kennedy from his staff is even more shocking. Kennedy is informed of the request of Elaine Jones, head of the NAACP Legal Defense Fund, that Democrats "hold off" on confirming Sixth Circuit Court of Appeals nominee Julia S. Gibbons until the court could issue its decision on the affirmative action case involving the University of Michigan Law School's admissions policy. The memo stated, "The thinking is that the current 6th Circuit will sustain the affirmative action program, but if a new judge with conservative views is confirmed before the case is decided, that new judge will be able, under 6th Circuit rules, to review the case and vote on it."

The memo admits staffers "are a little concerned about the propriety of scheduling hearings based on the resolution of a particular case. We are also aware that the 6th Circuit is in dire need of additional judges. Nevertheless we recommend that Gibbons be scheduled for a later hearing: the Michigan case is important, and there is little damage that we can foresee in moving Clifton first."[28]

This is all the more astounding when we learn that Ms. Jones was lead counsel to certain Michigan students who were parties in that very case. She was apparently concerned that a Bush appointee might vote against her clients. As the *Wall Street Journal* editorial page put it, "Democrats on Judiciary were being asked to delay confirmations for a desperately understaffed court not because the nominees were unqualified but because of how they might rule in a particular case. Now, that's 'politicizing' the judiciary."[29] As it turned out, Judge Gibbons was confirmed July 29, 2002, but not before the Sixth Circuit upheld the University of Michigan Law Schools' affirmative action policy by a 5–4 vote.

That wasn't the only case of liberal interest groups trying to influence the scheduling of hearings for nominees. Another memo to Durbin, of October 15, 2001, informed him that the groups were seeking to delay a second hearing on Judge Pickering to complete their "research" on him. The memo said that since Senator Leahy, and not his staff, had scheduled the Pickering hearing, the rescheduling request might have to come from Durbin personally. The staffers also warned Durbin that the groups wanted assurances that they would receive ample warning of "future controversial nominees."[30]

But Democrats were neither caught off guard nor intimidated by revelations of their own misconduct. Having learned at the feet of Bill Clinton, they simply adopted his tactics of turning the tables on their accusers. Senator Durbin demanded to know how two of his memos fell into the hands of the *Journal* and called for an investigation. He wondered whether someone had hacked into his staffers' computers.[31] The *New York Times* and *Washington Post* dutifully fell in line, editorializing against the leaks.

Senate Majority Leader Bill Frist responded to the Democrats' threats. In an interesting twist, he called on Democrats to disavow the memo. "They have not done so," said Frist's spokesman Bob Stevenson, "and no amount of political slight of hand should distract the American people from that reality."[32] Unfortunately, as it turned out, Republican leaders, including Frist and Hatch, caved in to the Democrats' political pressure and capitulated to their demand for an investigation of the leaks.[33] Senator Hatch also placed one of his staffers, Jason Lundell, on administrative leave for accessing the memos on the computer.

The Republican leadership's fecklessness, though, was not universally adopted by Republicans. Some were furious at the surrender and strenuously objected. But that didn't stop the investigation from proceeding or the Senate's sergeant-at-arms from seizing computers and interrogating myriad staffers. Nor did it cause Republicans to demand a reciprocal investigation against Democrats over the contents of the memos.

Conservatives were furious. Kay Daly, of the Coalition for a Fair Judiciary, said, "By giving the impression some sort of crime had been committed, Democrats were able to change the argument. They very artfully did this and they did it with the aid and comfort of Orrin Hatch, there is no denying it."[34] Concerning the allegation of crimes having been committed, Senate Democrats eventually demanded a criminal investigation be launched against the culprits.[35]

Meanwhile Senator Frist's counsel, Manuel Miranda, who was one of those responsible for revealing the contents of the memos, became a sacrificial lamb—a significant development, since he was considered the Republican "point man" on judicial nominees.[36] Miranda admitted that he had retrieved information from Democrats' computers, but insisted he wasn't searching for dirt, only trying to find out hearing dates for nominees. He said his actions were not illegal because the files were not protected (private), but on a shared network.

"I knew that there is no privacy expectation to documents on a government server, documents that are regularly backed up and stored in a government facility," said Miranda. "I knew that these were not confidential or classified documents." Miranda even said that Senator Leahy's staff had been told their files were unprotected, but they did nothing to secure them. Indeed, Democratic staffers were quite cavalier about protecting their memos—and about their content. In one memo, a Durbin staffer referred to Bush nominees as "Nazis." But, it wasn't as though the staffer had sunk lower than the senators themselves. Senator Ted Kennedy, at one point, referred to President Bush's judicial nominees, such as Miguel Estrada and Janice Rogers Brown, as "Neanderthals."[37] Democrats ultimately denied their memos were accessible to Republicans, saying that access across party lines was prohibited.[38]

Miranda did not take his sacrificial role lying down. He fought back by filing a complaint with the Senate Ethics Committee, alleging that further memos, "perhaps thousands," which so far had been undisclosed to the public, point to evidence of "public corruption . . . [including] the direct influencing of the Senate's advice and consent role by the promise of campaign funding and election support in the last mid-term election."[39]

The Senate's internal investigation was concluded in March, essentially blaming two Republican staffers for combing through the computer files, but saying that the files were not adequately protected. Senator Chuck Schumer was disappointed that so little blood was drawn from Republicans over the incident. He insisted that the "incomplete" investigation be pursued by "a special counsel with full investigative powers."[40] Not long after, six members of the Judiciary Committee, three Republicans and three Democrats, sent a letter to Attorney General John Ashcroft, asking him to appoint a special counsel, "if appropriate." Two of the three Republican Senators, not surprisingly, were those who would later become part of the "Gang of Fourteen," Lindsey Graham and Mike DeWine. The other was Saxby Chambliss.[41] In response, the Justice Department directed the U.S. attorney in New York to initiate an investigation.[42] As of late March 2006, there was still no word from the Justice Department on the investigation.[43]

Republicans steadfastly refused to demand an investigation into the contents of the memos, much less to make the Democrats otherwise accountable for them. Manuel Miranda said the Republican leaders reneged on a promise they made to him that if he would just resign, they would initiate an investigation into the shocking contents of the memos. Certain Republican senators, like John Cornyn, pushed for an investigation, but his efforts ultimately failed.[44]

"The Raw, Ugly Underside"

The current state of the judicial confirmation process is another testimony to the depth to which the modern Democratic Party has sunk. Unfortunately, the Republican response to the shameful Democratic tactics has been pathetically anemic, despite a few intermittent moments of hope. Republicans have even refused to call the Democrats' bluff and force them into real filibusters, instead of idle threats to invoke the remedy. If Republicans would revert to the old system and force Democrats genuinely to filibuster, perhaps Democrats would quickly tire of their shenanigans. But as it stands now, the mere threat of a filibuster often results in Republicans running for the tall grass, with the effect that a supermajority is required to confirm judicial nominees—something clearly out of line with the Framers' original understanding. Republicans haven't even been able to muster sufficient party support to invoke the "nuclear option" to end this filibuster madness. An aggressive, mad-dog minority party too often rules the roost, and the judiciary and the Senate are its casualties.

Democrats will continue to use bogus moral equivalency excuses to justify their vilification of conservative nominees. But the fact remains that the "Borking" of judicial nominees overwhelmingly emanates from the Left. One would be hard-pressed to cite examples of Republicans personally vilifying a Clinton nominee like Democrats have routinely vilified nominees of Republican presidents. This practice has damaging consequences to the judiciary. Walter Dellinger, a former Democratic solicitor general, wrote, "One wonders how much longer many lawyers of distinction will even agree to have their names submitted for a process that is so uncertain, disruptive and perilous to reputation."[45]

Thwarted nominee Charles Pickering agrees. He wrote, "During the . . . [Alito confirmation hearings], the American public saw the raw, ugly underside of the judicial confirmation battle: Ted Kennedy's self-righteous, judgmental, holier-than-thou grilling of Judge Alito, and Mrs. Alito's obvious hurt over how her husband was treated. With good lawyers making far more money than federal judges, with nominees now facing a virtual firing squad at confirmation, it is no wonder studies now show half of those approached about being nominated to the federal judiciary say 'no thanks.' And it is not surprising the 'brightest and best' young lawyers are deciding to direct their legal careers away from a judicial trac[k]. . . . This battle not only threatens the quality, independence and diversity of the judiciary, it holds hostage civility and collegiality in the U.S. Senate and weakens that body's ability to discharge its constitutional legislative responsibilities."[46]

In the spring of 2006, about a year after the Gang of Fourteen made its pact to avert the "nuclear option," Senate Democrats started flexing their muscles again, threatening to filibuster appellate court nominees Terrence W. Boyle and Brett Kavanaugh. Democrats raised their standard objections. They said Boyle's rulings show little concern for minorities and the disabled. He was voted out of the Judiciary Committee on a strict party line vote; but before his full Senate hearing on his nomination to the Fourth Circuit Court of Appeals, Democrats found some new dirt on him: that he held stock in companies who were parties to lawsuits before his court.

Senator Reid said, "I can't imagine how President Bush could bring him to the Senate for confirmation." Yet the supposed concern over Boyle's stock holdings appeared to be another cynical political ploy—similar to the noise they made over Judge Alito's Vanguard holdings. White House spokesman Dana Perino said, "Judge Boyle has never intentionally participated in any matter in which he should have recused himself, nor has there been any suggestion that Judge Boyle knowingly overlooked any conflict or used his office for private gain."[47] Nevertheless, Reid promised, "without question," a filibuster.

Kavanaugh's nomination for the D.C. Circuit had been lingering since July 2003. The Democrats saw his nomination as another opportunity to showcase their opposition to the president's policies. Since Kavanaugh had been a White House staff secretary during the administration's NSA warrantless surveillance program and detention of enemy combatants, Democrats said they wanted to ensure that he hadn't played a major role in the implementation of those policies. Reid said Kavanaugh was subject to "a possible filibuster." Once again, the Democrats attempted to hold the judiciary hostage to their political whims.[48] In the end their threats turned out to be empty and Kavanaugh was confirmed by a 57–36 vote.[49]

CHAPTER EIGHT

Politicizing Race

While Democrats like to believe they are the exclusive protec-tors of minorities, they are unapologetically vicious to blacks and Hispanics who are conservative. They have attacked Justice Clarence Thomas, Secretary of State Condoleezza Rice, Judge Janice Rogers Brown, Attorney General Alberto Gonzales, and other conservatives, often in explicitly racial terms.

Just ask Michael Steele, a black Republican running for the Senate in Maryland, who was pelted by Democrats with Oreo cookies during a campaign appearance and called an "Uncle Tom." Worse, two staffers on the Democratic Senatorial Campaign Committee, chaired by Democratic senator Chuck Schumer, allegedly used Steele's Social Security number to dig up a confidential credit report. Schumer, it should be noted, is a "leading critic of identity theft and breaches of sensitive personal data like credit reports,"[1] and has ongoing and feigned outrage over president Bush's NSA surveillance program. We saw little Democratic outrage at the revelation of these alleged illegalities at the hands of staffers for the self-styled Fourth Amendment guardian and racially enlightened Senator Schumer. Also consider Otto Banks, a black Republican who ran for city council in Harrisburg, Pennsylvania. The Democratic State Committee sent out mailings depicting him as a sellout. People marked "whitey" on his campaign signs, and called him "Uncle Bush Tom."[2]

But none of this counts against Democrats because liberals consider minorities who reject liberalism as traitors. Democrats regard blacks as one of their indispensable constituencies, consistently garnering some 90 percent of the black vote in presidential elections. To keep this lock on the black vote, Democrats stoke racial fires by casting Republicans as, at best, insensitive to minorities, and, at worst, racists. Democrats cast every issue, from immigration to natural disasters to phony allegations of voter suppression in terms of race.

DNC chairman Howard Dean aggressively pushes this idea. Concerning alleged voter fraud and black voter suppression in Ohio in 2004, he said, "It's been widely reported over the past several years that Republicans do target African Americans for voter suppression. It's very clear here while there was no massive voter fraud, and I concur with the conclusion—it's also clear that there was massive voter suppression.[3] ... This is bad for America. We need to repair and restructure the way we conduct elections in America."[4] Dean had so grossly mischaracterized a scholarly report on the alleged voter fraud that one of its authors, Cornell University professor of government Walter Mebane Jr., publicly contradicted him. Mebane said, "Where the partisan biases came from, where it went, we really have no basis for making any assertion about that and I don't believe the report makes any statements about that."[5] In fact, the U.S. Commission on Civil Rights launched an exhaustive investigation to prove allegations of black voter intimidation in Florida but found no evidence for it.

Since Democrats have so polarized the race issue, rational debate and evenhanded dialogue is difficult, with Republicans often finding themselves on the defensive and Democrats on the offensive. By playing the race card, Democrats do more harm to racial relations than those they falsely accuse of racism. They masquerade as champions of minorities but alienate them, by design, from a huge percentage of the white population—all for their own political gain. Howard Dean knows Republicans do not suppress the black vote, like his party once did in the South, or like they did in 2000 to our men and women in uniform. Their persistence in spreading this lie to depict Republicans as racists is illustrative of the ugly arrogance and ill-will that afflicts their party today. By emphasizing race consciousness instead of color blindness they exacerbate racial divisions. By treating blacks as their wards they foster a dependent relationship, which ultimately retards the ability of minorities to improve their lot in life.

"Clinton's Lies Didn't Kill Anyone"

When it comes to religion and politics, liberals are hypocrites. They condemn conservative Christians for getting involved in politics, but they love to exploit racial politics in black churches.[6] Democrats routinely ignore issues like abortion, homosexual rights, and school choice—on which black churchgoers are strongly conservative—and instead try to wrap themselves in the mantle of Dr. Martin Luther King and accuse Republicans of racism.[7]

During a Martin Luther King, Jr. Day event at the Canaan Baptist Church of Christ in Harlem, Hillary Clinton condemned the Bush administration, predicting it "will go down in history as one of the worst." As for Congress, she said it is run like a "plantation," where dissenting voices are suppressed. Republican congressman Peter King responded, "It's always wrong to play the race card for political gain by using a loaded word like 'plantation.' It is particularly wrong to do so on Martin Luther King Day."[8]

Former vice president Al Gore also couldn't resist exploiting the holiday with divisive racial rhetoric in an hour-long speech to liberal activists, mostly of MoveOn.org. Gore likened targets of President Bush's NSA surveillance program to Martin Luther King, Jr. Gore said, "On this particular Martin Luther King Day, it is especially important to recall that for the last several years of his life, Dr. King was illegally wiretapped." Gore neglected to mention that one of the principal architects of the King wiretapping was Democratic icon Robert Kennedy, then attorney general of the United States.[9] Gore also did not mention his boss Bill Clinton's Echelon spying program (which allegedly pried into millions of domestic e-mails, faxes, and phone calls) or his use of warrantless searches.[10]

President Bush chose a different path to honor Dr. King's legacy. In a speech at Georgetown University's "Let Freedom Ring" celebration, he praised King and civil rights figure Rosa Parks, whom he called the "mother of the civil rights movement." Bush said that King and Parks shared a "deep belief in a hopeful future" and that segregation would end when exposed to the light. King and Parks also believed, said Bush, "that the answer to hate and discrimination was love." He added that "These two leaders knew that freedom was not a grant of government, but a gift from the author of life" and that both King and Parks helped African Americans gain their God-given rights.[11] Bush's speech, unlike Hillary Clinton's and Al Gore's, was bereft of partisan themes or rhetoric and did not exploit racial issues.

But the Democrats' racially charged tone was music to the ears of certain civil rights leaders, who traffic in such inflammatory rhetoric. Activist Lawrence Guyot told radio and television host Sean Hannity the Bush administration was shutting down dissent and compared President Bush's practices to those of Adolf Hitler. "Hitler burned the Reichstag. This president says, 'I'm going to do eavesdropping, and I understand there's some laws, and I understand there was a court especially established for me, but I'm not going to do that.'"[12] But Guyot's remarks were mild compared to those of NAACP chairman Julian Bond, who said in a speech, "The Republican Party would have the American flag and the swastika flying side by side."[13] Bond also said Bush was a liar whose lies were worse than Clinton's because Clinton's lies didn't kill anyone.[14]

Marshaling Academic "Evidence"

Some on the Left have even attempted to use "science" to demonstrate the intrinsic tendency of racism among Republicans. A group of social psychologists presented a theory at a conference at the University of California postulating that Bush supporters and other conservatives have stronger admitted and implicit biases against blacks than liberals do. Republican National Committee spokesman Brian Jones rejected the study's conclusions and noted that researchers involved in it had biases themselves, having made campaign contributions to Democrats.

One of the researchers, Harvard psychologist Mahzarin Banaji, said, "Obviously, such research does not speak at all to the question of the prejudice level of the president, but it does show that George W. Bush is appealing as a leader to those Americans who harbor greater anti-black prejudice." Another researcher, Jon Krosnick, a psychologist and political scientist at Stanford, said "If anyone in Washington is skeptical about these findings, they are in denial. We have fifty years of evidence that racial prejudice predicts voting. Republicans are supported by whites with prejudice against blacks. If people say, 'This takes me aback,' they are ignoring a huge volume of research."[15] So there you have it. End of discussion. Racism and conservatism go hand-in-hand.

It might be interesting to ascertain how these scholars would explain historical data adduced by conservative columnists Larry Elder[16] and Bruce Bartlett, among many others, documenting, in the words of Bartlett, that "the historical record clearly shows Democrats, not Republicans, have been the party of racism in this country."[17] Blogger La Shawn Barber also provides excellent links and commentary tracing the Republicans' superior record on civil rights legislation through the years.[18] Indeed, National Black Republican Association chairman Frances Rice says her organization is committed to returning "black Americans to their Republican Party roots by enlightening them about how Republicans fought for their freedom and civil rights, and are now fighting for their educational and economic advancement."[19]

Today, Republicans are appointing and electing blacks to prominent government positions and an increasing number of black "heavyweights" have chosen the Republican Party as a better vehicle to represent their political views and to advance an agenda that is in the best interests of blacks as well as all Americans. As political commentator Dick Morris noted, "A quiet revolution is taking place in the role African Americans play in politics. In the very heartland of the nation—in Pennsylvania and Ohio—the Republican Party is getting set to nominate black candidates for governor in the coming elections. In a nation that has not a single African American governor—not one—from either party, this is its own little revolution.... A Democrat takes the black vote for granted... [but] if the black vote becomes 'in play' as the Hispanic vote has, there will be a whole new politics in this country of ours."[20]

A Snowball's Chance

Despite these hopeful signs, a word of caution is in order. As the inimitable Thomas Sowell has warned, Republicans will never succeed in garnering a greater percentage of the black vote by emulating Democrats. Sowell wrote, "Why would anyone who wants liberalism go for a Republican imitation when they can get the real thing from Democrats? Republicans do not have a snowball's chance in hell of winning the votes of liberal blacks.... It is not rocket science to see that whatever chances the Republicans have of making inroads into the black vote are more likely to be better among more conservative blacks. Black religious groups opposed to abortion or homosexual marriage are an obvious group to try to reach. So are black business owners or military veterans."[21]

Republicans must also do a better job of reaching black voters on the issue of affirmative action, which the Democrats have racially politicized. Republicans should affirm that their stand against race-based preferences is the moral high ground. Equal protection of the law guarantees that individuals will not be favored by government on the basis of race, gender, and certain other defined categories. When government gives one group an advantage, it discriminates. This policy is not justified even as a means to correct past discrimination. You can't establish respect for a principle by violating that principle. The Constitution's prohibition against discrimination doesn't contain an exception permitting discrimination to correct past discrimination. It's not the prerogative of judges to create such an exception, though liberal activist judges have done precisely that.

You can never move toward racial colorblindness and true equality as long as you sanction government bean-counting or scorekeeping on the basis of race. No matter how well meaning affirmative action programs may be, they harm and demean the individuals and groups they purport to benefit, creating further, needless divisions among Americans. Society will have great difficulty making progress toward improving racial relations until it eradicates race-based preferences and encourages racial colorblindness.

Unfortunately, the Democratic Party, whether or not it actually believes affirmative action is beneficial to blacks, *knows* it is beneficial to the Democratic Party. Democratic senators Biden, Leahy, Schumer, Kennedy, and others routinely condemn conservative nominees as opponents of civil rights if their records reveal or if they express a judicial philosophy of racial colorblindness, a commitment to genuine equal protection, and a rejection of race-based preferences. These senators will keep engaging in such polarizing practices as long as they yield political benefits.

Politicizing Katrina

Perhaps the most shameless example of Democratic race-baiting in recent times was their accusation that President Bush and other

Republicans deliberately or at least negligently delayed the federal response to Hurricane Katrina because a disproportionate number of its victims were black. While the American people themselves were focusing, constructively, on tackling the horrendous problems Katrina wrought, many politicians were playing the blame game. Individuals, businesses, and churches throughout America, motivated by a genuine spirit of altruism, were pouring their resources into helping the victims while Democratic politicians were calculating how they could best capitalize on the widespread hardship.

Today's Democrats don't hint at Republican racism, they come right out and say it. They have sponsored radio ads saying more churches would burn if Republicans were elected. Democratic National Committee chairman Howard Dean told the Baptist Political and Social Justice Commission, "We have to come to terms with the ugly truth that skin color, age, and economics played a deadly role in who survived [Katrina] and who did not. And this question, forty or fifty years after Dr. King and the civil rights movement, is, 'How could this still be happening in America?' "[22] Liberals seem to take their rhetorical cues from the likes of rapper Kanye West, who during a hurricane relief concert accused President Bush of racism. "George Bush doesn't care about black people." America, said West, was set up "to help the poor, the black people, the less well-off as slow as possible."[23]

Democrats saw in Katrina an opening to finally unify around an issue other than Iraq that would further demonize President Bush. The *New York Times* was quick to recognize their palpable sense of glee in parlaying the misfortune of others into great political advantage. The *Times* wrote, "From Democratic leaders on the floor of Congress, to a speech by the Democratic National Committee chairman at a meeting of the National Baptist Convention in Miami, to four morning television interviews by Senator Hillary Rodham Clinton, Democrats offered what was shaping up as the most concerted attack that they had mounted on the White House in the five years of the Bush presidency.... The display of unity was striking for a party that has been adrift since Mr. Kerry's defeat, struggling to reach consensus on issues like the war in Iraq and the Supreme Court nomination of Judge John G. Roberts Jr."

And why were the Democrats so blissful, according to the *Times*? Simple: they could "question the administration's competence without opening themselves to attacks on their patriotism." Some Republicans rightly called Democrats on their shameless opportunism. Congressman Thomas M. Reynolds of New York said, "Democrats throw stuff at the wall almost every week looking for something to stick. This is something they have now chosen to politicize during a national disaster, versus let's get people taken care of and then move on to what we have learned from it."[24]

"It Put the Wind in His Face"

As viciously as the Democrats consistently slandered President Bush over Iraq, there was even greater blood lust over Katrina. With the breaking of the levees in New Orleans there was an unmistakably new spring in the Democrats' step. They obviously saw Katrina as another chance to bring President Bush to justice and to expose him as a poster child for Republican and conservative racism and insensitivity. The "illegitimate" gravitas the President serendipitously acquired after September 11 had now rightly evaporated.

In their minds, Katrina had vindicated their half-decade-long character assassination and reduced President Bush to the small

fraction of a man they believed him to be. *New York Times* columnist Thomas Friedman told NBC's Tim Russert, "Well, I believe September 11 truly distorted our politics, Tim, and it gave the president
and his advisers an opening to take a far hard-right agenda, I
believe, on taxes and other social issues, from September 10, that
was not going anywhere from September 10, and drove it into a
September 12 world. It put the wind at his back. And Katrina
brought that to an end. It put the wind in his face." Only through
a "fundamental recasting of his position and his administration"
could Bush redeem himself, in Friedman's view. In other words, it
was time for Bush to start governing like a liberal.[25]

Friedman's observations were representative of the attitude of
Democrats and liberal commentators. To them, a national disaster
had discredited the conservative blueprint and validated their
worldview.

Senator Kennedy even injected Katrina into Judge Roberts's confirmation hearings, pretending it was relevant to constitutional
jurisprudence. In his opening remarks, Kennedy said, "The stark
and tragic images of human suffering in the aftermath of Hurricane
Katrina have reminded us yet again that civil rights and equal rights
are still the great unfinished business of America. The suffering has
been disproportionately borne by the weak, the poor, the elderly
and infirm, and largely African Americans, who were forced by
poverty, illness, unequal opportunity to stay behind and bear the
brunt of the storm's winds and floods. I believe that kind of disparate impact is morally wrong in this, the richest country in the
world."[26] Kennedy failed to articulate the connection between current Supreme Court decisions and the persistence of poverty among
African Americans.

Senator Patrick Leahy said, "But if anyone needed a reminder of the need and role of a government, the last two days have provided it. If anyone needed a reminder of the growing poverty and despair among too many Americans, we now have it. And if anyone needed a reminder of the racial divide that remains in our nation, no one can now doubt we still have miles to go." Leahy then added, "I believe that the American people still want and expect and demand the government to help ensure justice and equal opportunity for all and especially for those who, through no fault of their own, were born into poverty."[27]

Without question Americans see the government as a guarantor of justice and equal opportunity. But the context of Leahy's statement reveals that he does not really envision government as provider of equal opportunity—he favors race-based privileges. He sees government as the great economic equalizer, a role the founders never contemplated. Neither Leahy nor Kennedy explained how the courts could or should remedy the supposedly disproportionate effects of a natural disaster.

The senators' invocation of Katrina was obscene and manipulative. They exhibited their willingness to use that tragic event to promote their affirmative action and wealth redistribution agenda, fully aware that their approach would divide, polarize, and alienate people on the basis of race.

"Stuck on Stupid"

After politicizing Katrina, liberals tried again with Hurricane Rita. At a press conference to respond to questions about Rita, General Russel Honore, the National Guard officer in charge of post-Katrina operations in New Orleans, admonished reporters who insisted on asking him about Katrina and playing the blame game, "Don't get stuck on stupid"—stupid, as in stupid "gotcha" politics—and instead focus on the present problem.

Honore's admonition could just as easily be addressed to today's Democratic Party, which has been so obsessively absorbed with hating President Bush that it has paralyzed itself as a constructive political institution. Whether it's the War on Terror, Social Security, the economy, race relations, disaster relief, values issues, national security, or the judiciary, Democrats have all but abandoned policy advocacy, and focused exclusively on thwarting President Bush's agenda.

Almost two months after the hurricane struck, Democrats were still milking the disaster for political gain, continuing to sound race and class warfare themes. Democrats in the Senate and House implied they were the only ones interested in providing relief to the minority victims because Republicans were determined to give tax cuts to the wealthy. Senator Reid said, "We believe that Katrina's victims should be one of the top priorities that we have in Congress. But we Democrats are the only ones that believe that." Nancy Pelosi couldn't have agreed more. She said, "They're using the victims of Katrina to give tax cuts to the wealthy. It's a cruel hoax on the victims of Katrina to use their plight to have a budget that doesn't address their needs, that increases the deficit and gives tax cuts to the wealthiest people in our country.... First we had a natural disaster, then we had a second man-made disaster by the Bush administration in the emergency recovery and now we're going to have a third disaster in terms of the long-term recovery because of the decisions they are making in favor of their friends. It's all connected through the budget. We have a budget that is a reflection of their distorted values."[28]

It is difficult to understate the seriousness of the Democrats' charge that Republicans responded slowly because of their racism. When people in positions of authority make such outlandish allegations, significant numbers of people will doubtlessly believe they are true. How can today's Democratic Party pretend to be compassionate when it devotes such enormous polemic energy not to mending race relations but to fanning the flames of suspicion and distrust among minorities and the poor?

"Mean-spirited Dimness"

Immigration is yet another issue on which Democrats practice racial politics. Many conservatives—but by no means all—oppose a policy of open borders and lax enforcement of our immigration laws. They are not only concerned with the threats to our national security, but with the increasing balkanization of this nation.

Generally speaking, conservatives reject the politically correct rage over multiculturalism, believing it's perfectly proper to celebrate our multiethnicity, but destructive to promote multiculturalism. Multiculturalism would be harmful enough if it just segregated different ethnic groups into balkanized enclaves, but at its core it's anti-American and anti–Western Civilization. It doesn't merely defend other cultures; it denigrates American culture, our Judeo-Christian tradition and values, capitalism and the American ideal. It even scoffs at the concept of national sovereignty, preferring a globalist perspective.

Opponents of illegal immigration are not racists or nativists. Most of them rightly fear that American culture and the American ideal are being diluted, that those entering our borders are not being encouraged to learn about America's history, her Constitution, her freedom tradition, her dedication to the rule of law, and other hall-marks that make America unique. They are not encouraged to develop a spirit of patriotism and nationalism. Open borders opponents realize that a nation cannot last long if it loses its identity as a nation, which is why the naturalization process was instituted, whereby legal immigrants learn American civics and come to identify with the American ideal. Unbridled and illegal immigration threatens the very existence of this nation.

Nevertheless, Democrats see immigration as another wedge issue and an opportunity to acquire an entirely new constituency. Just as they have attempted to inspire distrust of conservatives among blacks, they are trying to convince Hispanic immigrants that it is racist to enforce America's immigration laws. DNC chairman Howard Dean, during the debate over a proposed Senate immigration bill, accused President Bush of "scapegoating" Hispanics for political gain.

This was odd, considering that Dean and Bush happened to be in agreement on the proposed legislation. It was also bizarre, given Bush's long-standing open-borders policy—to the point that he has been in trouble with his conservative base over it. Bush, in fact, has been eager to welcome Hispanics to the United States and has appointed individuals from that community, like Alberto Gonzales, to important government positions. But Howard Dean naturally fell back on the Democrats' "Republicans are racists" routine. Dean said, "In 2006 it's immigrants. That's what their strategy is on the Republican side: divide people, scapegoat them, set them aside, point the finger at them. Well, that may be good for the Republican Party, but it's bad for America, and we're not going to do that."[29]

Senate Minority Leader Harry Reid, during a debate on the Senate floor, shamelessly called a proposal to make English America's official language "racist." Reid said, "This amendment is racist. I think it's directed basically to people who speak Spanish." If it was racist—which it wasn't—it was a racism shared by an overwhelming majority of Americans. A Zogby International poll revealed that 84 percent supported such a measure, with 77 percent of Hispanics agreeing.[30] Despite Reid's demagoguery the bill passed 63–34 with all but eleven Democrats opposed.

On April 25, 2006, the *New York Times* called the House immigration bill, passed in December 2005, "xenophobic," presumably because it contained tough measures to seal the borders and enforce existing laws. Somehow an advocacy of the rule of law on the immigration issue means, according to the *New York Times*, a fear of foreigners.[31] A month later, the *Times* was outraged again with the Senate's passage of the English language provision. They referred to it as "mean-spirited dimness" and "xenophobic." According to the *Times*, the measure is "exclusionary, potentially discriminatory and embarrassingly hostile to the rest of the world."[32] To the *Times*, obviously, it is "exclusionary" for America to celebrate its unity and common culture.

CHAPTER NINE

Class Warfare

For Democrats, fomenting racial division is second only to encouraging class warfare. Their message contradicts the American ideal, which celebrates opportunity for all and discourages envy. It inspires resentment of the successful and discourages personal achievement and entrepreneurship, teaching that the best way for lower income groups to improve their lot is through the redistributive largesse of government. It says that government produces and should control wealth through taxing and spending policy.

Despite President Bush's professions of "compassionate conservatism," and his willingness to massively increase federal spending on education and other programs liberals support, liberal rhetoric has remained as hostile as ever. *New York Times* columnist Bob Herbert accused Bush of having "contempt for the poor," for deciding to alter the terms of the State Children's Health Insurance Program.[1] The *Buffalo News* was incensed that Bush's 2004 budget called for a mere 1 percent increase in domestic spending while proposing a 7 percent increase in military spending. It wrote, "Could President Bush show his contempt for the poor any more clearly than he does in his budget plan?"[2] Senator John Edwards, a veteran practitioner of class warfare, said, "George Bush's economic policy is the most radical and dangerous economic theory to hit our shores since socialism."[3]

With Hurricane Katrina, Democrats used class warfare to supplement their politics of racial exploitation. DNC chairman Howard Dean said, "Shall we give to the wealthiest people in the country, or should we rebuild New Orleans?"[4] Liberal PAC MoveOn.org organized a rally across from the White House to insist that Bush "acknowledge that budget cuts and indifference by his administration led to the disaster in New Orleans and along the Mississippi Gulf Coast." Though it was precisely such liberals who were pointing fingers of blame and contributing more to the problems than the solution, they nevertheless issued the bizarre suggestion that Bush should "stop blaming the victims of Hurricane Katrina and get to work helping them."[5]

Senator Edwards also used Katrina as a platform to resurrect his "two Americas" theme. "The truth," said Edwards, "is the people who suffer the most from Katrina are the very people who suffer the most every day."[6] Senate Minority Leader Harry Reid said that the inadequacy of the federal response was in part due to Bush's refusal to tear himself away from his vacation. Reid said, "How much time did the president spend dealing with this emerging crisis while he was on vacation? Did the fact that he was outside of Washington, D.C., have any effect on the federal government's response?"[7] Tennessee congressman Harold E. Ford, Jr. said that he was struck by Bush's "cavalier attitude toward the plight of the poor people across Louisiana, Mississippi, and Alabama....Now is not the time in the face of pain, anguish, and death to be weak and uncertain." Democratic New Jersey senator Frank R. Lautenberg said, "Instead of looking out the window of an airplane, [Bush] should have been on the ground giving the people devastated by this hurricane hope."[8]

The Rich Got Richer, but So Did the Poor

Democrats contend that Republican-sponsored tax cuts disproportionately benefit the wealthy, reduce revenues, increase deficits and the national debt, and wreck the economy—all because Republicans insist on favoring the rich at the expense of everyone else. But none of this is true, and a brief review of the record is essential to understanding the extent of the Democrats' duplicity on economic policy to this day.

The Reagan tax cuts of the eighties, according to a 1990 Bureau of Census report, resulted in financial improvement of all income groups, not just the wealthy. They also shattered the myth that upward mobility was a thing of the past. A study by the Treasury Department revealed that 86 percent of people in the lowest 20 percent of income in 1979 graduated into higher categories during the eighties. More people in every income group moved up than down, except the top 1 percent of earners.[9]

The Reagan tax cuts led to the largest peacetime economic growth to date in the history of the country. Real economic growth averaged 3.2 percent during the Reagan years, which was more than in the years immediately preceding or following. The economy was almost a third larger at the end of the Reagan years than at the beginning. Real median family income grew by $4,000, compared to almost no growth in the preceding Ford-Carter years. Reaganomics shattered certain economic theories, such as the Phillips Curve, which taught that there was a trade-off between unemployment and inflation. With the Reagan cuts, we enjoyed unprecedented growth and high levels of employment. Seventeen million new jobs—some say twenty million—were created from 1981 through 1989, with virtually no upward pressure on inflation. Interest rates dropped dramatically as well from the Carter period.[10] The economic pie truly was expanding and one man's growth was not another man's loss.

Unfortunately, President Reagan was unable, especially with a recalcitrant Congress, to rein in federal spending, so deficits and the national debt grew at what were then considered alarming rates. But even here, there are mitigating factors. Military spending constituted much of the spending increases—the defense budget doubled from $158 billion to $304 billion from 1981 to 1989. Contrary to popular understanding, the rate of domestic spending grew slower under Reagan than under all his immediate predecessors. As a percentage of GDP, domestic spending fell from 15.3 percent to 12.9 percent from 1981 to 1989.[11] And while the annual federal deficit grew rapidly during the Reagan years, it had begun to decrease substantially by the end of his second term—down from $237 billion and 6.3 percent of GDP to $141 billion and 2.9 percent of GDP.[12]

Given the empirically undeniable growth in revenues during the Reagan years, there could be no intellectually honest dispute that the source of the deficit explosion was unbridled spending. Yet during that period and ever since, President Reagan's dreaded tax cuts have been fraudulently scapegoated for triggering our exploding deficits and national debt. President Reagan, according to the liberal revisionism, destroyed the working class and nearly bankrupted the nation, all for the sinister purpose of bestowing a windfall on the wealthiest individuals and "big" corporations.

Democrats used this same fraudulent premise to oppose President Bush's proposed tax cuts, predicting enormous deficits and deliberately disproportionate benefits to the wealthy. These predictions have fallen flat on their face. Democrats have also deceitfully denied and covered up the strength of the Bush economy. As so many of the evils in today's Democratic Party can be traced to its godfather, Bill Clinton, so can their perennial misrepresentations about the economy under Republican administrations.

When Bill Clinton was running against President George H. W. Bush, he described the Bush economy as "the worst economy in fifty years"[13] or "the worst recession since the Great Depression." He blamed the deficits on "Reagan-Bush" "trickle-down economics." He said that under Reagan and Bush only the wealthy thrived while the middle and lower income groups struggled and suffered. None of his claims were true. The 1990–1991 recession, to which Clinton was referring, was—according to *Investor's Business Daily*—one of the mildest on record and was clearly over while the presidential campaign was still in full swing. As *IBD* noted, by definition, a recession requires two straight quarters of economic shrinking and the 1990–1991 recession "barely qualified." It was the third mildest recession since World War II. From its high point to its low point the economy only dipped 1.3 percent, as compared to a plunge of 3.9 percent in the 1973–1975 recession or a 3.4 percent fall during the 1957–1958 recession.[14]

In fact, the economy that President George H. W. Bush bequeathed to incoming President Clinton was growing at 4 percent with most key economic indicators, like orders for durable goods and personal income, having reached their highest points in four and a half years. But the liberal media wouldn't allow that to stand. According to the Center for Media and Public Affairs, negative reporting on the economy reached 96 percent from July through September 1992, its highest point in two years. Even in October, despite the undeniably positive data that was continuing to emerge on the economy, negative reporting remained as high as 90 percent.[15] But in November, when President Bush's quest for re-election ended, so did negative reporting on the economy. It stopped dead in its tracks, having served its purpose.

Even if the Bush economy had remained in a mild recession at its lowest point, it was nowhere near the "worst economy in fifty years." The Jimmy Carter malaise of the mid-seventies certainly earned that distinction, with the worst of all worlds, and no end in sight—short of a Reagan revolution. Interest rates and inflation were off the charts, reaching 15.27 percent and 13.5 percent, respectively, unemployment grew to 7.8 percent,[16] and Carter had virtually resigned himself to gloom and doom. The Bush economy at its worst was booming out of control compared to Carter's disaster. But Bill Clinton had set the precedent for grossly mischaracterizing the economy and getting away with it, and his party would follow in his shameless footsteps, aided by the mainstream media.

Though the economy under President Clinton thrived, it finally petered out toward the end, and President George W. Bush inherited a recessionary economy, for which the Democrats would hold him to account. When Bush was campaigning for president he argued that the economy was in a downturn and needed a boost through tax cuts. His critique was far from personal. His focus was not on blaming Clinton and Gore, but simply to cite the statistics and lobby for tax relief.

"Talking Down the Economy"

The media never challenged Clinton and Gore for their deceptive indictment of George H. W. Bush over "the worst economy in fifty years." But when George W. Bush called attention to the economic slowdown of the Clinton-Gore economy, Democrats and the media pummeled him for "talking down the economy," as if a candidate's accurate portrayal of a recessionary economy in order to garner support for a program to relieve it was out of bounds. They suggested that whatever problems the economy was experiencing were largely the result of Bush's undermining of public confidence through his negative campaigning. His negative critique, they said, caused the stock market to fall and other economic indicators to slide toward a recession. As economics professor William Anderson showed, the charge was unfounded: "The president of the United States, simply by citing economic indicators that demonstrate that the economic book is turning into a bust, is not 'talking down the economy.'"[17] Moreover, Bush had merely cited the empirical evidence; he had not targeted and threatened wealth producers like Clinton had during the regrettable period in 1993 and 1994 when he was enabling his wife's crusade for nationalized health care.[18] Of course, once Bush was inaugurated Democrats quickly forgot their rule that badmouthing the economy makes it worse, as they have been doing it ever since.

While Bush was trying to push his economic growth plan through Congress, Democrats did their best to delay and obstruct, which exacerbated the sluggishness of the economy. Yet they continued to blame him for the problems he inherited and on which they were preventing remedial action. After Bush's tax cuts were enacted and the economy began to grow again, Democrats refused to acknowledge the turnaround and continued to characterize the economy as anemic. The same held true for the changes wrought by Bush's 2003 capital gains tax cut. Business investment contracted at an annualized rate of 1.14 percent during the fourteen quarters preceding the 2003 capital gains tax cut, but grew at a rate of 13.03 percent over the three quarters following it.[19]

Though the economy has been consistently strong since at least as far back as the middle of Bush's first term, the Democrats and the media have portrayed it as sluggish in general and particularly hard on the poor. When running for president, John Kerry denied the good economic news and robust Bush recovery and, along with the mainstream media, recast it as a "jobless recovery,"[20] which was hardly accurate.[21] He said we were outsourcing too many jobs to foreign countries to the detriment of the economy, which was also highly questionable.[22] Never once was Kerry accused of "talking down the economy."

Despite Democratic naysaying, the economy continued to thrive and Democrats continued to deny it. During the Clinton years, the media routinely praised the Clinton economy based on benchmarks including the stock market, unemployment, economic growth, and inflation. But with unambiguously positive data in all four categories in 2006, Democrats and the media refused to acknowledge the strength of the Bush economy. The Media Research Center documented that from April 12 through May 2, 2006, the major television network news programs aired 183 stories about rising oil and gas prices, contrasted with only four network stories even mentioning the low unemployment rate.[23] The Democrats just can't accept good economic news when we have a Republican president. They can't overcome their stereotype that Republicans don't care about the poor. Here are the facts under George W. Bush.

In 2005, the economy grew 3.5 percent—the fastest rate of any industrialized nation. In the first quarter of 2006, the economy grew at a rate of 5.6 percent, the fastest pace in two and a half years[24] and representing, according to the Bureau of Economic Analysis,[25] the eighteenth straight quarter of economic growth. As of May 2006, employment had grown for thirty-one straight months, with 5.1 million new jobs being created. The national unemployment rate was 4.7 percent (it later fell to 4.6 percent), which was lower than the average rate of unemployment for any of the last four decades.[26] Indeed, rates below 5 percent have always been considered robust by economists. The stock market had been climbing for three years in a row and inflation was still low.[27] In May 2006, the stock market reached another six-year high.[28] Construction spending was at an all-time high and real after-tax per capita income had grown by nearly 9 percent since President Bush began his first term.[29]

Economist and commentator Larry Kudlow described the untold story about the booming Bush economy as "the greatest story never told."[30] Kudlow said that toward the end of April 2006 production, retail sales, and employment were all stronger than expected and that huge gains were occurring in the ordering of big-ticket items, suggesting that the boom would last for the foreseeable future. There was also a 12 percent gain in the backlog of unfilled orders, which, said Kudlow, is "the best leading indicator of business activity."[31] In an earlier piece, written November 30, 2005, Kudlow said he couldn't understand why the Bush White House had not trumpeted its remarkable economic record like Ronald Reagan had during the 1980s. Real GDP had grown at least 3 percent for the past ten quarters and had averaged a 4.1 percent annual growth rate—the best since the middle 1980s. Also, business profits had increased at 10 percent or more for the last nine quarters, which had only happened two other times in the previous five and a half decades. After-tax earnings were at a record high, as were household net worth and total employment.[32]

This remarkable economic success story was all the more noteworthy considering the convergence of factors immediately preceding and during the Bush administration, including the collapsing of the high-tech bubble, the surge in energy prices, the devastating September 11 attacks, which cost the nation approximately $100 billion in economic losses and some one million jobs, the enormous financial burdens of prosecuting the War on Terror,[33] and the onslaught of Hurricane Katrina, reportedly the most costly natural disaster in U.S. history.[34]

Instead of heralding this great economic news, the Democrats and the media did their best to suppress and distort it. House Minority Leader Nancy Pelosi issued a press release in April 2006—in the face of all the economic good news—that the economy was going in the wrong direction. "President Bush should ask American families, millions of whom are struggling to make ends meet and going deeper in debt, if they believe that there is 'an economic resurgence that is strong, broad, and benefiting all Americans.' With tax cuts for the wealthiest few causing red ink as far as the eye can see, incomes falling, and our jobs moving overseas, the economic record of President Bush is dismal for middle-class families. The Bush economy is going in the wrong direction: gas prices are sky-high and health costs are an overwhelming burden for too many Americans."[35]

The Associated Press routinely reported the economy in terms of gloom and doom. Despite big jumps in employment and substantial wage increases and the stock market booming in mid-2006, the AP chose a negative slant on the news, as highlighted by *Investor's Business Daily*. "Payroll performance in April was weaker than economists were expecting," wrote the AP. "This suggests that companies are not aggressively hiring. Companies are showing some caution with expectation that rising energy prices, higher interest rates, and a slowing housing market may temper overall economic activity." As the *IBD* editors astutely observed, despite the good economic news, "most people seem to think the economy's in trouble. No doubt, they fear higher oil prices and interest rates and the damage they could do. So do we. But unlike the rest of the media, we don't ignore the good news. And right now, there's plenty of that to go around."[36]

An Administration Almost Marinated in Oil

Instead of acknowledging the positive signs, Democrats accused Republicans of being in bed with big oil companies, which they said were gouging the American consumers by raising prices. In the weekly Democratic Party radio address, Michigan congressman Bart Stupak said, "Gas prices keep skyrocketing, and in Washington, Republicans continue to turn a blind eye to the oil industry's activities."[37] Senator Chris Dodd said that what could decide the 2006 elections was "where you stand on this issue: on whether or not you stand with those that want to see a rebate going back or whether or not you're going to protect large oil companies."

Oregon senator Ron Wyden said, "This is an administration that is almost marinated in oil. One official after another has a history and background in this sector and yet, where was the Department of Energy, where was the Environmental Protection Agency, where was the Commodities Future Trading Commission at a key time in our country's energy future?" Senator Bob Menendez said, "It's crystal clear that the current spike in gas prices is at least partially due to an act of greed." Senator Chuck Schumer said that the exploding gas prices were "way beyond what supply and demand would merit."[38]

Meanwhile, Democrats were busy proposing demonstrably ineffective and unfair windfall profits taxes on oil companies, obstructing relief proposals to make America more energy efficient, such as drilling in the Arctic National Wildlife Refuge and the Outer Continental Shelf, more liquefied natural gas terminals, and the exploitation of nuclear power. (Admittedly, not all Republicans were blameless on this type of activity either, including President Bush, who regrettably called for an investigation of the oil companies.[39]) Democrats also cherry-picked certain statistics to paint a bleak economic picture. The major print media and network newscasts lamented that American automobile sales cratered in 2005 compared to 2004. What they deliberately omitted was that 2004 saw record auto sales because automobile companies offered employee pricing deals, which stimulated sales, and in 2005 the sales settled back to normal rates.[40]

The Democrats' big lies worked to erode public confidence in the economy. Despite the unambiguously positive economic indicators, polling data indicated that the public was nevertheless skeptical about the good news. In March 2006, Gallup reported that only about one-third of Americans perceived the economy as excellent or good, while 60 percent said it was getting worse. Unsurprisingly, opinion split on partisan lines: Republicans believed the economy was good, while Democrats and independents did not, which tends to prove that the Democratic rank and file (and independents) are more receptive to Democratic misinformation.[41]

A Rising Tide Lifts All Boats

One of the Democrats' favorite arguments against tax cut policies is that they increase the deficit and national debt. But Reagan tax cuts led to a near doubling of nominal revenues during the 1990s ($517 billion to $1.031 trillion), and a substantial increase (20 percent) even after adjusting for inflation.[42] The Bush tax cuts, similarly, led to increases in federal revenues. This was true with both the income tax rate cuts of 2001 and the capital gains cuts of 2003, because tax cuts stimulate economic growth.

On May 17, 2006, at the ceremonial signing of the Tax Relief Extension Reconciliation Act of 2005, in which the tax rate reductions were extended for another two years, President Bush reported that in 2005 federal tax revenues grew by $274 billion, which represented an increase of almost 15 percent from 2004. He said that so far in 2006 the revenues were 11 percent higher than at the same point in 2005.[43] (A later report said that tax revenues were 12.9 percent higher than in 2005 and the deficit through May 2006 was down to $227 billion compared to $273 billion through May 2005. This led some economists to project that President Bush would make good on his pledge to cut the deficit in half by 2006.)[44]

As Daniel Clifton of the American Shareholders Association observed, "A capital gains tax cut spurs the growth of new businesses, increases the wages of workers, enhances consumer purchasing power, and grows the economy at large, resulting in more overall gains to be taxed. When capital is taxed at a lower rate, any revenue losses are offset because there is more overall capital being produced, and thus more total revenue being generated."[45]

In fact, Donald Luskin, chief investment officer of Trend Macrolytics LLC, points out that the same phenomenon occurs in reverse—increases in income tax rates reduce revenues. Democrats assert that Bill Clinton decreased the deficit through his tax increases, but the evidence, as Luskin shows, is that federal revenues increased because of the *decrease* in capital gains rates passed by the Republican Congress in 1997. As Luskin indicates, the Congressional Budget Office, using static analysis, had projected huge increases in revenues from Clinton's enormous income tax hikes of 1993. But the actual revenues generated from 1993 to 1996 beat the 1992 CBO revenue estimates for those years by less than 1 percent.[46]

While Democrats point to how Bill Clinton balanced the budget, truth be told the budget was balanced only because Newt Gingrich's Republican Congress decreased the capital gains rate and *forced* the Clinton administration to restrain its spending. If Clinton had his way, we could have ended up with nationalized health care, an enormous tax and spend economic "stimulus plan," increased government spending, and no welfare reform—which Clinton twice vetoed before reluctantly signing it. What spending Clinton did reduce was at the expense of the military. Similarly, while John Kerry campaigned for president saying he would rein in federal spending, he never explained how his grandiose spending proposals would do that.

Another Democratic criticism of the Bush tax cuts—as with the Reagan cuts—is that they are skewed in favor of the wealthy. In fact, the rates on lower levels of income—just considering the income tax and not the payroll tax—were reduced more sharply than on higher levels, making the income tax structure, by definition, more progressive. The Bush tax cuts shifted a *greater* burden of federal income taxes onto the higher income earners.

The top 1 percent of income earners paid a 1.5 percent higher share of the federal income tax burden after the Bush cuts than before. The top 3 percent paid 5 percent more of the revenues after the tax cuts. The top 5 percent paid 3 percent more of the revenues than before the cuts.[47] Moreover, the income tax monies paid by the top 3 percent of earners roughly equals that paid by the bottom 97 percent. And, the tax payments of that top 3 percent increased at twice the rate of the tax payments from all others from 2001 to 2004, according to the *Wall Street Journal*.[48]

It is hard to fathom how anyone with a scintilla of intellectual honesty could characterize as unfair to the poor a tax structure where the bottom half of income earners pay approximately 4 percent of total income taxes and the top half pay the other 96 percent, and the top 25 percent pay about 83 percent.[49] White House chief of staff Josh Bolten exposed the lie that the Bush tax cuts disproportionately benefit the wealthy by pointing out that the top 10 percent of income earners are paying a greater share of the federal revenues (66 percent) after the Bush tax cuts than they would if the cuts had not been implemented (64 percent).

Democrats have used another ploy to dupe people into believing the Bush tax cuts disproportionately benefit the "wealthy." They treat money as being owned by the government and the portion that is not taxed is what the government, in its beneficence, bestows upon individuals. In fact, tax cuts allow taxpayers to keep more of their own money. And if the rich get to keep more money in total dollars it is only because they pay more in total dollars and are taxed on higher income. They are also more likely to invest that income to create new jobs—private sector jobs that stimulate the economy, create opportunity, and benefit everyone.

Kicking the Can Down the Road

Democrats have also employed class warfare strategies on Social Security reform. Not that long ago—during the Clinton-Gore era and during the 2000 presidential campaign—Democrats themselves were calling for Social Security reform. They stressed the importance of segregating and preserving Social Security funds in a "lock box" to "save Social Security."[50]

In his 1998 State of the Union address, Clinton said, "What should we do with this projected surplus? I have a simple four-word answer: save Social Security first. Tonight, I propose that we reserve 100 percent of the surplus—that's every penny of any surplus—until we have taken all the necessary measures to strengthen the Social Security System for the twenty-first century.... Let us make this commitment: Social Security first. Let's do that together."[51] Shortly thereafter, Clinton began traveling around the nation claiming that Social Security was in crisis. He warned that every economic achievement of his administration was "threatened by the looming fiscal crisis in Social Security." He said, pointedly, that there should be no further spending or tax cut initiatives "before we take care of the crisis in Social Security that is looming when the baby boomers retire."[52]

When Al Gore was still vice president, he also used the word "crisis" to describe Social Security, warning that by 2032, "Social Security faces a serious fiscal crisis." At a rally with congressional Democrats, Gore, Congressman Richard Gephardt, Senator Edward Kennedy, and Senator Barbara Boxer all said, "save Social Security first." Of course, as *National Review*'s Byron York pointed out, their motivation—and Clinton's—in talking up the Social Security crisis was probably to deflect attention from the Clinton impeachment effort and to prevent Republicans from using the surplus for other purposes, like rebuilding the military.[53]

Clinton's director of the National Economic Council, Gene Sperling, said that Clinton was determined to reserve the budget surplus "until we know how much is needed for a long-term Social Security solution." He said Clinton favored a bipartisan solution to Social Security and "doing something historic in preventing a crisis."[54] Clinton's secretary of the treasury Robert Rubin also acknowledged that the Social Security system needed to be reformed, even saying that the administration wanted to defer addressing the punitive marriage penalty in the tax code "until Social Security has been addressed." He said the projected fiscal surplus should not be used "for any other purpose" until "a sound Social Security fix" could be "put together."[55]

Rubin, in 1998, emphasized what Democrats denied later during President Bush's push to reform the system: that Social Security would become insolvent in 2029. "Essentially," said Rubin, "the problem comes even quicker. It is in 2012 in which the receipts coming into the Treasury are...not enough to cover the benefits going out....This is a serious matter and it is a serious issue to try and elevate this debate in a way that we can do this in 1999." Even more interestingly, and presciently, Rubin said, "Some of the biggest threats to Social Security reform will be the temptation of elected officials to kick the can down the road, that no matter what we do, that they will feel that this is a problem that can be dealt with later and that every Congress will kick the can down the road another year, another two years, until rather than preventing a crisis, we have a crisis."[56]

Many other Democratic politicians recognized—and admitted— that Social Security faced an impending crisis. Congressman Martin Frost, chairman of the Democratic Congressional Campaign Committee, said in 1998, "What people in this country care about is education, health care, and the future of Social Security." Congressman Richard Gephardt, laying out the Democratic agenda, said, "We want to dedicate the potential budget surplus to the Social Security trust fund until we agree on a plan to ensure the fund's long-term integrity."[57]

Clinton's 1998 emphasis on the Social Security problem was not just a temporary fixation. During a White House press conference on January 28, 1999, White House press secretary Joe Lockhart bragged that the president's plan was to "balance the budget each and every year, without using Social Security surpluses, for the first time since 1960." He said that by locking away those funds, Social Security solvency would be extended.[58]

But Clinton and his Democratic Party couldn't bring themselves to get beyond the rhetoric and implement serious reform. Instead, Democrats played on the fears of seniors, saying Republicans wanted to deprive them of their retirement security. New York Democratic senator Daniel Patrick Moynihan recognized the liberals' intransigence on the issue. He favored partial privatization of Social Security, even before President George W. Bush started promoting the idea. The Social Security issue, Moynihan said, represented a crisis for liberalism, because liberals stood in the way of reform. "It's the liberals who can destroy Social Security," said Moynihan, "by preventing any change."[59]

Al Gore, when running for president in 2000, opposed a partial privatization plan. Like Clinton, he proposed a "lock box," and said he would "veto anything that takes money out of the Social Security trust fund for anything other than Social Security. We'll keep it sound."[60]

Beyond the illusory lock box scheme, which would never materialize, President Clinton's approach to Social Security had been a bland call for a "national dialogue." But when President Bush had the courage to take on the "third rail of politics," Democrats poohpoohed any suggestion that Social Security was in crisis, even though leaders of both parties knew that absent drastic reform the system would become insolvent in the lifetimes of their children and grandchildren.

Regardless, Democrats steadfastly blocked President Bush's effort to reform the system. Senator Harry Reid was one of those who obstructed the president's efforts, denying a problem existed. Yet Reid was one of the many Democratic politicians who had earlier insisted the system was in trouble. During his Senate race against John Ensign in 1998, Reid adamantly opposed tax cuts, saying he believed Social Security was on shaky ground. And, he opposed a constitutional amendment for a balanced budget because it did not prohibit the spending of Social Security funds.[61]

"It's a Crisis the President's Created, Period!"

But in 2005, when President Bush was lobbying for reform, Harry Reid stood in the way, saying, "Social Security is not in crisis. It's a crisis the president's created, period.... The president has never seen a crisis he hasn't created.... [Bush is] exaggerating the solvency. I've indicated that the Social Security program is strong, it's viable." Reid said that his party would not sit down with the president to discuss the issue until "he takes privatization off the table." When CNN's Judy Woodruff responded that even Federal Reserve Board chairman Alan Greenspan believed problems existed with Social Security that needed to be addressed "urgently," Reid said, "Judy, you understand, I hope, that I'm not a big ... Alan Greenspan fan. I voted against him the last two times. I think he's one of the biggest political hacks we have in Washington." Reid closed the discussion by saying the president understands "Social Security is not in crisis ... and that's why he wants to privatize it, to destroy it."[62]

Congresswoman Nancy Pelosi echoed Reid's thoughts, telling *FOX News Sunday*'s Chris Wallace that Social Security was not in crisis.[63] Senator Edward Kennedy also scoffed at the idea that Social Security was in crisis.[64] Senator John Kerry, still campaigning after his failed presidential run, told NBC's Tim Russert that "President Bush is hyping a phony crisis.... All you need to do to move Social Security into safety, well into the twenty-second century ... is to roll back part of George Bush's tax cut today. His tax cut takes three times the deficit of what is contained in Social Security.... The president's plan on Social Security is not only dangerous for Social Security, it's dangerous for the fiscal long-term health of our country."[65] Russert, of course, did not follow up by pointing out to Kerry that President Bush's tax cuts did not deplete federal revenues, but increased them.

Senator Boxer, another Democrat leading the hypocrisy offensive against Social Security reform—since she had insisted, along with

Al Gore and the others, that we must "save Social Security first"—attacked President Bush, saying he was trying to destroy Social Security. "Social Security is not in crisis, is not bankrupt and is not collapsing," she said in a speech at the San Francisco Senior Center at Aquatic Park. Bush, she said, was using "scare tactics and false information" to trick the people into supporting his partial privatization proposal.[66]

In addition to saying Republicans were trying to destroy Social Security with Bush's partial privatization plan, Democrats said Bush had proposed the plan as a sop to his big corporate friends on Wall Street. That is, the president was interested in allowing people to invest some of their payroll tax monies into private accounts—not to generate greater returns on those monies, but to enrich the coffers of the brokerage firms and the corporations in which the taxpayers would invest their funds. John Kerry shamelessly made this point during his presidential campaign.

He argued that financial services firms would receive a windfall under the Bush plan. Jason Furman, Kerry's economic policy director, said, "This study makes it clear when you choose individual accounts, seniors get hurt, the economy gets hurt, and the only institutions that benefit are the financial institutions that get nearly $1 trillion in additional revenues."[67] As usual, Democrats were more interested in preventing corporate profits than in reforming the system. Even if these management fees could be more than absorbed through reform and the overall Social Security system made more flush, Democrats opposed it because the plan would *also* benefit "big" corporations.

Liberal pundits also tried to block Social Security reform. The *New York Times*'s Paul Krugman had written in 1996 that there was a Social Security crisis "just over the horizon." But when President Bush promoted his reform proposal Krugman flatly denied there was much of a problem at all. Like the Democratic politicians, Krugman argued that the Republicans' motivation in pushing for private accounts was to destroy, not save, Social Security.[68]

Regardless of what Democrats now say, there truly is a looming crisis concerning Social Security—and Medicare, for that matter. Democrats are being dishonest to claim otherwise. They grossly distort the financial picture when discussing Social Security by implying that Social Security has some great asset pool that will extend its solvency long into the future. Most Social Security assets are not cash, but government bonds, which are, essentially, accounts receivable. The payment of these bonds is guaranteed by the government. So far, so good. But since they are guaranteed by the very same government, these accounts receivable are offset by an equal government liability. The problem is that when the accounts come due, the same government that is paying Social Security benefits has to pay off the bonds. The money to pay off those bonds isn't sitting around in some vault somewhere. It will have to come from future general revenues. It would be different if the bonds were guaranteed by third parties so that their payment would not cause an equal depletion of government assets. But such is not the case.

The time is rapidly approaching (2018 is the current estimate) when Social Security benefits will exceed payroll-tax collections. Not long thereafter (around 2042), the interest on the bonds will also be depleted. It is true that there will still be payroll taxes coming in, but because of demographic changes, they will only cover a projected 75 percent of the benefits to be paid out—and it will get increasingly worse from that point forward.[69] The government, to fund the Social Security shortfall, will have to call in its I.O.U.s. The bonds can only be paid off by increases in taxes, reductions in Social Security benefits, or further government borrowing. To make matters worse, it has been estimated that we will lose $600 billion for every year we ignore the problem.[70]

Proponents of partial privatization insist the entire crisis can be averted if we restructure Social Security to permit people to divert some of their payroll taxes into private accounts. Jack Kemp reports that "the chief actuary of Social Security has scored several different reform proposals based upon personal retirement accounts as achieving full solvency without cutting benefits, raising taxes, or raising the retirement age." According to Kemp, numerous studies have shown that through this type of plan, benefits can actually increase "while totally eliminating the program's long-run unfunded liability."[71]

While reasonable people can certainly disagree with Kemp's assertions, reasonable people can't conduct a debate when one party insists on scaremongering instead of addressing the issues. As long as Democrats refuse to treat this subject seriously and instead choose to inject fear into the hearts of seniors with the lie that President Bush and Republicans want to destroy Social Security, meaningful reform is nearly impossible.

Democrats demonstrated their true "commitment" to bipartisanship and Social Security reform during the president's State of the Union speech in 2006. When President Bush criticized Congress for not acting on his Social Security proposal, Democrats stood in self-congratulatory, mocking applause. Nothing could have better illustrated their penchant for unapologetically placing their obstructionist partisan politics above the national interest.

PART III

The Roots of the Bankruptcy

CHAPTER TEN

"I Hate the Way He Walks"

The solo unifying theme of today's Democratic Party, its raison d'être, is its singular hatred for President George Bush.

In September 2003, liberal columnist Jonathan Chait outlined this hatred:

> I hate President George W. Bush. There, I said it. I think his policies rank him among the worst presidents in U.S. history. And, while I'm tempted to leave it at that, the truth is that I hate him for less substantive reasons, too. I hate the inequitable way he has come to his economic and political achievements and his utter lack of humility (disguised behind transparently false modesty) at having done so....I hate the way he walks— shoulders flexed, elbows splayed out from his sides like a

teenage boy feigning machismo. I hate the way he talks—blustery self-assurance masked by a pseudo-populist twang. I even hate the things that everybody seems to like about him. I hate his lame nickname-bestowing—a way to establish one's social superiority beneath a veneer of chumminess....And, while most people who meet Bush claim to like him, I suspect that if I got to know him personally, I would hate him even more.

To make clear his feelings were not unique, Chait went on to explain that others share his view:

There seem to be quite a few of us Bush haters. I have friends who have a viscerally hostile reaction to the sound of his voice or describe his existence as a constant oppressive force in their daily psyche. Nor is this phenomenon limited to my personal experience. Pollster Geoff Garin, speaking to the *New York Times*, called Bush hatred "as strong as anything I've experienced in twenty-five years now of polling." Columnist Robert Novak described it as a "hatred...that I have never seen in forty-four years of campaign watching."

It is an intense, widespread, and persistent hatred indeed. As recently as July 7, 2006, the *San Francisco Chronicle*'s Mark Morford wrote:

It is like some sort of weird, painful rash on your face that makes you embarrassed to walk out the door, and so you sit there day after day, waiting for it to go away, slathering on ointment and Bactine and scotch. And still it lingers. Some days the pain is so searing and hot you want to cut off your own head with a nail file. Other days it is numb and pain-free and seemingly OK, to the point where you think it might finally be all gone and you allow yourself a whisper of a positive feeling, right up until you look in the mirror, and scream.

George W. Bush is just like that.

Everyone I know has had enough. Everyone I know is just about done. There is this threshold of deadened disgust, this point where the body simply resigns itself to the pain, where the disease, the poison, has seeped so deeply into the bones that you just have to laugh and shrug it all off and go for a drink. Or ten.[1]

A website called LinkCrusader reportedly provided links to some nine hundred anti-Bush websites, including SmirkingChimp, BushOnCrack, BushandCheneySuck, Bushes of Hazard, and AmBushed.[2]

Bush has been accused of stealing the 2000 election, lying about Iraqi WMD to get us into the war, and invading Iraq for oil—not in the sense of protecting the free flow of oil for America, but to enrich Dick Cheney and other corporate pals. His critics say he let Osama bin Laden's family escape the country before the September 11 attacks, which he knew about in advance and permitted to happen. He timed the capture of Saddam Hussein for maximum political benefit. He is intentionally abusing and torturing enemy detainees and spying on unsuspecting American grandmothers. He orchestrated a negligently delinquent federal response to hurricane Katrina because of his racism. Truth be told, he was even responsible for the hurricane itself, because he has refused to agree to the Kyoto

Protocol on global warming. There is just no issue, no calamity, no mishap, no unfortunate turn of events the Democrats will not blame on Bush for political gain.

The Democrats have become a one-note traveling band. Their devotion to undermining the president has been unremitting since 2000—even at the expense of damaging America's reputation, something they profess to care about. According to their unquestioned dogma, he is at once a simpleton puppet of Vice President Dick Cheney and a Machiavellian schemer. He is a unidimensional man without vision and relentlessly set in his ways, unable to admit mistakes and adjust his policies. He is an enemy of free speech, an autocrat, a theocrat, and a neoconservative imperialist. He promotes democracy for the rest of the world, but suppresses it here at home. He is the biggest liar in the history of the presidency—and he lies about things that matter, that get people killed. He is the personification of evil.

"We Need to Remember the Enemy Here Is George Bush"

Democratic politicians and pundits alike have been beside themselves over Bush—and have spoken about him in almost apocalyptic terms. Senator Robert Byrd said, "This republic is at its greatest danger in its history because of this administration." Commentator Bill Moyers, in a June 2003 speech at the Democrats' Take Back America conference, described the Bush presidency as a "deliberate, intentional destruction of the United States of America." He also condemned "the unholy alliance between government and wealth" and said "compassionate conservatism" was just conservative spin that makes "the rape of America sound like a consensual date."

"Right-wing wrecking crews" commissioned by Bush and his congressional allies, charged Moyers, were trying to bankrupt the government and privatize public services to pay off corporate campaign contributors. If not stopped, they would dismantle "every last brick of the social contract."[3]

Senator Hillary Clinton, in an NPR interview during her book tour, echoed Moyers's sentiments. "There's a very concerted effort with a right-wing agenda to turn the clock back on America, and the administration in Washington today is one of the most radical and reactionary...that we've ever had in American history."[4]

Their animosity for Bush is so consuming that many Democrats lose all sense of decorum. Senator Harry Reid, speaking to a group of high school students in Las Vegas, called the president "a loser," while discussing civics, of all things.[5] The statement was particularly inappropriate given that President Bush, at the time Reid uttered it, was landing on foreign soil. Though Reid called the White House to apologize for the remark, he refused to apologize for having called him "a liar" a few weeks before[6] and even seemed proud of it. When an interviewer for *Rolling Stone* told him, "You've called Bush a loser," Reid responded, "And a liar." When the interviewer pointed out he had apologized for the "loser" remark, Reid said, "But never for the liar, have I?"[7]

This bravado is typical of Reid, the Democrats' Senate minority leader. He has accused Bush and the Republicans of being "drunk with power" and destroying public education.[8] He called Justice Clarence Thomas an "embarrassment"[9] and California Supreme Court justice Janice Rogers Brown—an Alabama-born African American nominated by Bush to the federal appeals bench—a "woman who wants to take us back to the Civil War."[10]

Some Democratic leaders let slip their view of the identity of America's real enemy. Howard Dean said, "We need to remember the enemy here is George Bush.... This president has told more lies than George Washington ever denied telling." The president, according to Dean, has "no understanding of defense" and conducts diplomacy by "petulance."[11] Senator John Edwards said Bush is "incapable of cracking down on corporate cheating, and has declared war on work." And Congressman Dick Gephardt called Bush both a "miserable failure" and "the worst president."[12]

Mainstream liberal pundits were no more restrained than Democratic politicians. Columnist Michael Kinsley wrote, "In terms of the power he now claims, without significant challenge, George W. Bush is now the closest thing in a long time to dictator of the world."[13] The *New York Times*'s Maureen Dowd wrote, "Mr. Bush, whose administration drummed up fake evidence to trick us into war with Iraq, sticking our troops in an immoral position with no exit strategy, won on 'moral issues.'...With [the Bush] crowd, it's hard to imagine what would constitute overreaching. Invading France?"[14]

The *Times*'s Paul Krugman wrote, "There is no way to be both honest and polite about what has happened in these past three years.... On the fiscal front, this administration has used deceptive accounting to ram through repeated long-run tax cuts in the face of mounting deficits.... On the foreign policy front, this administration hyped the threat from Iraq.... It's impolite to say that Mr. Bush has damaged our national security with his military adventurism, but it would be dishonest to pretend otherwise...[Bush's] business career is a story of murky deals and insider privilege."[15]

Bush Derangement Syndrome

The Left's antipathy for George W. Bush is so irrational that columnist and psychiatrist Charles Krauthammer coined a term for it: Bush Derangement Syndrome. He described the condition as "the acute onset of paranoia in otherwise normal people in reaction to the policies, the presidency—nay—the very existence of George W. Bush."[16] The irrationality of the Left's visceral hostility toward Bush is all the more apparent, considering he has governed as a moderate on a number of issues. His domestic budgets, from a conservative viewpoint, were indefensible. His federal expenditures on education have been astronomical. He created a new federal entitlement for prescription drugs. For way too long he doggedly resisted conservative demands for more border control. He signed a draconian, First Amendment–encroaching campaign finance bill—favored by the Left—while saying the Supreme Court would probably declare it unconstitutional.

But the president's moderate policies don't register with the Left; facts can't appease its voracious hatred of this president.

Entertainment Hatred

Much of Hollywood, of course, hates Bush with a white-hot passion. America is regularly treated to Bush-hating rants from the stars. *Two Towers* actor Andy Serkis carried a "no war for oil" poster at the 2003 Academy Awards ceremony.[17] In his Academy Award acceptance speech, film producer Michael Moore said, "We like non-fiction and we live in fictitious times. We live in the time where we have fictitious election results that elect a fictitious president. We live in a time where we have a man sending us to war for fictitious reasons. Whether it's the fiction of duct tape or fiction of orange alerts we are against this war, Mr. Bush. Shame on you, Mr. Bush. Shame on you."[18] Moore, who has been elevated and glorified by the Left, showed his support for our troops in Iraq with this gem, "The Iraqis who have risen up against the occupation are not 'insurgents' or 'terrorists' or 'The Enemy.' They are the revolution, the Minutemen, and their numbers will grow—and they will win."[19]

Actor Charlie Sheen donned his tinfoil cap to join the kooks— to call them mere conspiracy theorists would be unduly harsh to conspiracy theorists—who believe that the World Trade Center Twin Towers were felled by "controlled demolitions." Sheen said on the GCN Radio Network he doesn't believe the government's official story that "nineteen amateurs with box cutters [took] over four commercial airliners and [hit] 75 percent of their targets."[20] Reportedly, actor Ed Asner applauded Sheen's "bold and brave stance" and called for a real investigation of the events of September 11.[21]

New York theatrical productions routinely deride President Bush. *Bush Wars: Musical Revenge* attacks "the disgraceful agenda" of the Bush administration. One of its dance numbers depicts Bush and Osama bin Laden taking their mothers to lunch. It features a mock duet between the characters of Bush and Karl Rove and has Vice President Cheney in a bedroom scene. *Bush is Bad*, "the musical cure for the blue-state blues," lampoons the president's "colorful turns of phrase" and promotes his impeachment. In the website for the musical a grand piano is dropped on the president's head. *Laughing Liberally* bills itself as an evening of stand-up comedy at Bush's expense.[22]

Bashing Bush has become a cottage industry for New York book publishers. A sampling: *The Lies of George W. Bush*, by David Corn; *Bushwacked*, by Molly Ivins and Lou Dubose; *The Great Unraveling*, by Paul Krugman; *Big Lies*, by Joe Conason; *The Five Biggest Lies Bush Told About Iraq*, by Christopher Scheer, Lakshmi Chaudhry and Robert Scheer; *Big Bush Lies, The 20 Most Telling Lies of President George W. Bush*, edited by Jerry Barrett; *The Bush-Haters Handbook: A Guide to the Most Appalling Presidency of the Past 100 Years*, by Jack Huberman; *All the President's Spin; George W. Bush, the Media, and the Truth*, by Ben Fritz; and *Lies and the Lying Liars Who Tell Them*, by Al Franken.[23]

Listeners of Air America, the upstart liberal radio network, were routinely hateful about President Bush. *New York Daily News* columnist Michael Goodwin received a number of voice-mail and e-mail messages after a column in which he "panned" Air America Radio. Goodwin noted that the network's hosts made frequent sex jokes at the expense of the Catholic Church and said President Bush and Defense Secretary Donald Rumsfeld should be shot.

A seventy-seven-year-old lady from Connecticut told Goodwin, "I think Air America is a breath of fresh air, and we liberals love it....You didn't like what they said about the president on the Randi Rhodes program? Too bad about you. I believe that Osama bin Laden had it right: His throat should be slit." Goodwin said he received this call on the very day Americans were seeing the horrible pictures of the terrorists' beheading of Nick Berg. Though host Al Franken assured Goodwin there was no literal intent of violence, others who responded to Goodwin's column were certainly venomous. One wrote—after calling Goodwin "a brainless right-wing idiot," "Hating Rumsfeld is the most patriotic thing anyone can do."[24]

The Worst President in History

Many liberals deny their animosity toward President Bush is emotionally based. In their "objective" view, he is a terrible president whose policies are destroying the country. In its May 2006 issue, *Rolling Stone* magazine featured a cover story by liberal professor Sean Wilentz titled "The Worst President in History?" Wilentz wrote, "Barring a cataclysmic event...there seems to be little the administration can do to avoid being ranked on the lowest tier of U.S. presidents. And that may be the best-case scenario. Many historians are now wondering whether Bush, in fact, will be remembered as the very worst president in history."

Wilentz reported that in 2004 an informal poll was conducted of 415 historians by the "nonpartisan" History News Network. Eighty-one percent of these "objective" analysts deemed the Bush administration a failure. Wilentz conceded that historians tend to be more liberal than the citizenry as a whole. But to him that's largely irrelevant, because, "Contrary to popular stereotypes, historians are generally a cautious bunch. We assess the past from widely divergent points of view and are deeply concerned about being viewed as fair and accurate by our colleagues. When we make historical judgments, we are acting not as voters or even pundits, but as scholars who must evaluate all the evidence, good, bad or indifferent."

University of Virginia professor of politics Gerard Alexander disagreed. Wilentz's list of Bush's supposed failures, he pointed out, "is rather selective." Wilentz cited Bush's "unprovoked, preventive warfare," his "discredited" supply side economics, his "anemic" job growth, and every liberal's current favorite, "Bush's subversion of the other branches of government to create a 'presidential absolutism.'" These examples are hardly conceded to be objective policy failures; many believe they are demonstrable successes. That Wilentz depicts them as objective failures is a stunning admission of liberalism's arrogant mindset.

Bush, the Simple-Minded, "The Dapples and Howevers"

Liberals depict Bush as simple-minded, devoid of nuance, and seeing the world in crude, absolute terms of good and evil, not unlike the way they tagged President Reagan. Just as they hysterically recoiled when Reagan dared to call the Soviet Union an "evil empire," their sensibilities were offended when the unpolished, brazen cowboy president identified Iraq, Iran, and North Korea as an "axis of evil." President Clinton's secretary of state Warren Christopher said "It was a speechwriter's dream and a policymaker's nightmare." Harvard's Kennedy School of Government professor Graham Allison said, "It was harmful both conceptually and operationally... The reaction of the world and the North Korea debacle demonstrate that it was a mistake."[25]

Former secretary of state Madeleine Albright said Bush's "axis" designation was a "big mistake" because it lumped together the three countries with a "cookie-cutter approach" and could cause America to lose international support.[26] She was particularly miffed that Bush had "single-handedly destroyed" the relationship with North Korea she had begun to establish for the Clinton administration. She lamented that many in the international community believed the United States had "lost [its] mind."[27]

"Evil" is "too heavy and radioactive a word," said Joseph Montville, director of the Preventive Diplomacy program at the Center for Strategic and International Studies in Washington, D.C.

"You can't make a deal with evil. You can only kill it." University of Hawaii professor Dae Sook Suh said the "cowboy language" was considered rude in Asia.[28]

Liberal editorialists everywhere were wringing their hands over Bush's supposed alienation of our European allies. He "surprised, alarmed and irritated many in Europe."[29] They dubbed the "axis of evil" slogan "simplistic." The *Kansas City Star*'s Bill Tammeus wrote, "Bush drifts into unsupportable sermonizing when he sets up a stark 'evil versus good' dichotomy with 'no in-between.' Americans can stand for the good, represent the good, support the good, but we cannot claim we are always and everywhere good. Life—especially public life—is too complicated to make such simplistic claims. History is complex. When told fairly, it cannot be reduced to morality tales in which all actors proceed from pure motives. Bush's claim that either 'you're with us or you're against us' also represents a simplicity that can't be sustained.... Language that recognizes only black and white but not gray may seem politically useful, but, in the end, it's destructive because it doesn't reflect nuanced reality—all the shades and flaws, the dapples and howevers of the world."[30]

The *St. Louis Post-Dispatch* called it "the rhetorical and ideological progeny of Ronald Reagan's 'evil empire'—both bold and simplistic."[31] The *Boston Globe* said it was "a gratuitous blunder" and "simplistic."[32] David Lazarus, in the *San Francisco Chronicle*, called it a "simplistic slogan."[33] Former career diplomat Jack Perry wrote, "There is stark danger in the belief that we Americans represent Good while our adversaries represent Evil.... There is peril in shouting to the world that we see an 'axis of evil' in Iran, Iraq, and North Korea, and to assert our right to remove their rulers from power. There is folly in the claim that America has every right to 'weapons of mass destruction' but others do not—and that we have the entire right to say who has the right and who does not."[34]

Former president Jimmy Carter, like others, also criticized Bush's "axis" language as "overly simplistic and counterproductive." "I think it will take years before we can repair the damage done by that statement," he said at a conference on terrorism's impact at Emory University.[35] Carter said that the statement has "thrown a monkey wrench in the efforts to bring peace to Korea," and it set back our move toward reconciliation with Iran.[36]

Bush Is Hitler

One of the fringe Left's favorite smear tactics is to compare President Bush and Republicans to Hitler, or Nazis in general. Conservative writer Victor Davis Hanson reported that this "crazy popular analogy"—Bush=Hitler—yielded some 1,350,000 matches on a Google search. Leftist PAC MoveOn.org produced political ads likening Bush to Hitler. In one ad Hitler appears ranting in German with the "translation" on the screen, "We have taken new measures to protect our homeland. I believe that I am acting in accordance with the will of the Almighty Creator." Hitler gradually morphs into Bush, who then says, "God told me to strike at al Qaeda, and I struck them, and then He instructed me to strike at Saddam, which I did." The ad closes with the words, "Sound familiar?"[37]

Another ad was replete with waving Nazi flags and fawning German crowds looking on at Hitler in one of his vintage speeches under the caption "A Nation Warped by Lies." Other captions in various clips were "Lies Fuel Fear," "Fear Fuels Aggression," "Invasion," and "Occupation." The clincher caption is "What Were War Crimes in 1945 Is Foreign Policy in 2003." The ad closes with a picture of Bush raising his hand at his inauguration, in a Nazi "Sig Heil!" gesture.[38] After Republican complaints, MoveOn.org promised to discontinue the ads.

All over the web, you could find Photoshopped images of Bush as Hitler or in Nazi uniform. Garrison Keillor said Republicans had:

> transmogrified into the party of hairy-backed swamp developers and corporate shills, faith-based economists, fundamentalist bullies with Bibles, Christians of convenience, freelance racists, misanthropic fratboys, shrieking midgets of AM radio, tax cheats, nihilists in golf pants, brownshirts in pinstripes, sweatshop tycoons, hacks, fakirs, aggressive dorks, Lamborghini libertarians, people who believe Neil Armstrong's moonwalk was filmed in Roswell, New Mexico, little honkers out to diminish the rest of us, Newt's evil spawn and their Etch-A-Sketch president, a dull and rigid man suspicious of the free flow of information and of secular institutions, whose philosophy is a jumble of badly sutured body parts trying to walk. Republicans: The No.1 reason the rest of the world thinks we're deaf, dumb, and dangerous.[39]

Author Hugh Pearson was repulsed enough by the Republican National Convention that he invoked Hitler in describing it. "As I watched Tuesday night's network coverage of the unrelenting political propaganda hour known as the Republican National Convention, the first thought that came to mind was of old newsreels of those self-congratulatory Nazi rallies held in Germany during the reign of Adolf Hitler." Pearson then strained, laboriously, to substantiate his claim, culminating in this rich, final paragraph: "Given the tone of what Republicans have been telling us—and the way they are delivering the message—let us not forget one other thing: Hitler was decisive, too."[40]

Hollywood also became part of the Bush-Hitler mania. Michael Moore, in his book *Dude, Where's My Country?* wrote, "The Patriot Act is as un-American as *Mein Kampf.*" In a television interview he said, "The Patriot Act is the first step.... If people don't speak up against this, you end up with something like they had in Germany."[41] In the movie *The Matrix: Reloaded*, when one character tells another about evil, images of Hitler and Bush appear on video screens. In CBS's mini-series *Hitler: The Rise of Evil*, an implicit comparison was reportedly made between "the burning of the Reichstag and the suspension of Germany's constitution" and September 11 and the enactment of the Patriot Act.

Liberal academia dabbled in the Bush-Nazi comparison as well. Retired Western Michigan University professor Edward Jayne said, "Like Hitler, Bush curtails civil liberties and depends on detention centers (i.e. concentration camps) such as Guantánamo Bay."[42] Radford University professor of philosophy and religious studies Glenn T. Martin wrote, "Notice that these titles, 'Patriot' and 'Homeland,' sound very much like the language of the Nazis. A common slogan of the Nazi regime was 'the highest freedom is a noble slavery of the heart.'...Do we have the courage and integrity to speak out now, before it is too late? Or will we continue to freely shop in our large department stores for gifts for family and friends—as they did in Nazi Germany?"[43]

Comedienne Margaret Cho took umbrage at the uproar over the Bush-Hitler comparison. At the MoveOn.org Award ceremony she said, "Despite all of this stupid bulls— that the Republican National Committee, or whatever the f— they call them, that they were saying that they're all angry about how two of these ads were comparing Bush to Hitler? I mean, out of thousands of submissions, they find two. They're like f'ing looking for Hitler in a haystack... George Bush is not Hitler. He would be, if he f-ing applied himself."[44] Bob Fertik, of Democrats.com, wrote, "Americans did not vote for fascism—but the fascists now control all three branches of our government."[45]

After taking heat for comparing Bush to a Nazi, cartoonist Ted Rall attempted to defend himself. Rall wrote, "Lately we're being told that it's either (a) inappropriate or (b) untrue to refer to Bush's illegitimate junta as Nazi, neo-Nazi, or neofascist. Because, you know, you're not necessarily a Nazi just because you seize power like one, take advantage of a national Reichstag Fire-like tragedy like one, build concentration and death camps like one, start unprovoked wars like one, Red-bait your liberal opponents like one or create a national security apparatus that behaves like something a Nazi would create and even has a Nazi-sounding name... Of course there are differences [between the Bush administration and Hitler.] Hitler, for example, was legally elected... I'll be happy to stop comparing Bush to Hitler when he stops acting like him."[46] Ted Rall, you might remember, made himself a poster boy for leftists who insist they oppose the war, but support the troops. He said, "The word 'hero' has been bandied about a lot to refer to anyone killed in Afghanistan or Iraq. But anyone who voluntarily goes to Afghanistan or Iraq is fighting for an evil cause under an evil commander in chief."[47]

Other entertainers couldn't resist offering their wisdom. Singer Linda Ronstadt used the Nazi analogy—indirectly—to smear Bush supporters. "People don't realize that by voting Republican, they voted against themselves....I worry that some people are entertained by the idea of this war. They don't know anything about the Iraqis, but they're angry and frustrated in their own lives. It's like Germany, before Hitler took over. The economy was bad and people felt kicked around. They looked for a scapegoat. Now we've got a new bunch of Hitlers."[48]

This was the same tolerant Linda Ronstadt who said, "It's a real conflict for me when I go to a concert and find out somebody in the audience is a Republican or fundamental Christian. It can cloud my enjoyment. I'd rather not know."[49] Comedienne Sandra Bernhard said, "The real terrorist threats are George W. Bush and his band of brown-shirted thugs." Musician Rickie Lee Jones said, "My skin crawls when I think of the first week after September 11. I was looking out of the window and there were people marching down the street carrying flags. It reminded me of spontaneous, angry Nazis and I thought, 'Oh, man, we are in a lot of trouble.'"[50] Beastie Boys rapper MCA said, "[Bush] is just a sick f—. I think we'd be hard-pressed to get someone worse than Bush."[51]

Sheldon Drobny, co-founder of liberal talk radio network Air America, was also unhesitant to make the Bush-Nazi comparison. In a column he penned for MakeThemAccountable.com, he wrote, "War benefits the armaments and oil industries. The corporate masters and their current spokesman, George W. Bush, promote a dangerous policy of pre-emptive warfare. They use exactly the same excuses Hitler used to sell to the public his maniacal desire to conquer Europe....The [businessmen] who were rational must have known Hitler was an extremist. Nevertheless, they were willing to ignore a dangerous and self-destructive policy for a shortsighted profit incentive. Among the results were the deaths of nearly forty million people and the destruction of Germany. A similarly shortsighted profit incentive by today's war entrepreneurs may lead us into a holocaust far greater than the one caused by Nazi Germany."[52]

Actress/activist Janeane Garofalo, who would later become a talk-show host for Air America, said that "the dumb and the mean love patriotism." Concerning conservatives, she said, "What you have now is people that are closet racists, misogynists, homophobes, and people who love a titled playing field and the politics of exclusion identifying as conservative."[53] Of the Patriot Act she said, "It is in fact a conspiracy of the 43rd Reich."[54]

Leftist billionaire George Soros, who has poured untold funds into MoveOn.org and other leftist organizations and causes, was also fond of the Bush-Hitler analogy. Speaking of his desire to see President Bush defeated in 2004, he said, "It is the central focus of my life." The presidential race "is a matter of life and death." "America, under Bush," he said, "is a danger to the world. And I'm willing to put my money where my mouth is.... When I hear Bush say, 'You're either with us or against us,' it reminds me of the Germans." This statement, said Soros, brought back memories of his experiences under Nazi and Soviet regimes.[55]

Commentator Dave Lindorff wrote, "It's going a bit far to compare the Bush of 2003 to the Hitler of 1933. Bush is simply not the orator that Hitler was. But comparisons of the Bush administration's fear-mongering tactics to those practiced so successfully and with such terrible results by Hitler and Goebbels on the German people and their Weimar Republic are not at all out of line."[56] According to

Lindorff, in his piece for the leftist website Counterpunch, Hitler "would be proud that an American president is emulating him in so many ways."[57] *National Review*'s Byron York noted that "Lindorff is not an obscure, solitary blogger." He "has contributed to *The Nation* and *Salon*, and has appeared on National Public Radio." York also pointed out that Counterpunch is hardly an unknown website, claiming to have some sixty thousand daily visitors. These daily visitors were treated, for example, to Wayne Madsen also accusing Bush of "borrowing liberally from Hitler's play book."[58]

York pointed out that the ideas of left-wing blogs have a habit of moving into the mainstream. *Vanity Fair*—not long after Lindorff's piece was published—printed a letter from a reader who compared a photo of arch-villain neoconservative Richard Perle to a photo of Nazi propaganda master Joseph Goebbels. The reader said, "Here it is: the same arrogance, the same malice toward the photographer, the same all around creepiness. Perle isn't the first government official to use deceit and fear mongering to force an extremist, irrational, and ultimately violent view on an entire nation or globe." Instead of throwing the letter in the garbage, notes York, *Vanity Fair* gave it prominent placement "in a special box with Perle and Goebbels photos side-by-side."[59]

Comparing Bush to Hitler has hardly been the exclusive province of the fringe blogs. Mainstream media and some Democratic politicians have been every bit as guilty. Former vice president Al Gore said, "The administration works closely with a network of 'rapid response' digital brownshirts who work to pressure reporters and their editors for 'undermining support for our troops.' "[60] Senator Dick Durbin compared Guantánamo Bay guards—serving under Bush as commander in chief—to Nazis and Communists. Robert F.

Kennedy, Jr., in his book *Crimes Against Nature: How George W. Bush and His Corporate Pals Are Plundering the Country and Hijacking Our Democracy*, couldn't resist the Hitler temptation—as if his title weren't slanderous enough. He wrote, "These elected governments used the provocation of terror attacks, continual wars, and invocations of patriotism and homeland security to privatize the commons, tame the press, muzzle criticism by opponents, and turn government over to corporate control. 'It is always a simple matter to drag the people along,' noted Hitler's sidekick, Hermann Goering, 'whether it is a democracy, or a fascist dictatorship.'... The White House has clearly grasped the lesson."[61]

He Stifles Dissent and Calls Us "Unpatriotic"

The Nazi comparisons weren't the only outrageous hyperbole in the Left's anti-Bush arsenal. Columnist Mark Morford, for the *San Francisco Chronicle*, said that the good news about America's dire state of affairs was that "it really can't get much worse.... George W. Bush gives me hope... because he has led the country into a zone where the only way to go—morally, spiritually, economically—is up. Is out." Morford said that Bush's "narrow and myopic political ideology" is being discredited and his "vicious leadership circle" is being exposed. He said that Bush and the GOP, for over four years, have "shut down the media and demonized all voices of dissent."[62]

One of the Left's common complaints is that Bush is a menace to the Constitution and Bill of Rights. Journalist Jill Nelson wrote, "I feel more vulnerable and frightened now than I ever have in my fifty years on the planet. It is the United States government I am afraid of. In less than two years the Bush administration has used the attacks of September 11 to manipulate our fear of terrorism and desire for revenge into a blank check to blatantly pursue imperialist objectives intentionally and to begin the rollback of the Constitution, the Bill of Rights, and most of the advances of the twentieth century."[63]

To many liberals, Bush's reaction to the constant harangue of his attackers is tantamount to chilling speech. When President Clinton was perfecting the politics of personal destruction against those with bona fide claims against him—like Special Counsel Kenneth Starr—the Left vigorously defended his right to defend himself, even when it involved viciously slandering his opponents. But when President Bush so much as lifts a finger to answer his accusers, he becomes an enemy of free expression. When Bush questions the motives of his accusers, he is said to be deflecting attention from his inability to defend his policies. *St. Petersburg Times* columnist Robyn E. Blumner wrote that Bush is so incapable of formulating a response and articulating a defense for his policy that he resorts to bullying, name-calling, and using authorities to silence his critics.[64] Democratic National Committee chairman Howard Dean said the Bush administration had revived the "McCarthy era," in stifling political dissent.[65]

Democrats are especially sensitive to the suggestion that they're soft on security or insufficiently supportive of the troops. When Bush or other administration officials have criticized Democrats for failing to support the war effort, Democrats have interpreted it as a move to label them as "unpatriotic."[66]

On *FOX News Sunday*, in response to a question from host Chris Wallace about Congressman John Murtha's comments on Iraq, Defense Secretary Donald Rumsfeld said that our words have "effects." They have an effect on the morale of the troops: "they have to wonder whether what they're doing makes sense." And, they have an effect on the enemy, who may conclude "maybe all we have to do is wait, and we'll win. . . . The battle is here in the United States."[67] Similarly, Vice President Cheney argued that the Democrats' constant drumbeat that Bush lied and manipulated intelligence on Iraq's WMD could undermine the troops in Iraq. Cheney said that such critics were responsible for "one of the most dishonest and reprehensible charges ever aired in this city [Washington, D.C.]. President Bush said that it was "irresponsible to do what [the Democrats] had done" in falsely claiming he deliberately misled the American people.[68]

Democrats were indignant that the administration was fighting back. Democrat strategist Robert Shrum said that Bush and Cheney were blaming Democrats for the situation in Iraq. But Bush and Cheney made no such claim, only that the Democrats' false charges could undermine our troop morale.[69]

On the Senate floor in November 2005, Senator John Kerry said it was disgusting that the administration would characterize Democratic criticism on Iraq as unpatriotic.[70] Kerry repeated the charge in a speech in Boston, in April 2006, thirty-five years to the date of his disgraceful remarks to the Senate Foreign Relations Committee slandering our soldiers in Vietnam. Referring to his 1971 remarks as "dissent," he said Americans have a right and an obligation to dissent against a president who is wrong. Kerry accused the Bush administration of stifling dissent and of wrongly branding critics as unpatriotic.[71]

Congressman John Lewis issued a press release scolding Cheney for trying to stifle dissent. He said, "It is the duty, it is the responsibility of American citizens and those who represent them in the U.S. Congress to speak up and speak out when they differ with the policies of their government. It is part of the noble tradition of our democracy. We have a constitutional right to dissent."[72]

Washington Post columnist Richard Cohen wrote, "Cheney, a man of ugly intolerance for dissent, should have been the first to go. His has been a miserable, dishonest performance—which he continues to this day."[73] One *Newsday* editorial, while admitting Democrats were exaggerating in their claims, still asserted that in defending himself, "Bush [was] equating dissent with treason."[74]

At no time have Bush or Cheney ever suggested that Democrats should not register legitimate dissent. They were not challenging their *right* to dissent, but the maliciously false content of their dissenting comments. The right to dissent is one of our most cherished freedoms and part of what makes America great. But that right carries with it a duty of responsibility and a measure of accountability, such as incurring the scorn of those you defame. The right to dissent does not exempt the critic's accountability for the substance of his remarks.[75] What Bush and Cheney were complaining about, in the words of Cheney, was the Democrats' "revisionism of the most corrupt and shameless variety."[76] To denounce someone for bearing false witness against you—and in the process undermining the troops and otherwise damaging the national interest—is completely different from trying to suppress noble dissent. But if the administration's response to the Democrats' attacks *was* an effort to curb free expression, *how much more so was* the Democrats counter-response?

Democrats can dish it out, but they can't take it. Based on their hysterical reaction, some liberals apparently believed Bush should stand silent before his accusers and refrain from defending himself. When Republicans accused Senate Minority Leader Harry

Reid of obstructionist tactics, Democrats, en masse, rose up to defend Reid by writing a group letter to President Bush to complain. "We urge you to keep your word about being a uniter and publicly halt these counterproductive attacks so that we are able to work together in a bipartisan manner and debate issues on the merits." Senator Schumer compared the Republican response to political knee-cappings.[77]

Funeral Politics

So deep is the liberals' hatred for Bush and Republicans that they've even been willing to contaminate the sacred atmosphere of funerals to vent their partisan animosity. They turned the funeral of Senator Paul Wellstone in 2002 into a veritable party convention.[78]

After the Wellstone theatrics, it was no surprise that Democrats reprised their m.o. at the funeral of Martin Luther King, Jr.'s widow, Coretta Scott King. During his remarks at the event, Reverend Joseph Lowery implicitly lit into President Bush, saying "We know now there were no weapons of mass destruction over there. But Coretta knew and we know that there are weapons of misdirection right down here. Millions without health insurance. Poverty abounds. For war, billions more, but no more for the poor."

Former president Jimmy Carter brazenly took shots at President Bush, who was sitting only three feet behind him as he spoke. He mentioned both wiretapping and the politics of race in his speech, alluding to Hurricane Katrina's victims. Carter said, "The efforts of Martin and Coretta to change America were not appreciated even at the highest level of our government. It was difficult for them personally, with the civil liberties of both husband and wife violated as they became the targets of secret government wiretapping, other surveillance, and, as you know, harassment from the FBI."[79] "We only have to recall the faces of those in Louisiana, Alabama, and Mississippi—those who were most devastated by Katrina—to know that there are not yet equal opportunities for all Americans."[80]

Not every black leader was appreciative of these comments. Roy Innis, chairman of the Congress of Racial Equality, described them as "crass" and "disrespectful." "It was an outrage for such behavior to be exhibited in the presence of the president of the United States, and it was particularly outrageous for it to occur at a funeral for a dignified lady, the wife of Martin Luther King, Jr.," said Innis.[81]

Some liberals rejected this criticism. Just as they accuse Bush of drawing first blood when he responds to his accusers, they argued that critics of the disgraceful politicization of the funeral were the ones at fault. John Nichols, in the *Capital Times*, said they were just trying to protect Bush "from even the mildest expressions of dissent." To Nichols, there was nothing inappropriate about the speakers' remarks. "The service provided the president with a healthy—if all too rare—dose of reality. Bush's policies are not popular, particularly with the African American community, and the president needed a gentle reminder of that fact,"[82] wrote Nichols—as if Bush could possibly forget the way he has been treated by the likes of Kweisi Mfume, Julian Bond, or Jesse Jackson.

CHAPTER ELEVEN

The Monster, the Witch-Burner, and the Architect of Torture

Democrats haven't limited their attacks to President Bush. They have also had a field day vilifying many in the president's inner circle. The presumption is that since Bush is bad, so are most of his people. The story line varies from Bush being the evil mastermind who surrounds himself with yes-men and women, to Bush being the puppet whose strings are pulled variously, by Rove, Cheney, Rice, or the neoconservative cabal.

Indeed, the press sometimes plays up the closeness of Bush's personal relationships, when it is not painting him as insular and isolated. National security analyst John Prados wrote that Condoleezza Rice learned early in Bush's first term that it was important that she establish a personal relationship with him. She talked sports and fitness and even worked out with him. It was because of the close relationship she cultivated with the president, according to Prados, that she was able to "stay out of the line of fire of the neocons who had fought her over Russia policy in the first Bush administration."[1]

At first the media line on Rice was that she was the only member of the Bush-Rice duo with any foreign policy expertise. They described her as "Bush's personal brain trust in foreign policy" whose job was "to make a complex and dangerous world seem simple and clear to President Bush" who sees "black and white" rather than shades of gray.[2] When *People* magazine named her one of "The 25 Most Intriguing People of 2001," it wrote, "Rice was a perfect choice to spackle over this president's geopolitical gaps and gaffes." She is "at the core of Bush's wartime brain trust."[3] Norman Kempster of the *Los Angeles Times* wrote, "Like Kissinger, who served in the Nixon and Ford administrations, Rice brings to the White House a reputation for intellectual brilliance that far outshines the public's perception of the president's brain power."[4] The *San Jose Mercury News* said that both Rice and Colin Powell "are what Bush is not, diligent students of U.S. foreign policy."[5]

"The Woman Is a Monster, a Monster, a Monster"

But it didn't take long for the media to turn on Rice. Given her "control" over administration foreign policy, she had to share much of the blame for the administration's bellicose proclivities, from identifying the "axis of evil" to its policies of preemptive military action and "unilateralism." *New York Times* columnist Thomas Friedman wrote, "President Bush thinks the axis of evil is Iran, Iraq, and North Korea, and the Europeans think it is Donald Rumsfeld,

Dick Cheney, and Condi Rice."[6] Later, the Left also began promoting the theory that both Rice and Bush were warned in advance about the September 11 attacks and did nothing to prevent them.

Congressman Henry Waxman requested a hearing of the House Committee on Government Reform into the question of whether the administration "misused the classification process" to conceal findings that federal aviation officials received multiple warnings of airline hijackings and suicide attacks before September 11. He wanted a committee inquiry into Condoleezza Rice's veracity in her statements, briefings, and testimony concerning this issue.[7] Uber-liberal columnist Joe Conason wrote that Rice dodged questions in her appearance before the 9-11 Commission and suggested that she and President Bush were too preoccupied with Iraq, missile defense, and other matters to pay sufficient attention to the "stream of warnings it received about al Qaeda."[8]

When President Bush nominated her to be secretary of state, the leftists stepped up their assaults. A series of liberal political cartoons took on a racist tone. Cartoonist Pat Oliphant depicted Rice as a parrot on Bush's arm. Daryl Cagle showed Rice with prominent buck teeth inside Colin Powell's enormous shoes. In a Matt Davies cartoon, a black couple, one named "Civil Rights Movement," and the other "Women's Rights Movement," were shown as disconsolate and standing under a banner that says "First Black, Female Warmonger Secretary of State—Historic Celebration." Jeff Danziger drew her "as a semi-literate mammy" with "big lips and buck teeth."[9]

Cartoonist Ted Rall actually referred in his caption to Rice as the president's "House Nigga." In his *Doonesbury* cartoon, Gary Trudeau had Bush calling Rice "Brown sugar." Bob Englehart depicted Rice as Mini-Me. John Sherffius showed Rice with her tongue sticking out and waving her hands under the caption, "The secretary of state is America's face to the world, George Bush."[10] Michelle D. Bernard of the Independent Women's Forum nicely summed up this disgrace. "The depiction of Dr. Condoleezza Rice by Jeff Danziger, Pat Oliphant, and Gary Trudeau as an Ebonics-speaking, big-lipped, black mammy who just loves her 'massa' is a disturbing trend in editorial cartoons. These cartoons take the racism of the liberals who profess respect and adoration for black Americans to a new level. It is revolting.'"[11]

Radio talk-show host Sly Sylvester, in Madison, Wisconsin, referred to Rice on the air as "Aunt Jemima." But when called on it, Sylvester didn't apologize, except to Aunt Jemima, saying, "It is with a heavy heart that I apologize this morning to Aunt Jemima. She wasn't a self-serving hack politician who got up in front of Congress and lied. Aunt Jemima didn't kowtow to Don Rumsfeld or Dick Cheney."[12]

Through all of this, where were Jesse Jackson and Al Sharpton to decry such overt racism? The Left, which is quick to denounce conservative racism where it doesn't exist, grants itself complete immunity from such charges. As La Shawn Barber wrote in her weblog, "If there is anyone left who believes all that liberal jive about how much they like black folks. . . . Just get your heads out of the sand. Don't expect any *high profile* liberal—black, white, or otherwise—to speak out against this. If they did, just one, I'd probably have a coronary."[13] Michelle Malkin wrote, "When it comes to minority conservatives, liberal bigotry knows no bounds. . . . There's nothing the Left hates more than a 'person of color' who is a person of substance and stature and intellect and independence first."[14]

Editorialists also weighed in on Rice. Whereas Rice was formerly depicted as Bush's foreign policy guru, she later became his loyal, unquestioning mouthpiece—changing from puppet master to puppet. The editors of the *New Republic* wrote, "[Rice] is absolutely loyal to the president, so deferential that, as *New York* magazine reported, at a Washington dinner party earlier this year, Rice casually and accidentally referred to her employer, George W. Bush, as her 'husband.'"[15]

Then, after detailing what they described as the miserable foreign policy failures of Bush's first term, they further commented on Bush's demand for loyalty. "Faced with these failures," they wrote, "you would think" Bush would retire the "architects" responsible for them—like Rice. But the Bush administration "doesn't punish incompetence. Instead it rewards it with extensions of tenure and promotions, so long as the incompetents prove their absolute loyalty." That is why Bush's decision to replace Colin Powell with Rice as secretary of state involved "perfect internal logic."[16] Powell wasn't enough of a team player and Rice was. It obviously didn't occur to the editors that President Bush didn't regard his first-term foreign policy record as one of failure and wanted to keep people on his team who shared his vision.

Liberal columnist Helen Thomas was more caustic. Newsmax.com reported that when its reporters asked her about President Bush's reelection she said, "My God, the man is a fascist—a fascist, I tell you." As for his nomination of Condoleezza Rice, she said, "I tell you, the woman is a monster, a monster, a monster." Thomas said Rice had lied about the Iraq war and "thousands had died." "The lady is a g-damn liar," she said.[17]

"Your Loyalty to the Mission Overwhelmed Your Respect for the Truth"

As Senate Democrats were gearing up to oppose Rice's nomination, they echoed, in substance, Helen Thomas's hysterical ranting. They sought to make Rice a scapegoat for all their complaints about Iraq. They said Rice had lied about the Iraq war and was an apologist for the president's failures. Senator Mark Dayton said she had repeatedly deceived Congress and the American public about the reasons we went to war.[18] Dayton said, "I don't like to impugn anyone's integrity, but I really don't like being lied to repeatedly, flagrantly, intentionally. It's wrong. It's undemocratic, it's un-American, and it's dangerous.... And it is occurring far too frequently in this administration. And this Congress, this Senate, must demand that it stop now."[19]

Senator Kennedy said Rice was the principle architect of our failed policy in Iraq and that she gave false reasons for going to war.[20] Senator Levin accused her of distorting and exaggerating intelligence. Senator Byrd said, "Dr. Rice is responsible for some of the most overblown rhetoric that the administration used to scare the American people."

But no one has been more demeaning and insulting to Rice during Rice's hearings before the Senate Foreign Relations Committee than Barbara Boxer was.[21] Boxer told Rice, "I personally believe—this is my personal view—that your loyalty to the mission you were given, to sell this war, overwhelmed your respect for the truth."

Rice responded, "Senator, I am more than aware of the stakes that we face in Iraq, and I was more than aware of the stakes going to war in Iraq.... I have to say that I have never, ever lost respect for the truth in the service of anything. It is not my nature. It is not my character. And I would hope that we can have this conversation and discuss what happened before and what went on before and what I said without impugning my credibility or integrity."[22] Boxer, after accusing Rice of lying, distastefully signed a Democratic Senatorial Campaign Committee fund-raising e-mail exploiting her grandstanding opposition to Rice. This ploy evoked a sharp response from Rice spokesman Jim Wilkinson, who said, "This disturbing letter puts to rest any doubts some may have had that this is all about politics."[23]

An Extremist on Abortion

No one received harsher treatment from the Left than Attorney General John Ashcroft. From the moment President Bush announced his nomination, they seized on him with a vengeance. In a more equitable world, news of Ashcroft's impending role at Justice, after the corrupt Clinton-Reno legacy, would have been met with welcome relief. But the Left has little tolerance for outspoken Christian conservatives like Ashcroft. The Reverend Carlton Veazey of the Religious Coalition for Reproductive Choice suggested the Ashcroft nomination signaled "a clear attack by Bush on safe, legal abortion services and an opening for a resurgence of abortion clinic violence."[24]

In his opening statement to the Senate Judiciary Committee at his confirmation hearings, Ashcroft emphasized that he knew "the difference between enacting and enforcing the law. It means advancing the nation's interest, not advocating my personal interest."

But Democrats dismissed Ashcroft's pledge out of hand. They questioned whether he could administer justice impartially, given his strong ideological and religious beliefs. Senator Ted Kennedy pounced on Ashcroft from the very beginning. Kennedy said, "Unfortunately, and often, [Ashcroft] has used the power of his high office to advance his personal views in spite of the law of the land." Ashcroft, said Kennedy, had often used litigation and legislation "in creative and inappropriate ways to advance his political and ideological goals."[25] He was one of the "principle architects" of the conservative strategy to undermine *Roe* v. *Wade*.

Senator Herb Kohl, striving mightily to pile on, told Ashcroft, "It is up to you to explain to us why your convictions will not permeate or dominate or even overwhelm the Department of Justice.... Your many years as a politician make some people wonder whether you are prepared to dispassionately administer the law."[26]

Senator Patrick Leahy accused Ashcroft of extremism, saying that in confirmation battles over both executive and judicial nominees, Ashcroft had not only been in the minority of the whole Senate, but a minority among Senate Republicans. But, as attorney Thomas Jipping pointed out, "Ashcroft voted against less than 5 percent of the judicial nominees he was asked to evaluate. He voted with a majority of Republicans on those nominees he opposed"[27]—quite the opposite of what Leahy fraudulently contended.

Leahy suggested—mystifyingly—that the role of attorney general was one of public peace-maker. He said, "The attorney general plays a role in bringing people together, in bridging racial divisions and inspiring people's confidence in their government."[28] But Senator Ashcroft, said Leahy, has often taken aggressively activist positions on a number of issues that deeply divide the American people. Leahy said it was the Senate's duty to "evaluate how these positions will affect his conduct as attorney general."

In labeling Ashcroft as "divisive," Leahy was referring to his conservative views, including his strong pro-life stance and his controversial opposition, while a senator, to the appointment of Ronnie White, a black Missouri Supreme Court justice, to the federal bench. Ashcroft's opposition, however, had nothing to do with race but was based on his view that Judge White was soft on crime.

Senator Biden said there was a "perception" based on the "cumulative weight of items" that Ashcroft was "not particularly sympathetic to African Americans' concerns and needs."[29] Maxine Waters, an African American congresswoman from Los Angeles testifying against Ashcroft, said, "I simply do not trust John Ashcroft.... Ashcroft has a record of opposing minorities nominated to key positions by President Bill Clinton, such as Bill Lann Lee, David Satcher, Judge Ronnie White." Ashcroft also took actions to "thwart voter registration" of blacks, the poor, and the disadvantaged in St. Louis. And, said Waters, "People like him are responsible for dashing the hopes and dreams of poor people and African Americans because of the kinds of decisions they make in their role as public policymakers." Waters also called him an extremist on abortion.[30] Senator Schumer agreed, questioning whether Ashcroft's "passionate advocacy of his deeply held beliefs over the past twenty-five years will limit his capacity to have the balanced worldview necessary for an attorney general. This is a man who had dedicated his career to eliminating a woman's right to choose."

Senator Durbin came right out and asked whether a strong conservative, like Ashcroft, would enforce laws with which he disagreed. "Can you guarantee," pressed Durbin, "fair and impartial administration of justice if you believe some Americans are undeserving or engaged in conduct which you find morally objectionable?"[31]

Ashcroft calmly and convincingly took exception to the senators' characterization, saying he had "lived within the rulings of the court in every one of those settings," meaning that he had enforced the law as it had been interpreted by the courts, even in cases where he might have disagreed with the rulings. Ashcroft made clear his view that when a public official believes a particular order is illegal, he has a duty to challenge it, "not to disrespect it" or "disobey it," but "litigate it." No matter how the decision turned, Ashcroft said, his office would "abide by the law."[32]

"The Scariest Man in Government"

After Ashcroft was confirmed he became an even bigger target, a virtual whipping boy for the angry Left. While Democrats showed grudging respect for President Bush for a time after the September 11 massacres, Ashcroft was accorded no such respect. He was maligned as a racist and a theocrat, and quickly became the symbol for all that was allegedly wrong with our prosecution of the War on Terror—military tribunals, abuse and torture, and "unlimited" detention of enemy combatants. He was cast as an enemy of civil liberties and a grave threat to the Constitution.

People for the American Way's Ralph Neas said Ashcroft was "the most dangerous threat to civil liberties in the federal government," who had mounted a "relentless assault on constitutional rights and civil liberties."[33] Ashcroft became inextricably associated with the Patriot Act, which, in the minds of liberals, symbolized a tyrannical government. He was also cast as a religious zealot who cavalierly violated the Left's sacred and mythical wall separating church and state. *Washington Post* columnist Richard Cohen wrote that people think of Ashcroft "as the scariest man in government."

Ashcroft, said Cohen, rounded up suspects in America "without the usual legal safeguards." He "has become the conservative point man for...[what] is a very conservative administration."[34]

In a Senate Judiciary Committee hearing on December 6, 2001, Democratic senators were particularly contentious toward Ashcroft concerning the Justice Department's tactics in the War on Terror that were allegedly threatening our liberties. Ashcroft fought back, denying the administration was trampling liberties and insisting that it always balanced constitutional liberties against the threat of terrorism. Ashcroft said, "Those who scare peace-loving people with phantoms of lost liberty...only aid terrorists, for they erode our national unity and diminish our resolve. They give ammunition to America's enemies and pause to America's friends. They encourage people of good will to remain silent in the face of evil."[35]

Ashcroft's "insubordination"—how dare he?—sent the Left into paroxysms of open-mouthed incredulity. Editorialists and critics called him arrogant,[36] insulting,[37] offensive,[38] McCarthyesque,[39] aggressive and specious,[40] polarizing, strident, and transparently ideological,[41] a bully-boy and stagily religious,[42] fearmongering,[43] pugnacious,[44] dismissive, indignant, and unresponsive,[45] dishonest,[46] bombastic,[47] over-the-line,[48] a small man,[49] and a Puritan minister obsessed with ridding the countryside of Evil with the same mentality as witch-burner Cotton Mather.[50]

Newsweek was so nasty in a hit piece on Ashcroft that it mocked the loss of his Senate seat to the widow of his opponent, Mel Carnahan, who had been killed in an aircraft accident days before the election. *Newsweek* referred to it as an "embarrassing political defeat—losing his Senate re-election to a dead man." In truth, Ashcroft almost surely would have won if Carnahan hadn't died.

Ashcroft was ahead in the polls by double digits shortly before Carnahan's death, but quit campaigning out of respect for Mrs. Carnahan, who ended up running and winning—largely on a sympathy vote.[51] Ashcroft's gentlemanly campaign style was beyond the comprehension of the "win at any cost" liberals.

Ashcroft's critics continued even when he resigned, panning him as a "polarizing" figure who resigned after a "tumultuous tenure."[52]

Refusing to Suffer Fools Gladly

When it comes to the Left's primary reason for hating President Bush—the Iraq war—no one symbolizes it more than Defense Secretary Donald Rumsfeld. There was no better way to discredit President Bush's Iraq war policy than to denigrate the top defense official in charge. Rumsfeld especially rankles the Left because of his self-confidence and refusal to take their flack lying down.

The media have done their best to demonize him because he has consistently exposed them for the incurious, biased charlatans that many of them are. In his combative press conferences, he has not suffered fools gladly—and reporters have resented it mightily.

Before the September 11 attacks Rumsfeld was considered controversial and some were predicting he would be the first of Bush's cabinet members to quit.[53] Immediately after September 11 and after our early successes in Afghanistan, he was celebrated for the tough-minded way he handled the press. But the honeymoon didn't last. The press hated his brusque, dismissive tone and his biting wit at their expense.[54] When asked, for example, whether the military should restrain itself to avoid arousing more Islamic terrorists, he replied, "Utter nonsense. It's kind of like feeding an alligator, hoping it eats you last."[55]

Rumsfeld's critics accuse him of arrogance, rudeness, and eva-siveness toward people who aren't his superiors. They accuse him of misjudgments, neoconservative imperialism, and militarism.[56] They say he is unconcerned about the safety of troops he is placing in harm's way, not sufficiently arming and "armoring" them. They are outraged that he doesn't grovel before the elite Old Media or pontificating, self-important politicians running investigative com-mittees. From the earliest opportunity, they have been demanding his resignation.

When he honestly answered "I don't know," to questions whose answers were truly "unknowable," such as how much the war would ultimately cost—they accused him of dodging and evading. When he insisted from the beginning that he couldn't possibly know how long the war would last, they recoiled in exasperation. But Rumsfeld was unflappable. He told a reporter, "There's never been a war that was predictable as to length, casualty, or cost in the his-tory of mankind."[57] Case closed.

From early on in Bush's first term, many have criticized Rumsfeld for his controversial plan to modernize the military with lighter, faster, and more lethal weaponry. Some of the top Pentagon brass resisted the overhaul, as did congressmen from states where soon-to-be mothballed weapons were manufactured and military bases were recommended to be closed.[58]

Opponents of Rumsfeld's plan said it would put soldiers at risk and lead to more U.S. battlefield deaths. They said he had created such a huge rift between Pentagon civilians and senior officers that it would threaten his plans for reform.[59] General Eric Shinseki has been one of Rumsfeld's critics at least as far back as Rumsfeld's deci-sion to reorganize the military. Shinseki and many other military men opposed Rumsfeld's plan to streamline the military bureaucracy of which they were a part—and have it run more like a business.[60]

An early illustration of their opposition to Rumsfeld's plan was their reaction to his decision to cancel the $11 billion Crusader artillery system because it was too cumbersome.[61] Rumsfeld noted it would take sixty to sixty-four C-17 transports—half our fleet—to take eighteen of these crusaders, loaded with troops and ammunition, into battle.[62] He said it was a good system, but if we funded every single item the services wanted, our defense budget would double or even triple within a decade or two.

Though liberals generally approve of canceling weapons systems, Rumsfeld didn't win any friends among the appeasement-oriented Democrats. They disapproved of his reputedly hawkish policies. They disapproved of his desire to develop a missile defense system, something the Left has always considered militaristic and provocative. Adding insult to injury was his alignment with President Bush to abandon the 1972 Anti–Ballistic Missile Treaty, which liberals, mystifyingly—since the Soviet Union repeatedly violated it—credited as "the cornerstone of nuclear deterrence."[63] And Rumsfeld also made the Left nervous with his initiative to reorganize the Pentagon's space programs, which, liberals argued, would give Russia and China "even more reason to be concerned."[64] Liberals tended to view anything that would make our defenses less penetrable a dangerous act of provocation.

The Left, however, focused most of its ire on Rumsfeld as one of the neoconservative demons behind our "preemptive" attack on Iraq. They blamed him for strategic and diplomatic errors,[65] for failing to support our troops, and for overhauling our military to the point that it couldn't do its job. Seymour Hersh, writing for the *New Yorker*, said that our ground campaign in Iraq had "faltered" with "attenuated supply lines and a lack of immediate reinforcements." He blamed Secretary Rumsfeld and "his inner circle of civilian advisers" for persuading President Bush to go to war and for "micromanaging the war's operational details."[66] Hersh tried to put meat on the bones of the argument that Rumsfeld's military reorganization plans were flawed and dangerous. He cited one unnamed "senior Pentagon planner," who said that Rumsfeld's streamlining plans were depriving the armed forces of the resources they needed to fight effectively. The planner said Rumsfeld had rejected the Pentagon's recommendation for more troops in favor of a "smaller, faster-moving attack force, combined with overwhelming air power."

Hersh played up a major schism between the military and their civilian superiors, led by Rumsfeld. *USA Today* wrote as early as December 2002 that Rumsfeld's abrasive style had alienated America's closest allies and strained his own working relationship with the military brass. It quoted "military officers and defense analysts" saying that "not since the Vietnam War have relations between a defense secretary and the armed forces been strained so badly." The paper fretted that Rumsfeld's style might hinder the Iraq war effort.[67]

The *Los Angeles Times* also wrung its hands over Rumsfeld, who "grossly underestimated how hard it will be to restore the oil fields, pump the gas, and turn on the lights and phones in Iraq." Rumsfeld, said the *Times*, had also bungled international diplomacy in failing to get allies to join us in the Iraq effort.[68] Rumsfeld fought back. He said that people lamenting over Europe's refusal to join the coalition were thinking of Europe as just Germany and France. "That's old Europe," said Rumsfeld. "If you look at the entire NATO Europe today, the center of gravity is shifting to the east and there are a lot of new members."[69] That remark evoked new claims that Rumsfeld was arrogant, by the French and congressional Democrats.

"An Architect of Torture"

Shamefully, Democrats and the media used the allegations of abuse and "torture" of enemy combatants in Abu Ghraib prison in Iraq and the detention center in Guantánamo Bay as an opportunity to indict the entire administration, but especially Rumsfeld. They said the administration established a permissive environment that led to the abuses at Abu Ghraib.[70]

Seymour Hersh said Rumsfeld's unconventional interrogation programs triggered the abuses. "The roots of the Abu Ghraib prison scandal," wrote Hersh, "lie not in the criminal inclinations of a few Army reservists but in a decision approved last year by Secretary of Defense Donald Rumsfeld, to expand a highly secret operation, which had been focused on the hunt for al Qaeda, to the interrogation of prisoners in Iraq."[71] The Pentagon categorically denied the charges, saying they were "filled with error and completely false." Pentagon spokesman Larry DiRita said, "No responsible official of the Department of Defense approved any program that could conceivably have been intended to result in such abuses as witnessed in the recent photos and videos."[72]

Senator Joseph Biden demanded accountability from Rumsfeld and others in the Pentagon.[73] Congressman Charles Rangel said he didn't just want Rumsfeld's resignation, but that he intended to sponsor a bill for his impeachment, charging that Rumsfeld "contributed to an atmosphere of lawlessness" and permitted a breakdown in discipline. "As a result of his malfeasance the secretary of defense has offended and embarrassed the American people, under-mined U.S. credibility around the world, and increased the danger to American troops and civilians around the world."[74]

The *New York Times*, in calling upon Rumsfeld to resign in May 2004, cited his "personal responsibility for the scandal at Abu Ghraib" as reason enough—though hardly the only reason—he should step down.[75] Rumsfeld, said the *Times*, "has morphed, over the last two years, from a man of supreme confidence to arrogance, then to almost willful blindness. With the approval of the president, he sent American troops into a place whose nature and dangers he had apparently never bothered to examine."[76] Other publications, including the *Boston Globe*, said that President Bush needed to do more than express his apologies for the abuse and should demand his resignation.[77] The incarceration and interrogation of enemy pris-oners at Guantánamo Bay became another opportunity for the lib-erals to accuse Rumsfeld and other administration officials of damaging our image in the world and setting back America's efforts to "win the hearts and minds of moderate Muslims." They seemed always willing to believe the allegations of the terrorists themselves, over the words of the administration.

In characteristic fashion, Rumsfeld did not cower from the accu-sations, but defended U.S. policy, saying that the rough interrogation tactics produced valuable inside information on al Qaeda from a would-be September 11 hijacker: the "twentieth hijacker," Mohammed al Qahtani. The information extracted from him and others, said Rumsfeld, led to the capture of the mastermind of Sep-tember 11, Khalid Shaikh Mohammed, the disruption of other planned terrorist attacks, and the identification of twenty of Osama bin Laden's bodyguards. Rumsfeld had approved of mild physical contact, stress positions, and isolation as interrogation techniques for a "select group of detainees, including al Qahtani."[78] Neither Rumsfeld nor the Pentagon considered these techniques to be "torture." Rumsfeld noted pointedly that the people against whom the rough techniques were used were "not common car thieves." They were "terrorist trainers, bomb-makers, extremist recruiters and financiers, bodyguards of Osama bin Laden and would-be suicide bombers."[79] None of these explanations mollified Democrats, who excoriated Rumsfeld and the administration and even demanded that the Gitmo facility be closed. The Democrats' rhetoric added fuel to the fire of fringe leftist groups, such as Amnesty International, whose U.S. director called Rumsfeld an "architect of torture."[80]

Going to War with the Army You Have

One Democratic complaint against Rumsfeld that appeared to resonate was that he was responsible for our military vehicles in Iraq being "underarmored." During a press conference with U.S. soldiers in Kuwait, a soldier—Specialist Thomas Wilson of the Tennessee National Guard—asked Rumsfeld about the lack of properly armed vehicles. Rumsfeld's blunt answer shocked liberals the world over. He said, "As you know, you go to war with the army you have, not the army you might want or wish to have at a later time."[81]

Democrats, who had been clamoring for Rumsfeld's resignation for over a year, seized on the opportune moment to attack Rumsfeld over his "insensitive" remarks to the troops.[82] Senator Joseph Biden said Rumsfeld's answers were an "insult to their service." He said "we didn't go to war with the army we have," because we didn't send enough troops to do the job in Iraq.[83] Democrats used the incident as a launching pad to revisit their claim that the administration had failed in its prewar planning. Congresswoman Ellen Tauscher said, "This is about faulty analysis and a failed strategy. We've never had enough troops on the ground since the fall of Saddam Hussein's government to deal with the insurgency because we didn't expect one."[84]

Senator John Corzine said that the issue was not one of just Humvees. "There has been miscalculation in interpretation of the intelligence before the war. There was a failure to secure all weapons dumps [in Iraq], there have been problems in the administration of prisons, and no one has been held accountable."[85] Senator Carl Levin also tied reports of our inadequately armored vehicles to the "poor planning and rosy scenarios" the administration had relied on before attacking Iraq.[86] Levin said the Senate Armed Services Committee would hold hearings on Iraq within a month, and would include in its investigation the question of whether we went to war with too few armored vehicles.[87]

As Matt Drudge reported, it turned out that an embedded reporter, *Chattanooga Times Free Press* employee Edward Lee Pitts, had sent an e-mail bragging that he had set up Rumsfeld by orchestrating hostile questions from two soldiers. Pitts said he brought the two soldiers along with him as escorts, worked on questions with them and arranged for the sergeant in charge of the microphone to call on the two soldiers for questions.[88] The mainstream media prominently featured the initial story, reporting it as if the soldiers' questions were heartfelt and spontaneous. But the revelation that it was a press-inspired, canned incident, received little play. When others, such as Drudge, raised the issue, the media and other reliable Rumsfeld critics refused to give ground, choosing to emphasize only Rumsfeld's callousness and lack of compassion.

Antiwar forces in the Democratic Party never tired of trying to oust Rumsfeld from his position. In March 2006, Senator Dianne Feinstein renewed calls for Rumsfeld's resignation. "I say it's time to change course, to bring in another team....I don't believe [Rumsfeld] listens to many people, and that's a problem. It's time for him to go."[89]

In April 2006, Feinstein received reinforcement when a group of retired generals publicly demanded that Rumsfeld resign or be removed. Some of these generals, of course, were critics of the war in general, not just Rumsfeld's pivotal role in it. One of the critics, retired Marine Lieutenant General Greg Newbold, wrote an article in *Time* magazine titled "Why Iraq Was a Mistake," blaming Rumsfeld, and saying, "we need fresh ideas and fresh faces."[90] A number of other retired generals agreed: Paul Eaton, Anthony Zinni, John Batiste, John Riggs, and Charles Swannack. Rumsfeld had to go.

Democrats jumped at this opportunity—once again—to begin a public outcry for Rumsfeld's head. In truth most of these retired generals had been longtime critics of Rumsfeld. Some appeared to have an ax to grind, such as John Riggs, who was demoted from three to two stars immediately before his retirement, and might have blamed Rumsfeld for it—because he had run into trouble with him for declaring publicly that the army was stretched too thin.

Greg Newbold had been publicly chastised by Rumsfeld for announcing that "the combat power of the Taliban has been eviscerated." When he requested early retirement in 2002, he said that he had grown tired of Rumsfeld's abrasive style. Newbold also endorsed the Democratic line that the administration had alienated our allies and distorted intelligence leading up to the war. He even adopted the liberals' familiar "chicken hawk" line of reasoning that those who had never served in the military had no right to give their opinions. Newbold wrote, "My sincere view is that the commitment of our forces to this fight was done with a casualness and swagger that are the special province of those who have never had to execute these missions—or bury the results."

Not all retired generals agreed with the Rumfeld critics. A group of retired generals who worked with Rumsfeld, including retired Air Force Gen. Richard B. Myers, former chairman of the Joint Chiefs of Staff under President Bush, vigorously defended Rumsfeld and decried calls for his resignation. Retired Marine Lt. Gen. Michael P. DeLong, who had been deputy commander of U.S. Central Command during the Afghan and Iraq invasions, also rushed to Rumsfeld's defense. He said, "When we have an administration that is currently at war, with a secretary of defense that has the confidence of the president and basically has done well—no matter what grade you put on there, he has done well—to call for his resignation right now is not good for the country."[91]

President Bush also stood by Rumsfeld without equivocation. He dismissed the claim that Rumsfeld runs roughshod over his military officers in the field. Bush said, "I have seen firsthand how Don relies upon our military commanders in the field and at the Pentagon to make decisions about how best to complete the missions. Secretary Rumsfeld's energetic and steady leadership is exactly what is needed at this critical period. He has my full support and deepest appreciation."[92]

But the antiwar Left persisted in their demand that Rumsfeld be fired, making it clear that as long as the war continued, they would view Rumsfeld as one of their main enemies and would never let up. But did the Democratic Party ever offer its own plans to modernize our military or to win the wars in Afghanistan, Iraq, and the broader War on Terror? No. Their "policy" was merely to condemn Rumsfeld and the administration and restate vague, general goals.

CHAPTER TWELVE

A Pair of Rasputins

Since Vice President Dick Cheney has been with President Bush from the beginning—meaning back to Bush/Gore/Florida 2000— the Left has harbored a special contempt for him. The only time he enjoyed any pretense of a honeymoon was right after candidate Bush named him as his running mate. Oh, he was dull all right, the liberals said, but he was a nice guy, smart and honest. But once they went into campaign mode, Democrats figured that a good way to discredit Bush and his claim to "compassionate conservatism," was to depict Cheney as a "real" conservative—the kind liberals believe is bereft of compassion.

Democratic politicians and operatives began to talk about his mean-spirited voting record. One said, "Cheney's anti-choice, he's opposed to gun control, he's anti-environment, he's against statistically measuring the census, and he voted for Clarence Thomas."[1] They also demonized his wife, Lynne Cheney, who was a bona fide conservative heavyweight in her own right. Oh, yes, and how could Bush hold himself out as the education candidate when his running mate voted against the Department of Education?

For a brief period during the Bush administration's first term, the Left regarded Cheney with grudging respect, as the brains behind the Bush administration, which was always a backhanded slap at the president. Fleeting respect aside, they have consistently reviled him from the beginning. He was criticized for secreting himself to an undisclosed location during and after the September 11 terrorist attacks for security reasons. But Cheney was acting no differently than federal officials had since the 1950s. The administration activated a "shadow government" plan that dated back to the Eisenhower administration, which involved keeping seventy-five or more senior government officials working outside Washington in case of a terrorist attack on the capital.[2] But the way Cheney's actions were reported, you would have thought he was the only government official to use an undisclosed location.

Media complaints about Cheney's penchant for secrecy transcended his retreats to undisclosed locations. They were convinced he was running important aspects of the government—especially concerning energy policy—under a cloak of secrecy.

Maureen Dowd wrote, "We are not allowed to know where Secret Agent Man sleeps. (Sometimes he'll entertain people at his residence, and then leave for his 'secure, undisclosed location' at the same time his guests leave for unsecure, disclosed locations.) We are not allowed to know whom he talks to in the White House. We are not allowed to hear how he shapes our energy policy or our war plans.... Cheney thinks he is entitled to put our energy policy behind closed doors with his oil and gas buddies and Republican donors." *Newsweek*'s Jonathan Alter wrote that Cheney had "taken secrecy about his whereabouts to inexplicable lengths."[3] The *American Prospect*'s Robert Dreyfuss said the office of the vice presidency under Cheney is "notoriously opaque," "very difficult for journalists to penetrate" and has "a fierce penchant for secrecy."[4]

The media even tried to carry forward the theme of Cheney's supposed secrecy in their reporting of the accidental shooting of his friend Austin attorney Harry Whittington while hunting. Cheney, Whittington, and one other hunter had separated from the ten-person hunting party and were pursuing a covey of quail. After the three had fired their shotguns, Whittington went to find the quail he'd hit. Unbeknownst to Cheney, Whittington had returned and was standing to his right when Cheney turned and fired at quail he heard in that direction, hitting Whittington. Cheney had difficulty seeing Whittington because the sun was in his face and Whittington was standing in a gully. A doctor traveling with Cheney assisted Whittington and went with him to the hospital.

Along with Democrats, the media did their best to manufacture a scandal out of the accident, saying Cheney had engaged in a cover-up because he failed to tell them about it immediately. At first, Harry Reid said Cheney had done nothing wrong. But the very next day, Reid, never willing to miss an opportunity to exploit a potential White House vulnerability, changed course and criticized Cheney for not being sufficiently forthcoming. "Talk about secrecy," said Reid. "The vice president accidentally shoots someone and keeps that a secret for nearly a day. That man is now very sick."

Reid added, "I think the reason it took the vice president a day to talk about this is part of the secretive nature of this administration. The American people are not entitled to know what's going on in their mindset."[5] Reid's sidekick Nancy Pelosi agreed, saying, "Open government demands that the vice president come clean with what happened.... There's probably a very simple answer to it, but we have to break this habit of the administration, of closed government without the openness that is healthy to a democracy."[6]

Slate's Jacob Weisberg wrote, "The Bush administration's aversion to openness reached the proportions of parody last weekend, when Dick Cheney shot a man in the face with a shotgun while hunting for quail in Texas." Weisberg complained that the White House "revealed nothing" about the incident and very well might have chosen not to report the "near-manslaughter" at all, if someone else had not spoken to the press. Weisberg even compared Cheney's "attempted cover-up" to Vice President Aaron Burr's effort to conceal his intentional shooting of Alexander Hamilton in a duel in 1804. Then again, if they can compare Bush to Hitler, why shouldn't they compare Cheney to Burr?

Weisberg tried to link Cheney's delay in reporting the incident to his and President Bush's "subterranean instincts" and their "disdain for the kind of disclosure and freedom of information that democracy demands." Throughout their term, said Wiesberg, "Cheney and Bush have indulged their urge to purge." The hunting incident "pretty much signals that Bush's resolution for a 'candorful' New Year failed."[7]

Cheney explained that his delay in reporting the incident had nothing to do with an intent to cover up the accident. There was nothing to hide. Cheney clearly took responsibility for the shooting.

"I'm the guy who pulled the trigger that fired the round that hit Harry," said Cheney. "It was not Harry's fault. You cannot blame anybody else." But he was unapologetic about his decision to let Katharine Armstrong, the owner of the ranch where the accident occurred and an eyewitness to it, first go to the press with the news. "I thought it made good sense because you can get as accurate a story as possible from somebody who knows and understands hunting." Cheney said he knew that Armstrong's report would instantly be reported on the "wires" and "posted on the website" and he "thought that was the right call. I still do," he said.[8]

Senator Lindsey Graham, who has hunted several times with Cheney, defended the vice president's conscientiousness about safety. Graham said Cheney made his decision not to go to the press out of respect for the privacy of his longtime friend Harry Whittington. Katharine Armstrong corroborated Graham's sentiment, saying, "What the vice president was doing was so respectful." She said that Cheney was concerned that a national news report might reach Whittington's daughters before the family could get word to them.[9]

But Cheney's political opponents and the media simply refused to accept his explanation or consider the idea that nothing sinister was involved. Former Democratic National Committee chairman Terry McAuliffe said, "This is the vice president of the United States of America who shot someone in the face. This is about personal responsibility. He hid. He didn't get the facts out."[10] The Left, typified by Jacob Weisberg, maintained that Cheney's delay in coming forward was characteristic of the administration's arrogance and contempt for the public's "right to know"—and consistent with its "imperial" nature. In an earlier piece on the administration's NSA wireless surveillance policy, Weisberg had written about the "power-madness of King George," and asked whether Bush was "turning America into an elective dictatorship.[11]

Throughout the media's reporting and commenting on the tragic incident, neither the mainstream media nor Democrats uttered a word of compassion. They were unmoved that Whittington had suffered a heart attack, probably due to a pellet that had lodged in his heart, or by Cheney's statement that the day of the accident was "one of the worst days of my life."[12] Always eager to believe the worst about him, they chose to hype certain exploitable tidbits—like Cheney's admitted consumption of a beer at lunch. To the Left this meant he was drunk and committed criminal negligence in shooting Whittington.[13] With that kind of treatment Cheney naturally chose to be interviewed by FOX News's Brit Hume, rather than by a "mainstream" media reporter, which further outraged the Left.

The worst Cheney could legitimately be accused of, as columnist Charles Krauthammer observed, was failing to notify the media on Saturday night after Whittington's family had been notified, instead of waiting until Sunday morning.[14] But this was a minor matter, considering there no was wrongdoing to cover up and no chance this information would be kept from the public for very long, thus no motive to cover up. The event revealed far more about the media and the Democratic Party, their antipathy toward the vice president and their willingness to jump to conclusions that conform to their prejudices, than it did about Cheney. As Old Media watchdog Brent Bozell noted, the media was way out of hand on the story. The "Big Three" networks aired thirty-four stories in the first forty-eight hours of evening and morning newscasts. "They treated this not as a mishap," wrote Bozell, "but as a brewing national scandal. 'The eighteen-hour delay in alerting the media!' 'The failure to pay a $7 hunting stamp!' 'Questions remain!' 'White House under fire!' 'Growing political fallout!' "[15]

For all the recriminations they issued against Cheney for not apologizing, none of them retracted a syllable of their hyperbole and distortions concerning the incident. A man of his ideological stripe is not worthy of their apology, since in their view he's guilty by virtue of his beliefs alone.

The Imperial Vice Presidency

From the beginning of Bush's first term, the Left also repeatedly peddled the myth that Cheney was the de facto president. Nicholas Lemann, in the *New Yorker*, wrote of Cheney's "Discreet Rise to Unprecedented Power." It analogized Bush's reliance on Cheney to getting "hooked up to the I.V. several times each day. . . . The power of that reassurance fix surely outweighs the political disadvantage of having had a running mate who brought with him only three electoral votes, which would have gone Republican anyway."[16]

NPR's Juan Williams described Cheney as historically "unique among vice presidents" in that he "plays a deeply important role for a president with limited political experience and no Washington experience." Williams said Cheney had the final word on budget proposals from Cabinet members and was "the pivot man on foreign policy, national security, and military matters." He was also "the man in charge" on energy policy.[17] In one column Maureen Dowd wrote, "Cheney may truly be the most powerful vice president in the history of the universe."[18] In another she said, "Like a buoyant Dr. Evil holding a napping Bush Mini-Me in a Snugli, Mr.

Cheney seems to relish running the world alone. Consider how primary the secondary man is."[19]

Robert Dreyfuss wrote that Cheney has a "Rasputin-like hold over the presidency." And, "Dick Cheney has ruled the White House roost for the past five years, amassing enough power to give rise to the joke that George W. Bush is 'a heartbeat away from the presidency.'" The vice president, said Dreyfuss, "wields...extraordinary authority."[20] The *Los Angeles Times* at one point suggested that Bush should relax "the unprecedented control" he had delegated to Cheney over agencies and departments.[21] *Newsweek*'s Jonathan Alter, calling Cheney "an imperial vice president," wrote, "Cheney has simultaneously expanded the power of the vice presidency and reduced its accountability." Alter argued that since Cheney's health prevented him from aspiring to the presidency, he felt he could "change the rules" with impunity.[22] Later, on a television appearance, Alter revealed his similarly low opinion of President Bush. In discussing the president's low poll numbers, Alter said, "There are not a lot of people who expect him to move very much in the polls. And once you're tagged as an incompetent, that's pretty hard to recover from."[23]

The Left has also depicted Cheney—the de facto president—as a key figure in the "neoconservative" fraternity reputedly behind our invasion of Iraq. They contend he was part of the grand conspiracy to distort and exaggerate intelligence on Iraqi WMD. And, he "forced the Central Intelligence Agency to provide false and tendentious reports," which "undermined the essential independence required of executive agencies if they are to provide objective information to the White House"[24]—though bipartisan investigations cleared him of that charge. *Los Angeles Times* columnist Robert

Scheer argued that Cheney and his fellow neocons, including Defense Secretary Donald Rumsfeld and Paul Wolfowitz, "began a whining chorus of demands" that September 11 be "exploited as an excuse to whack Iraq." Scheer urged candidate Kerry to make this a campaign issue.[25]

Robert Dreyfuss said that Cheney's team—"the neoconservative cabal"—operates "like disciplined Bolsheviks" and "with a single-minded, ideological focus on the exercise of American military power." The vice president's office, said Dreyfuss, was the command center for the cabal.

Senator Ted Kennedy essentially accused Cheney and his chief of staff Scooter Libby of obstruction of justice. In a letter urging supporters to sign a petition demanding the White House turn over documents following Libby's indictment by the special prosecutor, Kennedy characterized the indictment as being against more than one individual. "It's an indictment of the vicious and devious tactics used by the administration to justify a war we never should have fought. It's an indictment of the lengths to which administration officials were willing to go to cover up their failed intelligence, their distortions on Iraq's weapons of mass destruction and their serious blunders on the war. It is an indictment of their vindictive efforts to discredit anyone who challenges their misrepresentations. As we know, Scooter Libby and Vice President Cheney withheld critical documents in the Senate's investigation of the use and misuse of intelligence and the abuse of power in the decision to go to war and in the management of the war."[26]

Other liberals also tried to implicate Cheney in the Libby indictment[27] and insinuated he was behind a scheme to out "secret agent" Valerie Plame. After the indictment, the *Los Angeles Times* and others, like DNC chairman Howard Dean, said that Cheney should resign. But since that wasn't likely, at least he "should spend the bulk of his time at undisclosed locations and funerals for foreign dignitaries."[28]

Cheney, being one of the Left's favorite piñatas, was also said to be among the masterminds of the administration's much maligned treatment of enemy combatants—not to mention his role in the administration's "sinister" NSA surveillance program. The Left insisted that certain incidents of prisoner abuse were tantamount to a system-wide policy of abuse and torture, perpetrated at the direction of the White House and the Pentagon. Cheney, they said, along with Don Rumsfeld and Alberto Gonzales, was one of the chief architects of the administration's "torture policy." The *New York Times* referred to Cheney as "a prime mover behind the attempts to legalize torture" who was "leading a back-room fight to block a measure passed by the Senate, 90 to 9, that would impose international standards and American laws on the treatment of prisoners." Cheney, said the *Times*, wants to make the "CIA's camps legal" and "authorize the use of torture by intelligence agents."[29]

Halliburton

Early on, the Left challenged Cheney's ties to Halliburton, a Dallas-based oil services and engineering firm. Cheney was CEO of Halliburton from 1995 to 2000, but resigned when he accepted a position on the ticket with George W. Bush. Immediately, Al Gore exploited Cheney's Halliburton connection to demonize him and Bush as friends of "Big Oil." Gore's campaign spokesman, Doug Hattaway, said, "It seems big oil is making a big investment in the Bush-Cheney ticket. People would rightfully wonder whose side

Dick Cheney is on in taking on oil companies on the subject of gas prices and pollution controls."

Cheney's decision to pursue the vice presidency presented him with a dilemma. He owned stock as well as substantial unvested stock options in the company. The options were scheduled to vest over the next three years, but there was nothing Cheney could do to accelerate the vesting, and if elected, the options would vest while he was in office. This would create a potential conflict of interest because he would have a personal financial stake in a company that often contracts with the government and whose financial interests could be affected by his advice and decisions as a sitting vice president. He could transfer the stock that had already vested and avoid any conflict on that stock. But Halliburton had special rules preventing him from transferring stock options to anyone else, even children, charities or trust funds.[30]

As to the vested stock, Cheney could have transferred it into a blind trust before taking office on January 20, 2001. But after exploring all possible solutions, he decided he would have to forgo 233,000 Halliburton stock options if elected, worth more than $3.6 million at the time of his decision. Instead of being praised for his willingness to sacrifice several million dollars to pursue his commitment to public service, the Gore team decided to play the class warfare card. Gore operative Chris Lehane gloated, "Dick Cheney got his hand caught in the cookie jar. Now, far too late, he is trying to put the cookie back. No matter how hard he tries, he's not going to be able to break the connection the Bush-Cheney ticket has with big oil."[31]

Even though Cheney went the extra mile to do the right thing with his Halliburton stock options, Democrats continued to dog him over his ties to the company throughout the first term and into the second, especially as oil prices soared. Democrats, with complete disregard for the facts, accused Cheney of helping to secure lucrative contracts for Halliburton, including a no-bid contract for Iraqi reconstruction projects.[32] Candidate John Kerry said, "Dick Cheney's old company Halliburton has profited from the mess in Iraq at the expense of American troops and taxpayers. While Halliburton has been engaging in massive overcharging and wasteful practices under this no-bid contract, Dick Cheney has continued to receive compensation from his former company."[33]

But as Kerry knew, the administration's decision to award a no-bid contract for oil wells was because the company was already established in Iraq and to have made the bidding process public would have compromised the country's war plans. Kerry also doubtlessly knew that the nonpartisan Government Accountability Office had concluded that the administration's decision was prudent and proper because, among other reasons, Halliburton was the only company "in a position to provide the services within the required time." And, there was an "urgent need for reconstruction efforts."

Senate Minority Leader Harry Reid, in one hysterical utterance, blamed Cheney personally for virtually all the nation's major ills. Reid said, "The manipulation of intelligence to sell a war in Iraq, Vice President Cheney's involved in that. The White House energy policy that puts big oil ahead of the American consumer, Vice President Cheney is behind that. Leaking classified information to discredit White House critics, the vice president is behind that. Halliburton, contracting abuse, the list goes on and it goes on." Republican National Committee chairman Ken Mehlman fittingly described Reid's outburst as a "Lyndon LaRouche moment."[34]

"A Right-wing Rasputin"

Among the Left's nemeses, the granddaddy demon of them all is the mastermind par excellence, the evil one himself, Karl Rove. Rove drove the crazy Left utterly to distraction. Rove's unforgivable sin was masterminding Bush's election victories in 2000 and 2004 and his previous victories that positioned Bush to run for the presidency. Without Rove, there would be no President Bush, according to the Left. This alone would earn him enduring, irredeemable contempt.

They saw Rove as a superhuman political operative who would put Machiavelli to shame. He was dark and devilish,[35] White House consigliere, Bush's Svengali, an implementer of savage tactics,[36] and an unethical, take-no-prisoners operative.[37] Liberals depicted Rove not just as the boy genius of political consulting, but a cynical manipulator of policy decisions—often to influence poll results. He didn't just get Bush—and hundreds of others—elected, he helped craft Bush's policy agenda to hold the GOP base and attract swing voters. They were so paranoid about Rove that retired CBS anchor Walter Cronkite, who was once considered "the most trusted man in America," actually conjectured on *Larry King Live* that Rove might be behind the Osama bin Laden videotape released on the eve of the 2004 presidential election.[38]

From the media's perspective, Rove was long on political calculation and very short on principle. As one editorial put it, "Rove...is seen increasingly as a kind of right-wing Rasputin, shaping policy on issues as diverse as steel tariffs, family planning, and war with Iraq for political advantage." Almost every action of the Bush presidency, it said, "appears to be driven by domestic political considerations."[39]

Columnist Joe Conason wrote shortly after the 2000 election—and while its result was still uncertain—that Rove had the same "unscrupulous approach to political intrigue" as his late colleague Lee Atwater—another hated figure in the liberal imagination. Conason accused Rove of controlling Governor Bush's political appointments, and using his clout to secure state judgeships for his clients.[40] Many others, including the *Baltimore Sun*'s Jules Witcover, dubbed Rove "unscrupulous."[41]

So intense was the Democrats' obsession with Rove—some would call it paranoia—that they credited (or blamed) him with almost every one of the president's moves. In their minds, Bush didn't take a step without playing "Mother May I?" with Rove. The Democratic base had a singular antipathy for Rove, so merely to mention his name in connection with an event would place a black cloud over it. When anything was going wrong for a Democrat, the first person they suspected was Rove.

We saw this not only with the bin Laden tape, but also during the Democratic presidential campaign in late 2003. When a rash of mysterious e-mails flooded the inboxes of American Jews, stating that Howard Dean favored an "even-handed" Middle East policy, Dean was accused of being more sympathetic to the Palestinians than the Israelis. Dean attempted to deflect attention from the allegation by accusing Rove of being behind the message. But that was ridiculous, as Matthew Brooks, executive director of the Republican Jewish Coalition, pointed out. Rather, what got Dean in trouble was his statement that it was not in America's interest to "take sides" in the Israeli-Palestinian conflict. He had also selected as his foreign policy adviser Claude Prestowitz, who wrote, "U.S. aid to Israel should be conditional on Israel's withdrawal from the West Bank and Gaza Strip and a freeze on the development of settlements."[42]

"Bush's Brain"

During the 2004 presidential campaign liberals produced a brazenly partisan attack film, disguised as a documentary on Rove, called *Bush's Brain: How Karl Rove Made George W. Bush*, which purported to chronicle his career from Texas through Washington. Two Texas journalists in the film reportedly marvel at Rove's uncanny knack for turning his opponents' strengths into weaknesses, such as Texas governor Ann Richards's reputation for inclusiveness and John Kerry's war record.[43]

Democrats almost lost it when Rove, at a Republican fund-raiser in New York, depicted liberals as soft on terror. Rove said, "Conservatives saw the savagery of September 11 in the attacks and prepared for war. Liberals saw the savagery of the September 11 attacks and wanted to prepare indictments and offer therapy and understanding for our attackers." Rove added, "I don't know about you, but moderation and restraint is not what I felt when I watched the Twin Towers crumble to the ground, a side of the Pentagon destroyed, and almost three thousand of our fellow citizens perish in flames and rubble." Rove also asserted that Senator Durbin's likening of America's treatment of enemy detainees at Guantánamo Bay to what happened under Soviet gulags, the Nazis, and Pol Pot jeopardized the safely of our troops overseas. He noted that al Jazeera broadcast Durbin's words.[44]

Democrats, who had been politicizing the war for more than two years, now demanded that Rove resign for politicizing the war. Senator Chuck Schumer said, "In New York, where everyone unified after September 11, the last thing we need is somebody who seeks to divide us for political purposes." Senator Harry Reid said, "Karl Rove should immediately and fully apologize for his remarks or he should resign. Dividing our country for political gain is an insult to all Americans and to the common memory we all carry with us from that day." Senator John Kerry said that if Bush believes his own calls for national unity, he should fire Rove. Congresswoman Nancy Pelosi said that Rove "has decided to move to center stage in the theater of the absurd. He knows full well, as do all Americans, that our country came together after September 11."[45]

Six Democratic senators signed a letter to Rove, slamming him for his "inflammatory" comments and for trying "to score partisan, political points at the expense of three thousand victims and their families."[46] The White House defended Rove, saying he was just highlighting the different philosophies of the parties and accurately characterizing the positions of liberal groups like MoveOn.org, filmmaker Michael Moore, and DNC chairman Howard Dean.[47]

It greatly bothered the Left that Rove was not just a political operative, but a policy adviser as well. In May 2002, the *New York Times* reported, with obvious disapproval, that Rove was "inserting himself" into a panoply of policy issues, including "the Middle East, trade, terrorism, Latin America and other foreign policy matters." Certain administration officials, like Secretary of State Colin Powell, were said to be "rankled" by Rove's growing role. The *Times* stated that though Rove declined to comment for the story, he denied playing a major role in foreign policy. But the paper was not buying it, pointing to Rove's admission a few weeks earlier that he had expressed his opinions on the Mideast crisis to President Bush. Democrats also were horrified that such important decisions could be influenced by Rovian political calculations. The *New York Times*, which daily glorified the most political creature of the twentieth century, Bill Clinton, couldn't bear that a right-wing politico could be so close to the levers of ultimate executive power.[48] Rove's policy role did become more substantial when President Bush made him manager of policy development or "senior policy coordinator" in late 2005.

Like all others in Bush's inner circle, the Left painted Rove as a supporter of the abuse, torture, and other inhumane treatment of enemy war prisoners. One writer attributed Rove's (and the administration's) allegedly immoral outlook—and that of their "corporate-fundamentalist minions"—to the kind of deity they worship. "Bush-Rove's Master is a spiteful dictator," wrote Harvey Wasserman "defined by hate and greed, intolerance and hypocrisy. . . . If Christ came back today to resume preaching the Sermon on the Mount, Karl Rove would slime him in the media, then kill him outright, then turn his words into conservative hatespeak, then kill those who refuse to follow in his name. . . . But would Jesus stand for the slaughter of 100,000 Iraqis in his name for oil and dubious Biblical prophecy? . . . What would Jesus say about torture in American prisons, where much the same is being done to innocent inmates as was done to Christ himself on the way to Calvary? Mel Gibson's *Passion of the Christ* could serve as a documentary of the daily torture and slaughter among the 2.2 million prisoners held in the U.S. military and civilian gulag, a barbaric prison system that makes the Romans' seem benign by comparison."[49]

Democrats, who had been screaming for Rove's head for years, finally thought they'd been handed an ax in mid-2005, when his name surfaced in connection with the Valerie Plame/Joe Wilson scandal. Yes, it was always delicious to attack Dick Cheney and other Bush insiders, but nothing gave them greater pleasure than to wound Bush's alleged alter ego. To take Rove out would be to decapitate the president—figuratively speaking, of course. In the Plame affair they saw an opportunity to prove that Bush lied about Iraqi WMD, *and* to indict Rove and maybe even Cheney at the same time.

They were convinced that Rove—along with Cheney and every other Bush-connected villain—deliberately "outed" CIA "undercover agent" Valerie Plame. Rove did alert *Time* magazine's Matt Cooper to the fact that Joe Wilson was married to Plame, but not to reveal her identity. By all accounts he didn't even know her name—he merely knew she worked at the CIA. Much less did he know that she was a covert operative (it is disputed whether she was). Rove's motive was to impeach Wilson's credibility as a critic of the war in Iraq, not to exact revenge against him. If Cooper were to learn that Wilson was married to Plame, and that Plame had arranged for Wilson's "fact-finding" trip to Niger (Wilson fraudulently denied she'd done so), Cooper would be more likely to take Wilson's claims with a grain of salt.

Rove didn't initiate the call to Cooper; Cooper called him. Rove did absolutely nothing wrong. Indeed, a strong case could be made that he had an obligation to alert Cooper to Wilson's chicanery because it had a bearing on national security issues. Shouldn't Rove, in his position, do his part to correct the record about a matter so serious—especially when incessant liberal claims that Bush manipulated prewar intelligence were hurting America's image in the world? Those calling for Rove's firing were the same ones who refused to hold Wilson accountable for lying. They smelled the blood of the evil mastermind and were unwilling to consider mitigating evidence. The leftist antiwar group "Code Pink, Women for

Peace," began selling Karl Rove Condoms, saying "Some Things Should Never Leak."[50]

Not a Target

Rove's difficulties concerning this matter began because, by his own admission, he forgot to tell Special Counsel Patrick Fitzgerald until a year after the criminal investigation began that in his conversation with Matt Cooper he had mentioned Joe Wilson's wife. The Left's hopes continued to glimmer when Rove was called back to testify to the grand jury five times. It didn't seem to matter to the vultures that Fitzgerald assured Rove's attorneys that Rove was *not* a target of the investigation. Rove was mainly reappearing before the grand jury, according to his attorney Bob Luskin, to clarify details that remained unclear from his previous appearances, not to discuss new subjects.[51]

Those Democrats who knew better, like Senator Chuck Schumer, wanted to milk Rove's apparent limbo status before the grand jury as long as possible for maximum political effect. But once word was out that Rove had discussed Plame with Matt Cooper, the Democrats' rush to judgment was in high gear. Senator Harry Reid, who demanded Rove resign over his New York speech, called for his resignation again over the Plame affair—just for discussing Plame.[52]

Senator Chuck Schumer said, "While obviously no one knows what goes on in the grand jury, the fact that Karl Rove has been called back once again is ominous."[53] DNC chairman Howard Dean was less discreet, as usual, and conspicuously bereft of the facts. Though three years before he had urged caution in prejudging Osama bin Laden, he was quick to condemn Rove. Dean said,

"There's no question that Rove was the one that leaked the information about the CIA agent's name."[54]

Some in the mainstream media were sure Rove would be indicted. MSNBC correspondent David Shuster said on May 8, 2006, "Karl Rove's legal team has told me that they expect a decision will come sometime in the next two weeks. And I am convinced that Karl Rove will, in fact, be indicted."[55]

The Left was so hungry for a Rove indictment that one liberal website ran a story that Rove had actually been indicted by the grand jury. No matter how much contrary evidence emerged, they stuck to their story. When Patrick Fitzgerald made public his decision *not to indict* Rove on June 12, 2006, some on the Left were on the brink of psychological collapse. MSNBC's Chris Matthews couldn't quite absorb the shock. He said, "We know that Karl Rove will not be criminally charged, but we do know that he leaked twice to Matt Cooper and to Bob Novak. Is this the end of it, since he's not going to be indicted, we don't hear another word about this case? Is he just free to walk and serve in the White House?"[56]

"Ol' Buddy"

The list of Bush insiders and appointees the Democrats have slimed goes on and on, including UN ambassador John Bolton and Attorney General Alberto Gonzales. Their m.o. is almost always the same: trash and obstruct the nominee to hinder implementation of the Bush policy agenda, and taint the administration further through denigrating presidential nominees and cabinet members. The Democrats' nastiness was on full display in the nomination hearings for Gonzales, when the wholesome Ted Kennedy lectured Gonzales about torturing terrorists, and the self-important Joe

Biden patronizingly called Gonzales "Ol' Buddy," and told him, "I love you," before calling him, in effect, a liar.[57]

In their effort to smear John Bolton, Democrats said he was too mean-spirited, exacting, and insensitive toward subordinates and had a dismissive, disrespectful attitude toward the United Nations. Bolton, they said, cherry-picked intelligence data to support his policy objectives, sort of like what Democrats claimed Bush did. The Democrats who were outraged that Bolton didn't unquestioningly accept the judgment of intelligence people are the same ones who excoriated President Bush for too readily accepting the uniform judgment of all of our intelligence agencies that Iraq had WMD. The Democrats who were horrified that Bolton upbraided an insubordinate subordinate were the same lofty senators who routinely savaged Bush nominees from their Senate perches. And they were mortified when he stated that "if the UN secretary building in New York lost ten stories it wouldn't make a bit of difference."[58] Though that is probably the view of most Americans, to the Democrats the United Nations has more standing and credibility than the United States and certainly more than the Bush administration.

CHAPTER THIRTEEN

Hypocrisy and Sour Grapes

How did the Democratic Party—the party of the "little guy"— allow itself to become the party that embraces kooks who call an American president a Nazi and indescriminately demonize his confidants? How did the party of Harry Truman become so miserably derailed?

The party wasn't always this way. But in modern times it gave itself over to craven self-interest, the politics of personal destruction, and subordinating the national interest to its own. The party's savaging of Judge Robert Bork during his Senate confirmation hearings in 1987 and its character assassination of Clarence Thomas in 1991 were evidence of its decline.[1] It wasn't, however, until the Clinton years that the personal and political interests of a corrupt president thoroughly contaminated the entire party. Clinton and his party made the case that lying, perjury (a felony), obstruction of justice (a felony), and adultery were acceptable behavior, on the grounds that everyone lies about sex.

In the process, Clinton and his administration virtually declared war on the rule of law. The president infused the words "is" and "alone" with hopeless ambiguity[2] and Vice President Gore followed by describing Clinton's intentional acts of misconduct as "mistakes." At a town hall meeting in Derry, New Hampshire, Gore even referred to Clinton's alleged rape of Juanita Broaddrick as a "mistake."[3]

Clinton and his defenders treated the serious felonies of perjury and obstruction of justice as minor misdemeanors, provided they were committed by a president in the context of covering up an adulterous sexual encounter. "Lying about sex," even under oath, was hardly immoral, much less illegal. Clinton's accusers, like independent counsel Kenneth Starr, were the real misfits for dragging the nation (and Clinton's poor family) through the mud for what was essentially a "private matter about sex."

The country's chief executive urged Americans to accept the counterintuitive notion that president's "private" conduct—as if he is ever off duty—should be segregated from his public life. We were told that one's private character would not inform, or even spill over into, his public persona.

Clinton's licentiousness and duplicity were matched only by the despicable tactics he and his foxhole defenders employed against his accusers. He pulled out all the stops, from using seedy private investigators to dig up dirt on them to getting in bed with porn merchant Larry Flynt to smear them. Almost no tactic was beneath him. His thugs released Linda Tripp's confidential personnel files, slandered

Paula Jones as trailer park trash,[4] shamelessly slandered women with whom he'd engaged in affairs,[5] dismissed Monica Lewinsky as a stalker, and wrongfully accused independent counsel Kenneth Starr of a litany of crimes and other misconduct.[6]

Clinton's sins were one thing—every political party has its bad apples. But when his party rallied around him, unquestioningly condoning and ratifying his behavior, his cover-up, and his pernicious assault on our legal system and values, they crossed the line. They transcended a new threshold of decadence when they consciously chose to allow Clinton to escape accountability for his crimes and impeachable offenses. Democrats made a Faustian bargain: selling their souls to perpetuate the Clintons as their ticket to power.

When Republicans discovered they had a corrupt president in Richard Nixon, they pressured him to resign. Democrats, by contrast, did everything they could to defend the corrupt Clinton, including depicting him as the victim of a Republican witch hunt and viciously counterattacking those seeking to bring him to justice—a fatal blow to their integrity.[7] Democrats not only failed to vote to impeach; they also urged the extra-constitutional wrist slap remedy of "censure," and when they didn't get their way, filed out of Congress like whining children, something that hadn't occurred in more than ten years.[8]

Al Gore, who always liked to claim the moral high road, took the low road, proclaiming that Congress's vote to impeach Clinton "[did] a great disservice to a man I believe will be regarded in the history books as one of our greatest presidents."[9] When Tim Russert offered Gore a chance to retract or revise the statement a year later, Gore declined, reaffirming his assertion.[10]

Learning at His Master's Knees

Commentators differ on whether Gore hurt his presidential chances by failing to wrap himself sufficiently in Clinton's economic record or not sufficiently unwrapping himself from Clinton's scandals. But one thing Gore unmistakably acquired from Clinton was his penchant for shrewd, bare-knuckles, partisan warfare. Whether or not Gore had been a gentlemanly competitor in the past, he learned from the Clintons how to brawl in the political streets and manipulate the legal system to further his political ends—in short, how to engage in the politics of personal destruction.

During the Democratic primaries, Gore fought dirty, most notably in his debates with rival Bill Bradley. Right before the election, his operatives allegedly circulated rumors that Ralph Nader was gay[11] and recycled a story about George Bush driving under the influence over two decades earlier.[12]

From the moment it appeared the 2000 presidential election would turn on the close Florida vote, Gore and his team made a conscious decision not to bow out gracefully, no matter to what extent a protracted legal battle would undermine confidence in the electoral process. An hour after calling George W. Bush to concede the election, he called back and withdrew his concession, telling an incredulous Bush, "Your younger brother is not the ultimate authority on this."[13]

Before all the Florida ballots had even been counted (the first time), Gore dispatched a team of some seventy-two loyalists[14] by jet to Tallahassee to find something—anything—with which to challenge the election results. His rallying cry, delivered by his campaign chairman Bill Daley, was "Our campaign continues."[15] For the next thirty-six days, his army of lawyers manufactured countless phony claims to contest the election. The extent to which Al Gore was willing to go, the amount of damage he was willing to inflict on the electoral system, was stunning.

"Every Vote Must Be Counted"

By every measure, Gore lost the election, and lost, and lost and lost. He lost the initial vote count—this notwithstanding the fact that the major networks prematurely declared Gore the winner in Florida, directly resulting in an estimated net loss of 10,000 GOP votes according to one study and 11,500 according to another.[16] Gore next lost the "automatic" machine recount. He then fell short in the overseas and delinquent absentee ballots, which were added to the machine recount. Finally, he lost the manual recount ordered by the Florida Supreme Court.[17] Undeterred, Gore promised to press on (and drag the country through an agonizingly divisive ordeal). In his self-righteous, self-indulgent style, he told the *New York Times*, "I have an obligation to the fifty million plus voters who supported the agenda I laid out during the campaign."[18]

While Gore was insisting that "every vote must be counted," he and his team were circulating a memo with step-by-step directions on how to challenge overseas military ballots,[19] and Democratic operative Bob Beckel, though claiming to be acting independently, admitted he was trying to persuade Bush presidential electors to defect to Gore.[20] Gore had obviously learned well from his mentor, as his approach in contesting the presidential election bore striking resemblances to Clinton's underhanded tactics in fighting his impeachment. Just as Clinton's surrogates maliciously accused Ken Starr of leaking grand jury information they had leaked themselves,[21] Gore accused George Bush of being the one unwilling to abide by the will of the people. Just as Clinton used the full power of his office to marshal public opinion against his enemies, Gore launched this bitter, ill-conceived post-election war that exacerbated the animosity already polarizing the electorate.

One of the Left's knee-jerk responses to the charge it has gone over the line is: "Everybody does it; each party is equally guilty" of acts of misconduct. These efforts to reduce everything to moral equivalence and thereby dilute and diminish the significance are the height of cynicism. A sober examination of the evidence reveals that the unsavory tactics of the Gore team and their Democratic enablers in Florida were in a league of their own.

In December 1999, Gore bragged, "I'm not like George Bush. I'll do anything to win." During the post-election turmoil, also contrary to his stated desire to count every vote, Gore did everything he could to maximize Gore votes and minimize Bush votes. He requested recounts in only four counties: those that were the most Gore-favoring. Through his efforts, 40 percent of the overseas military ballots were disqualified, when many of them clearly shouldn't have been.

According to the *Los Angeles Times*, Gore flooded Florida with seasoned political operatives to find more Gore votes, with one Democratic lawyer telling them, "We only need 301 votes to win this. Our goal is to preserve the Al Gore vote. It's very important that if you see any kind of mark—a scratch, a dent, a pinprick in Al Gore's column—that you challenge." Yet when the operatives inquired how they should treat such marginal marks on Bush ballots, Gore's every-vote-must-count lawyer said, "Keep your lips sealed."[22]

Further stirring the pot, the Democratic National Committee hired Texas-based Telequest, a telemarketing firm, while polls were still open, to call thousands of voters in Palm Beach to agitate them into contacting local election officials to complain about their ballots. They tried to make it appear that these complaints independently originated with the voters. Within the last hour the polls were opened, the firm made some five thousand calls in less than forty-five minutes, according to Telequest's Wade Scott. The suggestive call script stated:

> Some voters have encountered a problem today with punch card ballots in Palm Beach County. These voters have said that they believe that they accidentally punched the wrong hole for the incorrect candidate. If you have already voted and think you may have punched the wrong hole for the incorrect candidate, you should return to the polls and request that the election officials write down your name so that this problem can be fixed.

The firm delivered the names and numbers of complaining voters to the Democratic Party. Even political science professor Candice Nelson, though opining the calls were legal, admitted that they "could have contributed to what appeared to most Americans to be a spontaneous explosion of concern in Florida the morning after the election."[23]

The Gore militia was praising county officials who followed their lead, but when Broward and Miami-Dade decided not to conduct a full manual recount, Gore threatened to file a suit to compel them to comply. Broward County Democrats changed a ten-year-old rule in the middle of a manual recount to more liberally construe ballots to enhance the Gore vote.[24] And some thirty-nine felons, mostly Democrats, managed to cast illegal absentee ballots in the Democratic counties of Broward and Miami-Dade. Those counties also reversed course, under heavy-handed pressure from Gore, and decided to conduct manual recounts.[25]

Miami-Dade then suspiciously closed its recount to the media. Gore lead negotiator Warren Christopher contacted the Democratic attorney for Palm Beach County's elections supervisor and urged him to use his influence to pressure the county to conduct a manual recount. The attorney made clear he thought Christopher's call was inappropriate. But Palm Beach proceeded with the recount.[26]

Five separate affidavits were filed in federal court alleging misconduct by Carol Roberts, a Palm Beach County Democratic election official, to help Al Gore in the manual recount.[27] One affiant swore, "I personally observed canvassing board counters and Ms. Roberts twisting and otherwise manipulating the paper ballots in an attempt to dislodge the chads. I personally requested that Ms. Carol Roberts review several ballots that were counted as valid Gore votes despite the fact that...there existed no hanging chads, and she refused...I observed Ms. Carol Roberts picking up numerous ballots from the questionable pile and the Gore pile and then interspersing ballots between the piles."[28]

Meanwhile, Gore personally contacted newspaper columnists to promote his cause. Democratic commentator Mort Kondracke conceded that the ongoing recount might send a signal to Democratic county commissioners about how many votes they would need to surpass Bush—but stated he wasn't suggesting the commissioners were corrupt.[29]

While anarchy was erupting in Florida at the behest of Gore's forces, his people were busy elsewhere drumming up support for the cause. Clinton-Gore operative Paul Begala wrote a scathing column painting the Bush states variously as racist, murderous, homophobic, and anti-Catholic.[30] Even columnist Camille Paglia, a Clinton supporter, noted there was an "upsurge in partisan warfare and racial animosity fomented in Florida by Democratic operatives after the election."[31] Al Gore feigned complete ignorance of his operatives' vitriol, and urged spokespersons in both parties "to do their part to lift up this discourse, to refrain from using inflammatory language and to avoid statements that could make it harder for our country to come together once the counting is over. This is the direction I have given to my own campaign."[32]

Micromanaging a Smear Campaign

Of all the shenanigans and dirty tricks orchestrated by Team Gore, nothing quite compared with its effort to destroy the reputation of Florida secretary of state, Republican Katherine Harris. Harris's reward for performing her nondiscretionary, ministerial duty of certifying the Florida election results was to be personally defamed and discredited in despicable fashion. No one had been more unjustly treated by the Clinton-Gore squads, with the possible exception of Ken Starr.

While Gore pretended not to be privy to this unconscionable assault on Katherine Harris, reports surfaced that he was directly behind the campaign to destroy her. *Human Events* reported that "Gore personally instructed his team to smear [Harris]. The vice president of the United States, micromanaging the Florida war from the dining room of his residence at the Naval Observatory in

Washington, was now directly engaged in the politics of personal destruction. Privately referring to Harris as Cruella De Vil...Gore told deputy campaign manager Mark Fabiani and press secretary Chris Lehane to plant damaging press stories that would discredit Harris as a Bush partisan."[33] They complied in spades.

Lehane proceeded to pronounce that Harris was "in the finest tradition of a Soviet commissar." Other henchmen stated she displayed an "astonishing abuse of authority," and tried "to steal the election."[34] Gore's aids warned that if Bush were to win with the help of Katherine Harris, "the investigation of her role in this entire situation will make Whitewater look like a picnic." Fabiani called Harris "a crony of the Bush brothers" who was "trying to steal this election away."[35]

Liberal editorialists also piled on. The *Boston Globe*'s Thomas Oliphant decried Harris's "astonishing abuse of authority,"[36] and the *New York Daily News*'s Lars-Erik Nelson charged that Harris was "trying to steal the election for George W. Bush. I also say she is doing it in a clumsy, nay, brutish way, with very little elegance. This is a mugging."[37] *New York Times* columnist Maureen Dowd said on the Don Imus show that Harris was "obviously trying to steal this election for Jeb."[38]

Then Gore's sympathizers began to insult Harris's appearance. *Boston Globe* columnist Joan Vennochi referred to her as "Florida's ghoulishly made-up secretary of state."[39] The *Washington Post*'s Robin Givhan wrote, "Her lips were overdrawn with berry-red lipstick—the creamy sort that smears all over a coffee cup and leaves smudges on shirt collars. Her skin had been plastered and powdered ....Caterpillars seemed to rise and fall with every bat of her eyelid....Her mouth is a jagged edge. One of the reasons Harris is so easy to mock is because she, to be honest, seems to have applied her makeup with a trowel."[40]

And mock they did. Harris immediately became fodder for late-night television skits and jokes. The *Boston Herald's* Margery Eagan said Harris would "be remembered for looking just ghastly Tuesday night. At least by Wednesday her appearance seemed almost—if not quite—transformed. Like Dr. Richard Sharpe, the transvestite and alleged wife killer. Or Marilyn Manson. Or Dustin Hoffman as Tootsie. Or Cruella De Vil. Or Leona Helmsley on Halloween."[41]

What Mandate?

In December 2000, in a column titled "The 4 Years' War," I predicted that "Gore's perpetual post-election tantrum is just a prelude to the next four years. Democrats, I'm afraid, are just getting warmed up for their Four Years' War."[42] I also observed that their dogged determination to undermine the election results would "square nicely with their aim to delegitimize Bush's presidency in the event their contest fails."[43] I couldn't have been more prescient, except that I guessed short on the number of years. I should have titled the column "The 8 Years' War," because the Democrats' bellicose behavior hasn't let up and will surely continue throughout Bush's second term.

After the U.S. Supreme Court spanked the Florida Supreme Court for judicially legislating changes in its state election laws *following the election*—such as establishing a new deadline for the secretary of state to accept returns—and officially ended Gore's chances of reversing the Florida results, Democrats and the liberal media had to grudgingly regroup. They would continue to complain bitterly about the "gross injustice" wrought by the Supreme Court, but they would also need to devise a more pragmatic strategy that could diminish the president's effectiveness.

One of the first themes they began to promote was that the U.S. Supreme Court "selected" this president, which meant that Bush's presidency was illegitimate and that he had no mandate,[44] ideas they would use often in the next four years and resurrect in a major way following the 2004 election. Bush would need to compromise, move to the center, engage in collegiality and bipartisanship, heal the wounds, and reach across the aisle. Democratic senator John Breaux said, "I think [Bush] needs to have some bipartisan memberships in his cabinet."[45] *Newsday* opined that "The success of Bush's presidency will lie in his willingness to ignore the hard right of the Republican Party and move toward the center."[46]

Congressman Charles Rangel, arguing against the implementation of President Bush's promised tax cuts, said, "Whatever challenges occur in the coming months concerning the U.S. and global economies, one thing is for sure: the only way to meet those challenges will be to act in a bipartisan manner. I urge our next president, George W. Bush, to reach out to his Republican friends and say it is time to negotiate with Democrats to accomplish targeted tax cuts."[47] In other words, even though Bush won, he should opt for the Democrats' tax plan. Only then would they deem him bipartisan.

CNN's Bill Schneider gleefully chimed in that: "There was no mandate here... he has to see that....And his job is to define a program, an agenda on issues that everyone cares about, like prescription drugs and education that both parties can rally around."[48] *CNN Live* aired a special event addressing whether President Bush, even if he wanted to compromise, could tame the "conservative beast."[49]

Liberal papers like the *Los Angeles Times* agreed that Bush had no mandate.[50] But such liberal papers seemed to have such reservations about mandates only when Republicans won presidential elections.[51] The *New York Times*, for example, opined that Ronald Reagan's mandate in 1980 had "little policy content."[52] Amazingly, it repeated this theme with his eighteen-point landslide victory over Walter Mondale in 1984, saying, "President Reagan's lonely landslide is a personal victory with little precise policy mandate or clear ideological underpinning."[53] This from a newspaper that consistently derided President Reagan as a right-wing ideologue.

Of course, when Clinton won in 1992 with only 43 percent of the vote, the paper that reports "All the News That's Fit to Print" said, "The test now will be how quickly President-elect Clinton can convert his mandate into momentum."[54] In 1996, when Clinton won with 49 percent, it said, "There can be no question about his mandate. The American people express their clearest opinion about what they want government to do through their choice of chief executive."[55]

Democratic leaders were acting as though Bush needed to be apologetic about his victory and tentative about his agenda, though the Constitution affords just as much executive power to a narrowly elected president as to a landslide victor. Bill Clinton, despite his victory by a mere 43 percent plurality in 1992, didn't voluntarily scale back his agenda. He engineered a plan hatched mainly by his wife for the government to take over one-seventh of the economy with nationalized health care and passed the largest tax increase in

American history—in lieu of the middle-class tax cut he promised—with Al Gore casting the deciding vote.

Yet Senate Minority Leader Tom Daschle said that nothing would divide the nation more quickly than for President Bush to try to push through his tax cut.[56] House Minority Leader Richard Gephardt made clear that Bush would have to engage in "honest compromise" to get anything done.[57] Democrats, snapped Gephardt, would not accept "dictation," a "take-it-or-leave-it approach," or a "my-way-or-highway agenda."[58] While Democrats painted Bush's tax cut proposal as extreme, it was decidedly more moderate than the tax cuts of President Kennedy or President Reagan.[59]

Other Democrats "remain[ed] incensed by the election outcome" and "determined to hold out for Al Gore's agenda," as they looked forward to 2004.[60] How dare President Bush presume to promote his own agenda! Democrats nationwide were said to be shocked at how quickly in his term Bush staked out conservative positions on "controversial" issues like abortion, school vouchers, and tax cuts.[61]

Academia weighed in as well. George Edwards, head of presidential studies at Texas A&M University, said, "You have a president coming in without a majority of the nationwide vote, without a plurality of the vote, without coattails, without a mandate, and with the additional polarization from an election whose legitimacy many people can question. He should look for small victories where there is a high probability of bipartisan cooperation rather than pushing the most notable aspects of his agenda."[62] Fort Lauderdale *Sun-Sentinel*'s Washington bureau chief, William Gibson, wrote, "Bush faces a far different kind of rebellion in the form of Democrats who remain convinced their candidate, Al Gore, actually won the 2000 election, but lost. The disputed outcome puts the president-elect's legitimacy under a cloud."[63]

Richard S. Dunham, *BusinessWeek*'s White House correspondent, wrote an article titled "Who Says Bush Has a Mandate? Bush. Despite losing the popular vote, George W. is pressing on as if he won in a landslide." Dunham quoted Princeton political science professor Fred Greenstein as saying, "Bush is very good at claiming victory. He has a 'Marlboro Man' approach to communication. His idea of having a mandate is to say 'I have a mandate.'"[64] *Time* magazine said that if Bush wins, it would be by a technicality. Democratic senator Chuck Schumer said, "The next president should call fifty Democrats and fifty Republicans to the White House and say, 'You're gonna be my base. He has to make a decision—work the middle or get nothing done."[65] The *Los Angeles Times*'s Ronald Brownstein wrote that the winner of the election must be a peacemaker who would offer olive branches to the loser.[66] Former New York governor Mario Cuomo said, "More people voted for Al Gore's agenda than voted for Bush's agenda. You can't neglect that."[67]

"It Will Be Scorched Earth"

Liberal public interest groups also wasted no time in issuing warnings to Bush that he better not even think about appointing conservative, originalist judges to the Supreme Court. Nan Aron, president of the Alliance for Justice, said, "It will be scorched earth. We won't give one lousy inch. There is no mandate to appoint a justice hostile to civil rights, women's rights, the environment. If the administration goes ahead and nominates someone like that, we will muster every resource to make sure that person is not confirmed."[68]

As President Bush picked his cabinet, Democrats and the main-stream media were aghast that Bush had the audacity to choose con-servatives. Why, he was choosing a cabinet that was "little different from one he would have chosen if he had won a resounding vic-tory."[69] They viewed his choices of John Ashcroft for attorney gen-eral and Gale Norton for interior secretary as breaches of his promise to seek a "new tone" and work toward reconciliation and unity. They were Bush's "first lies." In their view, they were in-your-face, divisive choices.[70] Democrats, who demand diversity, weren't the least impressed that President Bush nominated three women, two African American men, and one Hispanic man. They insisted on ideological diversity as well.

As Bush's first term got under way, the liberal establishment con-tinued to insist on "bipartisanship" from Bush, by which they meant unilateral compromise and conciliation on his part, while they would be free to practice bitter partisanship. Senator Edward Kennedy said that when Ashcroft was Missouri attorney general he exploited "racial tensions to promote his campaign for governor" and said that Ashcroft's opposition to school desegregation was "an outrage against the children of Missouri."[71] Senator Daschle told reporters he hoped to persuade at least forty-one senators—enough to sustain a filibuster—to oppose President Bush's nomination of Ashcroft to send a "signal to the Bush administration that Democrats have the clout to block future nominations."[72] The Democratic minority also slandered Gale Norton as anti-environment.[73] And, at a Democratic rally on the Capitol lawn, Senator Daschle and Congressman Gephardt accused the Bush administration of pandering to big busi-ness and naming "the most far-right, anti-woman, anti-environment, wealthiest, and best-connected cabinet in a generation."[74]

While still screaming for bipartisanship from Republicans, a number of liberal groups were organizing for "quick, brutal battles on nominations, tax cuts, the budget, and other issues." These groups were "energized and ready to fight"—hardly the vocabulary of conciliators.[75] When Bush had just completed his first week in office, then Democratic National Committee chairman Joe Andrew tore into him. "Whether it's imposing new restrictions on women's right to choose or delay new health, safety, and environmental initiatives, Americans are starting to ask what happened to the 'compassionate' George W. Bush they saw on Inauguration Day." Andrew then compared him to the reviled (by Democrats) former House Speaker Newt Gingrich. "Bush," said Andrew, "is ripping a page from the Gingrich playbook."[76]

Conspicuously absent throughout this period was any recognition by the Democratic minority that their own bipartisanship, compromise, and conciliation would have to be part of the mix to restore unity. Nary were calls from the mainstream media for Democrats to work with Republicans. Democrats did, after all, lose the election. Yet all the demands for compromise came from the Left.

Speaking as though President Bush had grievously wounded America (and minorities) by narrowly winning the election, Reverend Jesse Jackson said, "We want healing, but there's glass in the wound. There's an infection. A Band-Aid will not do. . . . Silence is betrayal."[77] Congresswoman Maxine Waters, railing against Bush's tax cut proposal, said, "George W. Bush speaks with a forked tongue. While he's trying to get photo opportunities with Democrats and send a message about cooperation and civility, in fact he's undermining us at every step."[78]

The Democratic Party proper, likewise, made it quite clear that it was not about to declare a cease-fire—but demanded unilateral disarmament by Republicans. One unmistakable signal of this was the party's brazen decision to elevate Bill Clinton's confidant and primo fund-raiser Terry McAuliffe to chairmanship of the Democratic National Committee. McAuliffe was the operative who had presided over Clinton's 1996 reelection effort, which the *Washington Post* described as "the most scandal-plagued harvest season in recent politics."[79]

Democrats made quite a statement by installing this man, who the Senate Governmental Affairs Committee found in 1997 was involved in one of the "most serious transgressions of the '96 campaign, in which the party agreed to trade donations with Teamsters Union officials who were then trying to secure the reelection of union president Ron Carey. The Teamsters were to give the party up to $1 million, in exchange for the party's pledge to find one or more donors to give $100,000 to Carey's reelection campaign."[80] This is how the Democratic Party rewarded the man who had operated under a cloud. This is how they demonstrated their commitment to bipartisanship.

No Honeymoon

In a conference call between Clinton, McAuliffe, and Andrew, McAuliffe's rival for the DNC post, McAuliffe threw down the gauntlet: "Let George W. Bush have a good week. Let him have a good inauguration. But we need to give these Republicans the same honeymoon they gave us: none."[81]

McAuliffe and his colleagues made good on his promise to deprive President Bush of his honeymoon. They drew the line on his tax cut proposal, his first major legislative initiative. Since Bill Clinton had been so successful in distorting the Reagan economic record and demagoging the tax issue with class warfare politics, his successors were not about to abandon the strategy.

Senate Minority Leader Tom Daschle, at a press conference announcing Democratic opposition to the Bush plan, stood before the cameras, held up an automobile muffler, and said, "If you make over $300,000 a year, this tax cut means you get to buy a new Lexus. If you make $50,000 a year, you get to buy a muffler on your used car. That's the difference. That's what we're talking about here, a Lexus versus a muffler. And I think we've really got to understand how imbalanced and how unfair this tax code is as it's been presented—or this tax proposal is as it's been presented to us."[82]

But the Democratic leadership didn't limit itself to mere class warfare. Certain Democrats, such as Congressman Robert Menendez, also played the race card. "As the highest-ranking Hispanic in Congress," said Menendez, delivering the Democratic response to the president's weekly radio address, "I can tell you that many Hispanic families will get little from the Bush plan."[83]

• • •

More than two hundred Democratic lawmakers, exhibiting the spirit of bipartisanship they had been lecturing Republicans so much about, snubbed President Bush's lunch invitation at the White House to celebrate his first one hundred days in office. Only fifty Democrats accepted the invitation, though all were invited.[84] But on their own turf, they still had plenty to say in assessing the president's first one hundred days. After lambasting him over tax cuts and health care, they accused him of trying to poison our drinking water (and our children) with arsenic, because he was willing to allow the EPA more time to study and implement a new rule regulating the levels of arsenic.

EPA administrator Christine Todd Whitman, in defending further study, said she wanted to examine the cost-benefit analysis, confirm they were using the best science, and make sure there would be no unintended consequences from implementing the new regulation.[85] Whitman told FOX News's Brit Hume she wanted "to ensure that we didn't force people into positions where they weren't able to afford their water."[86] Meanwhile the Democratic National Committee was airing a political ad showing a little girl holding out a glass of water and asking, "May I please have some more arsenic in my water, Mommy?" Next, a little boy is shown with a hamburger in his hand, saying, "More salmonella in my cheeseburger, please."[87]

Democratic politicians followed suit. Senator Barbara Boxer said President Bush ought to come with a warning label, "Hazardous to Our Health."[88] Senator Hillary Clinton said, "We've all heard about Bush's charm offensive. But now he's on a harm offensive doing harm to our environment and our children's health as he rolls back regulations designed to protect us from poisons like arsenic, and emissions that cause global warming. . . . A prior administration was known for calling ketchup a vegetable. I guess this administration wants to be known for calling arsenic a beverage."[89]

House Minority Whip David Bonior said, "Since taking office, the president has treated the big polluters to an all-you-can-eat smorgasbord of environmental giveaways."[90] Senator Daschle said, "Under FDR all we had to fear was fear itself. Now, we have to fear arsenic in our drinking water." He called the administration's action "an outrageous and indefensible decision." In his opportunistic fervor Daschle didn't disclose that he had been one of nineteen Democrats to vote with Republicans to grant the EPA more time to implement the arsenic regulation.[91] Nor did Daschle's fellow Democrats mention that Bill Clinton had left these same arsenic standards in place during his presidency.[92]

"Bully Bush"

About the time the president had completed his first six months in office, Democrats found friends in their ongoing war against Bush: our European allies. The Associated Press "reported" that "President Bush came into office promising a 'humble' foreign policy, yet his administration has managed to irritate friend and foe alike."[93] The *New York Times* agreed, saying, "Across Europe, there is little love of America's new president and a growing perception that the United States, under his leadership, is looking out only for itself these days—polluting the skies, breaking treaties, and flirting with arms races."[94] As a foreshadowing of the chorus the Left would sing throughout the lead-up to the war against Iraq and beyond, liberals began to complain about the United States' growing "unilateralism" and "a determination to go it alone," which, they complained, were a constant irritation to much of the rest of the world. "The rest of the world thinks we're a big bully," said former Clinton national security official Ivo Daalder. The German paper *Suddeutsche Zeitung* called the president "Bully Bush."[95]

Both National Security Adviser Condoleezza Rice and Secretary of State Colin Powell denied the Bush administration had adopted a unilateralist posture. But the Democrats' reflexive reaction was to concede Europe's criticism and blame America first. Daschle said, "I think [Bush] ought to listen to [European leaders]. I think he needs to hear their concerns because they're real." Of course, it just so happened that most of the European nations' complaints coincided with those of the Democratic leadership, including: Bush's plan for strategic missile defense, his withdrawal from the Kyoto treaty on global warming, his hard line against Saddam Hussein, and, yes, his support for the death penalty.[96]

As the president was preparing to leave for a summit of industrialized nations beginning in Genoa, Italy, Democrats continued violating the traditional rule that politics stops at the water's edge. Though forever complaining that Bush was hurting our image in the world, Senator Daschle and other Democrats, in siding with European leaders, themselves undermined America's image. For Democrats, it was all politics, all the time, irrespective of the detrimental impact to our national interests. Daschle said, "I think we are isolating ourselves, and in so isolating ourselves, I think we're minimizing ourselves. I don't think we are taken as seriously today as we were a few years ago."[97] President Bush disagreed with the Democrats' assessment that Republicans must be wrong if international leaders said we were. To Daschle's outburst, he responded, "The world leaders have found I am a person who speaks plainly and openly about key issues. We're willing to listen. But I will still continue to stand for what I think is right for America."[98]

It wasn't as though President Bush and Republicans were being particularly partisan or combative. Indeed, considering substantive policy alone, the Democrats' acrimonious assault against the Bush administration was nothing if not excessive. While President Bush and congressional Republicans were sticking to their conservative guns on certain big issues, like tax cuts, how could anyone deny that on many other issues—as noted—they were moving to the center?

The president allocated more federal money to public education than any of his predecessors, including Clinton. Republicans succumbed to the Democrats' manufactured complaints about the election and agreed to hold hearings on election reform. President Bush, after promising to oppose the campaign finance bill as unconstitutional, signed it into law.[99] Republicans even began to borrow the Democrats' euphemism "Patients' Bill of Rights" to describe their own HMO bill. Apparently, the Democrats' endless carping was yielding dividends with Republicans, who wanted to escape the label "uncompassionate" and allowed the Democrats to frame the terms of the national debate.

The Charm Offensive

Notwithstanding the Democrats' posturing, President Bush truly did try to woo Democrats and extend them the proverbial olive branch. How else could you describe Bush's anomalous courtship of Senator Ted Kennedy, from invitations to him and his family to watch the movie *Thirteen Days*—about JFK's handling of the Cuban missile crisis—at the White House[100] to virtually turning over the drafting of the No Child Left Behind Act to him? Yet cynics characterized his overtures to Democrats, including his unprecedented visit to their policy retreat and his meeting with lawmakers from both parties, as an insincere "charm offensive."[101]

Kennedy himself, instead of reciprocating with good will, trashed President Bush at the first expedient opportunity. He played a lead role in attacking the Bush tax cut as a sop to the rich. But an even worse betrayal was his assault on the president for spending too little on education. Kennedy said Bush's support of the education bill amounted to a hollow promise because his 2003 budget failed to adequately fund it. In a Democratic radio address, Kennedy said, "With the president's cuts in education, 18,000 fewer teachers will be trained next year. With the president's cuts in education, 33,000 children will be denied after-school programs that keep kids off the streets. With the president's cuts in education, 6 million needy children will be left behind."[102] While Kennedy was issuing this inflammatory rhetoric, Democrats were lacerating Bush for excessive government spending. Such was the Democrats' response to the president's bipartisan overtures. Such was their display of "bipartisanship."

President Bush—two of whose top cabinet members, Secretary of State Colin Powell and National Security Adviser Condoleezza Rice, are black—made similar overtures to the African American community. He spoke at an NAACP convention in Baltimore during the 2000 presidential campaign, but his overtures were continually rebuffed. The NAACP later produced ads implying that Bush's opposition to a hate crimes bill was tantamount to killing James Byrd, who had been dragged behind a truck by racist murderers, "all over again." In 2004, the NAACP ratcheted up the anti-Republican rhetoric even further when chairman Julian Bond depicted Republicans as enemies of African Americans.[103] NAACP president Kweisi Mfume accused the Bush administration of cynically courting the black vote while stifling black organizations such as the NAACP. Mfume said, "We're not fools. If you're going to court us, court us in the daytime, but not like we're a prostitute where you run around at night or behind closed doors and want to deal with us, but not want to deal with us in the light of day."[104]

Bush learned his lesson. Every year since 2000 he has declined the group's invitation, pointing to the leadership's ill treatment of him.

But he said that he admired some NAACP leaders and would seek the members' support "in other ways."[105] Bush's rejection of their later invitations caused the organization's leaders and other liberals to accuse him of snubbing the nation's largest and most effective civil rights organization.

The Democrats' bitter partisanship has continued through the president's first term and well into the second. We have seen it in their approach to almost all issues, from the economy, to Social Security reform, to tax policy, to judicial appointments, to Katrina, to Iraq.

President Bush has remained the focus of their wrath from the day he sprang onto the national scene, and they have pulled out all the stops to destroy him. The 2000 and 2004 defeats compounded their dramatic loss of congressional power in 1994, and they spiraled into a type of policy aimlessness that continues to this day.

CHAPTER FOURTEEN

Those "P.E.S.T.y" Democrats, or A Party in Search of Coherence

The Democrats remained furious throughout President Bush's first term. Party leaders were openly contemptuous of him. Democratic National Committee chairman Terry McAuliffe accused him of being AWOL. Howard Dean suggested that he knew about the September 11 attacks in advance. Senator Ted Kennedy called him a liar on the floor of the Senate. Al Gore repeatedly called him a liar in his shrieking speeches. Congressman Dennis Kucinich said he had targeted citizens for assassination in Afghanistan. Senator Joe Biden called him brain dead.[1]

As the 2004 elections approached, these estranged and bitter Democrats longed for vindication. Drunk on the illusion that Gore won Florida and that Republicans stole the election, they were fearful that it could happen again. Some even contemplated "an uprising" should that occur.

One informal election report posted on the web by a Kerry volunteer opened with this:

> I send you greetings from Florida, where I've been volunteering for the Kerry campaign here in Bushland. Feelings are running high and strong here, as people still remember the debacle of the 2000 election. I have never seen so much anger and frustration in this country. "I don't recognize my country any more," "This isn't democracy, it's fascism," "We can't trust the system after the 2000 election," "All three branches of government are suddenly in the hands of the same cabal—that's not how it's supposed to be," "We've got to take our country back," "If the Supreme Court decides the victor again without counting all the votes there's going to be an uprising in this country," are some of the comments I've heard this week.[2]

When Bush won re-election many Democrats were in a state of shock. John Kerry, within earshot of a *Newsweek* reporter, said, "I can't believe I'm losing to this idiot."[3] Democrats not only didn't get their longed-for vindication; they were repudiated. For four years they had been operating under the assumption they were the majority in the country, only to have been "robbed" by the "Republican" Court. By all rights, they should have significantly grown in numbers because of the mess Bush had made of things. They had been quite effective, had they not, in making that case? So how could they have started out with a majority in 2000, grown it continuously since that dreadful election, and yet lose again? This did not compute. Either they were delusional or America had gone mad—and they weren't sure which.

Not coincidentally, their response eerily resembled the five stages of grief, except for the last one: acceptance, for which they could be said to have substituted "revenge." They manifestly exhibited denial, anger, bargaining, and depression, though not necessarily in that order. Their various reactions ranged from "We were robbed again—in Ohio," to "Bush just barely won—a margin of only 136,000 votes in Ohio kept John Kerry from winning the electoral college—so he doesn't have a mandate," to "We fell short at grass-roots organizing and didn't get our voters out like Republicans did," to "We neglected rural America," to "It was that Osama tape—it scared [the American people]," to "Kerry wasn't the right candidate to make the Democratic case," to "No one could have convinced a majority of Americans because most are red-staters and Red America, frankly, is just too stupid," to "It's not our country anymore," to "The religious zealots divided the nation and won through fear," to "We believe in moral values too," to "They exploited national security; they played on our fears," to "We've got to figure out where we went wrong and how to better connect with voters," to "We're going to regroup and fight them like we've never done before."

Perhaps in his most intellectually honest moment of the period, incoming Senate Minority Leader Harry Reid, like a defeated pugilist who had just regained consciousness after being knocked out, confessed, "I don't think there's been a determination about what really happened. It's not that easy to figure out."[4]

Some were so beside themselves—not just the usual suspects in Hollywood—that they were considering leaving America. New

York City teacher Ireena Gurvich said, "I'm thinking of leaving the country" and going to Canada because "it's a kinder and gentler United States."[5] Manhattan architect Kate Dunham said her family might move to Barcelona. "We went there when the war was declared," said Dunham, "and Barcelona was actively against the war. For a long time we've been saying, 'If Bush wins, we've gotta leave.'"[6] Composer, environmental activist, and NPR host Bruce Adolphe agreed with Gurvich that Canada was a more attractive—and less scary—destination. "I imagine myself," said Adolphe, "in a beautiful country house in northern Canada, working on the Internet, doing my radio show, and traveling to concerts in New York, but not living in a scary environment."[7] Of course, none of them apparently followed up on their fantasy to leave. Adolphe, for one, said, "I love working in New York. I feel like it's a country, and it's the best country in the world."[8]

NBC Nightly News had a segment on "blue-state Americans packing up and moving to Canada." Anchor Brian Williams opened, "After the hard-fought election this nation has been through, after the victory for President Bush and the red states, a lot of those on the losing end, the bluest of the blue, find life so unbearable, they've made the ultimate decision to leave."[9] DemocraticUnderground.com, a militant leftist website that is quite popular among the growing fringe elements of the party, conducted a poll asking, "Which is more depressing, 9/11/01 or 11/3/04?" Not surprisingly, 73 percent picked the election date.[10]

"Bastardizing the Entire Psychological Field"

The Democrats' despair was so pronounced that they were engaging in "support-group-like conservations" with their friends about what had befallen them and what was yet to come.[11] Mental health experts advised that a healthy reaction to "post-election disappointment" was to talk about it with others.[12]

Psychologists were commenting on Democratic anguish, offering advice to the "vanquished partisans" who were having difficulty coping with their defeat. New York psychoanalyst Sherman Pheiffer said, "My patients were incredulous, depressed, angry, very frightened. Everyone talked about feeling frightened [about] the future of this country." Massachusetts psychologist Jane Darwin said her patients felt "the roller coaster had crashed. I think we all had a little post–Red Sox magical thinking."[13]

Melissa Healy, in the health section of the *Los Angeles Times*, wrote, "After an election marked by bitterness, high energy, and a sharply divided electorate, those who tend to Americans' mental health are worried about the emotional state of the losing side. Beyond the tears shed over an election lost, they see anger, uncertainty, paralysis, and downright denial among defeated Kerry backers. They see a depth and breadth of grief that many say they have never seen before."[14] Many "shrinks" anticipated that disgruntled Democrats would "lie awake at night fuming," "ponder[ing] revenge," "threaten[ing] to move to Canada," and "post[ing] screeds" on the Internet.[15]

Beverly Hills psychologist Cathy Quinn said, "I would actually use the word despair. That's what I sense from several patients who have come in since the elections."[16] Quinn believed that their angst over the election would drive many people to counseling for the first time in their lives. Other therapists even compared their patients' reactions to the horrible feelings people experienced after September 11. Washington, D.C., psychiatrist Justin Frank described it as "acute grief reaction." In some cases, he wasn't too far off. Actor/photographer Tony Sears lamented that when watching Kerry's concession speech, "I felt like someone had died. I was just very sad for what might have been."[17]

Dozens of Kerry supporters sought therapy—some had "intense hypnotherapy"—after the election. Boca Raton trauma specialist Douglas Schooler said one friend told him he had never been so depressed and angry in his life. "I observed patients threatening to leave the country or staring listlessly into space," said Schooler. They were emotionally paralyzed, shocked and devastated." The American Health Association (AHA) deemed the problem so widespread in South Florida that it adopted a phrase to describe it— reportedly coined by its executive director, Boca Raton psychologist Rob Gordon[18]: "post-election selection trauma (PEST)."[19]

Symptoms of the disorder were "feelings of withdrawal and isolation, anger and bitterness, loss of appetite, sleeplessness, nightmares, intense moodiness, and preoccupied with anxiety over the country's future."[20] One man melodramatically wrote to AHA that "to many of us, this was the key election about the future of our country, and with a Bush win that future is pretty much destroyed."[21]

Healthy skeptics are entitled to wonder whether liberal anxiety wasn't in a certain sense rational and largely predictable, given the endless demonization of Republicans by the Left since Bush's victory in 2000. If Bush and his party were really as awful as Democrats had been portraying them, grassroots liberals would have every reason to be steeped in a profound funk. But the AHA was not open to skepticism about its newfound "valid psychological problem." Its officials took umbrage when Rush Limbaugh lampooned the phenomenon on his national radio show, offering to provide his own free therapy to traumatized Kerry voters. "Rush Limbaugh has no clinical qualifications to counsel anyone," one therapist barked. "He's not only minimizing PEST, but he's bastardizing the entire psychological field and our clinical expertise."[22]

But PEST was not to be dismissed or discounted. It was hardly a localized phenomenon, nor was it—apparently—greatly exaggerated. The reports were too numerous. Fifty-year-old personal trainer Kate Schmidt said that after the election she was "just palpably, physically ill." State prosecutor Brad Levenson said he was feeling "rudderless, isolated, and—worst of all—powerless." Elizabeth Marshall, a Democratic volunteer worker in Pennsylvania, said people there showed "bereavement, almost. People feel that something they had, which was hope for imminent change, has been taken from them."[23] Irvine psychotherapist Jill Boultinghouse indicated that many of her clients were not eating or sleeping.

Washington, D.C., clinical psychologist Renana Brooks confirmed that in her observation, "People are in absolute post-traumatic stress and total despair and pretty much believe American society is permanently destroyed." She joined with Dr. Frank in comparing it to September 11. "That's what I've been hearing all day," said Brooks. "It looks to me like a worse trauma than September 11." A New York City rollerblader's T-shirt told the tale more succinctly, "Bush Wins: Upper West Side Put on Suicide Watch."[24]

Twenty-five-year-old Andrew Veal of Georgia reportedly committed suicide with a shotgun blast to the head over Kerry's defeat and girlfriend problems.[25] Speaking of September 11, Tina Brown wrote in the *Washington Post*, "What's eerie is that the feeling of drift and distraction in New York has an uneasy millennial echo.

This is just how it felt on the eve of September 11—except that now the drift is overlaid with a deep, unignorable anxiety. All those vengeful phantoms in Fallujah who have fled our conquering armies—are they out there somewhere?"[26]

New York psychiatrist Haddassah Brooks Morgan said that Kerry's defeat, together with the recent drubbing of the Yankees by the Red Sox, sent many of her patients into near-catatonic distress. "In my whole forty years of practice here I have never heard patients as bereft by a result as this. There was a feeling in session after session of the insult to one's tribe, a loss of purpose and direction."[27]

Yet another therapist, Alan Hilfer of Maimonides Medical Center in Brooklyn, New York, offered some advice to patients that many must have taken to heart. "Some at risk of post-election depression and anxiety may embrace fraud as an explanation, or subscribe to conspiracy theories to help protect themselves against their feelings of helplessness," he said. "For these people, it may be easier to attribute election results to nefarious misdeeds than to confront the limits of one's ability to influence a future in which one feels a strong stake."[28]

Thomas Lipscomb, writing for *The American Thinker*, reminds us that for all their hyperventilating over the election, this rush to "medicalize" problems is nothing new for the American Left. He notes that attaching the vocabulary of illness enables liberals to bring victimization into the equation, while simultaneously demonizing those—Republican voters—who brought about the condition. Lipscomb says that many on the Left indeed suffer from a psychological problem, the root of which is that they base much of their self-esteem on the "assumed virtue of their political alignment."[29] Others, including myself, have made similar observations. I wrote on July 8, 2000, that liberals "fool themselves into believing that their morality is defined more by the political policies they advocate than the way they conduct their lives."[30] An obvious example of this is their self-congratulatory advocacy of confiscating money from other people—those they pejoratively characterize as "the wealthy"—to give to the "poor."

Unilateral Bipartisanship

It wasn't just therapists putting themselves and others on couches. Mainstream journalists were also joining the fray. *New York Times* columnist Thomas Friedman lamented that he was living among people—a majority—who have a different vision for the nation than he does. He wrote, "But what troubled me yesterday was my feeling that this election was tipped because of an outpouring of support for George Bush by people who don't just favor different policies than I do—they favor a whole different kind of America. We don't just disagree on what America should be doing; we disagree on what America is."[31]

This was quite an admission for Friedman: one of wholesale alienation from the nation's majority. But it was more than that. Friedman wrote, "Despite an utterly incompetent war performance in Iraq and a stagnant economy, Mr. Bush held onto the same basic core of states that he won four years ago—as if nothing had happened. It seemed as if people were not voting on his performance. It seemed as if they were voting for what team he was on. This was not an election. This was station identification."[32] It apparently didn't occur to Friedman that people *were* voting on his performance, not in a vacuum, but weighed against John Kerry's policies and suitability for governance, especially in the War on Terror. The majority of people simply didn't share Friedman's negative assessment of the president's performance, a possibility he seemed unable to fathom.

Washington Post columnist E. J. Dionne displayed similar astonishment that America could be duped into electing a president who had intentionally divided the nation and used religion as a wedge issue. Dionne wrote, "Let's be honest: We are aghast at the success of a campaign based on vicious personal attacks, the exploitation of strong religious feelings, and an effort to create the appearance of strong leadership that would do Hollywood proud. We are alarmed that so many of our fellow citizens could look the other way and not hold Bush accountable for utter incompetence in Iraq and for untruths spoken in defense of the war.... And we are disgusted that an effort consciously designed to divide the country did exactly that—and won."[33]

Dionne, like Friedman, just assumes his version of disputed events and ideologies is objectively true. He assumes that conservative ideas—like upholding traditional marriage—are divisive, while liberal ideas are enlightened and "bipartisan." Liberals always do this. Somehow they assume that it was divisive for President Bush to try to advance his agenda after winning the election, but not divisive for Senate Minority Leader Harry Reid to say that his party would "make few, if any concessions, despite their setbacks" in the election.[34] Liberals assume it was not divisive for John Kerry, in his nomination acceptance speech, to accuse President Bush of lying us into war. "As president," said Kerry, "I will restore trust and credibility to the White House. I will be a commander in chief who will never mislead us into war."[35]

Red with Ignorance

Many liberal elites warmed to the idea that Bush supporters are just not very bright, much less decent human beings. To be fair, this is nothing new. The prolific economics writer and liberal icon John Kenneth Galbraith, in declaring conservatism dead in the '60s, also tagged conservatives as "bookless."[36] And it's common knowledge that the Left dismissed Ronald Reagan as a disengaged, "amiable dunce," though after he died the publication of his meticulously self-edited, brilliant letters and speeches exposed the Left's arrogant assessment for the foolhardy snobbery it was.

Garry Wills, adjunct history professor at Northwestern University, compared Bush "fundamentalist" voters to Muslim terrorists such as al Qaeda and "Saddam Hussein's Sunni loyalists." Wills wrote, "Can a people that believes more fervently in the Virgin Birth than in evolution still be called an Enlightened nation? . . . The secular states of modern Europe do not understand the fundamentalism of the American electorate. It is not what they had experienced from this country in the past. In fact, we now resemble those nations less than we do our putative enemies."[37]

University of Maryland investigators issued a report called "The Separate Realities of Bush and Kerry Supporters," in which they said that those who still had a favorable impression of President Bush "suppress awareness of unsettling information" and "cling so tightly to beliefs" that have been rejected (or "visibly refuted") by the media and "the majority of the people of the world."[38] Author Jane Smiley wrote, "The election results reflect the decision of the right wing to cultivate and exploit ignorance in the citizenry. I suppose the good news is that fifty-five million Americans have evaded the ignorance-inducing machine. But fifty-eight million have not. . . .

The error that progressives have consistently committed over the years is to underestimate the vitality of ignorance in America. Listen to what the red-state citizens say about themselves, the songs they write, and the sermons they flock to. They know who they are—they are full of original sin and they have a taste for violence."[39]

ABC's Carole Simpson was baffled by the nation's re-election of President Bush. At a National Press Club forum aired live on C-SPAN she said, "I look at the election, and I'm going, 'Well, of course our kids are not bright about these things because their parents aren't.'"[40] Slate columnist William Saletan, in his piece, "Simple but Effective, Why You Keep Losing to This Idiot," argued that Bush won because he "is a very simple man."[41] Kerry, on the other hand, was complex—probably too sophisticated for the majority of voters (red-staters, no doubt) to comprehend. "Bush had one message; Kerry had dozens, Bush had one issue; Kerry had scores." Next time, Democrats should find someone comparably simple (like Southerner John Edwards) who can resonate with voters. Once elected, that simple president can then "staff the executive branch" with those "legions" of liberals with "preparation, stature, expertise, and nuance."[42]

A liberal Internet posting ranked the states according to average IQ. And, you guessed it: Kerry's blue states purportedly outranked the red states with ease.[43] Many New Yorkers reportedly identified with the sentiment captured in the London *Daily Mirror*'s headline after the election, "How Could 59,054,087 People Be So Dumb?"[44] Cartoonist Ted Rall portrayed Bush voters as bigoted inbreds, typified by a big-toothed trucker, under the caption, "I need me lots of guns to shoot fags." Another slovenly white says, "And Darwinists! God hates them!"[45]

House Minority Leader Nancy Pelosi said Americans didn't hold Republicans accountable for things going badly in the country, "because the public didn't know that they controlled all three elements of government."[46] One wonders whether these pathetic red-state voters liberals continued to demean are the same ones Senate Minority Leader Harry Reid had in mind when he lamented, a few months after the election, "We neglected rural America. All we have to do is be there and let them know we care."[47] Perhaps it depends on what Reid means by "let[ting] them know we care."

Reid's incongruous comment aside, the fundamental disrespect liberals have for the common man they purport to champion is nothing new. Michael Gecan, of the Industrial Areas Foundation, a leftist critic of the Democratic Party, captured this liberal arrogance well in an op-ed for the *Washington Post*. He wrote, "Many in the hierarchy of the Democratic Party have contempt for ordinary Americans—for their red faces and moderate churches and mixed, often moderate, views."[48] Amen.

An Evangelical Jihad: Divide through Fear

Other Old Media liberals and Democratic politicians pushed a variation of the "red states are stupid" meme: Bush ran a divisive scare campaign and the gullible, vulnerable majority bought into it—especially "values voters." Hendrick Hertzberg, writing for the *New Yorker*, condescendingly groused, "Many of these formerly non-voting white evangelicals are remaining true to their unworldliness. In voting for [Bush] they have voted against their own material (and, some might imagine, spiritual) well-being."[49]

New York Times columnist Maureen Dowd wrote, "W. doesn't see division as a danger. He sees it as a wingman. The president got re-elected by dividing the country along fault lines of fear, intolerance, ignorance, and religious rule. He doesn't want to heal rifts; he wants to bring any riffraff who disagree to heel. W. ran a jihad in America so he can fight one in Iraq—drawing a devoted flock of evangelicals, or 'values voters,' as they call themselves, to the polls by opposing abortion, suffocating stem cell research, and supporting a constitutional amendment against gay marriage."[50] Speaking of the politics of fear, it apparently escaped Dowd's notice that Democrats have been trying to scare minorities and the poor for years. It often works, as illustrated when one distraught Texas lady on a fixed income called the American Health Association in south Florida, the mecca of post-election selection trauma, saying she was "absolutely terrified of what Bush will do."[51]

Dowd also did not mention the Democrats' bogus claim that Republicans had a secret scheme to reinstitute a military draft. Nor did she allude to the Democrats' campaign of exclusive negativity, one free of constructive solutions to any of the nation's major problems. In actuality, President Bush's victory was based more on hope and growth than fear. The *Economist* put it best: "In America, self-styled progressives look ever more the party of the past, and confessed conservatives are the ones focusing on the future."[52]

But not according to House Minority Leader Nancy Pelosi, whose analysis more closely resembled Maureen Dowd's. In a press conference after the election Pelosi said that people didn't vote on the substantive issues because Republicans didn't give them an opportunity to. Rather, "they had an election about wedge issues in our country, and you know what they are. They exploited the loveliness of the American people, the devoutness of people of faith... for a political end. That's one of the reasons they won the election."[53] In an NPR radio interview the day before, Pelosi had made the same point. The Democratic Party is "about the issues and about the future, and not about demagoguing the issues of faith, family, and patriotism to eclipse the important decisions...that are being made here."[54]

The "Reality-Based Community"

For all the Left's talk about Republican divisiveness, they were doing all they could to polarize further the red state/blue state dichotomy. Slate's Eric Alterman wrote, "Let's face it. It's not Kerry's fault. It's not Nader's fault (this time). It's not the media's fault (though they do bear a heavy responsibility for much of what ails our political system). It's not 'our' fault either. The problem is just this: Slightly more than half of the citizens of this country simply do not care about what those of us in the 'reality-based community' say or believe about anything." For Alterman, "reality-based community" is code for the blue-state enlightened— those who are not red-state redneck, Bible-thumping, dueling banjo-strumming conservative Neanderthals. Alterman added, "This is not a world of rational debate and issue preference. It's one of 'them' and 'us.' [Bush] is one of 'them' and not one of 'us' and that's all they care about."[55]

Perhaps Alterman had picked up the phrase "reality-based community" from liberal journalist and author Ron Suskind, who had used the term in a marathon piece for the *New York Times Magazine*, where he profiled President Bush as a close-minded, simplistic dogmatist who believes he is on a mission from God. Bush's faith leads him to demand blind obedience from his advisers and shut out facts or advice he doesn't want to hear or which doesn't comport with his faith. "Once he makes a decision—often swiftly, based on a creed or moral position," says Suskind, "he expects complete faith in its rightness."[56] Suskind seemed to be arguing a mutual exclusivity between faith and science, even faith and fact-based reality. Suskind quoted one person as saying that "when it gets complex, [Bush] seems to turn to prayer or God rather than digging in and thinking things through." In Suskind's mind, Middle American Bush supporters did not belong to the "reality-based community."

Secession, Anyone?

One group of despondent Democrats decided to assist "blue companies" to assuage their election pain. Ann and Bill Duvall created "Choose the Blue," a website encouraging readers to buy from companies whose employees donated to Democrats. The website's goal is "to shift vast amounts of wealth to people who support the Democrats' cause."[57] The website grew quickly, reaching at its peak over 300,000 hits a day, proving that grassroots Democrats were not as eager to apply to themselves their demands for unity.

Other Democrats suggested remedies transcending the financial realm, with some even hinting at secession. Democratic political consultant Bob Beckel said, "I think now that slavery is taken care of, I'm for letting the South form its own nation. Really, I think they ought to have their own confederacy."[58] A liberal map making the rounds on the Internet depicted the "United States of Canada," consisting of Kerry's nineteen blue states and Canada, with the thirty-one red states derisively designated "Jesusland."

Another web map promoted an "American Coastopia," which envisioned the joinder of the Northeast, the West Coast, and the upper Midwest in a new country—separate from the "rednecks in

Oklahoma" and the "homophobic knuckle-draggers in Wyoming."[59] The underlying e-mail circulating with that map said, indignantly, "We were all going to move to various other countries, but then we thought—why should WE move? We hold our noses as we fly over you. We are sickened by the way you treat people that are different from you. The rest of the world despises America, and we don't want to be lumped in with you anymore."[60] This, from the people who decry "hate" from the Right and express outrage at the suggestion their patriotism is wanting. *Washington Times* editorial page editor Tony Blankley remarked that the Democratic Party's bond with the "typical working American" lasted 176 years—until the 2004 election. Never before, said Blankley, had "either party in its loss reacted with such venomous contempt for the American people."[61]

E. J. Dionne started talking up the idea that the red states were living off the blue states. This is sheer hypocrisy on the part of conservative red-staters, argued Dionne, who "claim to be opposed to government but are eager to get as many benefits to them as they can." He suggested that to expose this "unbalanced system" could be part of a reform model.[62] *Washington Monthly*'s Paul Glastris agreed, saying, "Why shouldn't the Democrats become the party of federalism and smoke out the truth about how federal tax dollars flow from blue to red states?"[63] Author Matt Miller, writing for *Fortune*, said, "Between 1991 and 2001, 'winner' states got nearly $1 trillion more in federal benefits than they paid in taxes." He referred to the big blue states as "donor" states. Red states, he said, need to get off the "blue gravy train."[64]

Democratic strategist Lawrence O'Donnell said, "The segment of the country that pays for the federal government is now being governed by the people who don't pay for the federal government."[65]

Ninety percent of the red states, according to O'Donnell "are welfare-client states of the federal government."[66] The blue states, he complained, are footing most of the bill, but the people in those states still feel disenfranchised. The *Stranger*, a Seattle alternative weekly, suggested that blue-state liberals should abandon their compassionate instincts with respect to the red states. "To red-state voters, to the rural voters, residents of small, dying towns, and soulless sprawling exurbs, we say this: F— [the *Stranger* spelled out the entire word] off. Your issues are no longer our issues. We're going to battle our bleeding-heart instincts and ignore pangs of misplaced empathy. We will no longer concern ourselves with a health-care crisis that disproportionately impacts rural areas. Instead we will work toward winning health care one blue state at a time."[67]

Geraldine Ferraro, former Democratic vice presidential candidate, no less, snubbed her Eastern nose at the flyover hayseeds. "If, indeed, all those blue states all got together and seceded from the union," she said, "think what would be left for those red states: nothing. There would be no educational system. You would have nothing. What would be left to you? I mean, where is all of this talent in this country? It's on both sides, the Northeast corridor."[68]

In one newsletter/blog piece, "Democalypse Now," the editors of *Divided Times* newsletter expanded on the red-state dependency theory. They wrote, "Democrats have something Goldwater's GOP did not: A growing awareness that the Red States have no clothes, they're in full-blown parasitic dependence upon Blue States whose lifestyles they reject and whose populace they effectively oppress through electoral manipulation. Comparisons with the Civil War are rife, yet outrage over what amounts to taxation without representation recalls an earlier conflict with another King George. Tea, anyone?" These conspiratorial geniuses projected that the next shoe to drop would be "Phase Two of the Great Power Transfer: total lock-down of the electoral process, a.k.a. the Democalypse."[69]

Faux Centrism?

This rampant arrogance and hostility might explain why Democrats were simply unable to diagnose where they went wrong. They couldn't seem to decide whether to have unmitigated contempt for red-staters or to begin courting them all over again as they looked to the next national election. Al From and Bruce Reed addressed this conundrum in a *Wall Street Journal* op-ed following the election. From founded the reputedly centrist Democratic Leadership Council, whose most famous member was Bill Clinton. He had long argued that Democrats had become too liberal to appeal to mainstream Americans. In their piece, From and Reed said that the only way Democrats could recapture majority status would be to rehabilitate themselves in America's heartland by moving to the center.

More interesting than their prescription for a new Democratic policy agenda were their observations about fellow Democrats. Some of them, they said, "want to write off the red states, or pretend that the same old formula will make them turn blue." They took issue with Democratic strategist Joe Trippi, who had argued on his blog that the Democrats, to become successful again, needed to play to their liberal base.[70] From and Reed seemed to understand that the Democrats' electoral problem was not one of getting out the votes but making some connection with red-state voters and expanding their base. But even they betrayed their otherwise disguised contempt for Middle America by openly identifying it as "hostile territory." They also revealed their fundamental misapprehension of Midwestern values in saying, "Bill Clinton was able to carry a dozen red states in 1992 and 1996, with the same positions as Democrats today." Surely these coauthors realize that Bill Clinton played down his liberalism when in campaign mode. Surely they also realize that since Clinton's victories, Democrats have marginalized themselves, becoming a hodgepodge of such extreme positions that their base isn't big enough anymore. Their core platform doesn't resonate nearly as well with Middle America.

From and Reed clearly believe the Democratic Party still has much in common with flyover country voters; it's just a matter of emphasizing those common elements. What they and other self-designated centrist Democrats miss is that their difficulty in appealing to red-state voters has more to do with who they are and what they believe than how they package themselves. Democrats will continue to have major difficulties until they grasp that their inability to get sufficient traction is not due to election fraud or cheating, nor semantics or fund-raising, but their liberal policy positions, mainly concerning national security and cultural issues.[71]

Of course, every once in a long while, someone with the talents and charisma of Bill Clinton may come along and fool red-staters into believing he is one of them. But most Democrats are self-evidently not red-staters. Though Democrats generally don't subscribe to "assimilation" in immigration policy, if they hope to regain favor in the Midwest, they would be well advised to try to assimilate among us "foreigners." The *Washington Post*'s Harold Meyerson sarcastically acknowledged that, "So long as the boundaries between blue and red America seem so fixed, the Democrats must be able to come off as Americans behind the other guys' lines."[72]

From and Reed, despite flaws in their centrist analysis, were tame toward Republicans compared to most Democrats—and were roundly criticized for it. The *Pittsburg Post-Gazette* derided From's "corporate-sponsored Democratic Leadership Council," and "his wealthy cronies" for their "faux centrism" and for arguing that progressive policies were damaging the Democratic Party. Beltway Democrats weren't any better, according to the editorial. They were "sell[ing] out America's working class—the demographic that used to be the party's base."[73]

Outgoing Senate minority leader Tom Daschle, though having just been defeated by conservative John Thune while trying to mask his liberalism, also rejected the From-Reed approach. After the election, he insisted Democrats should not move to the right, but seek "common ground" on their own progressive principles. He added that "it wouldn't take much for the progressive movement in this country to be the majority movement again."[74]

The *New Republic*'s Peter Beinart had a radically different view. He argued that key liberal organizations "see liberalism's enemies almost exclusively on the right," which results in "a lack of liberal passion for winning the war on terrorism." This lack of passion, says Beinart, cost Democrats at the polls. Democratic leaders who did focus on defeating totalitarian Islam gained no traction in the party. Beinart argued that unless the Democratic Party could regain its credibility on national security issues—"by build[ing] institutions that make the fight against America's totalitarian foe a liberal passion"—it would remain the minority party.[75] On this point, Beinart's position closely resembled From and Reed's: the main reason Democrats lost was that voters did not trust them to be tough enough in the War on Terror. The party needed to develop its own "muscular strategy"[76] to compete with the Republicans.

Beinhart, From, and Reed would be right except for one crucial fact. The liberal fringe has, to a great degree, taken over the party and erected a wall against policy changes. What Beinart, From, and Reed seem to be suggesting is not some cosmetic makeover or even a different marketing approach. They are not proposing the party nominate people like John Kerry, who merely pretend to be hawkish in order to fool the voters. They're urging a dramatic, substantive transformation of the party, at least on national security issues. That may be smart advice, but it's tantamount to saying today's Democratic Party can only be successful if it ceases to be itself. Its problems on national security issues are inherent and systemic and Democrats cannot correct them without an institutional conversion and a change in values.

CHAPTER FIFTEEN

The Republicans' "Worst Nightmare"

At least for now, the power players in the Democratic Party are too consumed by hatred for President Bush and conservatives in general even to consider gravitating rightward. This couldn't have been made clearer when they deliberately picked the militant Howard Dean to be their new leader and vowed they would compete with the Republican Party "everywhere, everywhere, everywhere."[1] In February 2005, Democrats voted for Dean to head the Democratic National Committee, fully aware that just a few weeks before he had said, "I hate the Republicans and everything they stand for."[2] Like-minded party activist Billy Horton, of Austin, Texas, gleeful about Dean's elevation, said, "Republicans are laughing right now, but this is their worst nightmare: a Democrat who's ready to fight."[3]

Hastening to disabuse would-be party reformers that the party's leadership had the slightest intention of changing course, House Minority Leader Nancy Pelosi said that Democrats must continue "to speak from conviction, because we know what is morally right."[4] This was an in-your-face repudiation of those, like Al From, who were urging the party to abandon its "morality-grounded" opposition to the Iraq war. But Pelosi's prescription would be easier said than done, since the Democrats lacked any idea of what they stood for besides hating George Bush.

Shortly after the election, columnist Nicholas von Hoffman wrote a scathing editorial excoriating John Kerry for sending out more e-mails begging for money from grassroots volunteers and slamming Democrat strategists for convening conclaves of Democrats to discuss "What do we believe in?" Von Hoffman especially rejected the Democrats' plan to pursue so-called "values voters." He pointed out that 90 percent of those who attended church every week voted for Bush. "God is a registered Republican," he quipped, "which only leaves the Devil for the Democrats if they insist on messing with religion."[5]

But von Hoffman reserved his deepest criticism for the party's aimlessness in foreign policy and warned party leaders that "before the pros send out more of their mendicant e-mails, they might spell out for us what it is that they're asking people to back up with their dollars and their time. They might start with what the pros messed up the worst in the last campaign—foreign policy." Von Hoffman went on to propose certain foreign policy ideas the Democrats might consider adopting to distinguish themselves from Republicans that might at least "stand a chance of animating volunteers who are not up for another blast of blather from party headquarters."[6] What was telling about von Hoffman's piece was not his suggested policy prescriptions, but the fact that he felt he needed to advise Democratic Party leaders to develop a cohesive set of ideas—just a month after the election, no less, when there should have been no doubt what Democrats stood for.

"The Most Ridiculous Thing I've Ever Seen in My Life"

Liberal columnist Harold Meyerson correctly noted that the Democrats' policy aimlessness didn't begin in the aftermath of the 2004 election. Meyerson wrote, "Cover the Democrats for any length of time and you become expert in campaigns that don't seem to be about anything."[7] Even Senator Charles Schumer shockingly acknowledged that Democrats failed to lay out an alternative agenda should they win the White House.[8] Ruth Conniff of the *Progressive* expressed a similar sentiment, but with an optimistic twist. Immediately after the election, she conceded that most Democrats were perceived as not believing in anything. She contrasted the few who openly professed their "progressivism," such as Senator Feingold, and pointed to their electoral success. She said that if "progressives" would just have the courage to be who they are, they would do much better at the polls. She wrote, "That willingness to come out as who we really are, to speak the truth, and to spread the word makes me hopeful."[9] Despite her optimism, Conniff was tacitly admitting that Democrats didn't stand for much—but not so much because they didn't believe in anything. Rather, many of them obviously calculated that it would be political suicide to be completely honest about their liberalism.

There is something to this. Deny it though they will, liberals simply have difficulty getting elected when they are honest about who they are, except in the bluest of blue states. Liberalism just isn't in vogue like it was in the 1960s and 1970s. You rarely get a liberal activist to admit he's liberal. They prefer the euphemism "progressive," as witnessed by Ruth Conniff's writings. Liberal politicians are even more afraid of the label, with the possible exception of Ted Kennedy. Hillary Clinton is mortified by it. John Kerry, when reminded of his decidedly liberal record for two decades in the Senate (he was tagged by the bipartisan *National Journal* as having the most liberal voting record in the Senate in 2003),[10] tried to refute the label. Kerry said, "It's absolutely the most ridiculous thing I've ever seen in my life."[11] Even Howard Dean, whose fifteen minutes of presidential campaign fame can be directly traced to his leftist rants, sometimes denies his liberalism.[12] Dean's supporters included the mainstream media and the far Left. Their sole motivation for supporting him was his anti–Iraq war stance. Yet they invested considerable energy in presenting him as a moderate: "Why, he is pro-gun and balanced the budget as governor," they protested.

But one veteran Democrat understands that his party's leaders are going to have to do more than merely distance themselves from the liberal label to be competitive. Former New York mayor Ed Koch acknowledged that unless the party underwent a "major realignment" from "radical left" to "center left" it would not be able to reverse its losing trends.[13] Another Democrat pol who understands this—as much as she may resent it—is Hillary Clinton. In anticipation of a presidential run, she has done more than just flee from the label. She has engaged in a painstaking effort to remold herself into a values-based, hawkish centrist.

But John Kerry, despite his own feint to the center, strongly objects to the notion that his party's liberal ideas aren't salable. He said in an interview with *U.S. News & World Report* that he wasn't even convinced that his or the party's ideas didn't win in the 2004 election—perhaps the ultimate denial. "The naysayers," said Kerry, "are completely out to lunch, they don't know what they're talking about. On every issue that speaks to the qualities of people's lives, we won and will continue to win."[14] House Minority Leader Nancy Pelosi echoed similar sentiments. She specifically rejected the idea that Democrats were wishy-washy. They just weren't doing a good enough job of getting their ideas through the thick skulls of those pesky voters. She said, "It may be about how we can educate the American people more clearly on the difference between Democrats and Republicans." Pelosi also pooh-poohed the notion that Democratic leaders needed to engage in post-election soul-searching.[15] They needed to work on the voters, not themselves.

Framing

Pelosi was not alone in believing the Democrats' woes were, above all, a marketing problem. She found an ally in Berkeley linguist George Lakoff, who came along just as Democrats were reeling from the election, steeped in soul-searching, and analysis and susceptible to a variety of snake-oil remedies. Lakoff propounded a theory that was music to Pelosi's ears. It also comforted the likes of Senate Minority Leader Tom Daschle and Congressman George Miller, who distributed hundreds of Lakoff's book to their friends and staffs before the election.[16] Lakoff's theory was that the Democrats' election failures could be traced to linguistics. Lakoff said that people use mental structures, which he called "frames," when they think about words. Since conservatives are masters of "framing," as in their use of the phrase "tax relief," they are able to shape the political debate to their advantage. "For there to be relief there must be an affliction, an afflicted party, and a reliever who removes the affliction and is therefore a hero. And if people try to stop the hero, those people are villains for trying to prevent relief." Conservatives, Lakoff said, "had set a trap: the words draw you into their world view."[17] Surely Lakoff is aware of the Democrats' own stock phrases: "a risky tax scheme," "social security lock box," "the people against the powerful," "trickle down," or "it's the economy, stupid."

"I'm Reporting for Duty"

Regardless of the precise reason for it—political cowardice, marketing, or semantics—the Democratic Party had scarcely had a positive idea since President Bush was inaugurated in 2001, allowing all their mental energy to be drained in devotion to their anger against him. But the party's intellectual chaos came into sharpest focus during the 2004 election, when its presidential candidate, John Kerry, floundered for direction.

John Kerry had been a military-loathing dove most of his political career, which he had launched on the backs of his fellow Vietnam veterans, virtually accusing all of them of war crimes. He never apologized for his broad-brushed slander, and even later resurrected the same type of allegation against our troops in Iraq. On CBS's *Face the Nation* he told Bob Schieffer, "There is no reason, Bob, that young American soldiers need to be going into the homes of Iraqis in the dead of night, terrorizing kids and children, you know, women, breaking sort of the customs the historical customs, religious customs, whether you like it or not, Iraqis should be doing that."[18]

Yet during the campaign he tried to pass himself off as a hawk, best illustrated by his sophomoric entrance at the Democratic national convention where he saluted and announced he was "reporting for duty." It was nothing more than a shameless attempt to use his highly dubious—as his fellow Swift Boat veterans pointed out[19]—military record to drown out decades of opposition to all things military and present himself as a hawkish guardian of national security and defense, prepared to be commander in chief.

Beyond the amateurish symbolism, though, Kerry's attitude toward the most important issue facing the country, national security, was nearly inscrutable. Watching Kerry wrestle with his inner pacifist while trying to project himself as GI Joe was a painful experience on the order of witnessing a multi-personality patient struggle for identity. He knew he had to appeal to his base, which he could comfortably accomplish by following his natural antiwar instincts. But he also realized he would be entirely unelectable without convincing mainstream voters he could be trusted to safeguard our national security. Indeed, his very ascension to the nomination was facilitated by the recognition of party regulars and leaders that Howard Dean's extremist, rabid outbursts would not play well in a general election. Kerry was chosen by default not because anything he said was inspiring or coherent, but for his assumed "electability" compared to Mad Howard.

But when talking about the Iraq war, Kerry was obviously uncomfortable in his own skin. For the life of him, he just couldn't come up with a consistent strategy. He couldn't even decide whether he believed we should have attacked Iraq in the first place. At times Kerry savaged President Bush for his preemptive war policy, but in the first presidential debate admitted that "The president always has the right, and always has had the right, for preemptive strike. That was a great doctrine throughout the Cold War. . . . No president, through all of American history, has ever ceded, and nor would I, the right to preempt in any way necessary to protect the United States of America."[20]

We know now that Kerry voted for the Iraq war resolution—which gave the president unconditional authority to attack Iraq—because it was politically expedient. But, as we've seen, when Howard Dean's antiwar theme started resonating with Democrats and independents, Kerry and others backtracked and developed an ingenious but pathetically fraudulent line to explain their vote. They had supported the resolution, they said, because they were relying on assurances from President Bush that he would attack only as a last resort; they never thought he would make the mistake of actually using force. In one of the presidential debates, Kerry said "the president made a mistake in invading Iraq." But when moderator Jim Lehrer asked him whether Americans were dying now in Iraq for a mistake, Kerry responded, "No, and they don't have to, provided we have the leadership that we put—that I'm offering."[21]

What was he offering? Kerry said he had a plan to withdraw troops, but when pressed to elaborate said he couldn't be expected to formulate a plan since he wasn't president and thus not sufficiently privy to "conditions on the ground." He also denied he would delegate our national security to the United Nations or any other foreign power yet skewered President Bush for not following such a policy. He actually suggested that before an American president took military action he would have to pass a "global test," to "prove to the world [that the proposed action was] for legitimate reasons."[22] Kerry also slammed Vice President Cheney for saying America would be safer under Bush-Cheney, but in the next breath, promised that a Kerry presidency would lead to a safer America.[23]

And this was the Democratic Party's standard bearer? He was all over the map on the most important issue of the day. This bizarre state of affairs was not lost on the liberal media. The *Washington Post*, in its editorial endorsement of Kerry, even acknowledged Kerry's incoherence and inconsistency on Iraq. "We have been dismayed," wrote the editors, "most of all by Mr. Kerry's zigzags on Iraq, such as his swervings on whether Saddam Hussein presented a threat." The *Post* noted that Kerry had called Iraq a "diversion," yet promised he would not cut and run from it. It also questioned whether he was "decisive enough."[24] The *Los Angeles Daily News* offered a similarly tepid endorsement of Kerry, simply relying on Kerry's promise "to take a similar approach to terror as Bush," but pledging "to do it smarter." The *Daily News* went on to concede its uncertainty about whether Kerry "can live up to those promises," and, tellingly, acknowledged Kerry's "contradictory comments about the war and a lackluster twenty-year career in the Senate."[25]

Other liberal papers were reduced to admitting Kerry's flip-flops on Iraq, but saying his self-contradictions were the product of enlightened thinking—a refreshing change from President Bush's reputed stubborn myopia. They labored to present Kerry's vacillation as a positive—it showed admirable flexibility in a man who was willing to examine new evidence and adapt to changing circumstances. Kerry's twists and turns were proof of his sophistication, complexity, and ability to appreciate "nuance." This "thoughtful," "deliberate" John Kerry was the same guy who was so eager to undermine President Bush that he recommended that we adopt *all* of the 9-11 Commission's national security recommendations, before he'd had time to read, much less thoroughly study them.

In the end, Kerry was unable to come up with an enduring policy on Iraq, so he fell back to that with which he was most comfortable, and which had become his party's primary template: trash the president—and trust that "I can do it better. Just don't ask me how."

"Fifty-Four Million Voted for Unity in America"

After the election, Kerry, hoping to remain the party's main spokesman, continued sending out his e-mail blasts. In one message he ticked off a list of issues his "fifty-four-plus million" supporters had voted for, including health care, energy independence, stem-cell research, and protecting Social Security. But the most remarkable item on the list was "They voted for unity in America." Echoing the liberal columnists who had backed him, Kerry was apparently saying that a vote for him was a vote for harmony among the American people. This claim that Democrats stood for American "unity" was amusing in light of their obvious inability to unify themselves. Columnist E. J. Dionne would write, a full year after the election, "Almost every day Democrats seem to give their critics evidence of division. The party splintered over the nomination of John Roberts as chief justice" and even "the Katrina disaster. You know the party has a problem when even the politics of Katrina divides its members."[26] This was to say nothing of their coming disunity on withdrawing from Iraq, a proposed Alito filibuster, or Senator Russ Feingold's failed motion to censure the president over the NSA surveillance flap, among others.

Kerry's e-mail message was contradictory on its face, unless you understand liberal-speak and that "unity" had become another liberal buzzword. But how could it possibly be said that a minority of voters, who were militantly opposed to going along with the prevailing party's agenda, had voted for "unity"? It could be said only by liberals who believe that "unity" is virtually synonymous with their usages of "tolerance," "inclusiveness," and "open-mindedness." From their staggeringly arrogant perspective, "bipartisanship" means Republican acquiescence; "open-mindedness" means enlightened and broad-minded enough to embrace the liberal worldview; "divisiveness" means promoting the Republican agenda; "intolerance" means *rejecting* the Democrats' views on diversity, affirmative action, and "multiculturalism"; and "unity" means *endorsing all* the Democrats' views.

So according to their lexicon, a vote for Bush was an endorsement of divisiveness, intolerance, and bigotry. Liberal columnist Helen Thomas confirmed this narrow concept of open-mindedness in a piece in which she recited the definition of "liberals." "Various dictionaries," wrote Thomas, "describe liberals as open minded, generous, progressive, leaning toward individual freedom, broad-minded and ahead of the times. Those interpretations of the word liberal seem to add up to a compassionate person."[27]

Kerry's e-mail was just the beginning. About a week after the election, while he and his colleagues on Capitol Hill were still demanding conciliation from the GOP victors, they were huddling in D.C. "to try to devise a strategy to combat President Bush's agenda despite their weakened ranks in Congress."[28] Kerry spokesman David Wade seemed to be promoting a reverse mandate. Wade said, "There is a mandate for unity in the country, and there are fifty-four million Americans whose voices deserve to be heard as we move forward as a party." That was like saying, "Democrats lost, so their agenda should be followed."

At the meeting, Senator Dick Durbin was certainly not extending peace offerings to his GOP counterparts. He rallied Democrats to maintain their unity *against* Republicans. "I cannot, based on my constituents and principles," said Durbin, "back off." He dismissed Bush's 51–48 percent popular vote victory, saying, "It was not a landslide."[29] Nancy Pelosi, who similarly chided the president and his party for their divisiveness, said that Democrats were "ready for this lame duck, and we're ready for the next session, and we're ready for the next election."[30]

Liberal editorialists also, after lecturing us on how divisive Bush and his Rovian band of Republicans were, made clear that the unity admonition only went one way. Margaret Carlson, in the *Los Angeles Times*, wrote, "Get along? I don't think so. The truth is, we can't all just get along, not anytime soon, unless some things change. To start, President Bush has to quit saying his side is good (God told him so) and the other side is bad. . . . The hard part to take is that after a disputed election in 2000, Bush governed as if he were king by divine right. What kind of mandate does he think he has with a 51 percent win?"[31]

The *Washington Post*'s Richard Cohen, like other liberal commentators, was particularly miffed that President Bush was claiming a mandate with a mere 3.5 million popular vote margin. Such thinking, according to Cohen, borders on megalomania. Cohen wrote, sarcastically, "His reelection was no mere mandate, since, you will recall, he claimed that the last time, when he scratched out a win in Florida by only several hundred votes. No, this victory is a mandate of Rooseveltian dimensions. With precisely this sort of self-assurance, Napoleon crowned himself emperor of France."[32]

Paul Krugman wrote in the *New York Times*, "President Bush isn't a conservative. He's a radical—the leader of a coalition that deeply dislikes America as it is. Part of that coalition wants to tear down the legacy of Franklin Roosevelt, eviscerating Social Security and, eventually, Medicare. Another part wants to break down the barriers between church and state. And thanks to a heavy turnout by evangelical Christians, Mr. Bush has four more years to advance that radical agenda."[33]

The *New York Times*'s Bob Herbert wrote, "Mr. Bush's victory on Tuesday was not based on his demonstrated competence in office or on a litany of perceived successes. For all the talk about values we're hearing, the president ran a campaign that appealed above all to voters' fears and prejudices....He said, essentially, be afraid.... Tuesday's election was a dismaying sprint toward intolerance, sparked by a smiling president who is a master at appealing to the base aspects of our natures."[34]

Tina Brown wrote, "At a panel Thursday about who should be *Time* magazine's Person of the Year, the debate was whether the annual milestone cover should feature Karl Rove or God, which seems a false choice since everyone knows they are the same thing."[35] Noted liberal columnist Michael Kinsley said, "The election campaign made it official. These are the Disunited States. There is 'Red' America: conservative, Republican, religious. And there is 'Blue' America: liberal, Democratic, secular."[36] (At least Kinsley admits liberal secularism).

To Infinity and Beyond: Party Aimlessness
Extending Beyond the 2004 Election

The passage of time did not heal the party's disillusionment, bitterness, or disunity. Despite all the difficulties Republicans were encountering and President Bush's diving approval ratings, Democrats were unable to capitalize on them. They were careening out of control, like a fast-moving car without a driver.

About a year after the election, a Quinnipiac University poll revealed that Democrats were highly depressed. Though Republicans believed 2005 had been a better year than 2004 (65 percent to 22 percent), Democrats thought it had been worse (45 percent to 41 percent).[37] Powerline blogger John Hinderaker noted "that the question was not about the direction of the country, or about any aspect of current affairs; respondents were asked how 2005 was for 'you personally.'"[38]

As for the Democratic Party, it was still floundering in search of cohesion. Hillary Clinton, putative 2008 presidential candidate, seized an opportunity to project herself as party leader and issued a call for a cease-fire among disparate factions. But her power grab backfired when irate leftist bloggers turned their guns on her for sidling up to the turncoat centrists when she agreed to lead an initiative for the Democratic Leadership Council.[39]

This was a foreshadowing of the dilemma Hillary would face in trying to appear moderate, mature, and presidential without alienating the rabid, extremist base. Leftist blogs such as Daily Kos view Democrat centrists as pragmatic sell-outs more interested in power than principle. The blog's Markos Moulitsas said, "If she wanted to give a speech to a centrist organization truly interested in bringing the various factions of the party together, she could've worked with NDN [New Democrat Network].[40] Some liberals went so far as to say that in her call for unity from the DLC perch, Hillary was risking her chances for the nomination, an irony indeed considering her motive in calling for a truce.

The leftists' bullying did not intimidate all centrists. Like Al From, Democratic strategist Bill Galston was among the minority of moderate voices urging the dominant liberal wing to come back to sanity. In 1989, following George H. W. Bush's shellacking of the unapologetically liberal Michael Dukakis, Galston and Elaine Kamarck penned "The Politics of Evasion," a sober report card on the Democrats' slavery to liberalism, which the authors viewed as suicidal for the party.

After Kerry's defeat, the two wrote "The Politics of Polarization," a seventy-page analysis of the party's persisting problem with its extremists.[41] In addition to debunking the Democrats' hope for electoral salvation with increasing percentages of Hispanic voters, they criticized the party for evading the main categories of issues that matter most to Americans: national security and moral values. Democrats, they said—in so many words—will no longer be able to prevail on economic issues alone.[42] But even on economic issues, do voters really believe they need higher taxes and more government regulations?

Howard Dean wasn't interested in the debate over ideology, as long as the party could get sufficient mileage trashing President Bush and other Republicans. Dean made that quite clear in an interview on *Meet the Press* on November 13, 2005, when he conceded the party still had no substantive policy agenda—and wasn't in any particular hurry to craft one.

Tim Russert turned to Dean and said, "But there's no Democratic plan on Social Security. There's no Democratic plan on the deficit problem. There's no specifics. They say, 'Well, we want a strong Social Security. We want to reduce the deficit. We want health care for everyone,' but there's no plan how to pay for it." Incredibly, Dean responded, "Right now it's not our job to give out specifics.... It's our job to stop this administration from doing more damage to America. And that's what we're going to do." When Russert countered that this was tantamount to saying the people would have to trust Democrats can do things better, even without offering a plan, Dean said, "We will. When the time comes, we will do that." When pressed further, Dean disclosed that he would have specific plans in all of these areas—including Iraq—in 2006.[43]

Dean wasn't alone in maintaining that it was not incumbent upon Democrats to produce an alternative agenda. In December 2005, a day after the wildly successful elections in Iraq, House Minority Leader Nancy Pelosi told reporters that Democrats would "produce an issue agenda for the 2006 elections." But, she said, that agenda would "not include a position on Iraq." Even more incredibly, she went on to admit, "There is no one Democratic voice...and there is no one Democratic position."[44] This was astonishing, even for the modern Democratic Party. As one commentator noted, "Through either political cowardice or political calculation, one of America's two major parties has simply refused to take a stand on the greatest issue of our time—the front line in the War on Terror."[45] Pelosi's focus, like Dean's, was not on policy but on accusing the current Republican-controlled Congress of being "the most corrupt in history."

It's no wonder that Democrats wouldn't commit to a plan on Iraq. In the first place, they couldn't develop a consensus on it. Pelosi, for example, had endorsed Congressman John Murtha's proposal for an almost immediate withdrawal of our troops while Howard Dean had stated that his party was coming together on a strategy centered on withdrawal over the next two years.[46] But they really had little incentive to develop a unified position because once they did, they would risk becoming accountable for it and wouldn't have the luxury of shifting their criticisms as the situation on the ground changed.

But it wasn't just Iraq for which Democrats were reluctant to produce a plan. They promised to produce their domestic legislative agenda by November 2005, to give voters a full year before the 2006 elections to absorb their proposals.[47] But November came and went and they weren't any closer. Party leaders had changed their minds. It was too early to present a plan. They said they would wait until January. But again, they came up empty-handed. They set and ignored two more release dates when in March, Nancy Pelosi promised the document would be forthcoming in "a matter of weeks."[48]

There was some indication the delays were calculated. Senator Dick Durbin was among those arguing that it would be wiser for the party to release the plan closer to the election, when more voters would be engaged, and when Republicans would have less time to attack it. "When you bring it out early," said Durbin, "you are going to leave it open for the spinmeisters in Rove's machine, the Republican side, to tear it to pieces." House Minority Leader Nancy Pelosi argued that on some issues, like Social Security, Democrats have been able to defeat Republicans even without an alternative plan.[49]

Democratic governors, frustrated with Beltway Democrats, pressed Pelosi and Senate Minority Leader Harry Reid for just two or three central ideas they could promote in the states as national Democratic rallying cries for the 2006 election. Reid said he could only narrow it down to six ideas. Almost comically, Nancy Pelosi agreed there were six ideas—but her list was different from Reid's. Ultimately, the best the dynamic duo could offer was a tepid promise from Reid that "by the time the election rolls around, people are going to know where Democrats stand."[50]

Moonbats

Part of the reason for the party's ambivalence comes from the pressure it feels from its ever-growing fringe groups, especially those that dwell in the blogosphere. From MoveOn.org to DemocraticUnderground.com to the Daily Kos, the antiwar leftists are not to be denied or appeased; because they have money and commitment, they have clout. Following the 2004 election, MoveOn.org said, "Now it's our party: we bought it, we own it and we're going to take it back."[51]

Presumably, Beltway politicians concluded that the least unacceptable of the bad alternatives was simply to avoid a firm stand on the war, thereby irritating, but not irreversibly alienating the fringe. The leftists' ire, however, got intense. In January 2006, leftist bloggers conducted "relentless e-mail campaigns" denouncing the Democrats' lackluster opposition to President Bush's Supreme Court picks and the Iraq war[52]—about which you can never be critical enough. They also blasted Democrats for choosing the "too religious" Virginia governor Tim Kaine to deliver the response to President Bush's State of the Union address. The lefty bloggers had been lobbying for their newfound dovish hero, John Murtha, to speak and issue a tongue-lashing to the "imperialist" president.

They were particularly venomous about Hillary Clinton for her lurches to the right, on values issues, but especially concerning Iraq. The magnitude of her betrayal, considering her front-runner status for the 2008 campaign, drove them crazy—er, crazier. Code Pink, a women's antiwar group, was planning to use its website to encourage people to protest one of Hillary's fund-raising events.[53]

Democratic politicians like Hillary and John Kerry see these bloggers as an annoying, but necessary evil. Steve Elmendorf, a Kerry 2004 adviser and Democratic lobbyist, said, "The trick will be to harness their energy and their money without looking like you are a captive of the activist Left."[54] But how to pull that off when Jimmy Carter shares the presidential booth with Michael Moore at the Democratic Convention or Harry Reid gives a sycophantic speech at the 2006 annual convention of Daily Kos? Perhaps less noticeable to the general public, but obviously recognizable to the bloggers, are the frequent guest blogging appearances of high-profile Democratic politicians. Senators Barack Obama, Russell Feingold, and Harry Reid have all contributed to the Daily Kos, and John Kerry regularly blogs on his "diary" there.[55]

Other liberal activists were also hammering away at party leaders. A group of them met in January 2006 at the Busboys and Poets restaurant and bookshop in Washington, D.C., for a forum on "The Impeachment of President George W. Bush and Vice President Dick Cheney." The participants were quick to agree that the administration had committed "crimes against humanity," a "war on aggression," and "the supreme international crime," but they were equally eager to indict congressional Democrats for failing to stand up to Bush and the Republicans.[56] David Swanson, a disgruntled labor union official and head of "Impeach PAC," implied the Democratic Party had a death wish. "Does the Democratic Party want to continue to exist or does it want to ignore what 85 percent of its supporters want?" he asked. Also in attendance was activist Cindy Sheehan, who had just called President Bush a "terrorist" on foreign soil. Sheehan had few kind words for Democrats either, whom she predicted would "seriously screw up" the November elections.[57]

Some attendees argued that talk of impeachment was futile unless Democrats could regain control of the House. But others would not be deterred by such annoying appeals to pragmatism. An intransigent Swanson said, "Just go home if you're going to talk that way." One of the meeting's featured speakers was former U.S. attorney general, and volunteer lawyer for Saddam Hussein, Ramsey Clark. Clark called the Bush administration "the greatest threat to peace, to human rights, to economic justice worldwide." He called for a 75 percent reduction in military spending and also picked up on the theme of bashing Democratic leaders, saying they were just as militaristic as Republicans. Other highlights of the meeting were an antiwar activist comparing America's "shock and awe" attack on Iraq to the Nazi's World War II blitzkrieg and describing Bush foreign policy as "nationalistic triumphalism."[58]

"Why Can't We Get Any Traction against These Corrupt Republicans?"

Perhaps because of the tension between their leftist base and mainstream voters, Democrats were unable to gain ground on Republicans. Despite the collapsing approval ratings for President Bush and the GOP in the months leading up to the 2006 election, Democrats were still too confused and bumbling to provide an alternative vision. Senator Christopher Dodd, commenting on his party's health, said, "A lot worse than it should be. This has not been a very good two months. We seem to be losing our voice when it comes to the basic things people worry about."

The main obstacles preventing the party's cohesion were its inability to debunk its reputation as being weak on defense and its (by now) well-established impotence in crafting an agenda.[59] Democratic strategist James Carville, though claiming Democrats have been doing "pretty good" on the War on Terror, virtually admitted they'll never catch the Republicans on the issue. He said if polls show Democrats running ten percentage points behind Republicans on national security issues, that "is fine." There are other issues, said Carville, on which the Democrats can more than make up the difference.[60]

Perhaps the best illustration of the Democrats' predicament on national security issues is their harsh criticism of President Bush's NSA surveillance program. The louder they complain about the president flouting the rule of law—something they never seemed to be concerned about during the Clinton years—the more they risk being seen as soft on terror. Did they want to be known as the party that chased "phantoms of lost liberty"[61] or the guardians of America's national security?

Senator Evan Bayh expressed the Democrats' plight on national security when he said, "I think the Republicans are ripe for the taking on this issue, but not until we rehabilitate our own image. I think there's a certain element of denial about how we are viewed, perhaps incorrectly but nonetheless, by many Americans as being deficient on national security." Senator Barack Obama—perhaps unwittingly—summarized the Democrats' difficulties in formulating an agenda. "I think that two-thirds of the American people think the country is going in the wrong direction," Obama said. "They're not sure yet whether Democrats can move it in the right direction." And how could they, Senator, when Democrats haven't even bothered to tell the people what direction that might be?[62]

The Democrats' identity crisis is also exacerbated by their stance on social issues, especially abortion. The *New York Times* complained in early 2006 that while just a year earlier Republican and Democratic senators agreed that a Supreme Court nominee "who disagreed openly with the major abortion rights precedents" would face nearly insurmountable confirmation hurdles, the Alito hearings "cast doubt on such assumptions." The reason, they said, is that "the handful of Democrats from socially conservative states were reluctant to be perceived as voting against him on those grounds."[63] But another story in the *Times* a few days later said that Senate Democratic leaders "urged their members Tuesday to vote against [Alito] in an effort to lay the groundwork for making a campaign issue of his decisions on the court."[64] If the Democrats are ambivalent about their position on abortion, which galvanizes their liberal base, how can they be sanguine about their future?[65]

Meanwhile, Clinton strategists James Carville and Paul Begala ratified the growing view that Democrats were clueless and getting worse. In their book, *Take it Back: Our Party, Our Country, Our Future,* they chronicle the Democrats' state of disarray and argue that Democrats need to rethink their positions and revise their dogmatic thinking on abortion, gun control, and environmental concerns. Though they believe the Democrats actually "won" the 2000 election, they say that in the Democrats' "zeal" to blame others for their failures, they have "failed to ask the bigger question: How could the incumbent party, running in a time of peace and prosperity, make the election close enough for the Republicans to steal? If 2000 should have been a wake-up call, 2004 was an old-fashioned ass-kicking." But too many Democrats—the "No Problem" Democrats—remain oblivious, they argue, obsessing about the 2000 election being stolen instead of concentrating on how to address the party's obvious problems. "John Kerry's defeat," they say, "was a symptom of the catastrophe that has befallen the party we love."[66]

During a post-election press conference Carville, along with Clinton pollster Stanley Greenberg, insisted that Kerry lost because he didn't offer a "narrative" that explained what his presidency would be and that would give a clear choice to voters. Painfully, Carville made this admission, "I think we have to come to grips with the fact that we are an opposition party right now and not a particularly effective one. I'm out of denial. Reality has hit." Donald Fowler, former Democratic Party chairman, put it more pointedly. He said, "I think we have come to an ending point in a long transition that began in 1968. During that time, the old Roosevelt Democratic majority coalition has creaked and cracked away under various kinds of racial, religious, social, and international forces, and this election was the end point in that transition. I think we live in a country that is majority Republican now."[67]

Liberal columnist E. J. Dionne cited the 2004 network exit polls as demonstrating the "[Democratic] Party's problems are structural and [can] be explained by three numbers: 21, 34, and 45...21 percent of the voters who cast ballots in 2004 called themselves liberal,

34 percent said they were conservative, and 45 percent called themselves moderate."[68] White House deputy chief of staff Karl Rove made the same point in a speech to the American Enterprise Institute in May 2006. He said, "Ultimately, the American people are a center-right country, who, presented with a center-right party with center-right candidates, will vote center-right."[69]

As long as the Democratic Party continues to allow itself to be dominated by its fringe elements and treats mainstream conservatism as inherently offensive, it will have a built-in disadvantage in national elections. And as long as it prefers petty partisanship to responsible policy-making, it will deserve every defeat it gets.

ACKNOWLEDGMENTS

I want to thank Regnery Publishing and especially Marji Ross for their support of this project. I am grateful for the invaluable contributions of my editors Stephen Thompson and Harry Crocker, who couldn't have been easier to work with and whose talents and diligence greatly improved the final product. Thanks also to my project editor, Kate Morse, for her keen eye and patience for last-minute changes and to Paula Currall for overseeing the project.

I thank my friend Greg Mueller and Sean McCabe and the rest of the team at Creative Response Concepts for helping to promote this book as they have both of my previous ones. Additional thanks to Greg for introducing me to Regnery and for his steadfast support for my books.

I also owe a special thank you to my good friend Sean Hannity who has always been at the forefront in supporting my books and to my good friend Mark Levin for his advice and support.

Thanks also to my friends Ann Coulter and Michelle Malkin for their advice and support.

And, I again want to thank my brother Rush for his continued inspiration and example. He has tremendous and deserved success, but in the last few years he has demonstrated the quality of his character by overcoming adversity and achieving even greater levels of achievement. I am proud of his accomplishments and greatly appreciative of his support.

NOTES

PREFACE TO THE PAPERBACK EDITION

1. David Limbaugh, "Nancy Pelosi Colludes with a Terrorist Tyrant," Creators Syndicate, April 5, 2007.
2. Ibid.
3. "'They' Still Have No Plan," *Washington Times*, July 13, 2007.
4. Robert Burns, "Pace Declares 'Sea Change' in Iraq," Associated Press, July 17, 2007.
5. Pauline Jelinek, "Rice: Wait Until Fall for Iraq Decision," Associated Press, July 13, 2007.
6. Anne Flaherty, "Democrats Stage All-Night Debate on Iraq," Associated Press, July 18, 2007.
7. Deb Riechmann, White House Raps Hill Probes," Associated Press, July 5, 2007.
8. Alexander Bolton, "GOP Preps for Talk Radio Confrontation," *The Hill*, June 27, 2007.
9. Dianne Feinstein, "Transcript: Sens. Lott, Feinstein on 'FOX News Sunday,'" *FOX News Sunday with Chris Wallace*, June 24, 2007.

10. Frederic J. Frommer, "Democrats Block Amendment to Prevent Fairness Doctrine," Associated Press, July 14, 2007.
11. Roger Aronoff, "MSNBC Confirms Liberal Media Bias," Accuracy in Media, June 27, 2007.
12. Ruth Marcus, "The Democrats' Leap of Faith," *Washington Post*, June 6, 2007.
13. Rick Klein and Teddy Davis, "Democratic Candidates Moving Left," ABC News, June 18, 2007.
14. IBD Editors, "Party Like It's 1822," *Investor's Business Daily*, May 17, 2007.
15. John Edwards, "A National Goal: End Poverty Within 30 Years," John Edwards.com.

CHAPTER ONE: Iraq: Democrats Lied, and Their Credibility Died

1. Richard Sisk, "Patriot Slap Riles Dems, Rip Prez Over Comment," *New York Daily News*, September 26, 2002.
2. "Top US General Says US Drive Toward Baghdad Stalled, Longer War Likely," *The Bulletin's Frontrunner*, March 28, 2003.
3. Michael Cousineau, "Bayh Blasts Bush at NH Democrats Dinner," *New Hampshire Union Leader*, October 30, 2005.
4. "Top US General Says US Drive Toward Baghdad Stalled, Longer War Likely," *The Bulletin's Frontrunner*, March 28, 2003
5. Frank Rich, "And Now: 'Operation Iraqi Looting,'" *New York Times*, April 27, 2003.
6. Byron York, "Remember Al Qaqaa?" *National Review Online*, February 28, 2005.
7. "George and Ted's Détente; War Views Aside, Former President Hails Kennedy for Public Service," *Dallas Morning News*, November 7, 2003.
8. "Saddam 'Did not plan' Insurgency," *Daily Telegraph*, March 13, 2006.
9. Transcript, "President Talks to Troops in Qatar," *The White House*, June 5, 2003.
10. Maureen Dowd, "We're Not Happy Campers," *New York Times*, September 11, 2003.
11. Scott Goldstein, "Kennedy Renews Call for Exit Plan, Says Troops Should Leave Iraq by '06," *Boston Globe*, February 5, 2005.
12. Tommy Franks, "War of Words," *New York Times*, October 19, 2004.
13. Joel Engle, "They Left Him No Choice," *Weekly Standard*, November 17, 2005.
14. Eric Lichtblau and David E. Sanger, "Bush Was Warned of Possible Attack in U.S. Official Says," *New York Times*, April 9, 2004.

15. Joel Mowbray, "New York Times Bush Smear Campaign," Townhall.com, April 14, 2004.

16. "Bin Laden Determined to strike in U.S." Presidential Daily Briefing, August 6, 2001.

17. John H. Cushman Jr., "Threats and Responses: Politics; Congressman Says Bush Would Mislead U.S.," . *New York Times*, September 30, 2002.

18. Ibid.

19. National Briefing, "Daschle Starts Economic War to Fight Iraq Conflict," *National Journal's House Race Hotline*, September 19, 2002.

20. Paul J. Nyden, "Bush's War Plans Are a Cover-up, Byrd Says,": *Charleston Gazette*, September 21, 2002.

21. Norman Podhoretz, "Who Is Lying About Iraq?" *Commentary*, December 2005.

22. "The Truth About Iraq's WMD," *Federalist Patriot*, November 11, 2005.

23. "Howard Dean Goes Ballistic, Accuses Bush of Deliberately Lying to Start Iraq War," Worldnetdaily.com, November 13, 2005.

24. James Phillips, "Dispelling the Myths About Iraq," The Heritage Foundation, December 2, 2005.

25. See "WMDs – The Democratic Betrayal," FrontPageMagazine.com, November 2, 2005; See also "Words of Mass Destruction," Snopes.com, undated. url: http://www.snopes.com/politics/war/wmdquotes.asp.

26. "Clinton: Iraq Must Comply 'One Way or the Other,' GOP Leaders Say Any Strike Should Remove Hussein," CNN.com, February 4, 1998.

27. Christopher S. Bond, "Two Administrations Warned of Iraq's Weapons," *St. Louis Post-Dispatch*, October 21, 2003.

28. Transcript, "President Clinton Explains Iraq Strike," CNN.com, December 16, 1998.

29. "WMDs – The Democratic Betrayal," *FrontPageMagazine.com*, November 2, 2005.

30. Christopher S. Bond, "Two Administrations Warned of Iraq's Weapons," *St. Louis Post-Dispatch*, October 21, 2003.

31. Madeleine Albright, "Remarks Before the Chicago Council of Foreign Relations, Chicago, IL, November 12, 1999," U.S. Department of State Dispatch, November 1, 1999.

32. Bertha Rosson, "Bush Critics' Own Words Betray Them," *Roanoke Times*, November 6, 2003.

33. Ross MacKenzie, "The Usual Suspects Were on the Bandwagon All Along," *Richmond Times Dispatch*, October 12, 2003.

34. Ibid.

35. Larry Elder, "Who *Didn't* think Iraq had WMD?" *Washington Times*, May 28, 2006.

36. Ross MacKenzie, "The Usual Suspects Were on the Bandwagon All Along," *Richmond Times Dispatch*, October 12, 2003.

37. "If Bush Believed Iraq Had WMDs, He Wasn't Alone," *Sun Herald*, February 11, 2004.

38. Ross MacKenzie, "The Usual Suspects Were on the Bandwagon All Along," *Richmond Times Dispatch*, October 12, 2003.

39. "If Bush Believed Iraq Had WMDs, He Wasn't Alone," *Sun Herald*, February 11, 2004.

40. Edward Kennedy, "Remarks by Senator Edward Kennedy (D-MA) at the Johns Hopkins School of Advanced International Studies," Federal News Service, September 27, 2002.

41. Bob Schieffer, "Face the Nation, Edward Kennedy Discusses Iraq," CBS News Transcripts, October 6, 2002.

42. "Two-Faced War Lies; Dems' Bush-Bashing On Iraq Belied by Their Own Words," *New York Post*, November 20, 2005.

43. John D. Rockefeller IV, "Statement of Senator John, D. Rockefeller IV On the Senate Floor On the Iraq Resolution," Senate.gov, October 10, 2002.

44. Transcript, Meet the Press, "Senator Joseph Biden Talks About Senate Hearings On Iraq and the Possibility of a Military Attack," NBC News Transcripts, August 4, 2002.

45. Ross MacKenzie, "The Usual Suspects Were on the Bandwagon All Along," *Richmond Times Dispatch*, October 12, 2003.

46. "WMDs – The Democratic Betrayal," *FrontPageMagazine.com*, November 2, 2005.

47. Ibid.

48. John Edwards, "The Right Way in Iraq," *Washington Post*, November 13, 2005.

49. "If Bush Believed Iraq Had WMDs, He Wasn't Alone," *Sun Herald*, February 11, 2004.

50. David Horowitz, *Unholy Alliance: Radical Islam and the American Left*," (Washington, D.C.: Regnery Publishers, Inc., 2004), 224.

51. Ibid., 225.

52. Chairman: The Rt. Honorable The Lord Butler of Brockwell KG GCB CVO, "Review of Intelligence on Weapons of Mass Destruction, *Report of a Committee of Privy Counsellors*, July 14, 2004.

53. Transcript, "Press Briefing on Iraq and WMD and SOTU Speech, The White House, July 22, 2003.

54. While some say Tenet urged the president to remove the assertion from his Cincinnati speech, the Washington Post reports that the Senate Intelligence Committee found that the CIA did not tell the White House it had reservations about the reliability of the statement. Susan Schmidt, "Plame's Input is Cited on Niger Mission, Report Disputes Wilson's Claims on Trip, Wife's Role," *Washington Post*, July 10, 2004.

55. "Rice: 16 words dispute 'enormously overblown,'" CNN.com, July 14, 2003.

56. Susan Schmidt, "Plame's Input is Cited on Niger Mission, Report Disputes Wilson's Claims on Trip, Wife's Role," *Washington* Post, July 10, 2004; See also: Transcript, "Press Briefing on Iraq and WMD and SOTU Speech, The White House, July 22, 2003.

57. "Rice: 16 words dispute 'enormously overblown,'" CNN.com, July 14, 2003.

58. John E. O'Neill and Jerome Corsi, *Unfit for Command* (Washington, D.C.: Regnery Publishing, Inc., 2004).

59. Ramesh Ponnuru, "Democrats in a Time of War: We're Looking at Another Liberal Crackup," *National Review*, April 7, 2003.

60. David Horowitz and Ben Johnson, "The Wrong Argument, at the Wrong Place, at the Wrong Time," FrontPageMagazine.com, November 7, 2005.

61. Katharine Q. Seelye, "The 2004 Campaign: The Former Vice President; Gore Says Bush Betrayed the U.S. by Using 9/11 as a Reason for War in Iraq." *New York Times*, February 9, 2004.

62. Paul Krugman, "Who Gets It?" *New York Times*, January 16, 2001.

63. "Kerry Chides Bush for 'Fear and Smear' On Veterans Day," Associated Press, November 12, 2005.

64. "The Truth About Iraq's WMD," *The Federalist Patriot*, November 11, 2005.

65. Liz Sidoti, "Democrats Force GOP-controlled Senate into unusual closed session over Iraq Intelligence," Associated Press, November 1, 2005.

66. David Horowitz and Ben Johnson, "Unhinged," Frontpagemagazine.com, November 2, 2005.

67. Brian Wilson and Associated Press, "Democrats Mull Politicizing Iraq War Intelligence," *FOX News*, November 5, 2003.

68. Liz Sidoti, "Democrats Force GOP-controlled Senate into unusual closed session over Iraq Intelligence," Associated Press, November 1, 2005.

69. William L. Watts, "Senate Forced Into Closed Session on Iraq Rationale," *Market Watch*, November 1, 2005.

70. E-mail from Howard Dean, "Democrats Official Line: Demand Accountability for Manipulated Intelligence on Iraq," FreeRepublic.com, November 2, 2005.

71. Kenneth R. Timmerman, "Ex-Official: Russia Moved Saddam's WMD," Newsmax.com, February 19, 2006.

72. Kenneth R. Timmerman, "Found: Saddam's WMDs," *Insight* magazine via Frontpagemag.com, April 26, 2004.

73. Melanie Hunter, "Document Details WMD Recovered In Iraq, Santorum Says," CNSNews.com, June 21, 2006.

74. Bob Port, "France-Iraq Link In CIA Report," *New York Daily News*, October 10, 2004.

75. Georges Sada with Jim Nelson Black, *Saddam's Secrets, How An Iraqi General Defied and Survived Saddam Hussein* (Brentwood, TN: Integrity Publishers, 2006), 251-255.

76. Ibid.

77. Ibid.

78. Ibid.

79. Editorial, "Finding Answers to Iraq's WMD," *The Boston Herald*, March 12, 2006.

80. Stephen F. Hayes, "Finally," *The Weekly Standard*, March 13, 2006.

81. I made these points in my column "WMD: Don't Change the Ground Rules," *Creators Syndicate, Inc.*, June 4, 2003.

82. Kevin Woods, James Lacey, and Williamson Murray, "Saddam's Delusions: The View from the Inside," *Foreign Affairs*, May/June 2006.

83. Norman Podhoretz, "Who Is Lying About Iraq?" *Commentary*, December 2005.

84. James Phillips, "Dispelling the Myths About Iraq," WebMemo #932, The Heritage Foundation, December 2, 2005.

85. Ibid.

86. Norman Podhoretz, "Who Is Lying About Iraq?" *Commentary*, December 2005.

87. David Horowitz and Ben Johnson, "The Wrong Argument, at the Wrong Place , at the Wrong Time," FrontPageMagazine.com, November 7, 2005.

88. David Horowitz and Ben Johnson, "The Wrong Argument, at the Wrong Place, at the Wrong Time," FrontPageMagazine.com, November 7, 2005; George Tenet admitted in his speech at Georgetown that we didn't have enough of our own human intelligence. George J. Tenet, "Remarks as Prepared for Delivery by Director of Central Intelligence George J. Tenet at Georgetown University," *Central Intelligence Agency*, February 5, 2004.

CHAPTER TWO: The Defeatocrats

1. Report On The U.S. Intelligence Community's Prewar Intelligence Assessments On Iraq," U.S. Senate Select Committee On Intelligence, 7/7/04, 284-285.

2. Charles S. Robb And Laurence H. Silberman, The Commission On The Intelligence Capabilities Of The United States Regarding Weapons Of Mass Destruction, 3/31/05, 50-51)

3. George J. Tenet, "Remarks as Prepared for Delivery by Director of Central Intelligence George J. Tenet at Georgetown University," *Central Intelligence Agency*, February 5, 2004.

4. Kenneth R. Timmerman, "Ex-Official: Russia Moved Saddam's WMD," Newsmax.com, February 19, 2006.

5. "Bush Was Right," *Investors Business Daily*, February 21, 2006.

6. Rush Limbaugh, "W Was Right: Untold Story of Iraqi Documents," *The Limbaugh Letter*, May 2006.

7. President Bush, Remarks After Meeting With Members Of The Congressional Conference Committee On Energy Legislation, Washington, D.C., September 17, 2003.

8. Transcript, Nightline, "A Conversation with Condoleezza Rice," ABC News Transcripts, September 16, 2003.

9. "US Intelligence Officials Say Ranking Al Qaeda Members Hiding in Iraq," *The Bulletin's Frontrunner*, August 21, 2002.

10. Norman Podhoretz, "Who Is Lying About Iraq?" *Commentary*, December 2005.

11. Stephen F. Hayes, "Their Man In Baghdad," *Weekly Standard*, June 19, 2006.

12. Final Report of the National Commission On Terrorist Attacks Upon the United States," *The 9/11 Commission Report*, July 22, 2004, 66.

13. Final Report of the National Commission On Terrorist Attacks Upon the United States," *The 9/11 Commission Report*, July 22, 2004, 61.

14. Stephen F. Hayes, "Saddam's Philippines Terror Connection, And other revelations from the Iraqi regime files," *Weekly Standard*, March 27, 2006.

15. Stephen F. Hayes & Thomas Joscelyn, "The Mother of All Connections," *Weekly Standard*, July 18, 2005.

16. Ibid.

17. Ray Robison, "Terror Links to Saddam's Inner Circle," FoxNews.com, June 12, 2006.

18. Ray Robison, "Was Saddam Regime a Broker for Terror Alliances?" FoxNews.com, June 26, 2006.

19. "Ray Robison, "Iraq How-to Manual Directed Arab Military Operatives in Afghanistan," FoxNews.com, July 6, 2006.

20. Michael Barone, "Lurking in Saddam's Old Tent?" Creators Syndicate, March 7, 2006.

21. Transcript, "Interview with Joseph Biden, *FOX News Network*, November 20, 2005.

22. Transcript, FOX News Sunday Roundtable," *FOX News Network*, November 27, 2005.

23. "President Bush Outlines Iraqi Threat," The White House, October 7, 2002.

24. "President George Bush Discusses Iraq in National Press Conference," The White House, March 6, 2003.

25. Transcript, FOX News Sunday, "Interview With Senators Roberts and Rockefeller," *FOX News Network*, November 13, 2005.

26. Transcript, Newshour with Jim Lehrer, "Background: War and Politics," *PBS*, September 27, 2002.

27. Tom Curry, "Dean Assails Bush on 'Unilateralism,'" MSNBC.com, December 15, 2003.

28. David Limbaugh, "Multilateralism 'Til We're Blue in the Face," *Creators Syndicate, Inc.*, November 11, 2003.

29. Joseph R. Biden, Jr., "One Last Chance to Get Help," *Washington Post*, November 9, 2003.

30. Transcript: Jimmy Carter at Democratic National Convention, "Carter: 'At Stake is Nothing Less than Our Nation's Soul,'" CNN.com, July 26, 2004.

31. Dana Milbank, "For Clinton, a Chance to Evoke Better Days," *Washington Post*, April 13, 2006.

32. James Phillips, "Dispelling the Myths About Iraq," The Heritage Foundation, December 2, 2005.

33. Mona Charen, "Political Ambush," Creators Syndicate, June 6, 2006.

34. Jefferson Morley, "Who Gets the Credit in Iraq? Some Praise Bush's Policies, Others Say Election May Bolster Opponents of Occupation," *Washington Post*, February 1, 2005.

35. "Dean: US Won't Win in Iraq," WOAI.com, December 6, 2005.

36. Scott Goldstein, "Kennedy Renews Call for Exit Plan, Says Troops Should Leave Iraq by '06," *Boston Globe*, February 5, 2005.

37. Hans Nichols, "Dems' Iraq Group Seeks Unified Message On War," *The Hill*, February 10, 2005.

38. "Bush Touts Iraq Vote; Democrats Want Clear U.S. Strategy," Both See Hope in Poll on Draft Constitution," CNN.com, October 15, 2005.

39. Transcript, "News Conference With Senator Harry Reid (D-NV); Senator Carl Levin (D-MI); And Senator Jack Reed (D-RI)," Federal News Service, December 14, 2005.

40. Carl Limbacher, "Bill Kristol: Senate Democrats are 'Crazy,'" Newsmax.com, December 14, 2005.

41. Congresswoman Nancy Pelosi, "Pelosi Statement on Bush Administration Announcement on Troop Reduction in Iraq," Congresswoman Nancy Pelosi's Official Website, December 23, 2005.

42. "Final Vote Results for Roll Call 648," "Expressing the Commitment of the House of Representatives to achieving victory in Iraq," http://clerk.house.gov/evs/2005/roll648.xml, December 16, 2005.

43. Liz Sidoti, "House Disavows Calls for Iraq Withdrawal," Associated Press, December 16, 2005.

44. "Divided House Rejects Iraq Pullout Date, 42 Democrats Break Rank and Join Majority," CNN.com, June 16, 2006.

45. Paula A. DeSutter, "Libya Renounces Weapons of Mass Destruction," *eJournalUSA: Foreign Policy Agenda*, March 2005.

46. Transcript: Anderson Cooper 360 Degrees," CNN.com, March 10, 2005.

47. James Phillips, "Dispelling the Myths About Iraq," The Heritage Foundation, December 2, 2005.

48. See "The Underestimators: Sawyer, Clarke Claim Zarqawi Death Not 'Major' Blow to Terrorism," Newsbusters.org, June 8, 2006, and any number of other posts on that excellent Weblog.

49. Editorial, "Too Soon to Cheer in Baghdad," *New York Times*, June 14, 2006.

50. "Pelosi on Iraq: 'It's Time to Face the Facts,' "U.S. Newswire, June 16, 2006.

51. Susan Jones, " 'Murtha Democrats Believe America Can't Win,' GOP Says," CNSNews.com, June 19, 2005.

52. Text of a Document Discovered in Terror Leader Abu Musab al-Zarqawi's Hideout," Associated Press, June 15, 2006.

53. Internal Al-Qaeda Papers," discovered April 16, 2006, as referenced on *Bill Bennett's Morning in America*, May 10, 2006.

54. "Fear of Phoning," Strategypage.com, December 19, 2005.

55. "Brian Ross and Christopher Isham, "Three Foiled Hijack Plots Revealed in U.S. Document," *ACB News*, June 21, 2006.

56. "Plotters Sought to Bomb NY Tunnel: Paper," Reuters, July 7, 2006.

57. "Schumer: 'Intelligence Was on the Ball,' " CNN.com, July 7, 2006.

58. Kim Gamel, "Post-al-Zarqawi Raids Kill 104 Insurgents," Associated Press, June 15, 2006.

59. "17 Killed in Violence, Including Mosque Attack, U.S. Military: Top Al Qaeda Operative Captured," CNN.com, June 23, 2006.

60. "Insurgents Demand Withdrawal of U.S. Forces in Iraq in 2 Years," Associated Press, June 28, 2006.

61. Michael Isikoff and Mark Hosenball, "Catching Al Qaeda, Bush Now Claims that 75 Percent of the Group's Key Members Are out of Commission. Some Experts Say That Number is Meaningless," *Newsweek*, September 8, 2004.

62. Steven Komarow, "U.S. Chipping Away at Al Qaeda Leadership, But Attacks Climbing," *USA Today*, October 2, 2005.

63. James Phillips, "Dispelling the Myths About Iraq," The Heritage Foundation, December 2, 2005.

64. Donald Rumsfeld, "Do Some Soul Searching, Why Aren't the Media Telling the Whole Story About Iraq?" OpinionJournal.com, December 9, 2005.

65. Donald Rumsfeld, "Do Some Soul Searching, Why Aren't the Media Telling the Whole Story About Iraq?" OpinionJournal.com, December 9, 2005.

66. Donald H. Rumsfeld, "What We've Gained in 3 Years In Iraq," *The Washington Post*, March 19, 2006.

67. Donald Rumsfeld, "Do Some Soul Searching, Why Aren't the Media Telling the Whole Story About Iraq?" OpinionJournal.com, December 9, 2005.

68. Donna Miles, "Iraqi Progress Report Cites Successes, Challenges Ahead," *United States Department of Defense*, May 30, 2006.

69. "John Kerry Touts Al Qaeda Successes," Newsmax.com, January 22, 2006.

70. Lynda Hurst, "War on Terror Called Failure," *Toronto Star*, June 15, 2006.

71. Transcript, FOX News Sunday, "Interview With Josspeh Biden, Richard Lugar," *FOX News Network*, August 7, 2005.

72. Scott Goldstein, "Kennedy Renews Call for Exit Plan, Says Troops Should Leave Iraq by '06," *Boston Globe*, February 5, 2005.

73. Donald Lambro, "Democrats Split Over U.S. Troop Withdrawal," *Washington Times*, November 20, 2005.

74. Democratic Demand Total Iraq Pullout," *AFP*, November 18, 2005.

75. Byron York, "Murtha Fears a Withdrawal that 'Makes It Look Like There's a Victory,'" *National Review Online*, January 6, 2006.

76. "Democratic Demand Total Iraq Pullout," *AFP*, November 18, 2005.

77. "Iran and Qaeda Benefit From US in Iraq: Congressman," Reuters, March 5, 2006.

78. Donald Lambro, "Democrats Split Over U.S. Troop Withdrawal," *Washington Times*, November 20, 2005.

79. Donald Lambro, "Democrats Split Over U.S. Troop Withdrawal," *Washington Times*, November 20, 2005.

80. "Bush: U.S. to Stay in Iraq till War is Won," CNN.com, December 1, 2005.

81. Divided House Rejects Iraq Pullout Date, 42 Democrats Break Rank and Join Majority," CNN.com, June 16, 2006.

82. Donald Lambro, "Democrats Split Over U.S. Troop Withdrawal," *Washington Times*, November 20, 2005.

83. Dan Balz, "Pelosi Hails Democrats' Diverse War Stances," *Washington Post*, December 16, 2005.

84. Michael Kinsley, "It Hurts, but Don't Stop," *Washington Post*, November 21, 2004.

85. Liz Sidoti, "Democrats Offer National Security Platform," Associated Press, March 29, 2006.

86. "Rowan Scarborough, "Political Offensive Targets Bush," *Washington Times*, March 18, 2006.

CHAPTER THREE: King George

1. Arnold Beichman, "Frustrated Democrats," *Washington Times*, October 15, 2004.

2. Transcript, "U.S. Senator Patrick Leahy (D-VT) Delivers Remarks At Georgetown University Law School On the Nomination of Judge Samuel Alito to the U.S. Supreme Court," *Congressional Quarterly, Inc.*, January 19, 2006.

3. Matthew Cardinale, "30 US Reps for Bush Impeachment Inquiry," *Atlanta Progressive News*, March 11, 2006.

4. The United States Supreme Court might have just granted them their wish with its ruling in *Hamdan v. Rumsfeld* on June 29, 2006 holding that military tribunals for 10 terrorist enemy combatants held at Guantanamo Bay were illegal under U.S. law and Geneva conventions without congressional approval. "Supreme Court Blocks Guantanamo Bay War-Crimes Trials, FoxNews.com, June 29, 2006.

5. Douglas Jehl and Eric Schmitt, "The Struggle for Iraq: Investigations; Army Discloses Criminal Inquiry on Prison Abuse," *New York Times*, May 5, 2004.

6. Ibid.

7. Ibid.

8. Elisabeth Bumiller and Richard W. Stevenon, "Rumsfeld Chastised by President For His Handling of Iraq Scandal," *New York Times*, May 6, 2004.

9. Ibid.

10. Rick Lyman, "Scratching Behind Ears of Bush's 'Pit Bull,'" *New York Times*, May 16, 2004.

11. Transcript, FOX News Special Report with Brit Hume: Brian Wilson, Major Garrett, "Congress, The Pentagon And White House Negotiate How To Release Additional Photos Of Abused Iraqi Prisoners," *Fox News Network*, May 10, 2004.

12. "The Abu Ghraib Spin," *New York Times*, May 12, 2004.

13. Norman Podhoretz, "World War IV: How It Started, What It Means, and Why We Have to Win," *Commentary*, September 2004.

14. James Barron, "Citing a 'Shamed America,' Gore Calls for Rumsfeld, Rice, Tenet and 3 Others to Resign," *New York Times*, May 27, 2004.

15. "Al Gore Links Abu Ghraib Prison Abuses to Deep Flaws In Bush Policy," *PR News Wire*, May 26, 2004.

16. Maureen Dowd, "Marquis de Bush?" *New York Times*, May 27, 2004.

17. James Barron, "Citing a 'Shamed America,' Gore Calls for Rumsfeld, Rice, Tenet and 3 Others to Resign," *New York Times*, May 27, 2004.

18. Norman Podhoretz, "World War IV: How It Started, What It Means, and Why We Have to Win," *Commentary*, September 2004.

19. Norman Podhoretz, "World War IV: How It Started, What It Means, and Why We Have to Win," *Commentary*, September 2004.

20. Rowan Scarborough, "No Gitmo Torture, Senate Panel Told," *Washington Times*, July 14, 2005.

21. Scarborough, "No Gitmo Torture, Senate Panel Told," *Washington Times*, July 14, 2005.

22. It is unclear yet whether the Supreme Court's ruling in *Hamdan v. Rumsfeld* (see FN 4) governs the status of all Gitmo detainees.

23. Scarborough, "No Gitmo Torture, Senate Panel Told," *Washington Times*, July 14, 2005.

24. Jack Kelly, "Gitmo Grandstanding, Democrats Fulminate Over Guantanamo Prisoners, But They Are Treated Well," *Pittsburgh Post-Gazette*, June 19, 2005.

25. Aleksandr Solzhenitsyn, *Gulag Archipelago* (NY, NY: Harper & Row, Publishers, Inc. 1974).

26. "Shut Down Guantanamo? U.S. Eyes Options, Rumsfeld Joins Bush in Talking About Options," MSNBC.com, June 9, 2005.

27. Michael Adler, "US Defends Torture Charges," *Herald Sun*, May 5, 2006.

28. Editorial, "The Gitmo Suicides," *New York Post*, June 13, 2006.

29. "Carter Says U.S. Should Close Detention Center at Guantánamo," *New York Times*, June 8, 2005.

30. "Shut Down Guantanamo? U.S. Eyes Options, Rumsfeld Joins Bush in Talking About Options," MSNBC.com, June 9, 2005.

31. Jim Krane, "Gore Laments U.S. 'Abuses' Against Arabs," Associated Press, February 12, 2006.

32. Stephen Dinan, "Democrats Report No Abuse at Gitmo," *Washington Times*, June 28, 2005.

33. Dana Dillon, "Model Gitmo, Very Far Away From Anything Amnesty Claims," *National Review Online*, July 1, 2005.

34. "U.N. Says U.S. Should Close Gitmo Down," Associated Press, May 19, 2006.

35. Rich Tucker, "You Call This Abuse?" Townhall.com, June 2, 2006.

36. Ben Fox, "Gitmo Detainee Says Clash Involved Qurans," *Washington Post*, June 7, 2006.

37. Rich Tucker, "You Call This Abuse?" Townhall.com, June 2, 2006.

38. Editorial, "The Gitmo Suicides," *New York Post*, June 13, 2006.

39. Editorial, "The Deaths at Gitmo," *New York Times*, June 12, 2006.

40. James Risen and Eric Lichtblau, "Bush Lets U.S. Spy on Callers Without Courts," *New York Times*, December 16, 2005.

41. Ibid.

42. Ibid.

43. Ibid.

44. Ibid.

45. United States v. [Cassius] Clay, 430 F.2d 165 (5th Cir. 1970); United States v. Butenko, 494 F. 2d 593 (3rd Cir. 1974); United States v. Buck, 548 F.2d 871 (9th Cir. 1977); United States v. Truong, 629 F.2d 908 (4th Cir. 1980); and United States v. Duggan, 743 F.2d 59 (2nd Cir. 1984). John Hinderaker, of Powerline Blog has written a valuable memo on this legal question: See John Hinderaker, "On the Legality of the NSA Electronic Intercept Program," *Powerlineblog.com*, December 22, 2005.

46. States v. Duggan, 743 F.2d 59 (2nd Cir. 1984).

47. Sealed Case No. 02-001.

48. Sheryl Gay Stolberg and Eric Lichtblau, "Senators Thwart Bush Bid to Renew Law on Terrorism," *New York Times*, December 17, 2005.

49. Brian DeBose, "FISA Judges Say Bush Within Law," *Washington Times*, March 29, 2006.

50. Ibid.

51. Ibid.

52. Sheryl Gay Stolberg and Eric Lichtblau, "Senators Thwart Bush Bid to Renew Law on Terrorism," *New York Times*, December 17, 2005.

53. Ibid.

54. "Transcript, Statement of Sen. Patrick Leahy, Ranking Member, Senate Judiciary Committee Hearing on 'Wartime Executive Power and The NSA's Surveillance Authority,' Monday, February 6, 2006."

55. Transcript, "Senate Judiciary Committee Debates the Alito Nomination," *Washington Post*, January 24, 2006.

56. Robert B. Bluey, "Gore Calls Bush Threat to Democracy," *Human Events Online*, January 17, 2006.

57. Editorial, "Al-Qaida On Line Two," *Investor's Business Daily*, January 18, 2006.

58. Ibid.

59. Editorial, "Trust? Don't Think So," *Philadelphia Inquirer*, January 30, 2006.

60. Editorial, "Spies, Lies and Wiretaps," *New York Times*, January 29, 2006.

61. Tom Engelhardt, "King George," Salon.com, January 5, 2006.

62. Editorial, "Madness of King George," *The Nation*, February 13, 2006.

63. "Name That' President, Results of May, 2003 Eric Alterman Contest," *Talk-Left.com*, May, 2003.

64. Niall Ferguson, "The Monarchy of George II," *Vanity Fair*, September 2004.

65. "Democrats Seek Eavesdropping Special Counsel," Associated Press, February 27, 2006.

66. Transcript: Sen. Russ Feingold on 'FNS,' *FOX News Sunday*, April 3, 2006.

67. Gary Steven Corseri, "Liberate America, 25 Reasons to Impeach George W. Bush," Counterpunch.org, June 6, 2005.

68. Editorial, "The Data-mining Scare, Another nonthreat to your civil liberties," *Wall Street Journal*, May 13, 2006.

69. Ibid.

70. Ibid.

71. Editorial, "Dialing and the Democrats," *The New York Sun*, May 12, 2006.

72. Ibid.

73. Rich Noyes, "USA Today Reporter a Democratic Donor: Phone Company Demands Retraction," NewsBusters.org, May 19, 2006.

74. Ibid.

75. Eric Lichtblau and James Risen, "Bank Data is Sifted by U.S. in Secret to Block Terror, *New York Times*, June 23, 2006.

76. Andrew C. McCarthy, "The Media's War Against the War Continues," *National Review Online*, June 23, 2006.

77. Andrew C. McCarthy, "The Media's War Against the War Continues," *National Review Online*, June 23, 2006.

78. Eric Lichtblau and James Risen, "Bank Data is Sifted by U.S. in Secret to Block Terror, *New York Times*, June 23, 2006.

79. Editorial, "Finances of Terror," *New York Times*, September 24, 2001.

80. Transcript, FOX News Sunday, "FOX News Sunday Roundtable," *FOX News Network*, June 25, 2006.

81. Terrence Hunt, "Bush Condemns Leak of Terror Finance Info," Associated Press, June 26, 2006.

CHAPTER FOUR: We Have Values Too

1. "Should Democrats Get Religion?" *CBS News*, November 4, 2004.

2. Sheryl Gay Stolberg, "Democrats Getting Lessons in Speaking Their Values," *New York Times*, Feburary 11, 2005.

3. Ellen Goodman, "Winning Back Values Voters," *Washington Post*, November 6, 2004.

4. "Religion & Public Life, A Faith-Based Partisan Divide, *Pew Forum of Religion and Public Life*, January 20, 2005.

5. Greg Pierce, "Inside Politics," *Washington Times*, May 31, 2006.

6. "Democrats Sell Christian 'Hypocrite' Magnet, Fish Symbol With Hellish Flames Removed From Website After Exposure," Worldnetdaily.com, December 10, 2005.

7. Maureen Dowd, "Slapping the Other Cheek," *New York Times*, November 14, 2004.

8. Peter Steinfels, "Anti-Bush Criticism and the Fixation on 'Delusional' Christian Fundamentalism," *New York Times*, January 29, 2005.

9. David Crary, "Liberals Dismayed By 'Moral Values' Claims, Associated Press, November 9, 2004.

10. "School Bans History Materials Referring to God, California Teacher Prohibited from Giving Declaration of Independence,:" Reuters, November 24, 2004.

11. Tamara Henry, "The Very Picture of Patriotism," *USA Today*, January 2, 2002.

12. Ramesh Ponnuru, "Robert Reich's Religion Problem," *National Review Online*, July 6, 2004.

13. Shailagh Murray, "Roberts Hearings Likely to Enter Religious Territory," *Washington Post*, September 5, 2005.

14. ABC News Transcripts, "Interview with Howard Dean," *This Week With George Stephanopoulos*, October 23, 2005.

15. Rabbi Daniel Lapin, "Democrats' Dilemma: How to Sound More Spiritual," Worldnetdaily.com, November 29, 2005.

16. Jim VandeHei, "Dean Now Willing to Discuss His Faith, Campaign and Trips to Bible Belt States Changed Him, Candidate Says," *Washington Post*, January 4, 2004.

17. Rabbi Shmuley Boteach, "Howard Dean Gets Religion, Is Dean's Newfound Religious Conviction Sincere? Shmuley thinks not—and can prove it," Beliefnet.com, January 12, 2004.

18. Sheryl Gay Stolberg, "Democrats Getting Lessons in Speaking Their Values," *New York Times*, Feburary 11, 2005.

19. Steven Thomma, "Democrats Try New Tack: In God They Do Trust," Knight Ridder, December 17, 2005.

20. Michael Weisskopf, "Energized by Pulpit or Passion, the Public is Calling: 'Gospel Grapevine' Displays Strength in Controversy Over Military Gay Ban," *Washington Post*, February 1, 1993.

21. Noelle Straub, "Kerry: GOP Judge Talk Just God-Awful," *Boston Herald*, April 21, 2005.

22. Maureen Dowd, "Delay, Deny and Demagogue," *New York Times*, March 24, 2005.

23. Paul Krugman, "What's Going on?" *New York Times*, March 29, 2005.

24. Nicholas D. Kristof, "Apocalypse (Almost) Now," *New York Times*, November 24, 2004.

25. William Thatcher Dowell, "Made-in-America Wahhabism," *Los Angeles Times*, March 8, 2005.

26. Ellis Henican, "A Party That's Beyond Belief," Newsday.com, January 20, 2005.

27. Bill Moyers, "There is No Tomorrow," *Minneapolis Star Tribune*, January 30, 2005.

28. Jane Smiley, "Why Americans Hate Democrats—A Dialogue, The unteachable ignorance of the red states," Slate.com, November 4, 2004.

29. Thomas L. Friedman, "Two Nations Under God," *New York Times*, November 4, 2004.

30. Deborah Orin, "How Holy Howie Blasts GOP on Values," *New York Post*, February 12, 2005.

31. George Neumayr, "In Dean's Den," *American Spectator*, June 10, 2005.

32. Joe McDonald, "Rendell: GOP Not Last Word On Morals," *Morning Call*, April 24, 2006.

33. Steve Tetreault, "Political Notebook: Reid Makes Appeal to Religious on Democrats' Behalf," *Las Vegas Review-Journal*, July 25, 2005.

34. Steve Tetreault, "Political Notebook: Reid Makes Appeal to Religious on Democrats' Behalf," *Las Vegas Review-Journal*, July 25, 2005.

35. See Ann Coulter's excellent book, *Godless* (New York, NY: Crown Forum: 2006).

36. As Christian apologist Ravi Zacharias wrote, "Who we are in public is determined by what we have learned and cherished in private.... But it is a mindless philosophy that assumes that one's private beliefs have nothing to do with public office. Does it make sense to entrust those who are immoral in private with the power to determine the nation's moral issues and, indeed, its destiny? One of the most dangerous and terrifying trends in America today is the disregard for character as a central necessity in a leader's credentials. The duplicitous soul of a leader can only make a nation more sophisticated in evil." Ravi Zacharias, *Deliver Us From Evil* (Dallas, Texas: Word Publishing, 1996) 111.

37. Liberals even cite Jesus' admonition, "judge not lest ye be judged," to show that conservative views, such as upholding traditional marriage, are anti-Biblical and hypocritical. But as usual, they offer the scripture out of context. As evangelist John Stott wrote, the passage should not be understood as a command to "suspend our critical faculties in relation to other people, turn a blind eye to their faults, to eschew all criticism, and to refuse to discern between truth and error, goodness and evil. Much of Christ's teaching in the

Sermon on the Mount is based on the assumption that we will (indeed should) use our critical powers." John Stott, *The Message of the Sermon On The Mount, (Matthew 5-7),* (Leicester, England: Inter-Varsity Press, 1978), 175.

38. Christopher Flickinger, "Conservative Books Equate to 'Sexual Harassment,'" *Human Events,* April 17, 2006.

39. Carl Limbacher, "Ann Coulter Banned in New Jersey?" Newsmax.com, June 10, 2006.

40. David Limbaugh, *Persecution, How Liberals Are Waging War Against Christianity,* (Washington, D.C.: Regnery Publishing, Inc. 2003), 118.

41. Ramesh Ponnuru, *The Party of Death, The Democrats, the Media, the Courts, and the Disregard for Human Life* (Washington, D.C.: Regnery Publishing, Inc., 2006), 4.

42. Kathryn Jean Lopez, "I Am Against Abortion," *National Review Online,* October 30, 2004.

43. John Henry Westen, "Jim Cater's Son: 'I'm pro-choice as far as a woman choosing, but I'm against abortion." *LifesiteNews,* February 21, 2006.

44. Jonathan Finer, "Kerry Says He Believes Life Starts At Conception," *Washington Post,* July 5, 2004.

45. Kathryn Jean Lopez, "Pelosi Blames Catholics," *National Review Online,* November 18, 2004.

46. Daneen G. Peterson, Ph.D., "Seditionist Mahony Defies Pope," Mich-News.com, March 21, 2006.

47. Nedra Pickler, "Kerry: Religion Shouldn't Mix with Politics," Associated Press, April 23, 2004.

48. Ibid.

49. "Testing the Faith: Bush Ripped for 'God Talk'; Nader, Others Criticize Comments Included in Bob Woodward Book," Worldnetdaily.com, April 20, 2004.

50. "GOP the Religion-Friendly Party, But Stem Cell Issue May Help Democrats," *The Pew Forum on Religion & Public Life,* August 24, 2004.

51. Debra Rosenberg and Karen Breslau, "Culture Wars: Winning the 'Values' Vote," *Newsweek,* November 7, 2004.

52. "Voter Liked Campaign 2004, But Too Much Mud-Slinging," The Pew Research Center, November 11, 2004.

53. "John Kerry on Faith, An ongoing collection of quotes from Kerry about faith, his relationship with God, religion & politics, and more," Beliefnet.com, October 2004.

54. John Kerry, "Speech at the Broward Center for the Performing Arts," October 24, 2004.

55. "John Kerry on Faith, An ongoing collection of quotes from Kerry about faith, his relationship with God, religion & politics, and more," Beliefnet.com, October 2004.

56. Rush Limbaugh, "Liberals Sound Worried About Gay Marriage," Rush-Limbaugh.com, June 6, 2006.

57. Gloria Borger, "Democrats Need a Twang," *U.S. News & World Report*, November 22, 2004.

58. Lynn Sweet, "Toned-down Dean Finds Friendly Audience at Push," *Chicago Sun-Times*, June 13, 2005.

59. "Sen. Clinton Seeks Abortion Common Ground," *UPI*, January 25, 2005.

60. Michael Jonas, "Sen. Clinton Urges Use of Faith-Based Initiatives," *Boston Globe*, January 20, 2005.

CHAPTER FIVE: The Values Blues

1. "Democrats Jeer At Boy Scout Guests," Newsmax.com, August 18, 2000.

2. *Stenberg v. Carhart*, 530 U.S. 914 (2000).

3. Ibid.

4. Ramesh Ponnuru, *The Party of Death, The Democrats, the Media, the Courts, and the Disregard for Human Life* (Washington, D.C.: Regnery Publishing, Inc., 2006), 2.

5. Michael Kelly, "Arguing for Infanticide," *Washington Post*, November 6, 1997.

6. "Professor Who Killed Baby To Be Honored," *Boston Globe*, January 20, 2005.

7. Steven Pinker, "Why They Kill Their Newborns," *New York Times*, November 2, 1997.

8. Steven Pinker, "Why They Kill Their Newborns," *New York Times*, November 2, 1997; Pinker and Tooley are also quoted—disparagingly, by the late columnist Michael Kelly, "Abortion Rights Lead to Infanticide?" *Washington Post*, November 6, 1997.

9. Michael Kelly, "Arguing for Infanticide," *Washington Post*, November 6, 1997.

10. E. J. Dionne Jr., "The New Liberalism, Democrats Need to Show Their Family Values," *Washington Post*, January 14, 2005.

11. Transcript: Senator Hillary Rodham Clinton, "Remarks by Senator Hillary Rodham Clinton to the NYS Family Planning Providers," *Senator Hillary Rodham Clinton Official Website*, January 24, 2005

12. Ramesh Ponnuru, *The Party of Death, The Democrats, the Media, the Courts, and the Disregard for Human Life* (Washington, D.C.: Regnery Publishing, Inc., 2006), 73.

13. Ibid., 70.

14. Ibid., 74. Ponnuru explains in a footnote that "The National Cancer Institute held a workshop in February 2003 that concluded that there was no link, but Dr. Joel Brind wrote a dissenting report." One is entitled to what extent, if any, politics influenced the majority report.

15. Ibid., 69.

16. "Abortion's Physical and Emotional Risks," *Concerned Women for America*, January 18, 2003.

17. "Suicide Rate Higher After Abortion (MN, 1985: Medi-Cal, 1989; Elliot, 1993).

18. Garfinkle, B., et. Al., "Stress, Depression, and Suicide: A Study of Adolescents in Minnesota" (Minnesota: Univ Minnesota Extension Service, 1986).

19. B. Major, C. Cozzarelli, M.L. Cooper, J. Zubek, C. Richards, M. Wilhite, R.H. Gramzow, "Psychological Responses of Women After First-Trimester Abortion," Department of Psychology, University of California, Santa Barbara, *CA, Archives of General Psychiatry August, 2000.*

20. "The Psychology of Abortion: A Review and Suggestions for Future Research," (PandH, 4/05).

21. Charles Babington, "Democrats Wrestle With Choice and Choices," *Washington Post*, February 13, 2005.

22. Many Christians cite Genesis 9:6 on this very point: "Whoever sheds the blood of man, by man shall his blood be shed; for in the image of God has God made man."

23. E.J. Dionne Jr., "The New Liberalism, Democrats Need to Show Their Family Values," *Washington Post*, January 14, 2005.

24. Robert Knight, "Massachusetts High School to Celebrate 'Transgender, Gay Day,'" *Concerned Women for America*, December 13, 2004.

25. I cite a number of examples of this in my book *Persecution* (NY, NY: Regnery Publishing, Inc. 2004).

26. Fields v. Palmdale School District, 427 F. 3d 1197, 1200, (C. A. 9th Cir. 2005).

27. Transcript, CNN Reliable Sources, "War on Terrorism: What are the Challenges of Covering the War From Inside Afghanistan and Inside the Pentagon,' CNN, November 4, 2001.

28. Lee Bockhorn, "The Know-Nothing Press," *Weekly Standard*, November 7, 2001.

29. L. Brent Bozell, III, "Why Conservatives Should Be Optimistic About the Media," The Heritage Foundation, January 21, 1992.

30. Don Kowet, Sean Piccoli and Robin Berkowitz, "Notes on War Coverage," *Washington Times*, February 8, 1991.

31. Eric Pfeiffer, "Democrats Advised on Military Relations," *The Washington Times*, June 6, 2006.

32. Charles R. Kesler, Ph.D., "The Crisis of American National Identity," The Heritage Foundation, November 8, 2005.

33. Editorial, "America, the Indifferent," *New York Times*, December 23, 2004.

34. Editorial, "The Stingy U.S.; An Appalling Performance," *Minneapolis Star Tribune*, December 30, 2004.

35. Editorial, "Are We Stingy? Yes," *New York Times*, December 30, 2004.

36. John G. Sotos, "A Modest—and Slimming!—Proposal," *The Washington Post*, April 7, 2006.

37. Nina Burleigh, "Country Boy," Salon.com, April 17, 2006.

38. Thomas L. Friedman, "Read My Ears," *New York Times*, January 27, 2005.

39. Jim Krane, "Gore Laments U.S. 'Abuses' Against Arabs," Associated Press, February 12, 2006.

40. "Murtha Says U.S. Poses Top Threat to World Peace," *South Florida Sun-Sentinel*, June 25, 2006.

41. "Bil Clinton: Iraq A 'Big Mistake,'" *CBS News*, November 16, 2005.

42. Carl Limbacher, "Kerry Trashes Bush in Baghdad," Newsmax.com, January 6, 2005.

43. "Jimmy Carter Slams Iraq War," CBS News, July 30, 2005.

44. Editorial, "Jimmy's Follies," *Pittsburgh Tribune-Review*, March 8, 2006.

45. Ex-US President Jimmy Carter Slams 'Arrogant' US Foreign Policy," *Agence France Presse*, November 16, 2002.

46. Senate Secretary Travis McCoy, "Minutes of Washington University Student Senate," February 7, 2006.

47. Neal Boortz, "He Fought For Our Country....But He's Not Worthy," *Nealz Nuze at boortz.com*, February 15, 2006.

48. Midge Decter, "The Never-Ending War: The Battle Over America's Self-Meaning," The Heritage Foundation, November 21, 2005.

49. ABC News Transcripts, "Interview with Howard Dean," *This Week With George Stephanopoulos*, October 23, 2005.

50. Patrick Hynes, "Democrats Misplay 'God Card,'" Townhall.com, February 14, 2006.

51. Gary Bauer, "Values Voters and the Left," *Washington Times*, November 22, 2004.

CHAPTER SIX: The "Living Constitution"

1. "Breyer Says 'Zero' Politics on the Court," Associated Press, February 8, 2006.

2. John Nichols, "Karl Rove's Legal Tricks: Packing the Judiciary With Right-Wingers," *The Nation*, July 22, 2002; Rob Boston, "Attack of the Clones: President Bush and His Religious Right Allies Want to Stack the Supreme Court with Right-Wing Ideologues," *Church & State*, March 2005.

3. Edward M. Kennedy, "Kennedy Statement on Nomination of Judge Samuel Alito to Supreme Court," The office of Senator Edward M. Kennedy of Massachusetts, October 31, 2005.

4. *Planned Parenthood of Southeastern PA.* v. *Casey*, 505 U.S. 833 (1992).

5. Ibid., 505 U.S. 833, 852 (1992).

6. *Lawrence et al.* v. *Texas*, 539 U.S. 558 (2003).

7. Antonin Scalia, Transcript: "Antonin Scalia Delivers Remarks at the American Enterprise Institute on the Role That International and Foreign Law Should Play in American Judicial Decision-Making," *Congressional Quarterly, Inc.*, February 21, 2006.

8. Ruth Bader Ginsburg, "A Decent Respect to the Opinions of [Human]kind: The Value of a Comparative Perspective in Constitutional Adjudication," *Constitutional Court of South Africa*, cited on the official Supreme Court website under public info/speeches, February 7, 2006.

9. Transcript, Scalia-Breyer Debate on Foreign Law, "Subject: Constitutional Relevance of Foreign Court Decisions," *U.S. Association of Constitutional Law Discussion, American University*, January 13, 2005.

10. Sandra Day O'Connor, "Remarks by Sandra Day O'Connor, Associate Justice, Supreme Court of the United States," Southern Center for International Studies, October 28, 2003.

11. Jeffrey Toobin, "How Anthony Kennedy's Passion for Foreign Law Could Change the Supreme Court," *New Yorker*, September 12, 2005.

12. Charles Hurt, "Judiciary Democrats Assail Brown; Partisan Lines Clear as GOP Backs Court Pick," *Washington Times*, October 23, 2003.

13. Ibid.

14. Byron York, "Behind the Democrats' Attack, Democrats vs. Charles Pickering," *National Review Online*, February 11, 2002.

15. Ibid.

16. Pickering called Hunger to express his concern over the Justice Department's delinquency in getting back to him concerning the issue of the ambiguous mandatory sentencing guidelines and the disparity in the proposed treatment of the several defendants.

17. York, "Behind the Democrats' Attack, Democrats vs. Charles Pickering."

18. Editorial, "Smearing Judge Pickering," *Washington Times*, January 21, 2004.

19. David Firestone, "Blacks at Home Support a Judge Liberals Assail," *New York Times*, February 17, 2002.

20. I wrote about this in my syndicated column. David Limbaugh, "Using Race as a Weapon," Creators Syndicate, February 13, 2002.

21. Firestone, "Blacks at Home Support a Judge Liberals Assail."

22. Mario H. Lopez, "Masters of Obstruction," *National Review Online*, May 29, 2003.

23. Joan Biskupic, "Judicial Nominee Estrada Withdraws Name," *USA Today*, September 4, 2003.

24. "Estrada Withdraws as Judicial Nominee, Bush Slams 'Disgraceful Treatment,'" CNN.com/Inside Politics, September 4, 2003.

25. Bruce Fein, "Judicial Confirmation Sabotage," *Washington Times*, September 9, 2003.

26. Byron York, "Another Democratic Filibuster? Democrats Prepare to Obstruct Again—War or No War," *National Review Online*, March 28, 2003.

27. Ibid.

28. "Estrada Withdraws as Judicial Nominee, Bush Slams 'Disgraceful Treatment'."

29. Ex-solicitors General Weigh In on Estrada Probe," CNN.com/Law Center, June 26, 2002.

30. Editorial, "Kennedy & the Clowns," *New York Post*, January 14, 2006.

31. Eric Pianin, "A Senator's Shame, Byrd, in His New Book, Again Confronts Early Ties to KKK," *Washington Post*, June 19, 2005.

32. William Rusher, "Kennedy Strikes Out With Alito," *Human Events*, January 14, 2006.

33. Dale Russakoff, "Alito Disavows Controversial Group, Nominee Touted His Membership in 1985," *Washington Post*, January 12, 2006.

34. *Good Morning America*, "The Battle Cry; Alito's Wife Breaks Down," ABC News Transcripts, January 12, 2006.

35. State News Service, "Statement of Senator Patrick Leahy on Nomination of Samuel Alito," January 27, 2006.

36. Transcript, "Senate Judiciary Committee," FDCH Political Transcripts, January 11, 2006.

37. Brent Baker, "NBC, CNN & Wash Post Yet to Correct Kennedy's Smear of Alito Based on Satire," Newsbusters.org, January 17, 2006.

38. R. Jeffrey Smith, "Judge Participated in 2002 Vanguard Case Despite Promise to Recuse," *Washington Post*, November 1, 2005.

39. Senate Judiciary Committee, "U.S. Senator Arlen Specter (R-PA) Holds a Hearing on the Supreme Court Nomination of Judge Samuel Alito to the Supreme Court," FDCH Political Transcripts, January 10, 2006.

40. Ibid.

41. Ibid.

42. Thomas D. Morgan, "Letter to Honorable Arlen Specter, Chair, United States Senate Committee on the Judiciary, November 3, 2005.

43. David McGowan, "Judge Alito and the Vanguard Recusal Question," *Legal Ethics Forum*, November 5, 2005.

44. Senate Judiciary Committee, "U.S. Senator Arlen Specter (R-PA) Holds a Hearing on the Supreme Court Nomination of Judge Samuel Alito to the Supreme Court."

45. Professor Stephen Lubet of Northwestern University Law School, who Hatch also mentioned, believed that Alito had made an "oops" mistake in initially failing to recuse himself, but that it wasn't an episode that called his ethics into question. Professors Stephen Gillers of New York University Law School and David McGowan of the University of San Diego Law School agree with that assessment.

46. McGowan, "Judge Alito and the Vanguard Recusal Question."

47. State News Service, "Statement of Senator Patrick Leahy on Nomination of Samuel Alito," January 27, 2006.

48. Robert Kuttner, "Alito May Be the Worst Choice," *Boston Globe*, January 8, 2006.

49. Senate Judiciary Committee, "U.S. Senator Arlen Specter (R-PA) Holds a Hearing on the Supreme Court Nomination Of Judge Samuel Alito To The Supreme Court."

50. Transcript, "Reid Statement on Confirmation of Samuel Alito," State News Service, January 31, 2006.

51. I discussed this at some length in my column "Alito Not Extremist Enough for Left," Creators Syndicate, January 10, 2006.

52. Transcript, "Reid Statement on Confirmation of Samuel Alito."

53. Biden said, "As I've tried diligently to look at your record, you seem to come down more often and give the benefit of the doubt to the outfit against whom discrimination is being alleged. You seem to lean—in close cases, you lean to the state versus the individual." Senate Judiciary Committee, "U.S. Senator Arlen Specter (R-PA) Holds a Hearing on the Supreme Court Nomination of Judge Samuel Alito to the Supreme Court." Senator Stabenow said, "Judge Alito has been consistently outside the mainstream and has said no to the daily concerns of average Americans." Transcript, "Press Conference With Democratic Leaders and Members of the Senate Judiciary Committee Following Committee Vote on Nomination of Judge Samuel Alito to Be an Associate Justice of The Supreme Court," Federal News Service, January 24, 2006.

54. Transcript, "U.S. Senator Edward Kennedy (D-MA) Delivers Remarks on the Senate Floor on the Nomination of Judge Samuel Alito to the U.S. Supreme Court," *Congressional Quarterly, Inc.*, January 30, 2006.

55. Senate Judiciary Committee, "U.S. Senator Arlen Specter (R-PA) Holds a Hearing on the Supreme Court Nomination of Judge Samuel Alito to the Supreme Court."

56. William Tucker, "The Smear That Failed: Judge Alito, When Did You Stop Molesting Children?" *Weekly Standard*, January 23, 2006.

57. Senate Judiciary Committee, "U.S. Senator Arlen Specter (R-PA) Holds a Hearing on the Supreme Court Nomination of Judge Samuel Alito to the Supreme Court."

58. Adam Nagourney, Richard Stevenson, and Neil A. Lewis, "Glum Democrats Can't See Halting Bush on Courts," *New York Times*, January 15, 2006.

CHAPTER SEVEN: "Extraordinary Circumstances"

1. Audrey Hudson, "GOP: Bush Nominees Treated Unfairly; Have Relatively Low Confirmation Rate," *Washington Times*, April 3, 2002.

2. Thomas L. Jipping, J.D., "Fixing a Broken Confirmation Process: Ending Permanent Judicial Nominee Filibusters," May 9, 2003.

3. The Honorable Mitch McConnell, "The State of the Judicial Confirmation Process," Heritage Lecture #740, April 30, 2002.

4. Todd F. Gaziano, Testimony Before the House Judiciary Committee—Subcommittee on the Constitution, "A Diminished Judiciary: The Causes and Effects of the Sustained High Vacancy Rates in Federal Courts," October 10, 2002.

5. Hans S. Nichols, "Democrats Refuse to Act Judiciously: Democrats in Control of the Senate Have Stonewalled President George W. Bush's Nominees For the Federal Bench, Creating A Crisis in U.S. Law Enforcement," *Insight on the News*, December 3, 2001.

6. Byron York, "Much More Democratic Obstruction, Democrats Move to Kill An Entire Slate of Bush Nominees," *National Review Online*, March 20, 2003.

7. Byron York, "What Sort of Filibustering Has Taken Place In the Senate, Where Judicial Nominations Are Concerned?" *National Review*, June 6, 2005.

8. C. Boyden Gray, "A Filibuster Without Precedent," *Wall Street Journal*, June 10, 2003.

9. Charles Babington, "Filibuster Precedent? Democrats Point to'68 and Fortas, But GOP Senators Cite Differences in Current Effort to Bar Votes on Judges," *Washington Post*, March 18, 2005.

10. Gray, "A Filibuster Without Precedent."

11. Jipping, "Fixing a Broken Confirmation Process."

12. Gray, "A Filibuster Without Precedent."

13. John Cornyn, "Our Broken Judicial Confirmation Process and the Need for Filibuster Reform," *The Harvard Journal of Law and Public Policy*, Volume 27, Issue 1, 2003.

14. The Prowler, "Democrats Without a Prayer," *American Spectator*, April 4, 2005.

15. David Limbaugh, "A Betrayal of Historic Proportions," Creators Syndicate, May 27, 2005.

16. Charles Babington and Susan Schmidt, "Filibuster Deal Puts Democrats In a Bind, Pact May Hinder Efforts to Block High Court Nominee," *Washington Post*, July 4, 2005.

17. Peter Baker and Charles Babington, "Are a Nominee's Views Fair Game? As High Court Battle Nears, Parties Parse the Senate Filibuster Deal," *Washington Post*, July 6, 2005.

18. Ibid.

19. Jessica Wehrman, "'Gang of 14' Isn't 'Breaking Up'; Senators Taking 'Wait and See' Approach on Alito Nomination," *Dayton Daily News*, November 4, 2005.

20. Don Feder, "Bush Waging a Battle Against the Mentality of Judicial Imperialism," *Insight on the News*, June 18, 2001.

21. Audrey Hudson, "Democrats Raise Issue of Estrada's Politics; Judicial Nominee Targeted Over 'Ideology,'" *Washington Times*, September 27, 2002.

22. Some legal scholars, such as John McGinnis, argue that the Senate's "advice and consent" power over judicial appointments gives them the right to reject nominees for any reason at all. John McGinnis, "Advice and Consent: What the Constitution Says," The Heritage Foundation, WebMemo #800, July 19, 2005. Others, such as John C. Eastman and Timothy Sandefur, argue that "in the founders' view...the Senate's power in the confirmation of judicial nominees was extremely limited. It existed solely to prevent the President from exercising his power in an improper manner. Ideology—at least ideology of the kind that is unrelated to a candidate's ability to fulfill his oath of office—simply has no place in the Senate's decision...It was not that the founders believed the political views of judges were irrelevant; they were not that naïve. But in their view, the President was alone responsible for his appointments, and, in turn, the ideology of those he appointed." Under this view the presidential appointment power is entitled to much greater Senate deference and his nominees must be confirmed unless they are incompetent, morally unfit, or picked because of cronyism. John C. Eastman and Timothy Sandefur, "The Senate Is Supposed to Advise and Consent, Not Obstruct and Delay," The Claremont Institute, September 6, 2002.

23. Lino Graglia, "It's Not Constitutionalism, It's Judicial Activism," *19 Harvard Journal of Law & Public Policy*, 293, 298 (Winter 1996).

24. Robert H. Bork, *The Tempting of America* (New York: Touchstone, 1990), 130.

25. Senate Judiciary Committee, "U.S. Senator Arlen Specter (R-PA) Holds a Hearing on the Supreme Court Nomination of Judge Samuel Alito to the Supreme Court," *FDCH Political Transcripts*, January 10, 2006.

26. Mark Preston, "Durbin Demands Probe," *Roll Call*, November 17, 2003.

27. Ibid.

28. Editorial, "Memos of Special Interest on Hill; Democrats Plot Against Nominees," *Washington Times*, November 15, 2003.

29. Editorial, "Senate Inquisition: The Real Scandal Is What's in the Democratic Memos on Judges, Not Who Leaked Them," *Wall Street Journal*, January 29, 2004.

30. Bobby Eberle, "Score One for the Democrats in Memo-gate Spin," GOPUSA.com, February 20, 2004.

31. Preston, "Durbin Demands Probe."

32. Ibid.

33. Charles Hurt, "Senate GOP Backs Leak Investigation; Computer Memos Left Unprotected," *Washington Times*, November 25, 2003.

34. Christopher Smith, "Conservatives Attack Hatch for His Stance On Leaked Memos," *Salt Lake Tribune*, February 6, 2004.

35. Alexander Bolton and Geoff Earle, "Dems Seek Charges in Leak Probe," *The Hill*, February 10, 2004.

36. Eberle, "Score One for the Democrats in Memo-gate Spin."

37. Transcript, *FOX Special Report with Brit Hume*, "Campaign Money and Senator Edward Kennedy's Harsh Remarks Against the President," FOX News Network, November 14, 2003.

38. Eberle, "Score One for the Democrats in Memo-gate Spin," GOPUSA.com, February 20, 2004.

39. "Democrat Memogate: The Beginning of Political Scandal," *Confirmation Watch*, February 19, 2004.

40. Jesse J. Holland, "Senate Computer Snooping Blamed on Two Former Staffers, Inadequate Protection," Associated Press, March 4, 2004.

41. Keith Perine, "Six Judiciary Members Sign Letter Asking Ashcroft to Probe Memo Downloads," *Congressional Quarterly*, March 11, 2004.

42. Jesse J. Holland, "Justice Department to Investigate Judiciary Memo Scandal," Associated Press, April 26, 2004.

43. Editorial, "Bollinger on the Spot," *New York Sun*, March 24, 2006.

44. John M. Powers, "Hatch and Frist Fire Whistle-blower; Senate Republicans Have Reneged on a Pledge to Expose Hard Evidence of Collusion Between Democrats on the Judiciary Committee and Lobbyists for Special Interests," *Insight on the News*, April 26, 2004.

45. Walter Dellinger, "Broaden the Slate," *Washington Post*, February 25, 2003.

46. Charles W. Pickering, Sr., "Bench Repair," *Washington Times*, March 26, 2006.

47. Charles Babington, "Acrimony Over Bush Judicial Nominations Resurfaces, Senate Democrats Threaten to Filibuster Conservative Duo," *Washington Post*, May 3, 2006.

48. Ibid.

49. Laurie Kellman, "Kavanaugh Confirmed U.S. Appellate Judge," Associated Press, May 26, 2006.

CHAPTER EIGHT: Politicizing Race

1. Deborah Orin, "Schumer Staffers Eyed In Probe Of Political ID Theft," *New York Post*, September 22, 2005.

2. Salena Zito, "Rainbow Coalition Racism," *Pittsburgh Tribune-Review*, February 12, 2006.

3. Peter Kirsanow, "The Mass Confusion Act, The Push for Loose Elections Standards," *National Review Online*, June 29, 2005.

4. Carl Limbacher, "Dems Find No Vote Fraud in Ohio," Newsmax.com, June 23, 2005.

5. "Dean Charges Black Vote Suppressed in Ohio," FoxNews.com, June 23, 2005.

6. The antics of liberal black religious leaders have finally come under attack by conservative black groups such as Project 21. See "Black Activists Criticize Efforts to Politicize Black Churches," *Christian News Wire*, July 3, 2006.

7. Democrats have been getting away with this, but increasingly, black conservative groups like the National Black Republican Association (NBRA), are exposing the minority-disfavoring elements of the Democratic agenda— such as the party's complicity in trapping black children in inferior inner city schools. "Their actions," as NBRA Chairman Frances Rice says, "speak louder than words." Press Release, "Democrats Trap Black Children in Failing Schools," National Black Republican Association, January 7, 2006.

8. Bryan Virasami and Glenn Thrush, "Hillary's Hardball, In MLK Day Speech, Senator Clinton Slams the Bush Team, Saying GOP Congress Is 'Run Like a Planation,'" Newsday.com, January 17, 2006.

9. "Rev. Joseph Lowery Defends His Remarks at the King Funeral," FOX News.com, February 10, 2006.

10. Nathan Burchfiel, "Gore Likens Targets of Domestic Spying to MLK Jr." CNSNews.com, January 17, 2006.

11. Melanie Hunter, "King, Parks Believed 'Answer to Hate' Is 'Love,' Bush Says," CNSNews.com, January 17, 2006.

12. Transcript, "Hannity and Colmes, Interview With Lawrence Guyot," FOX News Network, February 2, 2006.

13. "NAACP Chairman Compares GOP to Nazis, Bond Delivers Blistering Partisan Speech in North Carolina," Worldnetdaily.com, February 2, 2006.

14. Ibid.

15. Shankar Vedantam, "Study Ties Political Leanings to Hidden Biases," *Washington Post*, January 30, 2006.

16. Larry Elder, "Black Support for Bush Drops Two Percent," Creators Syndicate, November 17, 2005.

17. Bruce Bartlett, "Party Tracks Records on Race," *Washington Times*, February 8, 2006.

18. La Shawn Barber, "Democratic and Republican Platforms Through the Years," *La Shawn Barber's Corner*, http://lashawnbarber.com/archives/ 2004/ 11/19/platforms/, November 19, 2004.

19. Dave Eberhart, "Black Republicans Returning to Their GOP Roots," Newsmax.com, February 3, 2006.

20. Dick Morris, "A Bigger, Blacker GOP," FrontPageMagazine.com, February 8, 2006.

21. Thomas Sowell, "Republicans and Blacks," Creators Syndicate, January 31, 2006.

22. "The Situation: Thursday, September 8, 2005," CNN.com, September 8, 2005.

23. "Kanye West Downs Bush During Relief Concert," Top News CBS2Chicago.com, September 2, 2005.

24. Adam Nagourney and Calre Hulse, "Democrats Intensify Criticism of White House Response to Crisis," *New York Times*, September 8, 2005.

25. Transcript, "*Meet the Press*, David Brooks, Maureen Dowd and Tom Friedman Discuss How the Hurricane Season Has Affected the Political Landscape," *NBC News* Transcripts, September 25, 2005.

26. Transcript, "U.S. Senate Judiciary Committee Holds a Hearing on the Nomination of John Roberts to Be Chief Justice of the Supreme Court," *Congressional Quarterly, Inc.*, September 13, 2005.

27. Transcript, "U.S. Senator Arlen Specter (R-PA) Holds a Hearing on Roberts Nomination," *Congressional Quarterly, Inc.*, September 12, 2005.

28. Jeff Johnson, "Democrats Say GOP Blocking Aid to Katrina Victims," CNSNews.com, October 26, 2005.

29. Scott Lindlaw, "Dean Blasts Bush for Scapegoating Hispanics," *Contra Costa Times*, March 31, 2006.

30. Charles Hurt, "Reid Calls Language Proposal Racist," *Washington Times*, May 19, 2006.

31. Editorial, "The Immigration Impasse," *New York Times*, April 25, 2006.

32. Editorial, "Press One for English," *New York Times*, May 20, 2006.

CHAPTER NINE: Class Warfare

1. Bob Herbert, "Sneak Attack," *New York Times*, February 4, 2002.

2. "Editorial, "Bush's Budget Plan Ignores the Poor," *Buffalo News*, February 11, 2004.

3. Greg Pierce, "Angry Democrats," *Washington Times*, June 23, 2003.

4. Denise Kalette, "Dean: Race Played a Role in Katrina Death Toll," Associated Press Worldstream, September 7, 2005.

5. "The Situation: Thursday, September 8, 2005," *CNN.com*, September 8, 2005.

6. Adam Nagourney and Calre Hulse, "Democrats Intensify Criticism of White House Response to Crisis," *New York Times*, September 8, 2005.

7. "Democrats Lash Out At Bush Over Katrina As GOP Leaders Announce Bicameral Panel," *The Frontrunner*, September 8, 2005.

8. Elisabeth Bumiller, "Democrats and Others Criticize White House's Response to Disaster," *New York Times*, September 2, 2005.

9. "The Reagan Presidency: An Overview," *The Eighties Club*, undated, http://eightiesclub.tripod.com/id363.htm.

10. William A. Niskanen and Stephen Moore, "Cato Policy Analysis No. 261, Supply Tax Cuts and the Truth About the Reagan Economic Record," The Cato Institute, October 22, 1996.

11. Ibid.

12. Ibid.

13. Anne Saker, "Gore Busing It; Bush Goes South," *Chicago-Sun Times*, August 23, 1992; A.L. May and Julia Malone, "Economy, Character Dominate as Debate Marathon Begins, Bush, Clinton Trade Blows On Trust, Patriotism, Perot Attacks Political System for Failure to Solve Problems," *The Atlanta Journal and Constitution*, October 12, 1992..

14. Editorial, "Truth and Consequences," *Investor's Business Daily*, February 1, 2000.

15. Editorial, "The Big Lie," *Investor's Business Daily*, February 7, 2000.

16. Mona Charen, "It's Clinton, Not Bush, Who's Taking Low Road," *Creators Syndicate, Inc.*, October 20, 1992.

17. William Anderson, "Talking Down the Economy," Ludwig von Mises Institute, March 16, 2001.

18. Ibid.

19. These statistics are from the Bureau of Economic Analysis, cited by Tim Kane, Ph.D., Rea S. Hederman, and Kirk Johnson, Ph.D., "WebMemo #582," The Heritage Foundation, October 7, 2004.

20. "What's Behind the Jobless Recovery?" Associated Press, October 1, 2003, "Transcript: NewsHour with Jim Lehrer, The Politics of Jobs," PBS, September 5, 2003.

21. Michael Barone, "The Jobless Recovery May Not Have Been Jobless At All,"*U.S. News & World Report*, April 7, 2004, Larry Kudlow, "Jobless Recovery? Try Again," *National Review Online*, April 2, 2004.

22. Larry Kudlow, "Jobless Recovery? Try Again," *National Review Online*, April 2, 2004.

23. Rich Noyes, "Media Reality Check, Hyping High Gas Prices, Hiding Good News," Media Research Center, May 4, 2006.

24. Jeannine Aversa, "Economy Zips Ahead at 5.6 Percent Pace," Associated Press, June 29, 2006.

25. Bureau of Economic Analysis, "Gross Domestic Product Percent Change from Preceding Period," http://www.bea.gov/bea/dn/gdpchg.xls, April 28, 2006, reported by The Republican National Committee, April 28, 2006.

26. "Fact Sheet: Growing Our Economy: Keeping Taxes Low and Restraining Spending," The White House, May 3, 2006.

27. Rich Noyes, "Media Reality Check, Hyping High Gas Prices, Hiding Good News," Media Research Center, May 4, 2006.

28. Editorial, "The Boom Goes On," *Investor's Business Daily*, May 5, 2006.

29. "Fact Sheet: Growing Our Economy: Keeping Taxes Low and Restraining Spending," The White House, May 3, 2006.

30. Larry Kudlow, "The Greatest Story Never Told," *National Review Online*, April 28, 2006.

31. Ibid.

32. Larry Kudlow, "Smart, or Stupid?" *National Review Online*, November 30, 2005.

33. Transcript: "Remarks By White House Deputy Chief of Staff Karl Rove to the American Enterprise Institute," Federal News Service, May 15, 2006.

34. Martin Crutsinger, "Economy Grows at Fastest Pace in 1 1/2 Years," Associated Press, December 21, 2005.

35. Press Release: Nancy Pelosi, "Pelosi: 'The Bush Economy is Going in the Wrong Direction,'" *Nancy Pelosi House Democratic Leader*, April 7, 2006.

36. Editorial, "The Boom Goes On," *Investor's Business Daily*, May 5, 2006.

37. "Democrats Accuse GOP of Aiding Oil Companies," Associated Press, April 30, 2006.

38. "Democrats Quick to Jump On Bush For High Gas Prices," FoxNews.com, April 25, 2006.

39. "Bush Takes Aim At Rising Gasoline Prices," CNN.com/Politics, April 26, 2006.

40. "Sssh, Don't Tell Anyone, Economy Booming," Avpress.com, January 14, 2006.

41. Frank Newport, "Republicans All Alone in Viewing the Economy as in Good Shape, Independents and Democrats Are Quite Negative," Gallup News Service, March 21, 2006.

42. Willaim A. Niskanen and Stephen Moore, "Cato Policy Analysis No. 261, Supply Tax Cuts and the Truth About the Reagan Economic Record," The Cato Institute, October 22, 1996.

43. White House Briefing: Remarks By President George W. Bush At The Signing of H.R. 4297, The Tax Relief Extension Reconciliation Act of 2005," Federal News Service, May 17, 2006.

44. Jed Graham, "Bush May Meet Vow to Halve the Deficit Three Years Early," *Investor's Business Daily*, June 12, 2006.

45. Daniel Clifton, "Cap Gains Tax Cut = More Revenue," *The Shareholders Corner blog*, January 26, 2006, as cited by Donald Luskin, "The 2003 Tax Cut on Capital Gains Entirely Paid for Itself," *National Review Online – Financial Section*, January 27, 2006.

46. Donald Luskin, "The 2003 Tax Cut on Capital Gains Entirely Paid for Itself," *National Review Online – Financial Section*, January 27, 2006.

47. Transcript: "Remarks By White House Deputy Chief of Staff Karl Rove to the American Enterprise Institute," Federal News Service, May 15, 2006.

48. Editorial, "The Tax Cut Record, Americans Are Better Off Despite Democratic Naysaying," *Wall Street Journal*, May 14, 2006.

49. "Do the Rich and Businesses Pay Their Fair Share?" National Center for Policy Analysis, undated, http://taxesandgrowth.ncpa.org/hot_issue/share/.

50. Gene Randall, "Social Security as a High Priority in Clinton's Agenda," *CNN Saturday*, March 21, 1998.

51. President Bill Clinton, "U.S. President Clinton Gives State of the Union Address, Delivered January 27 at the Capitol in Washington, D.C. to a Joint Session of Congress and a National Television Audience," *Facts on File World News Digest*, January 29, 1998.

52. Byron York, "'Save Social Security First'?" *National Review Online*, January 14, 2005.

53. Ibid.

54. Gene Randall, "Social Security as a High Priority in Clinton's Agenda," *CNN Saturday*, March 21, 1998.

55. Transcript, Evans and Novak, "Secretary of the Treasury Robert Rubin Discusses American Economy," CNN, March 21, 1998.

56. "Transcript of White House Press Briefing by Gene Sperling," U.S. Newswire, February 9, 1998.

57. Richard Gephardt, Congressman, House, "Gephardt Statement on the 1998 Democratic Agenda," *Congressional Press Releases*, February 12, 1998.

58. Press Conference, "Joe Lockhart Holds White House News Briefing On the Economy," FDCH *Political Transcripts*, June 28, 1999.

59. Greg Pierce, "Inside Politics," Washington Times, March 23, 1998.

60. George W. Bush, Al Gore Hold Campaign Rallies," CNN *Live Event/Special*, November 3, 2000.

61. Tony Batt, "Surplus Sets Stage for Debate," *Las Vegas Review-Journal*, February 22, 1998.

62. Transcript, Judy Woodruff's Inside Politics, "President Bush Vows to Catch bin Laden. Will Frist Delay Social Security Reform?" CNN.com, March 3, 2005.

63. Transcript, Nancy Pelosi on 'Fox News Sunday,' FoxNews.com, March 6, 2005.

64. Transcript, Meet the Press, "Guests: Secretary of Defense Donald Rumsfeld, Sen. Ted Kennedy, D-Mass.," MSNBC.com, February 6, 2005.

65. Transcript, Meet the Press, "Guests: Sen. John Kerry, D-Mass.; Brian Williams, Anchor and Managing Editor, NBC Nightly News, MSNBC.com, January 30, 2005.

66. Carolyn Said, "Boxer Comes Out Fighting, President's Aim Is to Undermine Social Security, She Says," *San Francisco Chronicle*, February 12, 2005.

67. Jonathan Weisman, "The Politics of Social Security, Kerry to Use Study to Call Bush Plan a Wall Street Windfall," *Washington Post*, September 22, 2004.

68. Donald Luskin, "Social Security Subterfuge," *National Review*, December 9, 2004.

69. Walter Updegrave, "Can You Count On Social Security? We Size Up the Health Of The System And Look At What The Proposals To Fix It Would Mean To You," *Money*, Fall 2002.

70. David Limbaugh, "Social Security Shell Game," Creators Syndicate, Inc., August 1, 2001.

71. Jack Kemp, "Social & Domestic Issues, False Facts Form Social Security Reform," *Human Events*, January 24, 2006.

CHAPTER TEN: "I Hate the Way He Walks"

1. Mark Morford, "The Question is Whether We Can Hold On For 2 More Years," *San Francisco Chronicle*, July 7, 2006.

2. Richard Tomkins, "Analysis: Climate of Hate in 2004 Contest," United Press International, January 14, 2004.

3. John Nichols, "Moyers Tends Flame of Democracy," *Capital Times*, June 10, 2003.

4. Editorial, "Destroying America," *Richmond Times Dispatch*, June 20, 2003.

5. "Senate Leader Calls Bush 'A Loser,'" Associated Press, May 7, 2005.

6. Mike Allen, "Reid Calls Bush a 'Loser," *Washington Post*, May 7, 2005.

7. Eric Bates, "The Gunslinger," *Rolling Stone*, June 2, 2005.

8. Dana Milbank, "Democrat Reid Shoots From the Lip," *Washington Post*, May 11, 2005.

9. Mark Leibovich, "Land of Hard Knocks, Long After It Gave Him Something to Escape, the Busted Boom Town of Searchlight Still Speaks to Harry Reid's Heart," *Washington Post*, July 17, 2005.

10. Erin Neff, "Del Sol High School Appearance: Reid Calls Bush 'A Loser,'" *Las Vegas Review-Journal*, May 7, 2005.

11. Howard Kurtz, "Dean Assails Bush on Defense; Rival Cites Combat Pay, Veterans' Health Benefits," *Washington Post*, December 1, 2003.

12. Gary J. Andres, "Dems Bicker," *Washington Times*, October 9, 2003.

13. Michael Kinsley, "Unauthorized Entry," *Slate* magazine, March 20, 2003.

14. Maureen Dowd, "The Red Zone," *New York Times*, November 4, 2004.

15. Paul Krugman, "Lessons in Civility," *New York Times*, October 10, 2003.

16. Charles Krauthhammer, "Bush Derangement Syndrome," Townhall.com, December 5, 2003.

17. Lorraine Fisher, "Gulf War 2: Battles Rage as Oscars Become Anti-Bush Demo: Shame on You, Shame on You;" *The Mirror*, March 25, 2003.

18. Anthony Breznican, "Michael Moore Criticizes U.S. War in Iraq During Oscar Acceptance Speech," Associated Press, March 23, 2003.

19. Michael Morre, "Heads Up . . . from Michael Moore," Michael Moore.com, April 14, 2004.

20. Inside Track, "Charlie Sheen Doesn't Buy 9/11 Spin," *Boston Herald*, March 23, 2006.

21. "The Dam is Breaking on the 9/11 Cover-Up, More Stars Go Public with Demands for 9/11 Investigation, Others to Follow," Infowars.com, March 28, 2006.

22. Claudia Parsons, "Bus-bashing Takes Center State in NY Theaters," ABC News, January 30, 2006.

23. Howard Kurtz, :"A Dislike Unlike Any Other? Writer Jonathan Chait Brings Bush-Hating Out of the Closet," *Washington Post*, October 19, 2003.

24. Michael Goodwin, "Left-wing Loonies Take on Right-wing Ragers; Radio for Rush Limbaugh Haters; Liberal Hot-line Callers Demonstrate a Remarkable Talent for Political Invective,: *New York Daily News*, May 19, 2004.

25. Maura Reynolds, "'Axis of Evil' Rhetoric Said to Heighten Dangers, Many Foreign Policy Observers Think Bush's Phrasing, Although Effective on the Home Front, Caused Serious Damage Abroad," *Los Angeles Times*, January 21, 2003.
26. Fox On The Record With Greta Van Susteren, "Interview with Madeleine Albright," Fox News Network, February 4, 2002.
27. "Clinton Chief Blasts Bush," The Sunday Times, February 3, 2002.
28. Maura Reynolds, "'Axis of Evil' Rhetoric Said to Heighten Dangers, Many Foreign Policy Observers Think Bush's Phrasing, Although Effective on the Home Front, Caused Serious Damage Abroad," Los Angeles Times, January 21, 2003.
29. Craig Gilbert, "America's Hawkish Tone Since Sept. 11 Alienates European Allies," The Milwaukee Journal Sentinel, March 2, 2002.
30. Bill Tammeus, "Bush's Bully Pulpit," *Kansas City Star*, February 23, 2002.
31. Editorial, "Carrying a Big Stick," *St. Louis Post-Dispatch*, February 3, 2002.
32. Editorial, "Bush's Evil Axis," *Boston Globe*, February 3, 2002.
33. David Lazarus, "Bush Can't Stomach Tough Talk," *San Francisco Chronicle*, February 20, 2002.
34. Jack Perry, "It's Perilous to Divide World Into Good, Evil: Why Should We Have the Sole Right to Decide Who Can Be Armed?" *Charlotte Observer*, February 20, 2002.
35. "Former President Carter Speaks Out Against Bush's 'Axis of Evil,'" Associated Press, February 21, 2002.
36. Reagan Walker, "Carter Decries Calling Nations 'Evil,'" *Atlanta Journal-Constitution*, February 22, 2002.
37. Jimmy Moore and Charles Mahaleris, "MoveOn Ads Compare Bush to Hitler; RNC, Jewish Leaders Urge Democrats to Denounce 'Hate Speech,'" Talon News, January 6, 2004.
38. Ibid.
39. Garrison Keillor, "We're Not in Lake Wobegon Anymore," *Truthout*, August 26, 2004.
40. Hugh Pearson, "Prime-time Republicans Are Hard to Take," *Newsday*, September 2, 2004.
41. Fred Barnes, "The Democrats and the Loony Left," *The Weekly Standard*, August 2, 2004.
42. Beth Gillin, "Misguided Bush-Hitler Comparisons Pervade Media," Philadelphia Inquirer, June 24, 2003.
43. Glen T. Martin, "Totalitarianism Nears" Without Protest, Americans are Giving Up Freedom," *Roanoke Times*, January 2, 2003.
44. Matt Drudge, "Raw Rage at Bush During MoveOn.org Awards; Transcript Revealed," Drudge Report, January 13, 2003.

45. Bob Fertik, "Starting the Fight Against Fascism in America," Democrats.com, November 4, 2004.
46. Ted Rall, "Is Bush a Nazi?" tedrall.com, January 6, 2004.
47. Andrew Sullivan, "An Evil Cause," *The Daily Dish*, May 5, 2004.
48. Elysa Gardner, "Linda Ronstadt, Hummin' an Outraged Tune," *USA Today*, November 16, 2004.
49. George Varga, "The Stuff That Comes Out of Their Mouths," *San Diego Tribune*, December 26, 2004.
50. Mark Yost, "Hey, Activist Musicians: Shut Up and Sing," *Saint Paul Pioneer Press*, October 5, 2004.
51. "Beastie Boys Hate Bush – So What?" Slantpoint.com, May 7, 2003.
52. Sheldon Drobny, "The Vast Right Wing Conspiracy," MakeThemAccountable.com, January 17, 2003.
53. CyberAlert, "CNN Gives Garofalo Liberal Crossfire Chair From Which to Rant," Media Research Center, August 19, 2003.
54. Jeff Jacoby, "Hate Speech of the Left," *Boston Globe*, December 28, 2003.
55. Laura Blumenfeld, "Soros's Deep Pockets vs. Bush; Financier Contributes $5 Million More in Effort to Oust President," *Washington Post*, November 11, 2003.
56. Dave Lindorff, "Bush and Hitler, The Strategy of Fear," Counterpunch.org, February 1, 2003.
57. Byron York, "Annals of Bush-Hating," *National Review Online*, September 4, 2003.
58. Ibid.
59. Ibid.
60. Mark Jacob, "Furor over Der Fuehrer," *Chicago Tribune*, June 26, 2005.
61. Robert F. Kennedy, Jr. Crimes Against Nature: How George W. Bush and His Corporate Pals Are Plundering the Country and Hijacking Our Democracy (New York, New York: Harper Collins Publishers Inc. 2004), 194-195.
62. Mark Morford, "George W. Bush Gives Me Hope, The Astonishing Collapse of the Bumbling One Surely Means Healthy Change is Imminent, Right?" *San Francisco Chronicle*, November 18, 2005.
63. Jill Nelson, "A Mean-Spirited America, Today I Fear My Own Government More Than I Do Terrorists," MSNBC, May 3, 2003.
64. Robyn E. Blumner, "President Seems Unable to Bear the Sight or Sound of Dissent," *St. Petersburg Times*, October 13, 2002.
65. Randy Hall, "Dean: 'We're About to Enter the '60s Again,'" CNSNews.com, June 28, 2006.
66. Mike Allen, "Bush Visits Army Post with Heavy Casualties in Iraq, Meeting with Families of Dead is His Third Since War Began," *Washington Post*, November 25, 2003.

67. Transcript, "Interview with Donald Rumsfeld," *FOX News Sunday*, November 20, 2005.

68. Edwin Chen, "Cheney Scolds War Critics as 'Dishonest'; He Says Democratic 'Opportunists' are Telling 'Pernicious Falsehoods' on Prewar Intelligence," *Los Angeles Times*, November 17, 2005.

69. CBS News Transcript, *The Saturday Early Show*, "Political Strategists Bay Buchanan and Robert Shrum Debate the Merits of the Dissent About the Iraq War," November 19, 2005.

70. "Democrats Defend Congressman Who Urged US Pullout From Iraq," Voice of America News, November 18, 2005.

71. Mark Pratt, "Kerry: Opposing Iraq War Is Patriotic," *Boston Globe*, April 22, 2006.

72. Press Release, "Rep. Lewis Responds to Vice President Cheney's Attack On Iraq War Critics," US Fed News, November 21, 2005.

73. Richard Cohen, "Iraq and the 'L' Word," *Washington Post*, November 22, 2005.

74. Editorial, "Straight Talk on Iraq; Americans Need it But They're Not Getting it From Bush and Democrats," *Newsday*, November 15, 2005.

75. David Limbaugh, "Dissent Does Not Equal Patriotism," Creators Syndicate, March 15, 2003.

76. James O'Toole and Maeve Reston, "Neither Side Gives Ground in War Debate," *Pittsburgh Post-Gazette*, November 22, 2005.

77. "Dems Accuse Bush of 'Political Knee-capping," Newsmax.com, February 11, 2005.

78. Transcript, "Paul Wellstone, Wife, Daughter Laid to Rest; Minnesota Senate Race Heats Up with Coleman, Mondale," CNN Inside Politics, October 28, 2005.

79. Jimmy Carter, Transcript of "Remarks by Former U.S. President Jimmy Carter at the Coretta Scott King Funeral," The Carter Center, February 10, 2006; Transcript, "Interview with Michael Brown, Michael Reagan," Hannity and Colmes, FOX News Network, February 7, 2006.

80. Martin Savidge, "Thousands, Including Four US Presidents, Say Goodbye to Coretta Scott King," NBC News Transcripts, February 7, 2006.

81. "CORE Blasts King Funeral 'Outrage,'" Newsmax.com, February 9, 2006.

82. John Nichols, "A Dose of Reality for Bush," *Capital Times*, February 13, 2006.

CHAPTER ELEVEN: The Monster, the Witch-Burner, and the Architect of Torture

1. John Prados, "Blindsided or Blind?" Bulletin of the Atomic Scientists, July/August 2004.

2. "Rice Shapes Bush's View of the World," Cox News Service, November 14, 2001.

3. "Condoleezza Rice; Right-Hand Woman," *People*, December 31, 2001.

4. Norman Kempster, "The Presidential Transition; Rice's Soaring Career Hits a New High," *Los Angeles Times*, December 18, 2000.

5. "Answering the Red Phone Bush Puts Foreign Policy in Capable Hands," *San Jose Mercury News*, December 20, 2000.

6. Thomas Friedman, "Crazier Than Thou," *New York Times*, February 13, 2002.

7. Rep. Henry A. Waxman, Congressman Carolyn Maloney, "Letter to the Honorable Tom Davis, Chairman Committee on Government Reform, U.S. House of Representatives."

8. Joe Conason, "The Artful Dodger," Salon.com, April 9, 2004.

9. Ambra Nykol, "The Protected Class of Bigots," Seaspot.com, December 13, 2004.

10. I got most of these examples from the Democracy Project website, "The Left and Black Authenticity," November 17, 2004.

11. Press Release, "IWF Denounces Racist Depictions of Dr. Condoleezza Rice in Popular Editorial Cartoons," Independent Women's Forum, November 17, 2004.

12. Bob Parks, "The Liberal Renaissance and the Racist Campaign to Denigrate Dr. Condoleezza Rice," *Mens News Daily*, November 22, 2004.

13. Will the DNC Chairmanship Go to a Black Man?" La Shawn Barber's Corner, November 17, 2004.

14. Michelle Malkin, "Liberal Racism and Condi Rice," Michellemalkin.com November 17, 2004.

15. Editorial, "End of Discussion," *The New Republic*, November 18, 2004.

16. Ibid.

17. "Insider Report: Helen Thomas: Condi a 'Monster,' 'G—damn Liar,'" November 22, 2004.

18. Anne Gearan, "Democrats Say Rice Misled About Iraq War," Associated Press, January 25, 2005.

19. Sonni Efron, "Senate Democrats Accuse Rice of Lying," *Los Angeles Times*, January 25, 2005.

20. "Democrats Blast Rice's Role in Iraq War, Senate Majority Leader Predicts Confirmation of Secretary of State," CNN.com, January 25, 2005.

21. Transcript, "U.S. Senator Richard Lugar (R-IN) Holds a Hearing On The Nomination of Condoleezza Rice To Be Secretary of State, Part Two (Continued from Senate-HRG-Rice-State)," Congressional Quarterly, Inc., January 18, 2005.

22. Transcript, "Day One, Morning Session Of A Hearing Of The Senate Foreign Relations Committee," Federal News Service, January 18, 2005.

23. Anne Gearan, "Democrats Say Rice Misled About Iraq War," Associated Press, January 25, 2005.

24. Jon Dougherty, "The Politics of Fear Align Against Ashcroft," Worldnetdaily.com, December 26, 2000.

25. "U.S. Senator Patrick Leahy (D-VT) Holds Confirmation Hearing for Attorney-General Designate John Ashcroft," FDCH Political Transcripts, January 16, 2001.

26. Ibid.

27. Thomas Jipping, "Outrage Over Ashcroft Hearings," Worldnetdaily.com, January 25, 2001.

28. Transcript, "U.S. Senator Patrick Leahy (D-VT) Holds Confirmation Hearing for Attorney-General Designate John Ashcroft," FDCH Political Transcripts, January 16, 2001.

29. Transcript, "U.S. Senator Patrick Leahy (D-VT) Holds Second Day of Confirmation Hearing for Attorney-General Designate John Ashcroft," FDCH Political Transcripts, January 17, 2001

30. Transcript, "U.S. Senator Patrick Leahy (D-VT) Holds Confirmation Hearing for Attorney-General Designate John Ashcroft," FDCH Political Transcripts, January 17, 2001.

31. Transcript, "U.S. Senator Patrick Leahy (D-VT) Holds Confirmation Hearing for Attorney-General Designate John Ashcroft," FDCH Political Transcripts, January 16, 2001.

32. Ibid.

33. Byron York, "The New War on Ashcroft, Patrick Leahy's Latest Strategy," *National Review Online*, November 28, 2001.

34. Richard Cohen, "Ashcroft on the Line," *Washington Post*, November 15, 2001.

35. "Ashcroft: Critics of New Terror Measures Undermine Effort," CNN.com, December 7, 2001.

36. Barbara Shelly, "He's Still Righteous, Still Wrong," *Kansas City Star*, December 8 2001.

37. Editorial, "Shades of Gray," St. Louis Post-Dispatch, December 9, 2001.

38. Robert Leger, "Ashcroft Wrong to Vilify Critics," *Springfield News-Leader*, December 9, 2001.

39. Editorial, "On Civil Liberties: Under Cloak of 'Security,'" *San Francisco Chronicle*, December 9, 2001.

40. Editorial, "Dangerous Power Grab," Orange County Register, December 9, 2001.

41. Editorial, "Zeal Rules Out Honest Debate," *Newsday*, December 9, 2001.

42. Cragg Hines, "The AG's Perpetual Adoration of Guns," *Houston Chronicle*, December 9, 2001.

43. Clarence Page, "More Questions for Ashcroft," *Chicago Tribune*, December 9, 2001.

44. Editorial, "Security vs. Justice?; Bush and Ashcroft Should Listen to Congressional Concerns," Charlotte Observer, December 9, 2001.

45. Editorial, "Ashcroft's Contempt," *St. Petersburg Times*, December 10, 2001.

46. Editorial, "Justice and the Attorney General," *Buffalo News*, December 10, 2001.

47. Jules Witcover, "The Real Ashcroft Stands Up," *Baltimore Sun*, December 10, 2001.

48. Kevin Freking, "Ashcroft 'Over the Line' In Attacks on Dissenters Groups Urge Debate, Ask Him to Refrain," *Arkansas Democrat-Gazette*, December 11, 2001.

49. Richard Reeves, "There is a Difference Between Dissent, Treason," Universal Press Syndicate, December 15, 2001.

50. John Powers, "Wyatt Earp and the Witchfinder General," *LA Weekly*, December 14, 2001.

51. David Limbaugh, "A True Smear Job," Creators Syndicate, December 11, 2001.

52. L. Brent Bozell, "Ashcroft Worse Than Arafat?" Media Research Center, November 20, 2004.

53. "Rumsfeld Said to Have the President's Backing For Military Overhaul Efforts," *The Bulletin's Frontrunner*, May 13, 2002.

54. "Rumsfeld's Reputation Takes a Turn," *Oakland Tribune*, November 18, 2001.

55. Ibid.

56. David Limbaugh, "In Defense of Secretary Rumsfeld," Creators Syndicate, February 18, 2005.

57. Dana Milbank, Secretary on the Offensive," *Washington Post*, February 17, 2005.

58. "Rumsfeld's Reputation Takes a Turn," *Oakland Tribune*, November 18, 2001.

59. Esther Schrader, "Pentagon's Biggest Fight May Come From Within; Rumsfeld is Shaking Up the Bureaucracy and the Brass with His Aggressive Approach to Reform," *Los Angeles Times*, January 4, 2003.

60. Paul Richter, "Bush's Defense Secretary Goes on the Offensive; Military: Rumsfeld Has Forcefully Pursued His Mission, To The Point Of Irking Potential Backers," *The Nation*, May 22, 2001.

61. "Fact Sheet: The Debate Over the Crusader," CNN.com, May 10, 2002.

62. "Transcript: Newsmaker: Donald Rumsfeld, NewsHour with Jim Lehrer," PBS.com, May 22, 2002.

63. Alison Mitchell, "Top Democrats Want of Battle on Missile Plan," *New York Times*, May 3, 2001.

64. Paul B. Stares, "Making Enemies in Space," *New York Times*, May 15, 2001.

65. When our troops were marching rapidly toward Baghdad at a record pace, Democrats blamed Rumsfeld. "It was his idea," they said.Concerning the rapidly advancing troops, one commentator said, "It was [Rumsfeld's] idea to move them very , very quickly, run the risk of outrunning their supply lines." "Lessons of War," PBS Online NewsHour, May 1, 2003.

66. Seymour M. Hersh, "Offense and Defense, The Battle Between Donald Rumsfeld and the Pentagon," *The New Yorker*, April 7, 2003.

67. Dave Moniz, "Rumsfeld's Abrasive Style Sparks Conflict With Military Command," USA Today, December 10, 2002.

68. Editorial, "New Spin Won't Fix Iraq," Los Angeles Times, October 7, 2003.

69. Leonard Pitts, "America Arrogant? Mais oui," *Milwaukee Journal Sentinel*, January 29, 2003.

70. "Editorial, "The Abu Ghraib Scandal; Reports Find Fault at the Top," *The Bergen County Record*, August 31, 2004.

71. Seymour Hersh, "The Gray Zone, How a Secret Pentagon Program Came to Abu Ghraib," *The New Yorker*, May 24, 2005.

72. Transcript, Inside Politics Sunday, "Did Rumsfeld Encourage U.S. Military to Abuse Prisoners?' Interview With Stephanie Cutter, Terry Holt," CNN, May 16, 2004.

73. Cynthia Hall Clements, "The Incompetence of Donald Rumsfeld," Cox News Service, December 14, 2004.

74. Ethan Wallison, "Rangel Threatens Articles of Impeachment Against Rumsfeld," *Roll Call*, May 6, 2004.

75. Editorial, "Donald Rumsfeld Should Go," *New York Times*, May 7, 2004.

76. Ibid.

77. Editorial, "Rumsfeld Must Go," *Boston Globe*, May 7, 2004.

78. Rowan Scarborough, "Rumsfeld Defends Gitmo," *Washington Times*, June 15, 2005.

79. Ibid.

80. Ibid.

81. Sharon Kehnemui Liss, "Durbin Apologizes for Nazi, Gulag, Pol Pot Remarks," FoxNews.com, June 22, 2005.

82. Ray Suarez, "Under Armored," PBS Online NewsHour, December 9, 2004.

83. Michael Bowman, "Criticism Mounts On Recent Rumsfeld Remarks," Voice of America News, December 12, 2004.

84. "Senator Joe Biden, "Biden Blasts Rumsfeld on Remarks to Our Troops," State News Service, December 9, 2004.

85. Pauline Jelinek, "Question to Rumsfeld Revives Charges of Poor Planning for War," The Associated Press, December 10, 2004.

86. Michael Bowman, "Criticism Mounts On Recent Rumsfeld Remarks," Voice of America News, December 12, 2004.

87. Walter Pincus, "Senate Panel to Set Hearings on Iraq Insurgency, Shortages; Democrat Criticizes Prewar Planning," Washington Post, December 15, 2004.

88. Frederic J. Frommer, "Dayton Calls on Bush to Investigate Shortage of Armored Vehicles," The Associated Press State and Local Wire, December 15, 2004.

89. Greg Pierce, "Inside Politics," Washington Times, December 10, 2004.

90. John Widemouth, "Feinstein Urges Regime Change – Rumsfeld Out, She Wants Troop Levels Cut, Focus Shifted to Training," San Francisco Chronicle, March 21, 2006.

91. Lieut. General Greg Newbold (Ret.), "Why Iraq Was a Mistake, A Military Insider Sounds Off Against the War and the 'Zealots' Who Pushed It," Time, April 17, 2006.

92. Rowan Scarborough, "Generals Defend Rumsfeld," Washington Times, April 15, 2006.

CHAPTER TWELVE: A Pair of Rasputins

1. David Limbaugh, "The Cheney Taint," Creators Syndicate, July 28, 2000.

2. "Bush Began 'Shadow Government' Hours After Sept. 11 Attacks; Defense: At least 75 or more senior officials who live and work secretly outside Washington D.C. in case of an assault ion the capital. The plan dates to the Eisenhower era," Los Angeles Times, March 1, 2002.

3. Jonathan Alter, "The Imperial (Vice) Presidency," Newsweek, February 27, 2006.

4. Robert Dreyfuss, "Vice Squad," The American Prospect, May 4, 2006.

5. Tony Batt Stephens, "Reid Criticizes Vice President For Not Disclosing Accidental Shooting Sooner," Las Vegas Review-Journal, February 15, 2006.

6. Steve Holland, "Top Democrats Urge Cheney to Come Forward on Shooting," Reuters, February 15, 2006.

7. Jacob Weisberg, "Smoking Gun, Dick Cheney's Assault on the Public's Right to Know," Slate.com, February 15, 2006.

8. Jane Roh, "Cheney: 'I'm the Guy Who Pulled the Trigger,'" Foxnews.com, February 15, 2006.

9. Ralph Blumenthal, "From Arrival to Errant Shot, a Timeline of Cheney's Hunting Accident," *New York Times*, February 16, 2006.

10. Jane Roh, "Cheney: 'I'm the Guy Who Pulled the Trigger,'" Foxnews.com, February 15, 2006.

11. Jacob Wiesberg, "The Power-Madness of King George, Is Bush Turning America Into An Elective Dictatorship?" Slate.com, January 25, 2006.

12. Jane Roh, "Cheney: 'I'm the Guy Who Pulled the Trigger,'" Foxnews.com, February 15, 2006.

13. Democrat analyst Lawrence O'Donnell implied as much when he said "Every lawyer I've talked to assumes Cheney was too drunk to talk to the cops after the shooting." Lawrence O'Donnell, "Was Cheney Drunk?" Huffingtonpost.com, February 14, 2006.

14. Charles Krauthammer, "Quell Quailgate, Cheney's Call Was Wrong but Understandable," *Washington Post*, February 16, 2006.

15. Brent Bozell, "The Media's Cheney Hunt," Creators Syndicate, February 15, 2006.

16. Nicholas Lemann, "The Quiet Man; Dick Cheney's Discreet Rise to Unprecedented Power," *The New Yorker*, May 7, 2001.

17. Juan Williams, "Pivotal Role That Vice President Cheney Plays in the Bush Administration, National Public Radio, March 12, 2001.

18. Maureen Dowd, "The Axis of No Access," *New York Times*, February 13, 2002.

19. Maureen Dowd, "Cheney Stays in the Picture," *New York Times*, August 11, 2002.

20. Robert Dreyfuss, "Vice Squad," *The American Prospect*, May 4, 2006.

21. Editorial, "Saving the Second Term," *Los Angeles Times*, October 30, 2005.

22. Jonathan Alter, "The Imperial (Vice) Presidency," *Newsweek*, February 27, 2006.

23. Noel Sheppard, "Newsweek's Alter Slams Cheney, Says Bush Has Been 'Tagged as an Incompetent,'" Newsbusters.org, April 14, 2006.

24. Sean Wilentz, "Democracy in America, 2003," *Dissent* magazine, Winter 2004.

25. Robert Scheer, "If Only Kerry Were From The Bronx; With Some Street Smarts, He Might Call Those Republican Bums Out," Los Angeles Times, September 14, 2004.

26. Senator Edward Kennedy, "Kennedy on the Libby Indictment," TedKennedy.com. A copy of Kennedy's e-mail was posted on John Conyers' blog: http://www.conyersblog.us/archives/00000292.htm, November 1, 2005.

27. Editorial, "The Prison Puzzle," The New York Times, November 3, 2005.

28. Editorial, "Saving the Second Term," The Los Angeles Times, October 30, 2005.

29. Editorial, "The Prison Puzzle," The New York Times, November 3, 2005.

30. John Mintz, "Stock Options Post Dilemma for Cheney," *Washington Post*, August 18, 2000.

31. Edward Walsh, "Cheney Says He'll Forgo Stock Options," *Washington Post*, September 2, 2000.

32. "Sources: Cheney Curses Senator Over Halliburton Criticism," CNN.com Politics, June 25, 2004.

33. David E. Rosenbaum, "A Closer Look at Cheney and Halliburton," *New York Times*, September 28, 2004.

34. Byron York, "Ken Mehlman on Harry Reid's 'Lyndon LaRouche Moment,'" National Review Online, November 9, 2005.

35. Tina Brown, "Taking the GOP Bait, Hook, Line and Stinker," *Washington Post*, April 29, 2004.

36. Joshua Green, "Karl Rove in a Corner," *Atlantic Monthly*, November 1, 2004.

37. "Sly as a Foxx," *Orlando Sentinel*, October 15, 2004.

38. Transcript, Larry King Live, "Bin Laden Releases New Videotape," CNN, October 29, 2004.

39. From the Rutland Herald, cited in Associated Press State & Local Wire, September 28, 2002.

40. Joe Conason, "Bush Camp's Pit Bulls Assert Their Entitlement," *New York Observer*, November 20, 2000.

41. Jules Witcover, "Incumbency Gives Bush Upper Hand," *Baltimore Sun*, December 3, 2003.

42. Matthew E. Berger, "Controversy Erupts Over E-mails as Dean Blames Rove for Online Attacks," Jewish Telegraphic Agency, December 17, 2003.

43. Tina Brown, "Taking the GOP Bait, Hook, Line and Stinker," *Washington Post*, April 29, 2004.

44. Patrick D. Healy, "Rove Criticizes Liberals on 9/11," *New York Times*, June 23, 2005.

45. Dan Baltz, "Democrats Call for Rove to Apologize, He Decried Liberals' Response to 9/11," *Washington Post*, June 24, 2005.

46. Patrick D. Healy, "Rove Criticizes Liberals on 9/11," *New York Times*, June 23, 2005.

47. Raymond Hernandez, "Democrats Demand Rove Apologize for 9/11 Remarks," *New York Times*, June 24, 2005.

48. Richard L. Berke and David E. Sanger, "Some in Administration Grumble As Aide's Role Seem to Expand," *New York Times*, May 13, 2002.

49. Harvey Wasserman, "If Jesus Returns, Karl Rove Will Kill Him," The Free Press, March 22, 2005.

50. http://codepinkalert.org/catalog/product_info.php?cPath=4_5&products_id=61.

51. "Rove Testifies to Grand Jury in CIA Leak Case," Foxnews.com, April 27, 2006.

52. "Sen. Reid Says Rove Should Resign, Democratic Leader Says Bush, Cheney Should Apologize for Leak," Associated Press, October 30, 2005.

53. "Rove Testifies to Grand Jury in CIA Leak Case," Foxnews.com, April 27, 2006.

54. "Howard Dean: Karl Rove Guiltier than Osama Bin Laden," Newsmax, May 2, 2006.

55. "Transcript, Countdown, Keith Olbermann, David Shuster, Dawna Friesen," MSNBC, May 8, 2006; Noel Sheppard, "Media Owe Rove an Apology – or at Least a Few Hugs," The American Thinker, June 14, 2006.

56. "Transcript, Hardball, Chris Matthews, Richard Engel, David Gregory, Lisa Myers, Bob Shrum, Pat Buchanan," MSNBC, June 13, 2006.

57. Editorial, "Dems Prove Again They're Out of Touch," New York Daily News, January 9, 2005.

58. Matthew Clark, "US ex-diplomats Slam Bolton Nomination," Christian Science Monitor, March 29, 2005.

CHAPTER THIRTEEN: Hypocrisy and Sour Grapes

1. Mona Charen, "Who Invented the Politics of Personal Destruction," Creators Syndicate, January 11, 1999.

2. CBS News Transcript, "President Clinton's Twisting of Words to Suit His Purposes," The Osgood File, September 16, 1998.

3. Transcript, "Vice President Al Gore Participates in Town Hall Meeting; Derry, New Hampshire, FDCH Political Transcripts, December 14, 1999; MSNBC Transcript, "How the Impeachment Will Effect Campaign 2000," Equal Time, December 17, 1999.

4. Thomas Sowell, "What Does It Tell You?" Creators Syndicate, November 6, 2000.

5. Let's not forget the way they tried to savage Kathleen Willey, Dolly Kyle Browning, Juanita Broderick, Gennifer Flowers, and countless others.

6. I cover this in meticulous detail in Chapter Four of my book Absolute Power, The Legacy of Corruption in the Clinton-Reno Justice Department, (Washington, D.C. Regnery Publishing, Inc., 2001), 93 – 138.

7. Professor Camille Paglia argues that "The Democratic establishment was cowardly and irresponsible in backing off from insisting that Clinton resign." Camille Paglia, "A Bland Antidote for Bill 'n' Al Fatigue: George W."

Salon.com, January 17, 2001. While I certainly agree the Democrats were "cowardly and irresponsible," I think they carefully weighed their options, and decided, with premeditation, to place politics over principle – not out of cowardice, but measured, political calculation.

8. Jonah Goldberg, "The Politics of Personal Destruction, As Practiced By Pros," *National Review Online*, December 21, 1998.

9. John F. Harris, "Clinton Vows to Finish Out Term; President Says He Will Keep Working to 'the Last Hour of the Last Day'," *Washington Post*, December 20, 1998.

10. NBC News Transcript, "Vice President Al Gore and Former Senator Bill Bradley Discuss Numerous Political Topics," *Meet the Press*, December 19, 1999.

11. Matt Drudge, "Gore Ops Target Nader's Sex Life: Move Called 'Desperate'," Drudge Report, November 1, 2000.

12. Thomas Sowell, "More Desperate, More Ugly," Creators Syndicate, November 17, 2000.

13. "How We Got Here: A Timeline of the Florida Recount," CNN.com, December 13, 2000.

14. Bill Sammon, *At Any Cost* (Washington, D.C.: Regnery Publishing, Inc., 2001), 54.

15. "How We Got Here: A Timeline of the Florida Recount," CNN.com, December 13, 2000.

16. Bill Sammon, *At Any Cost* (Washington, D.C.: Regnery Publishing, Inc., 2001), 19.

17. John J. Miller, "'The Campaign Continues': Gore in Florida, step by awful step," *National Review*, December 18, 2000.

18. Interview, "Counting the Vote; Excerpts From Interview with Vice President: 'Integrity of Democracy' at Stake," *New York Times*, November 27, 2000.

19. Alan W. Dowd, "No Ordinary Election," Hudson Institute, April 1, 2001.

20. Bill Sammon, *At Any Cost* (Washington, D.C.: Regnery Publishing, Inc., 2001), 201-215.

21. Transcript: "Hearing of the House Judiciary Committee To Consider Referral By the Independent Counsel In Matters Of Impeachment, Questioning by President Clinton's Attorney David Kendall, Federal News Service, November 19, 1998.

22. Elizabeth Mehren and Jeffrey Gettleman, "Decision 2000 / America Waits; Seasoned Democratic Army Hits the Shores of Florida; Partisans: Boston's Whouley Leads Troops in Florida to Oversee Recounts. The Party Operatives Have One Goal – Whittle Away At Bush's Slim Vote Margin," *Los Angeles Times*, November 17, 2000.

23. Allen G. Breed, "On Election Night, Democrats Called Florida Voters About Problem," Associated Press, November 11, 2000.

24. Terry Spencer, "Gore Gains Votes Halfway Through Broward Recount," Associated Press, November 19, 2000.

25. Review and Outlook, "The Will of the Lawyers, Al Gore Has Finally Found His Controlling Legal Authority: Democratic Judges," Opinion Journal.com, November 20, 2000.

26. Ibid.

27. Steve Miller, "Observers Say Ballots Manipulated By Examiner," *Washington Times*, November 16, 2000; "Democrat Election Official Manipulated Ballots, Witnesses Swear," Newsmax.com, November 16, 2000.

28. Jim Angle, Carl Cameron, William La Jeunesse, "Political Headlines," Fox News Special Report with Brit Hume, Transcript, November 16, 2000.

29. David Limbaugh, "Doing Anything To Win," Creators Syndicate, November 21, 2000.

30. Bob Clark, "As You Were Saying... It's Time for Gore Pit Bulls to Practice What he Preaches." *Boston Herald*, November 18, 2000.

31. Camille Paglia, "A Bland Antidote for Bill 'n' Al Fatigue: George W." Salon.com, January 17, 2001.

32. "Text of Remarks Wednesday by Vice President Al Gore About Florida's Vote Recount as Transcribed by eMediaMillWorks Inc., Associated Press, November 15, 2000.

33. Bill Sammon, "Al Gore's Fiasco in Florida," *Human Events*, May 21, 2001.

34. Editorial, "Katherine Harris, Heroine," *New York Post*, November 18, 2000.

35. Bob Clark, "As You Were Saying... It's Time for Gore Pit Bulls to Practice What he Preaches." *Boston Herald*, November 18, 2000.

36. Thomas Oliphant, "It's Easy to Figure Why Conservatives' Tune Has Changed," *Boston Globe*, November 14, 2000.

37. Lars-Erik Nelson, "Fla. Vote Chief's in W. Column," *New York Daily News*, November 14, 2000.

38. Bill Sammon, *At Any Cost* (Washington, D.C.: Regnery Publishing, Inc., 2001), 126.

39. Joan Vennochi, "Oh, What a Plot the Politicians Are Weaving in Florida," Boston Globe, November 17, 2000.

40. Robin Givhan, "The Eyelashes Have It," *Washington Post*, November 18, 2000.

41. Margery Eagan, "Election 2000; What a Surprise: Harris Look Draws Catty Comments," *Boston Herald*, November 16, 2000.

42. David Limbaugh, "The 4 Years War," Creators Syndicate, December 5, 2000.

43. Ibid.

44. David S. Broder, "Analysis; For Bush, Desire to Unite Will Be Tested," The Washington Post, December 14, 2000; Jill Darling Richardson, "Poll Analysis: Americans Support Bush's Presidency but Want Legislative Compromise," Los Angeles Times, December 17, 2000.

45. CNBC News Transcripts: Rob Reynolds, "Bush White House Will Have to Have Bipartisan Efforts to Accomplish Things Over the Next Four Years," Business Center, December 13, 2000.

46. Cover Editorial, "Surprise Us; To Succeed as President, Bush Should Move to Center," Newsday, January 21, 2001.

47. Rep. Charles Rangel, "Bipartisanship Best Way to Maintain Prosperity," Roll Call, January 8, 2001.

48. Transcript: Bobbie Battista, William Schneider, "What Does George W. Bush Want to Accomplish During His Administration?" CNN Talkback Live, December 14, 2000.

49. Transcript: Jeff Greenfield, Candy Crowley, "Can George W. Bush Tame the Conservative Beast," CNN Live Event/Special, December 15, 2000.

50. Jill Darling Richardson, "Poll Analysis: Americans Support Bush's Presidency But Want Legislative Compromise," Los Angeles Times, December 17, 2000.

51. Joshua Muravchik, "Why the Democrats Keep Losing," Commentary, January 2005.

52. Editorial, New York Times, November 5, 1980.

53. Adam Clymer, "Long-Range Hope for Republicans is Found in Poll," New York Times, November 11, 1984.

54. Editorial, "A Monumental, Fragile Mandate," New York Times, November 4, 1992.

55. Editorial, "The Road Ahead," New York Times, November 7, 1996.

56. MSNBC Transcript: "Can George W. Bush 'Change the Tone' in Washington?" Equal Time, December 18, 2000.

57. MSNBC Transcript: "Decision 2000: President-elect Bush Prepares for Transition," Hardball, December 14, 2000.

58. Jill Lawrence, "Democratic Party Walks a Fine Line After Impasse, Some Members Want to Hold Out for Gore's Agenda," USA Today, December 18, 2000.

59. John McCaslin, "Inside the Beltway," Washington Times, January 26, 2001.

60. Jill Lawrence, "Democratic Party Walks a Fine Line After Impasse, Some Members Want to Hold Out for Gore's Agenda," USA Today, December 18, 2000.

61. Will Lester, "Bush's Opening Act Surprises Democrats," Associated Press, January 26, 2001.

62. William E. Gibson, "Finally, It's Bush; Gore Concedes; Both Call for Unity; Bush Begins Task of Changing Tone," *Fort Lauderdale Sun-Sentinel*, December 14, 2000.

63. Ibid.

64. Richard S. Dunham, "Who Says Bush Has a Mandate? Bush, Despite Losing the Popular Vote, George W. is Pressing On as if He Won in a Landslide," *Business Week*, February 20, 2001.

65. Eric Pooley, "How Can He Govern?; With the Power of the Office Sapped and Congress Split, Will the Job Be Worth Having?" *Time*, November 20, 2000.

66. Ronald Brownstein, "Lack of a True Winner Calls for Creative Politic Reconstruction, Final Victor Must be a Peacemaker," *San Jose Mercury News*, November 21, 2000.

67. Transcript, "Supreme Showdown; Political Fallout; Supreme Court Decision, Election 2000 – It's History," The Newshour with Jim Lehrer, December 13, 2000.

68. Bill Rankin, "Move to Right Seems Certain; Expect Backlash If Nay Bush Nominees Are Seen As Too Conservative; The President-Elect: The Supreme Court," *Atlanta Journal Constitution*, December 17, 2000.

69. Mike Allen, "Bush's Choices Defy Talk of Conciliation; Cabinet is Diverse But Not Politically," The Washington Post, December 31, 2000.

70. James D. Bloom, "Bush Already Has Broken His Word, But the Old Teflon Standard is Back," Morning Call (Allentown, PA), January 9, 2001.

71. Margasak, "Daschle Predicts votes vs. Ashcroft," Associated Press Online, January 31, 2001.

72. Larry Margasak, "Daschle Predicts votes vs. Ashcroft," Associated Press Online, January 31, 2001.

73. Laura Ingraham, "A 'Get Along' Bush? Terrific – for Democrats," *USA Today*, January 22, 2001.

74. Marianne Means, "Where Are the Democrats and What Have They Been Doing?" *Seattle Post-Intelligencer*, May 2, 2001.

75. Robin Toner, "Contesting The Vote: The Liberals: The Left Vows To Be Ready for Battle in January," *New York Times*, December 4, 2000.

76. John McCaslin, "Inside the Beltway," *Washington Times*, January 26, 2001.

77. Larry Eichel, "The President-elect Speaks of Bipartisanship, but Not Electoral Reform," *Philadelphia Inquirer*, January 6, 2001.

78. Members of the Congressional Black Caucus, "Members of the Congressional Black Caucus Hold News Conference Regarding Tax Cuts," FDCH Political Transcripts, March 8, 2001.

79. Marjorie Williams, "The Cash Man Becomes the Chairman," *Washington Post*, December 20, 2000.

80. Ibid.

81. Morton M. Kondracke, "Bush, Democrats Can Deal – on Taxes, Medicare, Schools," *Roll Call*, January 4, 2001.

82. Press Conference, "Press Conference with Senate Minority Leader Senator Tom Daschle (D-SD) and Senator Kent Conrad (D-ND)," Federal News Service, February 5, 2001.

83. Transcript, "U.S. Representative Robert Menendez (D-NJ) Delivers Democratic Response to President's Weekly Radio Address;" FDCH Political Transcripts, March 16, 2001.

84. "Top of the Times; A Review of the Week's News," *Washington Times*, May 6, 2001.

85. Joyce Howard Price, "Bonior Blasts Bush's Record on Environmental Issue," *Washington Times*, April 22, 2001.

86. Brit Hume, "Interview With Christine Todd Whitman," *FOX Special Report With Brit Hume*, April 17, 2001.

87. Joseph Boris, "Bush Aides Defend Environmental Record," United Press International, April 29, 2001.

88. Betsy Rothstein, "Senate Dems Take Off the Gloves Against Bush," *The Hill*, April 11, 2001.

89. Editorial Page, "Clinton Pulls No Punches in Assailing Bush Policies," *Buffalo News* (New York), March 26, 2001.

90. Joyce Howard Price, "Bonior Blasts Bush's Record on Environmental Issue," *Washington Times*, April 22, 2001.

91. Rich Lowry, "Daschle's Love Affair with Arsenic," *National Review*, April 27, 2001.

92. Local Staff, "Johnson, Daschle Support Ultra-Left," *Argus Leader* (Sioux Falls, SD), May 5, 2001.

93. Tom Raum, "U.S. Seems at Odds With Rest of World on Important Issues," Associated Press, June 10, 2001.

94. Suzanne Daley, "President Facing Skeptical Europe on Trip This Week," *New York Times*, June 11, 2001.

95. Ibid.

96. Tom Raum, "U.S. Seems at Odds With Rest of World on Important Issues," Associated Press, June 10, 2001.

97. Jay Hancock, "Criticism of Bush Called Inappropriate; Daschle is Accused of Upstaging President Before International Talks," *Baltimore Sun*, July 20, 2001.

98. Ibid.

99. Kelly Wallace, "President Bush Signs Campaign Finance Bill, Court Challenge to Law Already Filed," CNN.com/Inside Politics, March 27, 2002.

100. NBC News Transcripts, "Surprising Political Friendship Between President Bush and Senator Kennedy," *Today Show*, March 4, 2002.

101. Oliver Knox, "Bush Pursues Unusual Courtship of Democrats," Ágence France Presse, February 3, 2001.

102. "Washington Dateline, "In Radio Address, Kennedy Says Bush is Short-changing Education," Associated Press, April 6, 2002.

103. Robert B. Bluey, "NAACP Chairman Compares Republicans to Terrorists," CNSNews.com, June 3, 2004.

104. William Douglas and Amy Worden, "Bush Snubs NAACP, Cites Leaders' Remarks," Chicago Tribune, July 10, 2004.

105. Ibid.

CHAPTER FOURTEEN: Those "P.E.S.T.y" Democrats, or A Party in Search of Coherence

1. Brit Hume, "Sen. Biden Says Bush is 'Brain Dead,'" FOX News, October 22, 2004.

2. Laura Shannon, "Election Report from Florida," *Government of the USA in Exile*, October 30, 2004.

3. Suzanne Fields, "Double-edged Politics," *Washington Times*, January 3, 2005.

4. Adam Nagourney, "So What Happened in That Election, Anyhow?" *New York Times*, January 2, 2005.

5. Anemona Hartocollis, "Becoming the Land of the Flee?" *New York Times*, November 7, 2004.

6. Ibid.

7. Ibid

8. Ibid.

9. Brian Williams, "Blue-state Americans Packing Up and Moving to Canada," *NBC Nightly News*, December 10, 2004.

10. Greg Pierce, "Inside Politics," *Washington Times*, November 15, 2004.

11. Panel Discussion, "What Now? A Discussion on the Way Forward for the Democrats; Democratic Party," Washington Monthly, December 1, 2004.

12. America Votes 2004, "Some Kerry Supporters Glum After Loss," CNN.com, November 5, 2004.

13. Ibid.

14. Melissa Healy, "Dejected Voters Find Themselves In an Even Bluer State: Feelings of Grief Can Be Severe for Those Who Backed the Defeated Candidate. Psychologists Say it's Important for Them to Forge Ahead," *Los Angeles Times*, November 8, 2004; See also Michelle Malkin's Unhinged,

Exposing Liberals Gone Wild (Washington, D.C.: Regnery Publishing, Inc., 2005), especially Chapter One, "Liberals On the Couch," 1-12.

15. Melissa Healy, "Dejected Voters Find Themselves In an Even Bluer State: Feelings of Grief Can Be Severe for Those Who Backed the Defeated Candidate. Psychologists Say it's Important for Them to Forge Ahead," *Los Angeles Times*, November 8, 2004.

16. Ibid.

17. Ibid.

18. Sean Salai, "Kerry Supporters Seek Therapy in South Florida, Boca Raton Trauma Specialist Has Treated 15 Patients," Boca Raton News, November 9, 2004.

19. Ibid.

20. "Democrats shellshocked By Bush Win Over Kerry, Mental-health Experts Publicize 'Post-election Selection Trauma,'" Worldnetdaily.com, November 11, 2004.

21. Sean Salai, "Psychologists Blast Rush Limbaugh for Mocking Traumatized Kerry Voters," Boca Raton News, November 16, 2004.

22. Ibid.

23. America Votes 2004, "Some Kerry Supporters Glum After Loss," CNN.com, November 5, 2004.

24. Melissa Healy, "Dejected Voters Find Themselves In an Even Bluer State: Feelings of Grief Can Be Severe for Those Who Backed the Defeated Candidate. Psychologists Say it's Important for Them to Forge Ahead," *Los Angeles Times*, November 8, 2004.

25. Sean Salai, "Kerry Supporters Seek Therapy in South Florida, Boca Raton Trauma Specialist Has Treated 15 Patients," *Boca Raton News*, November 9, 2004.

26. Tina Brown, "Those Post-Election, Pitiful Yankees, Big Apple Blues," *Washington Post*, November 18, 2004.

27. Ibid.

28. Melissa Healy, "Dejected Voters Find Themselves In an Even Bluer State: Feelings of Grief Can Be Severe for Those Who Backed the Defeated Candidate. Psychologists Say it's Important for Them to Forge Ahead," Los Angeles Times, November 8, 2004.

29. Thomas Lipscomb, "Misdiagnosis," *The American Thinker*, November 19, 2004.

30. David Limbaugh, "The Perplexities of Liberalism," Worldnetdaily.com, July 7, 2000.

31. Thomas L. Friedman, "Two Nations Under God," *New York Times*, November 4, 2004.

32. Ibid.

33. E.J. Dionne Jr., "... He Didn't Get," *Washington Post*, November 5, 2004.

34. Charles Babbington, "Reid Set to Lead Senate Democrats, Nevada Has Won Praise From Both Sides of Aisle," *Washington Post*, November 16, 2004.

35. John Kerry, "Text of Sen. Kerry's Convention Speech," Associated Press, July 29, 2004.

36. John Leo, "Liberalism: Can it Survive?" *U.S. News & World Report*, March 7, 2005.

37. Garry Wills, "The Day the Enlightenment Went Out," *New York Times*, November 4, 2004.

38. The Scrapbook, "Dumb Voters, Al Gore, and More," *The Weekly Standard*, November 22, 2004.

39. Jane Smiley, "Why Americans Hate Democrats—A Dialogue, The Unteachable of the Red States," Slate.com, November 4, 2004.

40. Notable Quotables, "Bush Selected by Dumb Voters...," Media Research Center, November 22, 2004.

41. William Saletan, "Simple But Effective, Why You Keep Losing To This Idiot," Slate.com, November 3, 2004.

42. Ibid.

43. Deroy Murdock, "Unhinged Left," *National Review Online*, November 24, 2004.

44. Vicki Woods, "New Yorkers Feel Like Strangers in Their Own Land," The *Daily Telegraph*, November 9, 2004.

45. Ben Shapiro, "I'm Just an Orthodox Jewish Hillbilly from Los Angeles," Creators Syndicate, November 24, 2004.

46. "The Scrapbook," "Dumb Voters, Al Gore, and More," *The Weekly Standard*, November 22, 2004.

47. Scott Sonner, "Reid: Democrats Failed to Take Message to Rural America, Nevada," Associated Press, February 23, 2005.

48. Michael Gecan, "In a Clueless Party," *Washington Post*, December 29, 2004.

49. Joshua Muravchik, Why Democrats Keep Losing," Commentary, January 2005.

50. Maureen Dowd, "The Red Zone," *New York Times*, November 4, 2004.

51. Sean Salai, "Pscyhologists Blast Rush Limbaugh for Mocking Traumatized Kerry Voters," *Boca Raton News*, November 16, 2004.

52. Editorial, "The Fear Myth, Actually, George Bush's Victory Had More to Do With Hope and Growth," *The Economist*, November 18, 2004.

53. Press Conference, "Press Conference with House Minority Leader Representative Nancy Pelosi (D-CA); And Representative Robert Matsui (D-CA)

Location: Democratic Congressional Campaign Committee Headquarters, Washington, D.C.," Federal News Service, November 3, 2004.

54. Melissa Block, Robert Seigel, "Nancy Pelosi Discusses the Mood of House Democrats Following Last Night's Wins By The GOP," National Public Radio, November 3, 2004.

55. Eric Alterman, "There They Go Again," Altercation, November 5, 2004.

56. Ron Suskind, "Faith, Certainty, and the Presidency of George W. Bush," *New York Times Magazine*, October 17, 2004.

57. Jennifer Skalka, "Blue Voters Now Urged to Buy Blue," *Chicago Tribune*, December 14, 2004.

58. Joseph Curl, "Blue States Buzz Over Secession," *Washington Times*, November 9, 2004.

59. Ibid.

60. Ibid.

61. Tony Blankley, "Secession," *Washington Times*, November 10, 2004.

62. Panel Discussion, "What Now? A Discussion on the Way Forward for the Democrats; Democratic Party," *Washington Monthly*, December 1, 2004.

63. Ibid.

64. Matt Miller, "This Land is Red land, Paid for by Blue Land ... America: Paid for By the Blue States," *Fortune*, November 29, 2004.

65. Editorial, "Stupid," *Richmond Times Dispatch*, November 29 2004.

66. Joseph Curl, "Blue States Buzz Over Secession," *Washington Times*, November 9, 2004.

67. Michelle Goldberg, "If at First You Don't Secede," Salon.com, November 17, 2004.

68. Transcript: Hannity and Colmes, "European Press Disappointed in Election," Fox News Network, November 5, 2004.

69. Editorial, "Democalypse Now?" *Divided Times Newsletter*, Issue 14, December 13, 2004.

70. Al From and Bruce Reed, "Get the Red Out," *Wall Street Journal*, December 8, 2004.

71. David Limbaugh, "Looking for Love in All the Wrong Places," Creators Syndicate, December 7, 2004.

72. Harold Meyerson, "Democrats in a Divided Land," *Washington Post*, November 5, 2004.

73. Editorial, "Debunking 'Centrism,'" Pittsburgh Post-Gazette, December 26, 2004.

74. Eric Pianin, "After an Often-Tumultuous Tenure, Daschle Exists Quietly, Defeated Democratic Leader Uncertain About Next Move," *Washington Post*, December 12, 2004.

75. Peter Beinart, "Can the Democrats Fight? Cold War Lessons for Reclaiming Trust on National Security," *Washington Post*, December 9, 2004.

76. Al From and Bruce Reed, "Get the Red Out," *Wall Street Journal*, December 8, 2004.

CHAPTER FIFTEEN: The Republicans' "Worst Nightmare"

1. Scott Shepard, "Democrats Attempt to Revitalize," *Palm Beach Post*, February 12, 2005.

2. Maggie Haberman, "Dean's Howling To Lead DNC," *New York Daily News*, January 30, 2005.

3. Shepard, "Democrats Attempt to Revitalize," *Palm Beach Post*, February 12, 2005.

4. Democratic National Committee, "Democratic National Committee Holds Plenary Session," Congressional Quarterly, Inc., February 11, 2005.

5. Nicholas von Hoffman, "Democrats Must Oppose Bush's Imperial Conquests," *New York Observer*, December 6, 2004.

6. Nicholas von Hoffman, "Democrats Must Oppose Bush's Imperial Conquests," *New York Observer*, December 6, 2004.

7. Harold Meyerson, "What Are Democrats About?" *Washington Post*, November 17, 2004.

8. Adam Nagourney, "So What Happened in That Election, Anyhow?" *New York Times*, January 2, 2005.

9. Ruth Conniff, "Reasons for Hope," *The Progressive*, December 2004.

10. Richard E. Cohen, "How They Measured Up," *National Journal*, February 28, 2004.

11. Craig Gilbert, "Democrats Scrappy in Likely Final Debate; Edwards Challenges Kerry in N.Y. Faceoff," Milwaukee Sentinel Journal, March 1, 2004.

12. CyberAlert, "CBS Backs Up Dean's Claim He's Not Liberal, But..." Media Research Center, May 5, 2003.

13. Ed Koch, "Democrats Must Make Changes," *Real Clear Politics*, December 1, 2004.

14. Roger Simon, "Dem Blues, Can the Democrats Find the Lyrics to Regain the White House?" *U.S. News & World Report*, February 14, 2005.

15. Press Conference, "Press Conference with House Minority Leader Representative Nancy Pelosi (D-CA); And Representative Robert Matsui (D-CA) Location: Democratic Congressional Campaign Committee Headquarters, Washington, D.C.," Federal News Service, November 3, 2004.

16. Edward Epstein, "UC Scholar to Help Democrats Refine Message, Party is Urged to Control Policy Debate," *San Francisco Chronicle*, December 5, 2004.

17. Holly Yeager, U.S. Democrats Try to Avoid Elephant Trap," *Financial Times*, December 5, 2004.

18. Bob Schieffer, "Senator John Kerry Discusses the War in Iraq and Politics," CBS News *Face the Nation*, December 4, 2005.

19. John E. O'Neill and Jerome R. Corsi, PH.D., *Unfit for Command* (New York: Regnery Publishing, Inc., 2004).

20. Debate Transcript, "The First Bush-Kerry Presidential Debate," Commission on Presidential Debates, September 30, 2004.

21. Mark R. Levin, "Slighting Substance, Kerry's Statements Deserve Greater Scrutiny," *National Review Online*, October 4, 2004.

22. Debate Transcript, "The First Bush-Kerry Presidential Debate," Commission on Presidential Debates, September 30, 2004.

23. David Limbaugh, "The Bizarre Candidacy of John Kerry," Creators Syndicate, September 14, 2004.

24. Editorial, "Kerry for President," *Washington Post*, October 24, 2004.

25. Editorial, "Kerry for President," *Daily News of Los Angeles*, October 24, 2004.

26. E.J. Dionne, "Democrats in Disarray," *Washington Post*, September 27, 2005.

27. Helen Thomas, "What's Wrong With Being Liberal? President's Use of L-Word Signals Desperation," Hearst Newspapers, October 14, 2004.

28. Geoff Earle, "Kerry Returns to Hill, Dems Ponder Strategy Seeking Key Role, Senator Confers with Reid, Pelosi," *The Hill*, November 10, 2004.

29. Ibid.

30. Press Conference, "Press Conference with House Minority Leader Representative Nancy Pelosi (D-CA); And Representative Robert Matsui (D-CA) Location: Democratic Congressional Campaign Committee Headquarters, Washington, D.C.," Federal News Service, November 3, 2004.

31. Margaret Carlson, "A Grim Study in Red and Blue, What Kind of Mandate is a Win of Only 51%?" *Los Angeles Times*, November 4, 2004.

32. Richard Cohen, "George Bush, Master of Delusion," *Washington Post*, January 20, 2005.

33. Paul Krugman, "No Surrender," *New York Times*, November 5, 2004.

34. Bob Herbert, "O.K., Folks: Back to Work," *New York Times*, November 5, 2004.

35. Tina Brown, "Those Post-Election, Pitiful Yankees, Big Apple Blues," *Washington Post*, November 18, 2004.

36. Michael Kinsley, "Am I Blue? I apologize for Everything I Believe In. May I Go Now?" *Washington Post*, November 7, 2004.

37. Polling Results, "December 26, 2005 – 2006 Will Be Better for Them, But No Peace on Earth, Americans Tell Quinnipiace University National Poll:

Most Will Watch Times Square Drop On TV," Quinnipiac University, December 26, 2005.

38. John Hinderaker, "Our Advice to Democrats: Cheer Up!" Powerlineblog.com, December 27, 2005.

39. Dan Balz, "Clinton Angers Left With Call for Unity," Senator Accused of Siding With Centrists," *Washington Post*, July 27, 2005.

40. Ibid.

41. Donald Lambro, "Soul-searching Democrats," *Washington Times*, October 20, 2005.

42. Ibid.

43. NBC News Transcripts, "Dr. Howard Dean Discusses Democratic Party Politics," Meet the Press, November 13, 2005.

44. Dan Balz, "Pelosi Hails Democrats' Diverse War Stances," *Washington Post*, December 16, 2005.

45. Carol Platt Liebau, "Democrats Take a Pass on Iraq," *Human Events*, December 19, 2005.

46. Dan Balz, "Pelosi Hails Democrats' Diverse War Stances," *Washington Post*, December 16, 2005.

47. Shailagh Murray and Charles Babington, "Democrats Struggle to Seize Opportunity, Amid GOP Troubles, No Unified Message," *Washington Post*, March 7, 2006.

48. Ibid.

49. Adam Nagourney and Sheryl Gay Stolberg, "Some Democrats Are Sensing Missed Opportunities," *New York Times*, February 8, 2006.

50. Shailagh Murray and Charles Babington, "Democrats Struggle to Seize Opportunity, Amid GOP Troubles, No Unified Message," *Washington Post*, March 7, 2006.

51. Sen. Elizabeth Dole, "Dems' Lurch to the Left Will Hurt Them in 2006," *The Hill*, November 3, 2006.

52. Jim VandeHei, "Blogs Attack From Left as Democrats Reach for Center," *Washington Post*, January 28, 2006.

53. Ibid.

54. Ibid.

55. Eric Pfeiffer, "Democrats Break Into Blogosphere; Likely '08 Hopefuls Walk fine Line Between Liberal Base, Mainstream," *Washington Times*, February 9, 2006.

56. Dana Milbank, "Tasting Victory, Liberals Instead Have a Food Fight," *Washington Post*, January 31, 2006.

57. Ibid.

58. Ibid.

59. Adam Nagourney and Sheryl Gay Stolberg, "Some Democrats Are Sensing Missed Opportunities," *New York Times*, February 8, 2006.

60. Fox News Transcript, "Carville & Begala Enter the No Spin Zone," *The O'Reilly Factor*, January 25, 2006.

61. This was a phrase Attorney General John Ashcroft coined during his Senate confirmation hearings, which incited the wrath of liberals and libertarians everywhere, as we'll see in Chapter Nine.

62. Adam Nagourney and Sheryl Gay Stolberg, "Some Democrats Are Sensing Missed Opportunities," *New York Times*, February 8, 2006.

63. David D. Kirkpatrick, "Alito Hearings Unsettle Some Prevailing Wisdom About the Politics of Abortion," *New York Times*, January 16, 2006.

64. David D. Kirkpatrick, "Democrats Urge Strategic 'No' Votes on Alito," *New York Times*, January 19, 2006.

65. David Limbaugh, "A Confused Party," Creators Syndicate, January 19, 2006.

66. James Carville and Paul Begala, *Take it Back, Our Party, Our Country, Our Future* (New York, NY: Simon & Schuster, 2006), 1-2.

67. Adam Nagourney, "Kerry Advisers Point Fingers At Iraq and Social Issues," *New York Times*, November 9, 2004.

68. E.J. Dionne, "Democrats in Disarray," *Washington Post*, September 27, 2005.

69. Transcript, Karl Rove, "Karl Rove at American Enterprise Institute," *Washington Post*, May 15, 2006.